Dr Savage seeks to understand the apostle Paul's apparently contradictory description of his ministry in 2 Corinthians as one in which power is manifested through weakness: 'When I am weak, then I am strong!' This paradox becomes intelligible when it is understood that Paul's critics were influenced by a perspective which was the exact opposite of his: they imbibed the self-exalting outlook of their contemporary world, while he embraced the self-emptying gospel of Christ. Drawing from archaeological data on first-century Corinth, this study is unique in establishing both the secular underpinnings of Paul's paradoxical language and the devastating critique which that language offers on the general outlook of the first century. Paul emerges as a radical foil to the spirit of the age.

SOCIETY FOR NEW TESTAMENT STUDIES

MONOGRAPH SERIES

General editor: Margaret E. Thrall

86

POWER THROUGH WEAKNESS

Power through weakness

Paul's understanding of the Christian
ministry in 2 Corinthians

TIMOTHY B. SAVAGE

*Senior Minister, Camelback Bible Church,
Paradise Valley, Arizona*

CAMBRIDGE
UNIVERSITY PRESS

Published by the Press Syndicate of the University of Cambridge
The Pitt Building, Trumpington Street, Cambridge CB2 IRP
40 West 20th Street, New York, NY 10011–4211, USA
10 Stamford Road, Oakleigh, Melbourne 3166, Australia

First published 1996

Printed in Great Britain at the University Press, Cambridge

A catalogue record for this book is available from the British Library

Library of Congress cataloguing in publication data

Savage, Timothy B.
Power through weakness: Paul's understanding of the
Christian ministry in 2 Corinthians / Timothy B. Savage.
   p.   cm. – (Society for New Testament Studies Monograph series; 86)
Rev. and updated version of the author's thesis (doctoral) –
Cambridge Univ., 1987.
Includes bibliographical references and index.
ISBN 0 521 49640 3 (hardback)
1. Bible. N.T. Corinthians, 2nd – Criticism, interpretation, etc.
2. Sociology, Christian – History – Early church, ca. 30–600.
3. Paul, the Apostle, Saint – Contributions in pastoral theology.
4. Pastoral theology – Biblical teaching. I. Title. II. Series:
Monograph series (Society for New Testament Studies); 86.
BS2675.2.S28   1995
227'.306 – dc20   95–44544

ISBN 0 521 49640 3 hardback

CE

CONTENTS

PREFACE

This monograph began its life as a doctoral thesis presented to and accepted by the University of Cambridge in 1987. Since then it has been revised and updated extensively.

Many people have cast a critical eye over this work at various stages of its development and their suggestions and encouragement have been invaluable. I am particularly grateful to my supervisor in Cambridge, the Lady Margaret Professor of Divinity, Morna D. Hooker, who enlarged my understanding of the cross of Christ in Paul and helped me to see its implications for the Christian ministry. I am also grateful to Mr A. G. Woodhead, a classical archaeologist and life-fellow of Corpus Christi College, who carefully supervised my work on first-century Corinth. My original readers, Dr Douglas R. de Lacey and the Rev. J. P. M. Sweet, sharpened many loose arguments and caught several errant details, as did Professor David Hellholm and Dr Margaret E. Thrall, who read the manuscript in preparation for publication. I wish especially to thank Dr Thrall who agreed to include this work in the SNTS monograph series. Several friends have provided important moral support: Dr Roy D. Clements; Professor Murray J. Harris; Professor Harold W. Hoehner; and the late Dr Colin J. Hemer. Mr Steven R. Laube compiled the indexes with admirable patience and accuracy. To each person, my debt is immense.

For the financial support which made the research possible I would like to thank the Rotary Foundation of Rotary International, the Tyndale House Council, Corpus Christi College, Cambridge and, above all, my parents.

The encouragement which I have received from my mother and father far exceeds the monetary. It was they who first challenged me to explore the teachings of scripture and they who undergirded my work with prayer. I trust this offering is worthy of their love.

Finally, I am grateful to my wife, Lesli, who unfailingly and without complaint put the demands of my research before her own interests. Without her support, the monograph would never have seen the light of day. For the abiding joy of her companionship I offer my deepest and humble gratitude.

ABBREVIATIONS
(and dates of ancient authors)

ABR	*Australian Biblical Review*
Ael.	Aelianus, c. AD 170–235
AJA	*American Journal of Archaeology*
AJP	*American Journal of Philology*
Alciphron	second century AD
ANRW	*Aufstieg und Niedergang der römischen Welt. Geschichte und Kultur Roms im Spiegel der neueren Forschung*, eds. H. Temporini and W. Haase (Berlin and New York: Walter de Gruyter, 1972–)
App.	Appian, c. AD 95–165
Apul.	Apuleius, b. c. AD 123
Arch	*Archaeology*
Aret.	Aretaeus, second century AD
Aristid.	Aelius Aristides, c. AD 117–180
Arist.	Aristotle, 384–322 BC
Artem.	Artemidorus Daldianus, second century AD
AS	*Anatolian Studies*
ASCSA	American School of Classical Studies in Athens
Ath.	Athenaeus, second century AD
August.	Augustine, AD 354–430
BA	*The Biblical Archaeologist*
BAG	Bauer, W. *A Greek-English Lexicon of the New Testament and other Early Christian Literature.*, translated and adapted by W. F. Arndt and F. W. Gingrich; 2nd ed. revised and augmented by F. W. Gingrich and F. W. Danker (see bibliog.)
BCH	*Bulletin de correspondance hellénique*
BDF	Blass, F. and Debrunner, A. *A Greek Grammar of the New Testament and Other Early Christian*

	Literature, translated and revised by R. W. Funk (see bibliog.)
BH	*Buried History*
Bib	*Biblica*
BJRL	*Bulletin of the John Rylands Library*
BZ	*Biblische Zeitschrift*
B. Mus. Inscr.	British Museum. *Ancient Greek Inscriptions in the British Museum*, eds. C. T. Newton, E. L. Hicks *et al.* (see bibliog.)
CAH	*Cambridge Ancient History*
Calabi-Limentani	Calabi-Limentani, *I. Epigrafia Latina* (see bibliog.)
CBQ	*Catholic Biblical Quarterly*
Cic.	Cicero, 106–43 BC
CIG	*Corpus Inscriptionum Graecarum*
CIL	*Corpus Inscriptionum Latinarum*
CN	*Coniectanea neotestamentica*
CP	*Classical Philology*
Crinagorus	b. c. 70 BC
D. C.	Dio Cassius, second century AD
D. Chr.	Dio Chrysostom, AD 40 – c. 120
D. S.	Diodorus Siculus, first century BC
Dig.	*Digesta Iustiniani Augusti*, second century AD
Edwards	Edwards, K. M. *Corinth: Coins 1896–1929* (see bibliog.)
Epict.	Epictetus, c. AD 50–120
ETL	*Ephemerides Theologicae Lovanienses*
Eusebius	AD 260–340
EvT	*Evangelische Theologie*
ExpT	*Expository Times*
Gal.	Galenus, second century AD
Gell.	Gellius, Aulus, second century AD
Hell	*Hellenica*
Hesp	*Hesperia*
Hicks	Hicks, E. L. *Greek Inscriptions from the British Museum* (see bibliog.)
Hist	*Historia*
Hor.	Horace, b. 65 BC
HTR	*Harvard Theological Review*
IEJ	*Israel Exploration Journal*
IG	*Inscriptiones Graecae*

IGRR	*Inscriptiones Graecae ad Res Romanas Pertinentes*
ILS	*Inscriptiones Latinae Selectae*
Int	*Interpretation*
ITQ	*Irish Theological Quarterly*
JAAR	*Journal of the American Academy of Religion*
JAC	*Jahrbuch für Antike und Christentum*
Jastrow	Jastrow, M. *A Dictionary of the Targumim, the Talmud Babli and Yerushalmi, and the Midrashic Literature* (see bibliog.)
JBL	*Journal of Biblical Literature*
JCE	*Journal of Christian Education*
JEA	*Journal of Egyptian Archaeology*
Jos.	Josephus, AD 37/38 – c. 100
JHS	*Journal of Hellenic Studies*
JKI	*Jahrbuch des Kaiserlich deutschen archäologischen Instituts*
JQR	*Jewish Quarterly Review*
JRH	*Journal of Religious History*
JRS	*Journal of Roman Studies*
JSNT	*Journal for the Study of the New Testament*
JSOT	*Journal for the Study of the Old Testament*
JTS	*Journal of Theological Studies*
Just.	Justinianus, sixth century AD
Juv.	Juvenal, first century AD
Kaibel	Kaibel, G. *Epigrammata Graeca* (see bibliog.)
Kent	Kent, J. H. *Corinth: The Inscriptions 1926–1950* (see bibliog.)
Lane	Lane, E. *Corpus Monumentorum Religionis dei Menis* (see bibliog.)
LCL	Loeb Classical Library (London: William Heinemann, Ltd., and Cambridge, Mass.: Harvard University Press)
Le Bas-Wadd.	Le Bas, P. and Waddington, W. H. *Voyage archéologique en Grèce et en Asie Mineure* (see bibliog.)
Livy	59 BC – AD 17 or 64 BC – AD 12
LSJ	Liddell, H. G. and Scott, R. *A Greek-English Lexicon*, revised and augmented by H. S. Jones, with the assistence of R. McKenzie (see bibliog.)
Luc.	Lucan, AD 39 – 65

Lucian	c. AD 125–180
LXX	The Septuagint
Mart.	Martial, c. AD 40–104
Meritt	Meritt, B. D. *Corinth: Greek Inscriptions 1896–1927* (see bibliog.)
Moretti	Moretti, L. *Inscrizioni Agonistiche Greche* (see bibliog.)
MT	The Massoretic Text
NDIEC	*New Documents Illustrating Early Christianity*
NT	New Testament
NT	*Novum Testamentum*
NTS	*New Testament Studies*
OCD	*Oxford Classical Dictionary*, eds. N. G. L. Hammond and H. H. Scullard, 2nd ed. (see bibliog.)
Origen	AD 185/186–254/255
OT	Old Testament
Ovid	43 BC – AD 17
Paus.	Pausanias, second century AD
Petron.	Petronius, first century AD
P. Fay.	Grenfell, B. P., Hunt, A. S. and Hogarth, D. G. *Fayûm Towns and their Papyri* (see bibliog.)
P. Flor.	*Papiri Fiorentini, documenti pubblici e privati dell'età romana e bizantina*. Eds. G. Vitelli and D. Comparetti (see bibliog.)
PGM	*Papyri Graecae Magicae*, ed. K. Preisendanz (see bibliog.)
Philo	c. 30 BC – AD 45
Philostr.	Philostratus, second century AD
PhilW	*Philologische Wochenschrift*
Plato	c. 429 – 346 BC
Pliny the Elder	AD 23/24–79
Pliny the Younger	c. AD 61–112
Plut.	Plutarch, c. AD 46 – c. 120
PLJP	*Paul, the Law, and the Jewish People*. E. P. Sanders (see bibliog.)
P. Lond.	*Greek Papyri in the British Museum*, eds. F. G. Kenyon and H. I. Bell (see bibliog.)
P&P	*Past and Present*
P. Par.	Brunet de Presle, W. *Notices et extraits des*

	papyrus grecs du musée du Louvre et de la bibliothèque impériale (see bibliog.)
P. Oxy.	*Oxyrhynchus Papyri*, eds. B. P. Grenfell, A. S. Hunt *et al.* (see bibliog.)
PPJ	*Paul and Palestinian Judaism.* E. P. Sanders (see bibliog.)
PW, PWSup	*Paulys Real-Encyclopädie der classischen Altertumswissenschaft, and supplementary volumes*, ed. G. Wissowa (Stuttgart: Metzler, 1894–)
Quint.	Quintilian, b. between AD 30 and 35 – c. 100
RAC	*Reallexikon für Antike und Christentum*, ed. T. Klauser (Leipzig: Hiersemann, 1941–)
RB	*Revue biblique*
RE	*Revue Épigraphique*
REG	*Revue des Études grecques*
RestQ	*Restoration Quarterly*
RevPhil	*Revue de Philologie*
RevQ	*Revue de Qumran*
RevScRel	*Revue des Sciences Religieuses*
RGG	*Religion in Geschichte und Gegenwart*
RHE	*Revue d'histoire ecclésiastique*
RS	*Religious Studies*
RSR	*Recherches de science religieuse*
Sen.	Seneca, b. between 4 BC and AD 1–65
S. E.	Sextus Empiricus, second century AD
SEÅ	*Svensk exegetisk årsbok*
SEG	*Supplementum Epigraphicum Graecum*
SG	*Studium Generale*
SIFC	*Studi italiani di filologia classica*
SIG³	*Sylloge Inscriptionum Graecarum*, 3rd ed. (see bibliog.)
SNTU	*Studien zum Neuen Testament und seiner Umwelt*
SO	*Symbolae osloenses*
Stat.	Statius, c. AD 45–96
Str-B	Strack, H. L. and Billerbeck, P. *Kommentar zum Neuen Testament aus Talmud und Midrasch*, 6 vols. (München: Oskar Beck, 1922–56)
Str.	Strabo, 64/63 BC – AD 21/22
Suet.	Suetonius Tranquillus, c. AD 69 – 115
Tac.	Tacitus, c. AD 56 – c. 115

Tat.	Tatianus, second century AD
TB	*Tyndale Bulletin*
TNIDNTT	*The New International Dictionary of New Testament Theology*, ed. C. Brown, 3 vols. (Exeter: The Paternoster Press, 1975–78)
TQ	*Theologische Quartalschrift*
Trypho	first century BC
TS	*Theological Studies*
TSK	*Theologische Studien und Kritiken*
TWNT	*Theologisches Wörterbuch zum Neuen Testament*, eds. G. Kittel and G. Friedrich, 10 vols. (Stuttgart: W. Kohlhammer, 1933–78)
TZ	*Theologische Zeitschrift*
Vett. Val.	Vettius Valens, second century AD
Vidman	Vidman, L. *Sylloge inscriptionum religionis Isiacae et Serapiacae* (see bibliog.)
VT	*Vetus Testamentum*
West	West, A. B. *Corinth: Latin Inscriptions 1896–1927* (see bibliog.)
WZKM	*Wiener Zeitschrift für die Kunde des Morgenlandes*
YCS	*Yale Classical Studies*
ZAW	*Zeitschrift für die alttestamentliche Wissenschaft*
ZNW	*Zeitschrift für die neutestamentliche Wissenschaft*
ZTK	*Zeitschrift für Theologie und Kirche*

The method of citation

Abbreviations of primary sources follow established usage: for classical literature see LSJ and *OCD*, for Jewish material see *JBL* 95 (1976) 335–38 and for Philo and Josephus see LCL. Commentaries on 2 Corinthians are cited by author only. All other books and articles are cited by author and short title.

INTRODUCTION

No student of the New Testament who wishes to come to grips with the nature of the Christian ministry can afford to neglect the second epistle of St Paul to the Corinthians. In this letter the apostle paints a remarkably candid picture of his own experience as a minister of Christ. His autobiographical sketch reaches a climax in 2 Corinthians 12:10, in the words 'When I am weak, then I am strong!'

At first glance Paul would seem to be indulging in a meaningless contradiction. How can he be both weak and strong? How can he sum up his vocation in terms which are normally thought to be mutually exclusive? Yet on further reflection we discover something very different: what appears on the surface to be a clear absurdity is for Paul a profound teaching. Over and over in this epistle he describes his ministry in terms of two completely different, yet overlapping, experiences. In chapter one he defines his vocation in terms of comfort experienced through suffering; in chapter three in terms of glory manifested through shame; in chapter four in terms of life working in death; in chapter six in terms of riches won through poverty; and in chapters twelve and thirteen in terms of power expressed through weakness. It is clear from this general overview that at the core of Paul's teaching in 2 Corinthians lies an important paradox – a paradox which finds expression in a number of different antitheses and which drives to the heart of what it means to Paul to be a minister of Christ. It will be the aim of this book to make sense of this paradox. We shall seek to discover what Paul means by the cryptic words ὅταν γὰρ ἀσθενῶ, τότε δυνατός εἰμι.

The problem

The task before us will be complicated by the fact that 2 Corinthians is an occasional epistle. Most of what Paul says in this letter represents a careful response to a very specific set of problems

I

within the Corinthian church. If we are to make sense of his teaching, we must reconstruct the situation which lies behind it. But here we encounter a problem. Paul never reveals the precise nature of the situation he is addressing. He merely alludes to the various issues and events which trouble him and assumes that his readers, the Corinthians, can fill in the details.[1] This leaves us with the delicate task of trying to piece together the 'background' of the epistle using only the scattered and oblique references to it which Paul himself provides. Such an endeavour is naturally fraught with difficulties, yet it is not without reward. With due care and diligence we can construct a fairly convincing picture of the situation which gave rise to Paul's teaching. We begin the process in what follows.

The situation at Corinth

Most scholars would agree that 2 Corinthians contemplates a different set of problems from that of 1 Corinthians. The sort of party strife and misuse of wisdom, knowledge and glossolalia which we find in the earlier epistle have largely disappeared from view in the latter.[2] Instead Paul turns his attention to an intruder (ὁ ἀδικήσας, 7:12), one who appears to be attacking him personally (cf. οὐκ ἐμὲ λελύπηκεν, 2:5; ὃ κεχάρισμαι, 2:10). What troubles Paul is not so much that he is being assailed, but that his converts have not rallied to his support. For this reason, he addresses a harsh letter to the Corinthians and calls on them to punish the intruder (2 Corinthians 2:3–4; 7:12). To his great relief they quickly demonstrate both their 'innocence' in the matter (ἁγνοί, 7:11) and their loyalty to him (7:7) by bringing the offender to justice (2:6). Paul's joy is renewed (7:7, 16) and his confidence in his converts restored (7:14).

This, however, represents only part of the picture. One of the most puzzling features of 2 Corinthians is that in a space of a few verses Paul can both rejoice in the loyalty of his converts (7:7) and bemoan their lack of affection for him (στενοχωρεῖσθε δὲ ἐν τοῖς σπλάγχνοις ὑμῶν, 6:12), applaud their earnestness on his behalf (7:12) and wonder at their failure to make room for him in their

---

[1] Cf. Munck *Paul* 168: 'of all Paul's letters II Corinthians is probably the most difficult to understand in detail. He alludes again and again to events of which we otherwise know nothing'.

[2] Thus Barrett 'Christianity at Corinth' 286–87; 'Opponents' 236–37; Kümmel *Introduction* 284–85; Georgi *Gegner* 14; Oostendorp *Another Jesus* 5; *pace* Schmithals *Gnosis* 274–75 who envisages the same 'background' for both epistles.

hearts (cf. 6:13: πλατύνθητε καὶ ὑμεῖς; 7:2: χωρήσατε ἡμᾶς). It would seem that, despite their outward obedience, the Corinthians harbour reservations about their apostle (1:14).[3] Indeed, according to 2 Corinthians 7:2, they feel betrayed by him. Paul suggests that this is because they understand him only in part (ἐπέγνωτε ἡμᾶς ἀπὸ μέρους, 1:14) and he spares no effort trying to redress this deficiency. Hopefully, on hearing his case, they will again have reason to be proud of him (ἀφορμὴν διδόντες ὑμῖν καυχήματος ὑπὲρ ἡμῶν, 5:12).

This is the situation as it is implied in chapters 1–7. In chapters 10–13, which probably comprise a separate epistle written shortly after chapters 1–9 (see the appendix below), everything becomes more explicit. It is clear, for instance, that Paul is indeed coming under intense criticism. Not only is his character impuned, but his entire position as a minister of Christ is openly disputed as well (10:10; 13:3). The Corinthians seem more reluctant than ever to embrace him (cf. 11:1) and instead show deference to his more impressive rivals, the so-called opponents (11:4, 18–20). It appears that the factors which led the Corinthians initially to tolerate the person referred to as ὁ ἀδικήσας and not to rally to Paul's defence have now caused them to embrace a number of such rivals, and to the almost complete exclusion of their own apostle Paul.

It is of cardinal importance to identify the factors which have caused the Corinthians to express dissatisfaction with Paul, for it is in response to their criticisms that Paul sketches the paradoxical picture of his ministry. In other words, if we are to understand what Paul means when he describes his ministry in terms of power through weakness we must identify the criticisms which evoked that teaching.

1 The opponents: a survey of recent scholarship

It has been a reflex of modern scholarship to attribute the criticisms levelled against Paul to his opponents. This is probably due to the fact that the opponents emerge as such a prominent force in 2 Corinthians and serve as the object of some of Paul's most scathing attacks.[4] It is natural to assume that much of what Paul writes in

---

[3] Cf. Barrett 'Titus' 13–14.
[4] There are more references to opponents in 2 Cor. than in any other Pauline epistle, both explicit – ψευδαπόστολοι, ἐργάται δόλιοι (11:13) and οἱ διάκονοι αὐτοῦ (where αὐτοῦ refers to Satan, 11:15) – and implicit – οἱ τοιοῦτοι (11:13), οἱ πολλοί

this epistle represents a direct response to his rivals. It is thus incumbent on the interpreter to discover both the identity of the opponents and the nature of their criticisms.[5]

Much energy has been invested in this pursuit, but little consensus has been reached.[6] There are no less than 13 different views of the nature of Paul's opposition in 2 Corinthians alone.[7] These may be grouped conveniently into three categories.

a. Palestinian Jewish Christians. Many scholars believe that the opponents were Jews who came from Palestine. This view is based largely on 2 Corinthians 11:22 where Paul implies that his rivals are 'Hebrews'. Here the term Ἑβραῖοι is thought to denote not only the Jewish nationality of the opponents, but also their Palestinian origin.[8] Allegedly this finds confirmation in 2 Corinthians 5:16 where Paul seems to be defending himself against the charge that he never knew the earthly Jesus, a charge which presumably could have been levelled only by those who *did* know Jesus and thus who hailed from Palestine.[9] The position is well summarised by W. Kümmel: 'Er ergibt sich aus diesem Sinn von Ἑβραῖοι, dass die Gegner des Paulus in Korinth palästinische Juden waren, die dem Paulus auch das Fehlen persönlicher Kenntnis des irdischen Jesus vorwarfen (5:16)'. ('It is clear from the sense of the term Ἑβραῖοι that the opponents of Paul in Corinth were Palestinian Jews who reproached Paul also for his lack of personal knowledge of the earthly Jesus.').[10] Those who adopt this view may be divided further into two schools.

(2:17; 11:18) and τινες (3:1; 10:2, 12); and cf. the singular τις (10:7), ὁ τοιοῦτος (10:11), ὁ ἐρχόμενος (11:4), which may refer to a ring-leader among the opponents (thus Barrett 260) or perhaps to 'anyone' of the rivals.

[5] Barrett 'Opponents' 233 even claims that 'a full understanding of both New Testament history and New Testament Theology waits on the right answering of the question [of the identity of the opponents]'.

[6] Cf. Fascher 'Korintherbriefe' 291: 'Die Frage der Gegner des Paulus in Korinth bleibt . . . umstritten' ('The question of the opponents of Paul in Corinth remains . . . disputed').

[7] See the list in Gunther *Opponents* 1.

[8] Cf. Käsemann 'Legitimität' 36; Barrett 'Opponents' 235–36; Ellis 'Opponents' 289–90; Gutbrod "Ἰσραήλ' 391–94; Kümmel *Introduction* 285; Gunther *Opponents* 76; Theissen 'Legitimation' 212–13.

[9] So Käsemann 'Legitimität' 49; Oostendorp *Another Jesus* 17; Lietzmann 125; Strachan 110; Héring 42.

[10] Kümmel 211. The seminal work on the Palestinian origin of the opponents was done by Baur *Paulus* 259–332, see esp. 294; other scholars taking this position include Thrall 'Super-Apostles' 42–57; Héring 109; Windisch 23–26; and cf.

i. Judaizers. Some scholars draw a further implication from 2 Corinthians 11:22. By claiming to be 'Hebrews' and 'Israelites', the opponents inevitably declare their loyalty to the religious traditions of Judaism, and especially to the Law. It would seem to follow that they are Judaizing Jews, perhaps in the mould of the opponents in Galatia. If so, they are probably accusing Paul of failing to uphold the law.[11]

The difficulty with this view is the lack of explicit evidence in 2 Corinthians to indicate that the law was ever an issue between Paul and his rivals in Corinth. Unlike the epistles to the Romans and the Galatians, the matter of circumcision is never even mentioned.[12] Although it is not impossible that Paul was dealing with a brand of Judaism in which circumcision played only a minor role,[13] the complete absence in 2 Corinthians of the word νόμος itself would suggest that he was not dealing with Judaism at all.[14]

ii. A Delegation from the Jerusalem Apostolate. According to E. Käsemann, the opponents were not legalistic Jews but a delegation sent ostensibly from the pillar apostles to discover whether Paul was a legitimate apostle.[15] In particular, they sought to determine whether he had properly subordinated himself to the Jerusalem apostolate – a regulation already established as a *Traditionsprinzip* ('principle of tradition') – for only then could he rightly claim to possess apostolic authority. The outward marks of a true apostle included a personal commission from Jesus, evidence of the signs of an apostle and acceptance of monetary support. Since Paul was deficient in each of these respects, his relation to Jerusalem, and hence his authority as an apostle, was open to question. Accordingly, his opponents accused him of being 'no legitimate apostle'.[16]

Georgi *Gegner* 58 who regards the opponents as hellenistic Jews with Palestinian roots (see below pp. 8–9).

[11] Cf. Barrett 'Opponents' 251: 'the intruders were Jews, Jerusalem Jews, Judaizing Jews'; and 'ΨΕΥΔΑΠΟΣΤΟΛΟΙ' 396: 'there is a close relation between 2 Corinthians and Galatians'; see also Baur *Paulus* 278, *et passim*; Gunther *Opponents* 63–64, 211, 299–302; Oostendorp *Another Jesus* 82–83, *et passim*; Barnett 'Opposition' 9–11; Schoeps *Paul* 80–82; Lietzmann 108–9; Héring 79; Plummer 296; and cf. Borse *Galaterbriefes* 84–91.

[12] Thus the criticism by Lütgert *Freiheitspredigt* 62–68.

[13] Thus Barrett 'Christianity at Corinth' 296; 'Opponents' 238, 251.

[14] So Friedrich 'Gegner' 192–93; Munck *Paul* 172–84; Kümmel *Introduction* 285; Furnish 53.

[15] Cf. Käsemann 'Legitimität' 34–52.

[16] Thus Käsemann 'Legitimität' 35: 'Die mangelnde apostolische Autorität verrät die pseudoapostolische Existenz.' ('The absence of apostolic authority betrays his pseudo-apostolic existence.').

R. Bultmann has rightly challenged the view of Käsemann. There is no evidence to suggest that the right of Jerusalem to confer apostolic authority had been established as a *Traditionsprinzip*,[17] nor that the marks of a true apostle had been set out in any codified form.[18] More importantly, there is no explicit evidence in the text of 2 Corinthians to confirm that the opponents were specifically disputing Paul's office as an apostle, nor that they were drawing a link between that office and his authority.[19] Indeed, for all the emphasis on apostleship in scholarly work on 2 Corinthians, the notion itself plays a relatively minor role in the epistle. The word ἀπόστολος occurs only four times in 2 Corinthians 10–13 (the passage where we should most expect to find criticisms of Paul's 'apostleship'), twice in reference to the 'superlative apostles' (11:5; 12:11), once in reference to the false apostles (11:13) and once in reference to the 'signs of an apostle' (12:12). In none of these instances are we compelled to infer that Paul is responding to charges that he is not a true apostle. Any suggestion that it is specifically Paul's 'apostleship' that is being disputed rests on slim evidence.

We are on much firmer ground if we acknowledge that it is his status as a *minister of Christ* that is being questioned. The term διάκονος and its cognates are used 19 times in 2 Corinthians, which represents half of their total occurrences in Paul.[20] Moreover, it is specifically his *ministry* which Paul defends (6:3–4), and seemingly in response to those who claim that they, not he, are true ministers of Christ (cf. 11:15, 23). The distinction between apostleship and ministry may seem to be over-subtle and doubtless Paul himself would have regarded the two as nearly the same. Nevertheless, when it comes to the matter of how Paul replies to his critics the distinction becomes important.

According to Käsemann, Paul responds to complaints against him by defending his apostleship, and specifically his *authority* as an

---

17 Thus Bultmann *Exegetische Probleme* 20–23.
18 Cf. Georgi *Gegner* 43: 'zur Zeit Paulus noch kein allgemeines, inhaltlich gefülltes Apostelverständnis vorhanden war, noch kein festes Apostelbild.' ('In the time of Paul there was not yet a full understanding of the content of an apostle, nor a firm picture of an apostle.').
19 Cf. Best 'Apostolic Authority?' 3–25 who argues that Paul never defends his 'apostolic authority': although he is an *apostle* and does exercise *authority*, he never appeals jointly to both. This represents a healthy corrective of the view which is almost axiomatic in Pauline studies – e.g. in Schütz *Apostolic Authority*; Käsemann 'Legitimität'; Holmberg *Paul and Power*; Shaw *Authority* 119–25.
20 In 2 Cor. cf. διακονία (3:7, 8, 9 [2]; 4:1; 5:18; 6:3; 8:4; 9:1, 12, 13; 11:8), διάκονος (3:6; 6:4; 11:15, 23) and διακονέω (3:3; 8:19, 20).

apostle.[21] The problem with this view is the implication that Paul, like his opponents (cf. 11:18–20), is eager to project his *own* authority. Yet that, Paul argues, is precisely what he does not want to do (cf. 11:12).[22] He will not defend *himself*, either his authority or his apostleship (11:19).[23] Instead it is specifically his 'ministry' which he defends (6:3–4), a term which is better suited to underscoring his humility, not his authority, his service, not his office. While he may commend himself, it is only as a minister *of God* (cf. 6:4: ἐν παντὶ συνιστάντες ἑαυτοὺς ὡς θεοῦ διάκονοι). His position thus differs markedly from his opponents: he does not seek to glorify himself, but God (4:15; 5:13).

Finally, even the general assumption that the opponents come from Palestine is based on dubious grounds. It is by no means certain that the term Ἑβραῖοι in 2 Corinthians 11:22 carries geographical significance. It may merely point to the Jewish heritage of the opponents.[24] In the same way, it is unnecessary to interpret Paul's affirmation in 2 Corinthians 5:16 as though it were a response to a criticism which could have been uttered only by those of Palestinian origin. There is a more satisfactory way in which to take this verse (see below p. 143).[25] We may conclude, therefore, that there is no compelling reason to hold that Paul's opponents came from Palestine.

b. Gnostic Jewish Christians. A second group of scholars identify the opponents with Gnosticism. They suggest that the intruders are Christian Jews of the diaspora who put great emphasis on the gifts of the Spirit – ecstatic speech, knowledge, signs and wonders, visions, etc. The opponents thus represent the same group that caused the problems in 1 Corinthians. They continue to criticise Paul for his failure to demonstrate the powerful signs of the Spirit. He is, they allege, no true πνευματικός.[26]

---

[21] Thus Käsemann 'Legitimität' 35–36; and cf. Kümmel 208: 'Paulus in [2 Cor] 10–13 seine Autorität . . . verteidigt.' ('Paul in [2 Cor] 10–13 defends . . . his authority.'); see also Schütz *Apostolic Authority* 184–86; Furnish 37.

[22] Cf. Best 'Apostolic Authority?' 11: 'Paul does not assert his authority . . . but says he [is] too weak to do such a thing'.

[23] Cf. Barrett 'Opponents' 246: 'One might have supposed that Paul was defending himself, his integrity and also his position and authority. This is not so'.

[24] Thus Munck *Paul* 174, 178; Friedrich 'Gegner' 182; Betz *Paulus* 97; Kee 'Super-Apostles' 66; Allo 271–72; Furnish 534.

[25] Cf. Barrett 171–72; Furnish 330–33.

[26] Cf. Lütgert *Freiheitspredigt* 62–70; Bultmann 'γινώσκω' 708–11; *Exegetische Probleme* 4–5, 23–30; Schmithals *Gnosis* 166–67, 184, *et passim*; Wilckens 'σοφία'

But this view neglects the fact that the difficulties which arose from a false conception of the Spirit in 1 Corinthians have largely receded from view in 2 Corinthians. The word πνεῦμα is infrequent in 2 Corinthians;[27] and in chapters 10–13, where evidence of the opponents' criticisms is most explicit, it hardly occurs at all.[28] In addition, each of the so-called 'gnostic' or 'spiritual' charges registered against Paul – his failure to manifest signs and wonders, visions and knowledge – must be inferred from positive affirmations which Paul makes of himself. Such affirmations may well represent Paul's own creative teaching and hence have no basis in the prior charges of the opponents at all. Finally, it must be conceded that there is little historical evidence to suggest that Gnosticism (or even 'gnosticism' with a small 'g') was ever a viable presence in the Mediterranean world of the first century.[29]

   c. Hellenistic Jewish missionaries.   There is, finally, a third position. Some believe that the opponents were hellenistic Jews who imitated the methods of propaganda used by the itinerant prophets, magicians and saviours of their hellenistic environment.[30] This view takes two different forms.
   i.   θεῖοι ἄνδρες. According to D. Georgi, the opponents claimed to be θεῖοι ἄνδρες, a category of religious persons which Georgi alleges was common in hellenistic antiquity.[31] These individuals sought to display their divine status by performing signs, accepting monetary support and presenting letters of commendation. Above all, they strove to emulate Moses and Jesus, the quintessential 'divine men'. In contrast, Paul did not cultivate a lofty or divine status, nor did he imitate the powerful and impressive Jesus of the

---

[27]   519–23; *Weisheit passim*; Güttgemanns *Apostel* 96, *et passim*; Dinkler 'Korintherbriefe' cols. 17–18; Bieder 'Gegner' 319–33; and see Windisch 23–26 who believes that the opponents were gnostics, but not hellenists; others hold that they were pneumatics, but not gnostics: thus Käsemann 'Legitimität' 35, 40; Georgi *Gegner* 288; Lührmann *Offenbarungsverständnis* 57, 64.

[27]   It appears seventeen times in 2 Cor, less than half its occurrences in 1 Cor. and roughly the same as in Romans and Galatians.

[28]   Cf. 11:4, 12:18 and 13:13 – where in 12:18 it is probably used non-theologically ('Did we not behave in the same spirit, walk in the same footsteps?') and in 13:13 as part of a benediction formula ('The grace of the Lord Jesus Christ, and the love of God and participation in the Holy Spirit').

[29]   Cf. the criticisms of Wilson 'How Gnostic were the Corinthians?' 65–74; 'Gnosis' 102–14; Nock 'Gnosticism' 277; MacMullen *Paganism* 68–69.

[30]   Cf. Georgi *Gegner*; Friedrich 'Gegner'; Bornkamm *Paul* 169–72; Rissi *Studien* 42–44; Collange 18–20, 323–24; Kuhn 'Jesus bei Paulus' 295–320.

[31]   Cf. Georgi *Gegner* 145–82, 192–99.

opponents. It was because of his failure to measure up to the ideal of the 'divine man' that he incurred the abuse of his rivals.[32]

In one sense the category of θεῖοι ἄνδρες makes good sense of the self-exalting tendencies of Paul's rivals in 2 Corinthians (cf. 11:20). In another sense, however, it goes beyond those tendencies. There is, for example, no suggestion in 2 Corinthians that the opponents consciously regarded themselves as *divine* men. Had they done so they would have had no need to present letters of commendation.[33] Another weakness of this view is the absence of historical attestation to θεῖοι ἄνδρες in Paul's day. The silence of the literary and archaeological sources would suggest that there was no such category of religious person in the first century.[34]

ii. Adherents of Stephen. G. Friedrich is rightly critical of the view that the opponents regarded themselves as 'divine emissaries' (*göttliche Sendboten*),[35] yet he remains convinced that they were diaspora Jews influenced by their Greek environment. He suggests that they were members of the circle of hellenistic Jews surrounding Stephen in Acts 6 and 7. They performed signs and wonders (cf. Acts 6:8), indulged in inspired speech (6:10) and advocated a community of goods (6:1). It is because Paul did not do the same that he incurred their reproach.[36]

The weaknesses of this position have been well exposed by C. K. Barrett. His most trenchant criticism is that it is by no means clear 'how disciples of Stephen found their way to Corinth, and why, if they did so, they should have formed an opposition to Paul'.[37] It seems unlikely, therefore, that the opponents were followers of Stephen.

d. A critique of the various positions. It is clear from the observations above that none of the traditional attempts to identify

---

[32] Georgi *Gegner* 301–3.

[33] Cf. the criticism of Friedrich 'Gegner' 196; for further internal evidence against the position of Georgi see Theissen 'Legitimation' 213–14 n. 3.

[34] Cf. Smith 'Divine Men' 174–99, esp. 194–95; Judge 'Classical Society' 34; Holladay *Theios Aner* 235–42; Tiede *Charismatic Figure* 290; Moule 'Distinctiveness of Christ' 563; Barrett 276–77; 'Opponents' 235; Furnish 244; but see Betz 'Gottmensch' 248–49.

[35] 'Gegner' 196; though see p. 212 where Friedrich comes close to viewing the opponents as θεῖοι ἄνδρες.

[36] Thus 'Gegner' 199–200, 205–8; see also Wolff 7–8 who argues that the opponents were hellenistic-pneumatic-charismatic-wandering missionaries after the model of Acts 13:1–3.

[37] Thus 'Opponents' 236; cf. Martin 340.

Paul's opponents has been fully successful. Each puts accusations in the mouths of the opponents which the text cannot sustain. In short, there is simply too little evidence to suggest that Paul is being faulted on the grounds that he is not sufficiently legalistic or apostolic or pneumatic or ecstatic. The reason for this negative outcome is certainly not a lack of enterprise on the part of scholars. Probably no area of Pauline research has received more attention than the identity of the apostle's opposition.[38]

What has hindered scholars is the paucity of explicit information on the opponents. All we *really* know is that they were Jewish (2 Corinthians 11:22) and outsiders (11:4). Beyond that we may infer that they preached a different Jesus from Paul (11:4), were intruding into his sphere of ministry (10:12–18), were receiving financial support (11:12) and were behaving in a heavy-handed manner (11:18–20). Much more we cannot say. We simply know too little about the opponents to construct an adequate background to Paul's teaching.[39]

But this does not mean that our attempt to make sense of Paul's paradoxical language is bound to fail. For it is possible to reconstruct the background to his teaching without recourse to a full understanding of the opponents. The way forward will require some modification in the assumptions which have normally governed this area of research.[40] In particular:

i.   The assumption that the criticisms levelled against Paul originate with the opponents. If this were the case, our ability to understand Paul's teaching would indeed depend on whether we could reconstruct the identity of his rivals. But this assumption neglects the possibility that there may well have been discontent with Paul long before the opponents arrived on the scene. If so, the criticisms could go back to the Corinthians themselves, in which case the opponents would merely be exploiting a situation which had already turned against Paul. On this reckoning, it would be Paul's own converts who represent his chief opposition.[41] Indeed it is certainly

---

[38] Cf. the survey of the vast history of research in Ellis 'Opponents' 264–92.

[39] Cf. the assessment of Hickling 'Second Epistle to the Corinthians' 287: 'we must be content to remain largely in ignorance of the doctrinal position or tendencies of Paul's rivals'; and Munck *Paul* 184: 'we know nothing at all of their doctrine'.

[40] For a helpful critique of the methods which have been used in this field of study see Berger 'Die impliziten Gegner' 373–400.

[41] Thus McClelland 'Super-Apostles' 85: 'the true opponents of Paul are the misguided church members themselves'; and Munck *Paul* 186: 'the real opponents of Paul . . . are the Corinthians themselves'.

to them, and not to the opponents, that he directs his teaching in 2 Corinthians.[42]

ii. The assumption that the criticisms are of a religious nature. It is nearly an axiom of Pauline studies to regard the complaints against Paul as essentially religious in character. As we have seen, most commentators believe that Paul is responding to the charge that he neglects the law or his apostleship or the Spirit or his divine status or his ecstasy. But this ignores the possibility that he is not responding to religious criticisms at all. Indeed it is conceivable that the Corinthians are evaluating Paul on essentially secular grounds, though perhaps framing their criticisms in religious language.

iii. The assumption that the criticisms may be inferred directly from Paul's own teaching. Too often students of Paul interpret his teaching as though it represented nothing more than a direct contradiction of the accusations of his rivals. A case in point is Paul's affirmation in 2 Corinthians 12:12 that he performs the signs of an apostle. This is often understood to be an answer to the charge that he does not manifest such signs.[43] The weakness of this approach is that it fails to recognise in Paul the exposition of truth for its own sake. For instance, it is possible that in calling attention to the signs of his apostleship Paul intends to go far beyond all criticism and break new ground in the defence of his ministry.[44]

It is clear, then, that we need to remain flexible in the assumptions which govern our enquiry into the situation which gave rise to Paul's teaching in 2 Corinthians. In particular, we must be open to the possibility that he is responding to the criticisms of his converts themselves and that these criticisms are secular as well as religious in nature. Moreover, we must not interpret what the apostle says as though it were always a simple denial of charges levelled against

---

[42] Cf. Harvey 'Opposition' 320–21: 'Paul's arguments are not to be understood as answering the theological objections of his opponents, but as awakening his correspondents from their theological thoughtlessness'; and Munck *Paul* 186: 'the letter . . . is meant for the Corinthians. The [opponents] are only a subordinate theme, which has become important because the Corinthians saw something great in them and their demeanour'.

[43] Thus Käsemann 'Legitimität' 61–71; Furnish 555; Bultmann 233; Kümmel 213; though see Barrett 321; 'Opponents' 245.

[44] Cf. the warning of Hickling 'Second Epistle to the Corinthians' 285: 'we should not assume that Paul's choice both of subjects and of phraseology [is] dictated by the arguments of his competitors'; 286: 'this approach fails to do justice to the proportion in Paul's writing between controversy and exposition of the truth for its own sake'; and 287: 'by unwarrantably reading a subtle and oblique polemic into [Paul's] words, we may fail to hear all that they are really saying'.

him. It may well represent a radical critique of those charges.[45] In brief, we need to be extremely cautious in our attempt to establish the background of Paul's paradoxical language in 2 Corinthians. At least initially, we must confine ourselves to what the text makes explicit.

2   *The criticisms: the evidence*

It is possible to identify at least four specific areas in which the Corinthians find fault with Paul.

a.   Boasting.   First of all, they seem to be critical of his refusal to boast. They gladly receive those who do boast, namely, the opponents (ἡδέως γὰρ ἀνέχεσθε τῶν ἀφρόνων, 2 Corinthians 11:19), and spurn Paul for refusing to boast (cf. 11:18–21a). When he finally does boast, it is, he says, because the Corinthians have compelled him to do so (12:11).

b.   Physical presence.   The Corinthians are also unhappy with Paul's physical demeanour. His letters are impressive, but his bodily presence is weak (ἡ παρουσία τοῦ σώματος ἀσθενής, 10:10).

c.   Speech.   They express further dissatisfaction with Paul's speech. It is contemptible (ὁ λόγος ἐξουθενημένος, 10:10) and, as Paul himself concedes, unskilled (ἰδιώτης τῷ λόγῳ, 11:6).

d.   Support.   Finally, the Corinthians disapprove of his refusal to accept monetary support (11:7–10; 12:14). It makes them feel inferior to other churches (12:13) and causes them to question whether Paul really loves them (11:11).

3   *The criticisms: an analysis*

It is immediately noticeable that none of these criticisms is essentially religious in nature. Each represents the sort of charge which anyone living in the first century – religious or non-religious – might bring against Paul. In other words, the criticisms have cultural overtones. They reflect the social prejudices of the day.[46] This

---

[45] Cf. Judge 'Radical Critic' 191-203; Malherbe *Social Aspects* 13; Keck 'Ethos' 450.
[46] So Judge 'Classical Society' 35-36.

suggests that we need to learn something about the way in which people in antiquity evaluated each other. It would be helpful, for instance, to know what sort of traits the typical Corinthian would look for in a minister like Paul – what sort of physical demeanour, speech and attitude to money would be desired in a leader. Only by discovering answers to questions like these will we be in a position to understand the nature of the criticisms levelled against Paul.

It is also clear that in the minds of the Corinthians these apparently 'secular' criticisms had important 'religious' implications. For instance, we see that Paul's failure to measure up to the social standards of his converts (if that is indeed the case, a point which still needs to be established) caused them to question his position in Christ (10:7; 13:3). They were using their secular prejudices to assess the legitimacy of his ministry. This suggests that we must also learn something about the way in which people in antiquity evaluated religion, and especially how they related the religious realm to the secular.

The task before us, then, is two-fold. We need to establish how people in Paul's day evaluated (i) each other and (ii) religion. That of course will mean conducting a fairly extensive enquiry into the routine environment of the first century. Only in this way will we be able to gain insight into the nature of the criticisms levelled against Paul and hopefully, in turn, the meaning of his paradoxical reply.

The method of this study

The sort of historical enquiry which we are envisaging must be governed by sound method and hence the following precautions will be observed.

1 Social facts

There is currently great interest among NT scholars in developing a 'social description' of early Christianity.[47] Such a description would seem to call for a careful gathering and sifting of social facts. Yet much of the work completed so far gives only passing attention to such facts and focusses instead on reading the NT in the light of modern sociological models.[48] The reason for this is probably due

---

[47] Cf. the survey of scholarship in Scroggs 'Sociological Interpretation' 168–77.
[48] Cf. the criticism by Judge 'Social Identity' 209–12; Smith 'Community' 123–30.

both to the current vogue of sociological analysis in historical studies in general and to the very scattered nature of the historical evidence relevant to biblical studies.[49] The danger of this approach is that social history is reduced to modern sociological theory and consequently that we learn more about contemporary social models than the actual situation in antiquity. In the enquiry which follows, we shall give priority to the gathering of social facts and to an interpretive process which allows those facts to speak within the context of their own time.

2   Breadth of scope

There has been a tendency among historians in general to regard small sectors of society as though they represented the whole. The entire history of Rome, for example, has often been depicted in terms of the lives of the Caesars and their wars. Similarly, the history of early Christianity has sometimes been viewed narrowly in terms of gnosticism or mystery religions.[50] Our enquiry will require greater breadth, for we are seeking to identify the habitual thoughts of ordinary people, thoughts which cannot be attributed to isolated factors or influences. Here we shall find the work of the classicist R. MacMullen especially helpful for, unlike many others in his field, he seeks to discover the 'feelings that governed the behaviour of broad social groups'.[51]

3   Accurate dating

The time when Paul ministered in Corinth was one of rapid change. Styles of speech, in particular, underwent profound revision.[52] If we are to be at all confident of our understanding of the attitudes of first-century Corinthians we shall need to pay close attention to the dates of our sources. Accordingly, we shall focus on evidence which can be dated with some measure of certainty to the period one hundred years on either side of Paul's sojourn in Corinth – that is to say, the period roughly between 50 BC and AD 150. If reference is made to sources outside this period it will be duly noted. The dates

---

[49] Cf. Judge 'Social Identity' 216.
[50] Cf. the criticism by Judge 'Classical Society' 23.
[51] MacMullen *Social Relations* vii.
[52] Cf. Früchtel 'Attizimus' 899–900; Peters *Hellenism* 541–42.

of literary figures cited in the text are set out in the list of abbreviations above.

4 Diversity of sources

There has been a tendency among biblical scholars to rely heavily on ancient literature as a source of historical background. But the record left on parchment and paper was almost exclusively the province of the intellectual elite and thus not always reflective of the thoughts and behaviour of people like the Corinthian Christians.[53] Of course if used carefully literary sources can still be of great value. But of much greater relevance is the testimony left on stone and metal – the witness of inscriptions, coins and other archaeological artifacts. The advantage of these sources is 'the closeness of contact which they give us with the ancient world'.[54] Unlike literature, the evidence of, say, epigraphy brings us more consistently into touch with the thoughts and feelings of ordinary men and women.[55] We shall therefore make use of such sources whenever possible. The best approach is undoubtedly to employ a diversity of sources, both non-literary and literary.

5 Evidence from Corinth

At first glance, the condition of the epigraphical and archaeological evidence from first-century Corinth is disappointing. Much of it is mutilated or lost.[56] Nevertheless, it can still be of immense value, especially when used in conjunction with evidence gleaned from the Graeco-Roman world at large.[57] Accordingly, our approach will be to seek first to answer our questions using data drawn from the Graeco-Roman world in general, where evidence is abundant and generalisation safer, and then to compare and contrast our findings with data taken from Roman Corinth in particular.

[53] Cf. MacMullen *Paganism* 9, 65, 68.
[54] Thus Woodhead *Greek Inscriptions* 1–5 (citation 3).
[55] Cf. Tod *Greek History* 24: 'While the illumination afforded by a literary record is often dim and diffused, inscriptions . . . illuminate vividly, intensely, one small spot, leaving all around in darkness'; and Dill *Roman Society* 196: 'The silence of Roman literature generally as to social life outside the capital is very remarkable . . . For the municipal system and life, the relations of its various social grades, the humdrum routine of shops and forums, the rustic rites and deities, the lingering echoes of that dim common life with its vices and honest tenderness, its petty ambitions or hopeless griefs, we must generally go to the records in stone'.
[56] Cf. Powell 'Inscriptions from Corinth' 26–27; Kent 17.   [57] Cf. Kent 20.

6   Tentative conclusions

The tentative nature of our enquiry and its conclusions hardly needs to be stressed. One can never be confident of having captured the essence of an age, if indeed an age can be distilled to a single essence. Our study will therefore be suggestive, not definitive. It will be a beginning of research, on which firmer conclusions can be built as further evidence comes to hand.[58] Its value will rest on whether what we discover about the ways in which the early Corinthians evaluated people and religion can be seen to shed light on the criticisms which the Corinthian Christians are levelling against Paul, and whether this in turn serves to illuminate Paul's paradoxical teaching of power through weakness. Before we embark on this study we must set out the plan for the book as a whole.

The plan

The enquiry into first-century Corinth will form the first chapter of the book. In chapter two we shall attempt to discover from the standpoint of the biblical text whether this historical analysis has served to illuminate our understanding of the criticisms directed against Paul. These two chapters together will comprise the first part of the study, the 'background' to Paul's teaching of power through weakness.

In part two we shall examine the paradox itself. In particular, we shall seek to establish not only why Paul expresses himself in paradoxical terms (here the insights of part one will be particularly useful), but also what he means by these terms – that is, how he *himself* understands his teaching of power through weakness. This will feature in chapters three, four, five and six, an examination of key portions of 2 Corinthians 2:14–7:4, and especially of 4:1–18, where the paradox emerges in a particularly striking light.

[58] The rate of publication of *new* data – epigraphical and papyriological – is greater now than ever before; cf. Judge 'Social Identity' 216 n. 40.

PART I

Power through weakness: the background

I

THE SOCIAL SETTING OF FIRST-CENTURY CORINTH: AN HISTORICAL EXAMINATION

The Graeco-Roman world

We may begin our historical analysis by looking at the way in which people evaluated their peers and religion in the Graeco-Roman world at large.

The appraisal of fellow-humans

1 Individualism

The hellenistic age was marked by the decline of the city-state with its close-knit social bonds and by the rise of individualism. No longer was corporate solidarity the ideal. Instead people cultivated a rigorous self-sufficiency (αὐτάρκεια).[1] Philosophers stressed human autonomy and ethicists called for individual initiative. Consequently, people began to focus on themselves and in particular on cultivating their self-worth.[2] For many, self-appreciation became the goal and self-glorification the reward.[3]

---

[1] Thus Dihle 'Ethik' 652: 'Alle hellenist. E(thik) ist im Kern streng individualistisch u. lehrt die Autonomie u. Autarkie des Einzelnen' ('The entire hellenistic ethic is at its core strongly individualistic and teaches the autonomy and self-sufficiency of the individual'); see also Wendland *Die hellenistisch-römische Kultur* 45; Grant *Roman Hellenism* 15; Ferguson *Roman Empire* 190.

[2] Cf. again Dihle 'Demut' 738: 'Alle antike Ethik basiert geradezu auf einem ausgesprochenen Selbst- u. Wertgefühl des einzelnen Menschen.' ('The entire ancient ethic is really based on a pronounced feeling of self and of worth in the individual man.') While the Stoics placed importance on duty to others (see Cicero's *De Officiis*), even this was meant to enhance individual esteem. On cultivating self-worth see Sen. *Ep.* 34.3–4, 66.46, 115.3–4; Plut. *Mor.* 76B-E.

[3] Cf. Judge 'Antike und Christentum' 5: 'All classical systems are based on the specific self-appreciation of the individual'.

2   Status

In Roman society rank was a prized possession. It determined one's behaviour, relationships and legal privileges. All people belonged to one of two classes: the *honestiores* or the *humiliores*, the high or the low. The former was made up of the nobility – senators, equestrians and, away from Rome itself, decurions. These were men who, together with their womenfolk, were esteemed for their *dignitas* and often possessed great power and fortune. The *humiliores* – plebs, freedmen and slaves – lacked *dignitas* and were held in no honour by the nobility.[4] Since rank was hereditary, movement from one class to the other was virtually impossible.[5]

Yet there *was* social mobility. In the early Empire the *honestiores* comprised a mere one percent of the population[6] and since they lived either in Rome or, to a lesser extent, in other parts of Italy, the rest of the Empire was theoretically a one-class system. However 'the feel of society, the living sense of its proportions' gave a very different impression.[7] In the cities civil magistrates sat at the top of a steep pyramid. At the bottom, representing nearly a third of the population, were the indigent and slaves. That left a huge mass of people, nearly two-thirds of the total, in the middle – men and women who were relatively free to manoeuvre, if not into the ranks of the nobility, at least into higher strata within their own hetero-geneous class. For these individuals upward mobility became a passion.[8]

Higher status was primarily a function of wealth.[9] The rich found

---

[4] For a full discussion of class structure in Roman times see Garnsey *Social Status* 221–80; cf. also Stambaugh 'Social Relations' 75; den Boer *Private Morality* 49; Finley *Ancient Economy* 87.

[5] Thus Hopkins 'Elite Mobility' 12–26.

[6] The senatorial stratum amounted to two-thousandths of one percent of the popu-lation and the equestrians totalled less than a tenth of one percent.

[7] MacMullen *Roman Social Relations* 90.

[8] It is largely to this group that Paul addressed his letters. For the relatively educated, upwardly mobile composition of Pauline congregations cf. Malherbe *Early Chris-tianity* 29–59; Meeks *First Urban Christians* 51–73; Judge 'Social Identity' 201–17; Gill 'Social Élite' 324–330; Kreissig 'Zur sozialen Zusammensetzung' 99; Hengel *Property and Riches* 36–39; Gülzow 'Soziale Gegebenheiten' 220–21; Grant *Early Christianity* 11; *pace* Deissmann *Light* 62–145; Scroggs 'Sociological Interpreta-tion' 164–79; Gager 'Social Class' 113; Gigon *Die antike Kultur* 16–17; Engels *Roman Corinth* 70.

[9] Thus MacMullen *Roman Social Relations* 109: 'To rise in the world, one must be a man of means' (cf. 88, 117); and cf. Lucian *Gall.* 11: the wealthy 'hold their heads

it easy to rise in the world, but the less prosperous were not without means. They too could ply some skill and rise to relative affluence and respectability. Their passage was easiest in the cities, particularly in maritime trading centres.[10] It was there that aggressive freedmen emerged as the Empire's merchants and some amassed fortunes which rivalled the nobility.[11] This naturally provoked the scorn of the free-born of lesser means.[12] Not surprisingly, people worshipped wealth – as Juvenal put it: 'no deity is held in such reverence among us as Wealth' (1.112–13). Poverty, on the other hand, was regarded with contempt. It was 'evil and unfortunate' (D. Chr. *Or.* 7.115), 'a disgrace and a dishonour' (Cic. *Tusc.* 5.15).[13]

Wealth was not the only means of scaling the social ladder. The philosophers taught that one could cultivate social respectability through virtuous living.[14] While this would have suited the lettered elite, the common person was more likely to choose other channels. He could advance socially by claiming some advantage or authority by virtue of his name,[15] occupation,[16] neighborhood,[17] talents,[18]

---

high' (ἐξυπτιάζειν), receiving 'the admiration and the envy of all beholders' (similarly *Cat.* 16; *Ind.* 21); see also Dill *Roman Society* 209; Kolb 'Statussymbolik' 239.

[10] Thus Meiggs *Ostia* 230; MacMullen *Roman Social Relations* 98.

[11] On the wealth of freedmen see below pp. 38–39.

[12] E.g. Juv. 1.24–30; and see Reekmans 'Juvenal's Views of Social Change' 121, 141–45; Reinhold 'Usurpation of Status' 275–302.

[13] Cf. Artem. 4.18: 'to be poor means good luck to no one'; and Lucian *Nigr.* 23: the poor 'speak as a slave'.

[14] Cf. Sen. *Dial.* 2.15.2–3: 'his virtue has placed him in another region of the universe'; and 7.26.7: 'give respect to those who have long pursued [virtue]'; see also *Ep.* 67.16; Plut. *Mor.* 75C, 76C–86A; and cf. Dihle 'Ethik' 653–54; Armstrong 'Greek Philosophy' 362.

[15] A name announced pedigree (cf. Lucian *Gall.* 14: 'Tell that pauper not to abbreviate my name: it is not Simon, but Simonides') — Greek names in Roman cities usually indicated servile descent (Taylor 'Freedmen' 125); hence freedmen often gave their sons a Latin *cognomen* (Gordon 'Freedman's Son' 67); cf. Lucian *Tim.* 22: 'a lewd slave held in high esteem ... changing his name from Pyrrhias'.

[16] Men proudly displayed their line of work on gravestones: see e.g. a 'carpenter' (ILS 7715; SEG 4.105); 'sculptor' (IG 2.2.9611; Calabi-Limentani no. 57); 'architect' (ILS 7733); 'engraver' (Calabi-Limentani no. 127); and for the shared prestige of craft guilds cf. CIL 6.9316, 10.6699, 7039; CIG 3629; see also Burford *Craftsmen*; and further examples below p. 85, esp. nn. 126 and 127.

[17] See the refs. in MacMullen *Roman Social Relations* 175 n. 52.

[18] Cf. Cic. *Off.* 2.10.

education,[19] religion,[20] political office[21] or athletic accomplishment.[22]

Whatever the means, elevating one's status was a cherished feature of urban life in the first century AD. And no wonder: an individual's worth and consequently his respect in the community was dependent on the status he was able to project.

3 Self-display

The projection of status was crucial. It was not enough simply to possess wealth or authority. The Greeks were people of eyes[23] and they sought to authenticate status visually.[24] As Plutarch observed: 'Most people think that to be deprived of the chance to display wealth is to be deprived of the wealth itself' (*Cat. Ma.* 18.4, here slightly paraphrased); similarly Lucian: 'the man who lives in a fine house gets no good of it, nor of his ivory or gold either, unless someone admires it all' (*Nigr.* 23).[25] Accordingly, the rich flaunted their wealth, erecting monuments and buildings in their own honour and purchasing political office.[26] The less fortunate were equally interested in self-glorification, though their methods were more simple.

The lack of privacy in the cities only encouraged public display. Life was lived in the streets in full view of the neighbour; little happened that was not known to all.[27] The wealthy paraded their riches in the full knowledge that it would win them instant

---

19 Cf. Vett. Val. 2.22 (p. 88): 'one enjoys good fortune from letters and learning — much loved, much known, worthy of honour, gifts and glory, and blessed by all'; see also Petron. *Sat.* 58; Artem. 2.12; and Hopkins 'Elite Mobility' 14.

20 See Gordon 'Mithraism and Roman Society' 109; Barton and Horsley 'Hellenistic Cult Group' 13, 39.

21 Cf. Vett. Val. 1.22 (pp. 45–46); and MacMullen 'Social History' 108.

22 See Finley and Pleket *Olympic Games* 81.

23 Thus Snell *Ausdrücke* 69.

24 Cf. MacMullen *Roman Social Relations* 109: '[people] sized each other up . . . according to . . . display'; see also Peters *Hellenism* 354; Boman *Hebrew Thought Compared with Greek* 200–15.

25 Cf. also Juv. 7.134–49; Petron. *Sat.* 32–38.

26 Cf. Artem. 4.17: 'a rich man must spend freely'; and 2.27: 'ever ambitious for honour, he will spend for the people'; see also Plut. *Cic.* 8.1; and MacMullen *Roman Social Relations* 61–62; Dill *Roman Society* 211, 217, 219–31; Meiggs *Ostia* 222.

27 Thus in Corinth large crowds gathered 'straightaway' to hear a new orator (D. Chr. *Or.* 8.10) or to see horses fighting (9.22); cf. also MacMullen *Roman Social Relations* 62–64; Meeks 'Urban Environment' 118.

acclaim.[28] The poor and the delinquent were less fortunate and their miseries brought instant scorn.[29] It was a time when everyone yearned for an admiring public. The pursuit of upward mobility thus turned into a quest for applause and esteem.[30] Not surprisingly, personal glory, δόξα, became an ideal.[31] The word itself conveyed the dual notions of visual splendour and lofty esteem.[32]

When people turned to evaluate their contemporaries they looked for the same evidence of personal worth and glory that they prized for themselves: impressive displays of status worthy of public applause and esteem.

4 Competition for honour

The first century AD was intensely competitive. People knew that glory was elusive and that they had to vie with others to keep it. Consequently, they struggled to remain one-up on their peers.[33] The rich spent lavishly and sometimes impoverished themselves in order to excel their rivals and retain their repute.[34] The common person clung tenaciously to whatever distinction might elevate him above the rabble.[35] It was an era of high incentive and great accomplishment, but also of anxiety and uncertainty.

[28] Cf. Lucian *Nigr.* 23: '[the rich are] admired for their possessions, praised for their plate, [and people] crowd their doorways'.

[29] On the poor being 'jeered' and the 'target of ridicule' see Petron. *Sat.* 57 and Juv. 3.153–54, respectively (cf. Pliny *Ep.* 9.6); on public scorn for 'those who have been struck by aediles with lashes' see *Dig.* 50.2.12 (Callistratus).

[30] Cf. Cic. *Off.* 2.9: 'The highest, truest glory depends upon . . . the admiration and esteem of the people'; Tac. *Ann.* 4.38: 'In the scorn of fame was implied the scorn of virtue'; and D. Chr. *Or.* 51.2: 'with us everybody lauds everybody'; see also Petron. *Sat.* 55, 57; D. Chr. *Or.* 8.32; Juv. 13.34–37; and MacMullen 'Women in Public' 215.

[31] Cf. the honorific inscriptions SIG³ 2.700 (35): ἀξίως δὲ καὶ τῆς ἰδίας δόξης τε καὶ ἀνδρείας ('and worthy also of his own glory and manliness'); and SIG³ 2.704E (20): δὲ τὰ πρός δόξαν καὶ τιμήν ('and our relation [?] to glory and honour'); see also Cic. *Arch.* 11.26.

[32] Thus Vermeulen *Gloria* 11.

[33] Cf. Cic. *Off.* 2.10: 'those are regarded with admiration who are thought to excel others in ability'; Tac. *Ann.* 4.38: 'the best men . . . desire the greatest heights'; and Dill *Roman Society* 231: 'The passion for prominence was probably never greater'; see also den Boer *Private* Morality 32.

[34] Thus D. Chr. *Or.* 46.3–4: 'he spent on public benefactions all that he had . . . so that he had nothing left at all . . . [and] was held in great friendship and esteem'; and cf. MacMullen *Roman Social Relations* 61–62: 'a thirst for honor' moved the wealthy to give 'with a generosity unequalled in any other period of human history'; also 106–9; 'Social History' 108; Jones *Greek City* 249; Kolb 'Status-symbolik' 259.

[35] For freedmen this distinction was material prosperity and they pursued it with unusual vigour; see Taylor 'Freedmen' 131; Gordon 'Freedman's Son' 75–77.

Competition for honour had two important side-effects. First, it encouraged outward expressions of pride and arrogance.[36] For many boasting itself became an activity worthy of honour.[37] Humility, on the other hand, was scorned.[38] The lowly had no self-respect, no public standing – they were 'slaves on a low scale' (Epict. 4.1.55).[39] It follows, secondly, that individuals grew indifferent to the needs of others.[40] Serving one's neighbour for his own sake was too self-effacing and so was avoided.[41] As a result, dissension and even hostility plagued the communities of the early Empire.[42]

In short, people assessed each other on the basis of how well they measured up to their neighbour: was their boasting more compelling, their self-assertion more arresting?

5   Cities

Competition also emerged on a larger scale. In particular, the material splendour of cities became the object of intense rivalry.[43]

---

[36] Indeed 'Roman arrogance' became proverbial, thus Tac. *Ad. Gr.* 35.

[37] Cf. D. Chr. *Or.* 57.5: '[It is the] mark of a foolish person to be ashamed to praise himself'. Further on self-praise cf. Epict. 3.14.12–14; Petron. *Sat.* 38, 50–51; Plut. *Mor.* 540A-B; MacMullen *Roman Social Relations* 110–14; Dill *Roman Society* 216–17.

[38] Cf. Dihle 'Demut' 737: 'Die D[emut] als Tugend ist der gesamten antiken Ethik fremd.' ('Humility as a virtue is foreign to the entire ancient ethic.'); see also Dihle 'Ethik' 687–88; 'Antike Höflichkeit' 184–85; Dodds *Greeks and the Irrational* 215, 238; *pace* Rehrl *Demut* 196–203.

[39] Cf. Lucian *Somm.* 9: 'the humble-witted [are] . . . neither sought by their friends nor feared by their enemies . . . [but are] ever cringing to the man above'; and D. C. 52.8.5: 'No one of servile background can develop any great pride'; also Lucian *Nigr.* 21, 23; Epict. 3.24.54–57; and cf. Origen *Cels.* 6.15. On the disgrace of humility Dihle 'Demut' 741 explains: 'verschmähen sowohl Griechen wie Römer jede Haltung oder Gebärde, die einer Minderung des Persönlichkeitswertes gleichkommt.' ('Both Greeks and Romans spurn any posture or gesture which amounts to a reduction of personal worth.'); for modifications of Dihle see den Boer '*Tapeinos*' 143–62.

[40] Cf. Petron. *Sat.* 48; and see Tarn and Griffith *Hellenistic Civilisation* 110. A few, of course, did consider such indifference a bad thing.

[41] Cf. again Dihle 'Ethik' 687: 'Die hingebende Liebe, die nicht nach der eigenen προκοπή fragt, sondern allein durch das Verlangen des Nächsten provoziert wird, ist dieser E[thik] fremd.' ('The sacrificial love which does not ask after its own "advancement" but is alone triggered by the desire of the neighbour is foreign to this ethic.'); see also den Boer *Private Morality* 72.

[42] Thus D. Chr. *Or.* 38.24: 'contending for primacy . . . has served as the cause of strife'; cf. MacMullen *Enemies* 94; Dill *Roman Society* 375.

[43] Thus D. Chr. *Or.* 44.9: 'although Prusa is not the largest of cities . . . it has long caused its citizens to rank . . . in competition with virtually all Greeks everywhere';

Loyal citizens would sacrifice large sums of money to support elaborate building schemes. Their sole reward was the proud boast of a finer agora, a grander temple. But that was reward enough. To rich and poor alike, boasting in one's city was a matter of personal standing.[44]

6   Summary

Late Hellenism stressed an individual's ability to determine his own worth. When the Roman emphasis on social stratification penetrated Greek society, people gained both a framework for measuring worth and an incentive to reach higher.[45] In theory, higher status was attained through wealth and/or some other social advantage. But this was meaningless unless acknowledged by others. Consequently, people competed for attention. They paraded their lives before their contemporaries in an attempt to earn applause and esteem. Assertiveness and pride characterised their efforts and boasting was *de rigueur*. When people turned to appraise their counterparts they looked for the same indications of worth and status which they valued for themselves: namely, impressive displays meriting public applause and esteem.

The appraisal of religion

I   Popularity of pagan cults

The first centuries AD witnessed a surge in religious interest. Lucian wrote that 'the large majority of Greeks and all of the non-Greeks' practise religion (*Trag.* 53). Aelian condemned the 'barbaric wisdom' of atheism (*VH* 2.31; cf. D. Chr. *Or.* 43.11; Lucian *Demon.* 11).[46] And inscriptions document a lively cult-life.[47] But was relig-

cf. Aristid. *Or.* 26.97–99; Jones *Roman World* 86–90; Jones *Greek City* 248–50; MacMullen *Roman Social Relations* 60–61.

[44] On civic pride see Cic. *Off.* 2.17; D. Chr. *Or.* 46.3; and Robert 'Le titre de "nourricier du peuple"' 569, nn. 35, 42; as well as the numerous benefactions to the city of Corinth below p. 41.

[45] Cf. Peters *Hellenism* 309–11; Meeks 'Urban Environment' 113–14; Dihle 'Demut' 742–43.

[46] Cf. Plut. *Mor.* 1125E: 'a city without holy places and gods, without any observance of prayers, oaths, oracles, sacrifices for blessings received or rites to avert evil, no traveller has ever seen or will ever see'.

[47] In Corinth, for example, cf. inscriptions honouring Neptune/Poseidon (West nos. 2 and 3; Kent no. 156; IG 4.201, 210, 211, 215–20), Venus (Kent no. 56), Serapis

ion deeply-felt? Did it penetrate the innermost heart of worshippers? Here the evidence is mixed. Seneca exposed the superficial in religion (*De superstit.* in August. *De civ. D.* 6.10); Juvenal highlighted naive belief (13.34–37); and Petronius' Trimalchio questioned the gods (Petron. *Sat.* 44). On the other hand, Chrysostom claimed that all people honour deity (*Or.* 12.60–61); Plutarch called attention to devout worship (*Mor.* 270D); and Ovid pointed to divine service (*Fast.* 6.249). With such disparate testimony it is natural to enquire what it was that worshippers wanted from religion.

Was it, as traditional historians believe, relief from an 'age of anxiety'?[48] The classicist R. MacMullen thinks not. He argues that an 'age' is too complex to be limited to a single characteristic – such as 'anxiety'. Moreover, he suggests that the wide spectrum of feelings and experiences conjured up by first-century cults shows that people were seeking much more.[49] The most prominent of their yearnings are highlighted below.

2   Rationalism and superstition

In the first century BC intellectualism fell on hard times. People became disillusioned with natural causes and began to focus on the activity of the gods.[50] The philosophers bore the brunt of criticism and many of them felt compelled to modify their teaching to accommodate the supernatural.[51] This alarmed traditionalists. They decried the religious and 'shallow' teachings of, say, Neoplatonism and Pythagoreanism and called for a revival of strict rationalism.[52]

---

and Isis (Kent no. 57), Demeter, Kore, Palaemon and Helios (IG 4.203), Asclepius (Kent no. 63), Janus (Kent no. 195), Victory (Kent no. 199), Saturn (West no. 6) and Nemesis (West no. 10). See also below p. 50.

[48] Thus Dodds *Age of Anxiety* 3; *Greeks* 253; Cumont *Les religions orientales* 38–40; Peters *Hellenism* 617.

[49] Cf. MacMullen *Paganism* 64, 122–24; *Roman Government* 13–15; Gordon 'Roman Society' 93–94.

[50] There were of course exceptions, such as the poet and philosopher Lucretius; but on the general anti-intellectual trend of the day see Peters *Hellenism* 426–27. By the second century AD Sextus Empiricus had applied an 'intellectual coup de grâce to the world of reason' (so Cramer *Astrology* 203–4), concluding οὐκ ἄρα ἔστι τι μάθημα ('there is then no learning') (*M.* 1.9).

[51] Cf. Sen. *Ep.* 5.2: 'the mere name of philosophy . . . is an object of sufficient scorn'; Quint. *Inst.* 1pr15: 'the name of philosopher has too often been the mask for the worst vices'; and Juv. 2.10: 'socratic reprobates'; see also Tac. *Agr.* 4.1, 3; D. Chr. *Or.* 34.52

[52] Thus Armstrong 'Greek Philosophy' 350; Dihle 'Ethik' 672–75; Nock *Conversion* 120; MacMullen *Enemies* 107–8.

This prompted an 'atticizing' trend in the first century AD, but it influenced little more than the conventions of speech among the lettered elite.[53] The general impulse of the age remained firm. People wanted contact with the supernatural, not logic and learning.

Magic provided that contact, and at every level.[54] Peasants and senators alike hung amulets round their necks to chase away evil spirits.[55] Recipes for magic written on papyri were perused in the streets.[56] Nero solicited rites from the magi in order to escape his mother's ghost.[57] Curse tablets inveighed against all kinds of malefactors.[58] Astrology,[59] oracles,[60] portents[61] and dreams[62] filled out an atmosphere of enchantment. The abundance of the evidence suggests that vast segments of first-century society were engrossed in superhuman schemes and engulfed in superstitition.[63]

3 Soteria

It is clear from the recurrence of *Soter* and *Soteria* in the inscriptions that 'salvation' played an important role in first-century religion. Yet it was not salvation as we would understand it – not deliverance from this world and safe passage to the next.[64] In fact the notion of afterlife receives only the faintest attestation in the evidence – for example, in the Dionysiac mysteries of the late second and early third centuries.[65] Otherwise, the record is very pessimistic

[53] Cf. Früchtel 'Attizismus' 899; Peters *Hellenism* 541–42.
[54] On the pervasive influence of magic in the first century cf. Lucian *Alex.* 6; Juv. 6.610–11; Pliny *HN* 17.267, 28.19–20, 47; Luc. 6.430–830; and see Aune 'Magic' 1507–57, esp. 1519; MacMullen *Enemies* 95–127; Nilsson 'Greek Religion' 264.
[55] Thus Artem. 5.26; Pliny *HN* 33.41; MacMullen *Enemies* 103; Bonner 'Magic Amulets' 25–53.
[56] Cf. Acts 19:19; Nock 'Greek Magical Papyri' 219–35, esp. 227–30.
[57] Thus Suet. *Nero* 34.4.
[58] Cf. Elderkin 'Curse Inscriptions' 382–95.
[59] Cf. Tac. *Ann.* 2.27, 12.22; Juv. 6.576, 582, 588; Dihle 'Ethik' 674–76; MacMullen *Enemies* 128–42.
[60] See D. C. 79.7.4; Pliny *Ep.* 7.27.   [61] See Suet. *Nero* 36; Pliny *HN* 28.17.
[62] On a city council acting on the advice of dreams see IG 1.568, 387; cf. also Hanson 'Dreams and Visions' 1395–1427, esp. 1396; Dodds *Greeks* 102–21.
[63] On δεισιδαιμονία ('superstition') in the first century see Plut. *Per.* 6.1; *Cleom.* 39; *Tim.* 26.1–2; *Nic.* 23; cf. other refs. in Erbse 'Plutarchs Schrift' 296–314, esp. 301–4; and further on superstition see Schneider *Kulturgeschichte des Hellenismus* 907–10; MacMullen *Paganism* 70.
[64] Simon 'Pagan Thought' 392 suggests that the ancient's quest for eternal life is 'a well known fact', but offers no supporting evidence; similarly Markus *Roman World* 29; in rebuttal see MacMullen *Paganism* 55, 172 n. 22.
[65] Cf. Nilsson *Dionysiac Mysteries* 147; and for traces of the belief in an afterlife elsewhere see MacMullen *Paganism* 53–56; Betz 'Apocalyptic Genre' 586–87.

and epitaphs even jest about annihilation. We may note, especially, the oft repeated *somno aeterno* ('sleep eternally', CIL 6.15983, 16472, 17430, 18850, 28875; 8.2506), *somno perpetuali* ('sleep forever', CIL 6.19966), *non fui, fui, non sum, non desidero* ('I was not, I was, I am not, I am free from wishes', CIL 8.3463; apparently reduced to the formula *n f f n s n c[uro]* in CIL 5.2893) and οὐκ ἤμην, ἐγενόμην, οὐκ εἰμί, οὐ μέλι μοι ('I was not, I became, I am not, I do not care', IG 14.2190; cf. EG 595; CIG 6745).[66] The outlook is often negative in the literature as well. Seneca denied eternal life (*Luc.* 24.18, 36.10) and Celsus belittled bodily resurrection (Origen *Cels.* 7.32).[67] Such fatalism seemed to engender a wanton lust for life – as the glutton Trimalchio observed: 'Well, well, if we know we must die, why should we not live?' (Petron. *Sat.* 72, cf. 32).[68]

This suggests that soteria had more to do with matters of this life. Indeed, as the inscriptions show, it encompassed such everyday needs as health,[69] wealth,[70] protection[71] and sustenance.[72] Salvation was thus envisaged in terms of present benefits received – what mattered was the service the gods rendered to people, not people

---

66 After a comprehensive study of first-century epitaphs, Lattimore *Latin Epitaphs* 342 concludes: 'the belief of the ancients, both Greek and Roman, in immortality, was not widespread, nor clear, nor strong'.

67 For some evidence of the belief in an afterlife in literary sources see Graf *Eleusis* 79–94.

68 See also the inscription from imperial times in Deissmann *Light* 295: πεῖνε, βλέπις τὸ τέλος ('Drink, behold the end.'); cf. 1 Cor. 15:32; and note the refs. in Bultmann 'εὐφραίνω' 772–73, n. 38.

69 Cf. the inscription from Corinth Παιηωνιεῷ Σωτῆρι ('Healing Saviour') (Kent no. 64); and σωθεὶς θεοῖς σωτῆρσι νόσων ('saved from disease by saviour gods') (LeBas-Wadd. 2343); see also the tribute to many gods ὅτι ὁλοκληροῦσαν με ('for they gave me good health') (Robert *Hell.* 10 [1955] 100); cf. Ael. *NA* 11.35: 'this same god . . . cured Chrysermus . . . lives are saved (σώζεσθαι) by them (viz. the gods)'.

70 Cf. the dedication Διὶ Ἡλίῳ μεγάλῳ Σαράπιδι Σωτῆρι Πλουτοδότῃ ('to divine Helios, great Sarapis, Saviour, Giver of riches') (Vidman no. 389); and Μηνὶ Σωτῆρι καὶ Πλουτοδώτι ('To Saviour Μήν [an astrological god], Giver of riches') (Lane no. 142).

71 See the tribute Σεράπει σωθέντες ἐκ πολέμων μεγάλων ('saved by Serapis from great wars') (CIG 2716 = Lebas-Wadd. 516); and Διὶ Ἡλίῳ μεγάλῳ Σαράπιδι . . . ὁ κράτιστος νεωκόρος ἐκ μεγάλων κινδύνων πολλάκις σωθείς ('to divine Helios, great Sarapis . . . the mighty νεωκόρος ['one who has charge of a temple'] who has often been saved from great hazards') (IGRR 1.107 = IG 14.1030).

72 See Lane no. 92; CIG 3792; LeBas-Wadd. 686.

to the gods.[73] Nock has described this as deity assimilated to the person.[74]

4 Power and display

The great allure of the cults may be summed up in a few words: 'the visible show of divinity at work'.[75] People yearned to see divine power. They wanted to be thrilled by it and even terrified by it.[76] Accordingly, the cults publicised the feats of the gods and tributes to deities appeared on every corner.[77] Temples, sacred fountains, majestic statues and beautiful murals assaulted the senses. Banquets, parades, festivals, dances and drama filled out an atmosphere of religious fervour. Passers-by were meant to stop, look, be filled with awe and believe.

Converts did not regard the god's power passively, but wanted to experience that power for themselves. The more powerful one's god the more strength one expected to receive and manifest.[78] For this reason the stature of the god often became a matter of personal pride.[79] This explains the frequent use of hyperbole – μέγιστος,[80]

---

[73] Cf. Artem. 2.33: 'men sacrifice to gods when they have received benefits'; thus CIL 5.3221: *quot se precibus compotem fecisset* ('how many prayers you [eternal God] have granted fruitfully'); cf. Nilsson 'Greek Religion' 259.

[74] 'Graeco-Roman Beliefs' 91.

[75] Thus MacMullen *Paganism* 126; see also pp. 96, 98; and Nilsson *Geschichte* 41–43.

[76] Cf. Cic. *Nat. D.* 2.6: 'reverence for the gods and respect for religion grow continually stronger [because] . . . the gods often manifest their power in bodily presence'; and see inscription Robert 'Hellenica' 200: ἐπιφανεῖ ἥρῳ ἀπὸ τῆς ἐργασίας ('to the hero who displays his work'); CIG 3646: Ἥρως ἐπιφανὴς ὁ Κράτης ('Hero Manifested [ἐπιφανής = a title of divinities] The Mighty'); and Acts 8:10: ἡ δύναμις τοῦ θεοῦ ἡ καλουμένη μεγάλη.

[77] It was universal knowledge that Asclepius (Plut. *Mor.* 745A; Str. 8.6.15) and Serapis (Str. 17.1.17) could heal, Poseidon could control the earth (Philostr. *VA* 6.41) and, in Corinth, the sea (Broneer 'Hero Cults' 139), and Nemesis could bring victory in war (CIL 6.2820; Wissowa *Religion* 377–79; and in Corinth: West no. 10).

[78] Thus the prayers in P. Par 1665: δὸς ἰσχύν καὶ θάρσος καὶ δύναμιν ('grant strength and courage and power'); P. Lond. 121: [δὸς] τὴν δύναμιν ('grant power'); and P. Par. 1616: δὸς δόξαν καὶ τιμὴν καὶ χάριν καὶ τύχην καὶ δύναμιν ('grant glory and honour and grace and fortune and power'); cf. further Nock 'Graeco-Roman Beliefs' 87; Kolenkow 'Greco-Roman World' 1482.

[79] On extolling the power of one's god cf. P. Oxy. 1381 (215–17): εἰς πάντα γὰρ τόπον διαπεφοίτηκεν ἡ τοῦ θεοῦ δύναμις σωτήριος ('for in every place roams the saving power of the god'); and IGRR 4.1529 (10–12): Ὦ μέγας ὢν καὶ δυνατὸς δυνάμει ('O Great One, powerful in your strength').

[80] Cf. IG 9.2.1201: βασιλέα θεὸν μέγιστον παντοκράτορα ('king, greatest god, almighty'); IGRR 1.107 (= IG 14.1030 = Vidman no. 389): Διὶ Ἡλίῳ μεγάλῳ ('to great divine Helios'); and Acts 19:28 and 34: Μεγάλη ἡ Ἄρτεμις Ἐφεσίων;

κράτιστος,[81] ὕψιστος[82] – in tributes to the gods. Such superlatives served ultimately to elevate and exalt the worshipper himself. It perhaps goes without saying that a weak or servile god was unthinkable.[83]

5 Preaching

In the mid first century BC Cicero expressed his 'regret at the decadence, not to say the utter extinction, of eloquence' (*Off.* 2.19).[84] Such sentiment prompted, one hundred years later, a return to classical oratory and in the second century the rise of the Second Sophistic. The latter was a movement of able communicators such as Quintilian and Philostratus, but it was primarily elitist and confined to the academies and the well educated.[85]

The popular orators of Paul's day were not highly trained. Nor was their stage a lecture hall. It was the agora, the temple precincts, the festivals – anywhere crowds might assemble. Speeches were geared to public tastes, to win applause, to gain a hearty 'Bravo!' or 'Marvellous!' (Epict. 3.23.24).[86] Since people wanted to be amused, preachers specialised in startling effects, sensational topics and powerful deliveries.[87] Truth and knowledge were sacrificed on the altar of popular acclaim.[88] When in Corinth the sage Diogenes proclaimed 'relief from folly, wickedness, and intemperance, not a

---

for further examples see Robert 'Le grand nom de Dieu' 86–89; IGRR 4.1529; Ramsay 'Inscriptions in Asia' 322–23; 'Artemis-Leto' 226, no.21.

81 Cf. IGRR 1.107 (= IG 14.1030) in n. 71 above.

82 See Ramsay 'Sepulchral Customs' 258–59, no. 9.

83 Cf. Cic. *Nat.D.* 1.38: 'what could be more ridiculous than to award divine honours to things mean and ugly, or to give the rank of gods to men'; and S. E. *P.* 1.157: 'we oppose the legendary belief . . . that Heracles . . . toiled at the spinning of wool, enduring slavery's burden'.

84 Cf. also Tac. *Dial.* 32.3–4: 'our clever speakers . . . [demonstrate] the shameful and discrediting blemishes of everyday speech . . . they degrade eloquence . . . to a few commonplaces and cramped conceits'; and see Kennedy *Rhetoric* 442–46.

85 On the elitism of the Second Sophistic cf. Bowersock *Greek Sophists* 11–21; Jones 'Philostratus' 12; Smith *Rhetoric* 130; Peters *Hellenism* 538–41, 545.

86 Cf. Epict. 3.23.10–11; 'when you were received with applause, you walked around and asked everybody "What did you think of me?"'; and 3.23.19: 'you gaped for men to praise you, and counted the number in your audience'; and see the advice to an orator in Lucian *Rh. Pr.* 21: 'make marvellous assertions about yourself, be extravagant in your self-praise'; and D. Chr. *Or.* 32.10: speak for '[your] own glory' (δόξης τῆς ἑαυτῶν); cf. 33.6; Plut. *Mor.* 45F; and Friedländer *Roman Life* 164; Dill *Roman Society* 344.

87 Thus Fantham 'Imitation and Decline' 115–16.

88 Cf. Plut. *Mor.* 1090A: 'Pherecydes and Heracleitus . . . courted applause with a bold display of hollow words'; and see D. Chr. *Or.* 4.33–35.

man would listen'; instead they applauded 'the wretched sophists around Poseidon's temple shouting and reviling one another', the 'many writers reading aloud their stupid works . . . jugglers showing their tricks . . . fortune tellers interpreting fortunes, lawyers innumerable perverting judgment' (D. Chr. *Or.* 8.8–9).[89] The literature further depicts street orators as proud and ruthless, whose sheer force of delivery could overwhelm an audience, prompting admiration and praise.[90]

6 Doctrine

It is not pure misfortune that we know so little about the teachings of first-century paganism. With so much emphasis on show there was little interest in doctrine.[91] The myths and legends underpinning the cults were largely forgotten.[92] People wanted to know the power, not the personality, of the gods. As Aristides puts it: 'If we have said what he (Serapis) can do and what he gives, we have found who he is and what nature he has' (*Or.* 8.52.1). The same preoccupation with the deeds of the gods emerges in the inscriptions. The bulk of religious people had little or no theology.[93]

7 Toleration

The high mobility of people in the early Empire brought various cults together.[94] Yet there was little religious friction, the relative absence of doctrine seeming to ensure against this. Instead the cults

---

[89] While this episode refers to the third-century BC orator Diogenes, it probably reflects the situation in Corinth at the time of its writing in the late first century AD; so Jones *Roman World* 47, 49; Murphy-O'Connor *Corinth* 94.

[90] Cf. the parody of street orators in Lucian *Vit. Auct.* 10: 'you should be impudent and bold and should abuse all . . . for thus they will admire you and think you manly. Let your language be barbarous . . . like the barking of a dog . . . In a word, let everything about you be bestial and savage . . . there will be nothing to hinder you from being wondered at, if only you have impudence and boldness and learn how to abuse people properly'; see also *Peregr.* 3; Epict. 3.22.50–51; 4.8.34.

[91] Thus MacMullen *Paganism* 67, 98, 104–5; Giversen 'Mysterienreligionen' 282; and in Corinth see Broneer 'Hero Cults' 128.

[92] Thus Tac. *Ad. Gr.* 27.2.

[93] Cf. Petron. *Sat.* 44: 'no one cares a button for dogma'; and see Simon 'Pagan Thought' 390.

[94] So Meeks 'Urban Environment' 113–14. Nilsson *Geschichte* 2.700 suggested that such mobility fostered religious syncretism; cf. also Köster *Einführung* 169. But MacMullen *Paganism* 93–94 disagrees: the gods seemed to retain their own identities.

offered basically the same fare: salvation, power and (as we shall see) entertainment. It was not uncommon for people to tolerate and even to enlist in more than one cult.[95] Indeed temples sometimes housed numerous deities[96] and priests performed rites for several gods.[97] The person who advocated one religion to the exclusion of the others brought ridicule and abuse upon himself.[98]

8   Cult and society

Religion provided for the social needs of communities by giving people a place to come together for food, drink and fellowship. Only temples had kitchens and dining rooms sufficient to host the great feasts so loved in antiquity. Secular groups, too, used these facilities.[99] The cult banquet was renowned for its ample servings of meat and drink and consequently for its gross indulgence of appetites.[100] While the gods were thought to be present at festive occasions,[101] the religious significance of banquets was often subordinated to merriment and revelry.[102]

---

95 On worshipping more than one deity cf. SIG³ 1153: πάντα θεὸν σεμνύνομεν ('we magnify every god'); and P. Oxy. 1766 (18) θεοῖς πᾶσιν εὔχομαι ('I pray to all gods.'); see also Robert *Hell.* 10 (1955) 100; Grant *Roman Hellenism* 17.

96 In Pergamum the temple of Demeter also had altars to Hermes, Helios, Zeus, Asclepius and Heracles; so Ohlemutz *Kulte* 218–19.

97 In Rome cf. inscription to ὁ ἱερεὺς τῶν ... θεῶν πάντων ('the priest of ... all the gods') (Kaibel *Epigrammata Graeca* no. 588); and see ILS 4413 where Rufus Volsinianus was *pater* (of the cult of Mithras), *ierofanta* (of the cult of Hecate), *profeta Isidis, pontifex dei Sol* (see Nock 'Graeco-Roman Beliefs' 89).

98 Thus Apul. *Met.* 9.14 who regards a certain baker's wife as 'an enemy of faith and chastity' because she is a 'despiser of all the gods whom others did honour'. On religious toleration in the ancient world see Momigliano *Claudius* 28.

99 On dining rooms in the Asclepieion at Troezen see Welter *Troizen* 32, near the sanctuary of Hera Akraia at Perachora cf. Payne *Perachora* 1.14, in the temple of Heracles at Thasos see Launey 'Le verger d'Héraklès' 402–3 and at Lato in Crete cf. Demargne 'Fouilles a Lato' 216. On 'the banqueting-hall (ἑστιατήριον) in the temple [of Artemis in Ephesus]' see Philostr. *VS* 665; and the gift of a ἑστιατήριον to the temple of Artemis cf. Reinach 'Notes' 239. See also τρίκλεινον δειπνιστήριον ('a dining room with couches on three sides') in the sanctuary at Chalcis (IG 12.9.906 [10]) and θυηπόλειον δειπνιστήριον ('a dining room with an altar') in honour of Aphrodite (Reinach 'Inscriptions' 242).

100 Cf. Petron. *Sat.* 21: 'swimming in wine'; and ILS 6328: 'all night celebration for the ancestral god'.

101 Cf. Aristid. *Or.* 8.54.11 who insists that the god Serapis sits 'before them as a guest and diner'; cf. also SIG³ 1109.

102 Thus Plutarch (*Mor.* 1102A) must remind his readers that 'it is not the abundance of wine or the roast meats that cheer the hearts at festivals, but ... the belief in the benign presence of the god'.

If the cults were vital to social life they were equally important for the cultivation of fine art. Hundreds, sometimes thousands, of people filed into great theatres to watch an essentially religious fare. The χορευταί ('choral dancers') of Dionysos or of Aphrodite (cf. Lucian *Salt.* 10–11) and the *ballatores* of Cybele (see CIL 6.2265) attracted large followings, but miming dancers, those enacting the lives of the gods, were most popular.[103] In temples entertainers found a second stage. The ἀκροβάται of Artemis danced on tiptoes while pouring wine onto altars (cf. B. Mus. Inscr. 3.481 [374–76]),[104] priests of Apollo acted the mime during sacrifices (CIL 10.3716; cf. 14.2113, 2977) and choirboys (B. Mus. Inscr. 3.481 [192–93, 328–29]; cf. Lucian *Salt.* 16) and trumpeters (Plut. *Mor.* 364F) provided music at holy services. If we take into account the architecture, frescos and mosaics of Graeco-Roman society, the best of which were reserved for sacred purposes – for temples, religious statues and monuments – we gain some impression of the imposing part which religion played in the arts. Without the cults, fine culture largely disappears.[105]

Religion was likewise a boon to commerce. Great temples attracted pilgrims to the cities – after paying homage to the gods they paid their money to local merchants.[106] This pattern was encouraged by the close proximity of shops and shrines, the former sometimes falling within the precincts of the latter.[107] The great religious festivals of the first century were generally commercial affairs, dominated by 'hucksters ... [in] booths of reeds and other improvised material ... [selling] slaves and all kinds of cattle, also garments, and silver and gold' (Paus. 10.32.14–16).[108] The link

---

[103] Thus Apul. *Met.* 10.30–31; Lucian *Salt.* 67; Tat. *Ad. Gr.* 32; and see Lucian *Salt.* 15: 'not a single ancient mystery cult can be found that is without dancing'.

[104] See further examples of sacred ἀκροβάται in Picard 'Ephèse' 255–57.

[105] Thus MacMullen *Paganism* 24: 'the whole culture ... was called into the service of the gods'.

[106] Thus Str. 5.3.10: 'the inhabitants of these cities meet ... to hold markets and to perform sacred rites'; see also IGRR 3.1020; and MacMullen 'Market-Days' 336–37.

[107] Cf. CIL 6.9969: *vestar[ius] ab aede Cerer* ('clothes-dealer from the sanctuary of Cerer'); 6.33922: *vestiari de Dianio*; and 6.10006: *unguentaria ab D[ianae]* ('perfume-sellers from the sanctuary of Diane'); further on shops in the temple area see Dudley *Urbs Roma* 123; Staehelin *Die Schweiz in römischer Zeit* 432.

[108] For crowds of shoppers attracted by the festival of Artemis see SIG³ 867; for a priestess thanked for 'attending to merchants and strangers coming ... to the religious/public festival' cf. IGRR 4.144; and for a priest of Dionysos giving τὴν τε στόαν καὶ τοὺς ἐν αὐτῇ οἴκους ('both the stoa and the shops in it') see SEG 1.444.

between cult and commerce would seem to have been intentional: the office of festival president and agora superintendent were frequently combined.[109]

Finally, and briefly (for more will be said about this later), religion was closely related to politics. In particular most civic leaders also performed religious duties.[110]

In short, the cults supplied the heart of daily life. They arranged the social, inspired the cultural, stimulated the commercial and assisted the political. With sacred and secular so intertwined it is natural to ask whether society secularised religion or religion sanctified society. Natural, that is, for the modern person, but unthinkable for the ancients. For the latter, cult and society were inseparable, hardly to be distinguished. We must be content, therefore, with two observations. First, the cults seemed to exact little appreciable change in a convert's manner of life.[111] Secondly, and not unrelated to the first, religion served not as a critic of, but as a warrant for, society. It uplifted, entertained, prospered and confirmed those it was designated to serve.

9 Summary

First century worshippers looked to religion for contact with the divine. But this was contact as they defined it, according to their wants. They wanted divine benefits, not enlightenment – health, wealth, protection and sustenance, not moral transformation. Naturally they were attracted to convincing displays of the gods' power, for they yearned to tap into and display that power for themselves. The stronger the god the more power they could manifest. They cared little for doctrine and thus little for those who excluded every god but their own. They honoured the one who preached with flair, force and pride. In short, they wanted religion to serve them on their own terms – not to change them, but to exalt them.

---

[109] For examples see MacMullen *Paganism* 154 n. 37.
[110] Cf. ILS 4326 where one is honoured for being *Iovis sacerdos* and *decurion*; such examples can be multiplied many times (see below p. 51). On the mix of the civic and the religious see Stambaugh 'Roman Temples' 581–85; Castrèn *Ordo Populusque Pompeianus* 68.
[111] Cf. Nock *Conversion* 160: 'the surprising thing is the slightness of the change which they (the cults) effected in the fundamental temper of the people among whom they took root'.

Corinth

The data assembled thus far give a general picture of the criteria used in Graeco-Roman society to appraise people and religion. But what of Corinth in particular, that city so different from its Mediterranean neighbours? Do the same criteria apply there? In order to answer this question we must discover what it was that distinguished Corinth from other cities.

The appraisal of fellow-humans

1 The City

Corinth was destroyed and its population dispersed by Mummius in 146 BC. In 44 BC, when Julius Caesar issued a directive that a Roman colony be established on the old Corinthian site, the Hellenistic past was largely forgotten. Epigraphy confirms this break. Unlike other cities in Greece, Corinthian inscriptions remained predominantly Latin, and not Greek, until the reign of Hadrian.[112] Interestingly, eight of the seventeen Corinthian names in the New Testament are Latin.[113] When Paul entered Corinth in AD 50 he thus found a young Roman city with shallow roots. There were few traditions, a changing aristocracy and a relatively open society. Perhaps no city in the Empire offered so congenial an atmosphere for individual and corporate advancement.[114]

And advance Corinth did, at a meteoric pace! Most of the inscriptions which testify to building activity fall within the short period

---

[112] Of 104 pre-Hadrian inscriptions 101 are Latin; see Kent 181–89 (a similar proportion of Latin names is found among signatures on Corinthian lamps; cf. Broneer *Isthmia, III: Teracotta Lamps*). The 'break', however, was not total (cf. Murphy-O'Connor *Corinth* 43; *pace* Theissen 'Soziale Schichtung' 262): there was some continuity in religion (cf. Wiseman 'Corinth' 495) and habitation (Cic. *Tusc.* 3.22.53; cf. Harris 'Coins' 158; Kent 20, n. 10; though see Paus. 7.16.7–8; Livy *Per.* 52). On Corinth as a Roman enclave on Greek soil see Dessau *Geschichte* 2.553; Cartledge and Spawforth *Roman Sparta* 104; Gill 'Corinth' 259–64; *pace* Willis 'Corinthusne' 233–4. In the second century AD Corinth became progressively hellenistic; thus D. Chr. *Or.* 37.26.

[113] Cf. Fortunatus (1 Cor. 16:17), Lucius (Rom 16:21), Tertius (Rom 16:22), Gaius and Quartus (Rom 16:23 – assuming, in the last three references, that the epistle to the Romans was written from Corinth), Aquila and Priscilla (Acts 18:2) and Titus Justus (Acts 18:7).

[114] On the contrast between the entrenched aristocracy of Athens and the relatively fluid hierarchy of Corinth see Stambaugh 'Social Relations' 79.

between Augustus and Nero.[115] The second-century historian Pausanias confirms this and attributes the city's finest buildings to this 'second ascendancy' (2.2.6). Archaeologists, too, agree – it was the burst of construction in AD 14–44 that brought Corinth to its final form and made it arguably the most dazzling and modern of Greek cities.[116]

At Paul's arrival Corinth was at the height of its glory, a tribute to human-made splendour.[117] Its South Stoa was, at 500 feet, one of the longest buildings in Greece[118] and its agora was among the largest in the Empire.[119] The city featured an abundance of temples,[120] three theatres (including the only Roman amphitheatre in Greece)[121] and countless shops.[122] Excavations reveal homes laid out handsomely,[123] adorned by mosaics, frescos and marble statues.[124] Baths, fountains and monuments rounded out the appeal of this elegant city.[125] The cumulative effect must have inspired awe. Surely it confirmed Horace's accolade: 'it is not the privilege of every man to visit Corinth' (*Epist.* 17.36).[126]

What kind of people created such a city? Certainly those impressed with material splendour and intent on raising their standing in the world.[127] Indeed Corinthians were famed for 'boasting' in their Corinthian citizenship (Mart. *Ep.* 10.65), for being easily 'puffed up' (D. Chr. *Or.* 9.21) and 'ungracious . . . among their luxuries' (Alciphron *Ep.* 3.15.1) and for 'assuming airs and priding themselves on their wealth' (D. Chr. *Or.* 9.8). In order to

---

115 Cf. the list in Kent 23–26.
116 See Scranton *Corinth: Monuments in the Lower Agora* 1.3.130; Lenschau 'Korinthos' 1035.
117 Thus Broneer 'Corinth' 82, 90; Hertzberg *Geschichte Griechenlands* 81–82.
118 Cf. Broneer *Corinth: The South Stoa* 1.4.5.
119 Larger in fact than the *Forum Romanum*; thus Scranton *Corinth: Monuments in the Lower Agora* 1.3.133.
120 See Paus. 2.2.6–3.1.   121 Cf. Broneer 'Corinth' 95.
122 Thus Scranton *Corinth: Monuments in the Lower Agora* 1.3.112–17, 130.
123 Thus Wiseman 'Corinth' 528; Theissen 'Soziale Schichtung' 262–63.
124 For a magnificent mosaic floor in a triclinium (dining-room) see Miller 'Mosaic Floor' 332–54; Wiseman 'Corinth' 528.
125 On baths πολλαχοῦ and πολλαί fountains see Paus. 2.3.5; and cf. Hill *Corinth: The Springs* 1.6.
126 Cf. as well Aristid. *Or.* 46.25, 28: 'Not even the eyes of all men are sufficient to take it (Corinth) in . . . so numerous are the treasures of paintings all about it, wherever one would simply look, throughout the streets themselves and the porticos'; cf. Alciphron *Ep.* 3.24.3; and see further Scranton *Corinth: Monuments in the Lower Agora* 1.3.153; Rostovtzeff *Roman Empire* 1.140–41. On the general allure of living in Corinth see Epict. 2.17.22; Lucian *Herm.* 27, 29, 45.
127 On the beauty of a city conferring personal status and esteem see above pp. 24–25.

learn more about this people we must turn to matters of descent and class.

2 The Corinthians

Strabo wrote that Caesar colonised Corinth with 'people belonging primarily to the freedman class' (ἐποίκους πέμψαντος τοῦ ἀπελευθερικοῦ γένους πλείστους, 8.6.23).[128] Elsewhere he added that 'some soldiers' (τῶν στρατιωτῶν τινας) were among the early settlers (17.3.15; cf. Plut. *Caes.* 57.5).[129] Pausanias noted that the colonists came from Rome (ἔποικοι ... ἀποσταλέντες ὑπὸ Ῥωμαίων, 2.1.2), indeed were 'Romanized' Greeks resettling by choice (πέμψαντος ἐποίκους Ῥωμαίων τοὺς προαιρουμένους, Str. 17.3.15),[130] perhaps seeking a more lucrative environment (cf. App. *Pun.* 8.xx.136).[131] Others followed later: Jews,[132] Syrians[133] and Egyptians.[134] But the bulk of the population continued to be of freedmen stock (ἐκ δούλων, Epict. 4.1.157). In Paul's day the presence of large numbers of ex-slaves is well attested by the many inscriptions paying tribute to *liberti* (West no. 140; cf. also nos. 142 and 151; Kent no. 281), to those identified simply by the letter *l* (Kent nos. 280 and 321; cf. West no. 69) and, more prestigiously, to *Aug[usti] lib[erti]* (Kent nos. 62 and 64; cf. no. 67; West nos. 69, 76 and 77; CIL 3.6099).[135] It will be helpful to look more closely at the distinctives of this class.

---

[128] Crinagorus *Anthologia Graeca* 9.284 refers derisively to the 'scoundrelly slaves' of Corinth; cf. Cic. *Tusc.* 3.53.

[129] See Kos 'Latin Epitaph of a Roman Legionary' 22–25; and cf. Kent nos. 134, 171.

[130] Thus Kent 20; Larsen 'Roman Greece' 446; *pace* Bowersock *Greek World* 66–67. Cf. the inscription describing the Greek-named Junia Theodora as a Ῥωμαίαν κατοικοῦσαν ἐν Κορίνθῳ ('Roman living in Corinth') (SEG 18.143 [63, 67]); and see C. Julius Laco who is honoured as a Roman in Corinth (West no. 67) and a Greek in Athens (SIG³ 788).

[131] Appian calls the new settlers *aporos*, i.e. those locked into a low social level and seeking a way out (cf. Murphy-O'Connor *Corinth* 113).

[132] Cf. Acts 18:1–16; Philo *Leg. Gai.* 281–82; and cf. the fourth century AD inscription Συναγωγὴ Ἑβραίων ('Synagogue of the Hebrews'), Meritt 111.

[133] See Wiseman 'Corinth' 497.

[134] Cf. Acts 18:24 and 1 Cor. 1:12; and for the presence of the Serapis-Isis cult see Kent no. 57; Smith 'Egyptian Cults at Corinth' 201–31.

[135] Demographic studies of Rome and Pompeii suggest that nearly half of their populations were of servile descent (so Rawson 'Lower Classes at Rome' 82; Day 'Life of Pompeii' 178). The proportion is much greater in Corinth, if the high incidence of Greek *cognomina* in the inscriptions is any indication (so Taylor 'Freedmen' 127 and Solin *Personennamen in Rom* 158). We may note the Augustan inscription to *liberti qui Corinthi habitant* ('freedmen who live in

On the whole freedmen were upwardly mobile. Manumission, itself a leap in status, encouraged ex-slaves to reach still higher. Sometimes prosperity was achieved by winning a place in a master's will. Trimalchio provides a classic example:[136] 'I was my master's favourite for fourteen years . . . [and] have come into an estate fit for a senator' (Petron. Sat. 75-76). Similarly, Juvenal observes: 'the royal road to high preferment – the favours of an aged and wealthy woman' (1.38-39).[137] Most freedmen, however, advanced through hard work, vigour and venture and aggressively converted the skills learned while slaves into financial gain. Even Trimalchio boasts: 'By my own merits I have come to this (fortune) . . . I buy well and sell well' (Petron. Sat. 75-76). Indeed ex-slaves were adept business-men[138] and dominated commerce and banking in Roman cities.[139] The most prosperous even owned land.[140] Their wealth became proverbial. Of a rich man Seneca wrote: 'he had the bank account . . . of a freedman' (Ep. 27.5).[141]

Freedmen had 'no family honour, no inherited code' to temper their quest for wealth and status.[142] At worst they pillaged Corinthian graves to make profits in Rome (Str. 8.6.23); in general they were exploitative, ruthless and willing to take great risks. Emerging as the nouveaux riches, ex-slaves purchased political office and hence power (cf. CIL 10.6104; D. C. 75.22.1, 79.14.4). Tacitus wrote that freedmen 'supplied the great part of the . . . decuries . . . the city cohorts . . . most of the knights, many senators' (Ann. 13.27). When Augustus denied these positions to freedmen,[143] they simply trans-ferred their civil ambitions to their sons.[144] For instance, we read of

Corinth') (West no. 121), which suggests the presence of a collegium libertorum in Corinth; and for further reference to freedmen see Kent nos. 240, 276; West nos. 56, 138.

136 The fictitious story of Trimalchio provides a typical, if satirical, sketch of a freedman.

137 For legacy hunters cf. Lucian Tim. 22; Pliny HN 34.11.

138 Cf. Trimalchio: 'I conceived a passion for business' (Petron. Sat. 75; also 57).

139 See Duff Freedmen 124; Hopkins Slaves 1.117; Gordon 'Freedman's Son' 75-76; and for an example see Geagan 'Tiberius Claudius Novius' 280.

140 See Petron. Sat. 36, 48, 76-77; Juv 1.106-9; D. Chr. Or. 46.5, 7; and cf. especially the herm of Herodes Atticus, a freedman, found at Corinth with the inscription, Ἡρώδης ἐνθάδε περιεπάτει ('Herod used to live here') (Philadelpheus 'Un hermès d'Hérode Atticus' 170-80).

141 Cf. further Mart. Ep. 5.13; Pliny HN 33.134-35; and see Hopkins 'Elite Mobility' 20.

142 Thus MacMullen Roman Social Relations 103.

143 Cf. Reinhold 'Status' 286; Crook Life of Rome 51.

144 Thus Gordon 'Freedman's Son' 66-74; Finley Ancient Economy 77.

M. Cornelius Valerianius, son of a freedman, who at age twelve was a member of the town council (CIL 14. 341; cf. 10.1268). Ex-slaves also penetrated the higher echelons of the cults. Of the 275 names of officials connected with the imperial cult in Rome 229 or 86 percent were freedmen (ILS 6073). Imperial freedmen, the *Familia Caesaris* (or *Aug Lib* in inscriptions), usually led other ex-slaves up the social ladder.[145] A case in point is the prosperous Claudius Etruscus (see Stat. *Silv.* 3.3.78).

As self-made people freedmen were renowned for their pride and for taking pains to display their accomplishments. Trimalchio 'picked his teeth with a silver quill . . . [and] bared his right arm where a golden bracelet shone' (Petron. *Sat.* 32–33); and his wife Fortunata 'counted her money [in public] by the bushel' (Petron, *Sat.* 37). A successful freedman was usually 'well pleased with himself' (*quam bene se habuit*, Petron. *Sat.* 38) and prone to boast: 'I am the owner of five shops . . . I possess more property than Pallas' (a man of great wealth; thus Juv. 1.105–6, 108–9); 'I am the sole owner of genuine Corinthian plate . . . I own a hundred engraved four-gallon cups' (Petron *Sat.* 50, 52). Furthermore, freedmen posted self-honouring inscriptions in conspicuous places – examples abound in Corinth (see below p. 41). All this provoked the ire of the lettered elite (cf. e.g. Sen. *Ep.* 86.7; Pliny *Ep.* 8.6) and of the freeborn of lesser means (Mart *Ep.* 2.29). But in Corinth there was no elite, no nobility. It was a freedman's city – a place where the traits mentioned in the last paragraphs emerged with particular prominence.

Four examples of successful Corinthians stand out in the evidence, all of servile descent. C. Babbius Philinus, a wealthy freedman and near contemporary of Paul, was perhaps Corinth's most important benefactor.[146] He built the majestic Babbius monument at the head of the agora (Kent no. 155),[147] the Southeast Building (the *Tabularium*) at the opposite end (West no. 122 = Kent no. 323),[148] a small circular temple housing a statue of Poseidon (West no. 132) and possibly much else, for his name appears in Corinthian inscriptions more than any other (at my count fourteen times). C. Julius Laco (West no. 67) and his son Spartiaticus (West no. 68; Meritt no. 70), also first-century benefactors of Corinth, were direct descendants of freedman C. Julius Eurycles, once the most influen-

---

[145] See Weaver *Familia Caesaris* 284–96.　　[146] See West 5, 108.
[147] See Scranton *Corinth: Monuments in the Lower Agora* 1.3.17–21, 72.
[148] Cf. Broneer 'Investigations at Corinth' 237–38.

tial man in Greece and donor of Corinth's fashionable baths (Paus. 2.3.5).[149] Reference may also be made to C. Cornelius Pulcher, a rich second-century patron of the city of freedman stock whose name is preserved no fewer than eleven times.[150]

Power was the reward and hence the aim of Corinthians on the rise socially. Philinus, for example, was honoured with the high civil and religious posts of *duumvir* and *pontifex* (Kent no. 155; West no. 132).[151] Laco bore the titles *duumvir quinquennalis, flamen Augusti* and, highest of all in Corinth, *agonothetes*, president of the Isthmian and Caesarean festivals (West no. 67). His son Spartiaticus shared these distinctions but added the most coveted priesthood in the region: *archiereus domus Augustae . . . primus Achaeon* (West no. 68).[152]

People of wealth could purchase power. T. Claudius Dinippus, a mid first-century freedman, earned the offices of *duumvir quinquennalis* and *agonothetes* through contributions to famine relief (Kent nos. 158–63; West nos. 80–86). Of special interest is one Erastus, a wealthy freedman and possible member of the Corinthian church (cf. Rom 16:23), who laid pavement in return for his aedileship (Kent no. 232).[153] These men admittedly represented the upper crust of Corinthian society and thus not necessarily the typical convert in Paul's young congregation. Nevertheless they do serve to illustrate something dear to *all* Corinthians – that with a little ambition and application one could rise from level zero to social respectability and a measure of power.

---

149 On C. Julius Eurycles and his descendants cf. West 47–53; Meritt 54; Taylor and West 'Euryclids in Latin Inscriptions' 389–400.

150 On C. Cornelius Pulcher see Kent 64–65.

151 In Corinth, unlike Rome and the rest of the provinces, freedmen were permitted to hold municipal office and priesthoods; see Duff *Freedmen* 66; West no. 108.

152 Here we see that loyalty to Rome (i.e. to Augustus) could lead to political office and power; cf. as well C. Licinius, the freedman patriarch of an important Corinthian family, who was called *Philosebastos*, 'friend of Augustus' (West no. 15).

153 In Rom 16:23 Paul refers to Erastus as οἰκονόμος τῆς πόλεως, possibly the Greek equivalent of *aedilis* (though ἀγορανόμος is the usual synonym – see e.g. in Corinth IG 4.203 = CIG 1104) or *quaestor*, the office just below aedileship (thus Kent no. 168; West no. 104a). Either way Erastus the Christian and the city administrator were probably the same person. No other Erastus appears in the evidence and the inscription in question dates to the middle of the first century AD (cf. Kent 99–100; Theissen 'Soziale Schichtung' 237–46; Broneer 'Corinth' 94; Clarke 'Erastus' 146–51; *pace* Cadbury 'Erastus' 42–58). If so, he was one of two aediles in Corinth and second in power only to two *duumviri*, hence among the οὐ πολλοὶ δυνατοί of 1 Cor. 1:26; cf. Gill 'Social Élite' 323–30.

3   Self-display

As in the Graeco-Roman world at large, Corinthians were intent on displaying their status. Philinus, as *duumvir*, approved and erected a monument in his own honour (Kent no. 155). So did one named Hicesius (Kent no. 231; cf. no. 334). Since public funds rarely covered such ventures (though see Kent no. 165), each man paid for his own tribute (*de sua pecunia fecit*). Freedmen also inscribed eulogies to successful sons, the freedman's name appearing prominently at the top of the stone in over-sized letters (cf. Kent no. 237).[154] An example of self-display within the means of most Corinthians is an inscription written by T. Flavius Antiochus and T. Claudius Primigenius, men of servile stock who proudly described themselves as 'the most outstanding members of the club' (*collegianis primis*, Kent no. 62). Given these illustrations it is hardly surprising that Corinth was the stage of Favorinus' speech asking for a statue of himself to be restored to public view (D. Chr. *Or.* 37);[155] nor that his pupil Herodes Atticus in an inscription to his wife should proclaim himself great (μέγας), pre-eminent above others (ἔξοχος ἄλλων), more famous than all (περίβωτον ἁπάντων), the flower of Achaia (ἄνθος Ἀχαιϊάδος) and one having attained the peak of every kind of excellence (παντοίης ἀρετῆς εἰς ἄκρον, Kent no. 128).

Putting oneself on show was not a ritual reserved for the elite. It was a passion played out at every level, though on lesser scales. In Corinth, perhaps more than anywhere else, social ascent was the goal, boasting and self-display the means, personal power and glory the reward.

4   The economy

As Corinthian citizens advanced materially so did the economic fortunes of their city. Strabo described Corinth as 'great and wealthy' (8.6.23); Aristides as 'everywhere full of wealth' (*Or.* 46.27); Alciphron as 'abounding in luxuries' (*Ep.* 3.24.3).[156] This

---

154 See also Bugh 'Roman Corinth' 45–53. For similar inscriptions to husbands cf. Kent nos. 173, 175; and to a father see Kent no. 153.

155 Only in this way, Favorinus reasons, will his 'fame never be destroyed' (D. Chr. *Or.* 37.47).

156 Further on wealth of Corinth see Athenaeus *Deipnosophistae* 13.573c–574c; and cf. Wiseman 'Corinth' 503; Elliger *Paulus in Griechenland* 246.

affluence is reflected in the large denominations of first-century coins[157] and also in the elegance of Corinthian buildings (see above p. 36).[158] Other Greek cities provided a stark contrast: 'wealth has deserted both Orchomenos and Delphi' (D. Chr. *Or.* 37.36); 'most of the country has become depopulated . . . particularly the cities have disappeared from sight' (Str. 7.7.3). Nero lamented that he could find so few cities worthy of his munificence (SIG³ 814). Alciphron posed the situation more bluntly: either one could 'munch green figs . . . at Athens [or] . . . take pickings from [Corinthian] gold' (*Ep.* 3.15.1).[159] No wonder Corinth attracted the likes of Philinus, Laco and Spartiaticus and more significantly the highly ambitious masses, mostly of freedman stock, eager to win a share of the wealth. Their arrival only served to increase the opulence of Corinth and to render it unsurpassed 'in exciting envy' (D. Chr. *Or.* 37.36).[160]

Perhaps Corinth's greatest asset was its location. Situated on the isthmus of Greece it was 'master of two harbours' (Str. 8.6.20), 'the cross-roads of Greece' (D. Chr. *Or.* 8.5), 'a meeting-place for Asia and Greece' (Livy 33.32.2), 'a passage for all mankind' (Aristid. *Or.* 46.27).[161] Trade was an inevitable source of income – in Strabo's words: 'Corinth is called "wealthy" because of its commerce' (8.6.20).[162] Taxes on goods in transit generated more wealth (Str. 8.6.20).[163] In addition Corinth was a centre both of banking (Plut.

---

157 Cf. Harris 'Coins' 158.   158 So Larsen 'Roman Greece' 465.
159 Further on the decay of Greek cities cf. Paus. 8.33.2; Sen. *Ep.* 91.10; and of Athens in particular see Geagan 'Roman Athens' 385. On Corinth as a stimulus to the stagnant Greek economy see Bowersock *Greek World* 68.
160 In Corinth one could earn 'much money' (Apul. *Met.* 10.19) and become a 'millionaire . . . owning a fleet of merchant ships' (Lucian *D. Mort.* 21.1). On rich Corinthians cf. Lucian *Tox.* 22; *D. Mort.* 22.7; *D. Meretr.* 5.2.
161 Served as well by three major roads (cf. Wiseman *Ancient Corinthians* 17–43), Corinth was the most cosmopolitan of all Mediterranean cities except Rome. This is confirmed by the fact that thirty-nine percent of the coins that have been excavated from Roman Corinth were not minted locally: 630 come from the west, seventy-seven from Argolis, sixty-six from the Peloponnesus, sixty-one from central and northern Greece and twenty-eight from the orient (Kahrstedt *Gesicht Griechenlands* 116); see also the cosmopolitan character of pottery found in the 'Cellar Building' (Wright 'Pottery Deposit from Corinth' 174–75); and cf. D. Chr. *Or.* 9.5; Aristid. *Or.* 46.22.
162 Chrysostom *Or.* 37.8 mentions the 'trader' (ἔμπορος) first of all in his list of visitors to Corinth; see also Aristides *Or.* 46.23 who calls Corinth a 'market place . . . common to all the Greeks'; cf. further Apul. *Met.* 10.35; Lucian *D. Mort.* 21.1; and Wiseman *Ancient Corinthians* 12; Rostovtzeff *Hellenistic World* 1025, 1043, 1273; Lenschau 'Korinthos' 994–97.
163 See Wiseman *Ancient Corinthians* 12–13.

Mor. 831A)[164] and of regional government (Str. 8.6.23)[165] and hence 'the principal town of all the province of Achaea' (Apul. *Met.* 10.18). Further revenue came from crowds attending the Isthmian and Caesarean games (Str. 8.6.20). These people were attracted not only by 'exhibitions in which there are trials of skill' but also by 'an abundance of all wares' (Livy 33.32.2).[166]

Mention should also be made of Corinth's artisan wealth, for the city was 'well equipped with men skilled . . . in the craftsman's arts' (Str. 8.6.23).[167] In particular, Corinthian bronze was 'valued before silver and almost before gold' (Pliny *HN* 34.1).[168] Other trades flourished as well, including the manufacture of lamps,[169] metals,[170] pottery,[171] perfumes,[172] ceramics,[173] textiles,[174] pigments[175] and tents.[176] Craftsmen were committed to financial prosperity and especially in Corinth. To them the saying is attributed: 'Great is the smell of profits from whatever derived' (Juv 14.204–5).[177]

In short, Corinth was a boom town. Many were making money hand over foot and everyone, no doubt, worshipped success. If in the Graeco-Roman world at large respect depended upon the size of one's earnings (see above pp. 20–21), then we can assume that it did even more so in Corinth.[178]

---

[164] Thus Kahrstedt *Gesicht Griechenlands* 116; Larsen 'Roman Greece' 491–92.

[165] Indeed the seat of the Roman governor, thus Kent 18; and cf. 'ambassador' (πρεσβευτής) in Chrysostom's list of visitors (*Or.* 37.8).

[166] Further on the games see Str. 8.6.20; D. Chr. *Or.* 37.8; Aristid. *Or.* 46.23.

[167] The ref. is to pre-146 BC Corinth, but probably equally descriptive of the later city at the time Strabo was writing (so Murphy-O'Connor *Corinth* 68). On the high esteem for Corinthian craftsmen see Wiseman *Ancient Corinthians* 13.

[168] According to Plut. *Mor.* 395B, the bronze 'was smooth and shining with a deep blue tinge'; cf. Paus. 2.3.3; Pliny *HN* 34.3.6–8, 17.48; 37.12.49; Str. 8.6.23; Petron. *Sat.* 31, 50, 119; D. Chr. *Or.* 37.4; Mart. *Ep.* 9.59.11; Jos. *V.* 68; Pliny *Ep.* 3.6; Suet. *Aug.* 70; *Tib.* 34; and see Murphy-O'Connor 'Corinthian Bronze' 23–36. For bronze foundries operating in the first century AD see Wiseman 'Ancient Corinth' 222; 'Excavations in Corinth' 67–69; *Ancient Corinthians* 13, 15 no. 40; Mattusch 'Corinthian Metalworking' 380, 389.

[169] Cf. Pliny *HN* 34.6; and see Broneer *Corinth: Terracotta Lamps* 4.2.76–78; 'Excavations in the Odeum at Corinth' 451; Davidson *Corinth: The Minor Objects* 12.21–22; Williams *Kenchreai: The Lamps* 35–48.

[170] On a first-century AD foundry with sophisticated metal-working techniques see Mattusch 'Corinthian Metalworking' 389; and cf. Pliny *HN* 34.6; Petron *Sat.* 50.

[171] See Str. 8.6.23; and Kahrstedt *Gesicht Griechenlands* 116.

[172] Cf. Plut. *Tim.* 14.2.   [173] See Petron. *Sat.* 50; Pliny *HN* 34.48.

[174] Cf. Kardara 'Dyeing and Weaving Works at Isthmia' 261–66.

[175] Cf. Petron. *Sat.* 119; and see Wiseman *Ancient Corinthians* 13.

[176] Thus Acts 18:3.

[177] Recently Meeks *Urban Christians* 49, 73 has suggested that the Corinthian congregation was made up primarily of craftsmen and merchants.

[178] Cf. Murphy-O'Connor 'Corinth' 147–48.

5   The games

By the first century AD athletic games in Greece numbered more than three hundred a year. But the Isthmian games were special, surpassed only by the games at Olympia.[179] They formed the high point of a biennial spring festival, the third of four great festivals in the Mediterranean basin.[180] Crowds flocked to Corinth from all parts of Greece and provided a vital stimulus to local business (Str. 8.6.20).[181] So important were the games for Corinth that the *agonothetes*, the president of the games, was the city's highest ranking and most honoured official.[182] Every four years a second series of competitions, the Caesarea, were added to the Isthmian program. A third series, named in honour of the reigning emperor and beginning with Tiberius, expanded the contests still further.[183] The games and festival of AD 51 must have deeply impressed a visiting apostle Paul, so charged was the atmosphere, so pervasive the merriment.[184]

Chrysostom describes some of that atmosphere in his 'Isthmian Discourse'. Multitudes would press 'to see the athletes and to gormandize' (ἵνα ἐμπλησθῶσιν, *Or.* 9.1). The victor was 'surrounded by a great mob . . . carried shoulder high by the throng, with some following after and shouting, others leaping for joy and lifting their hands towards heaven, and still others throwing garlands and ribbons upon him' (*Or.* 9.14). 'To be praised by the spectators, to become a man of mark' is the aim of all competitors, said Lucian (commenting on the Isthmian games in particular), adding, 'if the love of fame should be banished from the world . . . who would want to do any glorious deed' (*Anach.* 36). The practice of setting athletes on pedestals sheds penetrating light on what

179 On the Isthmian festival cf. Gardiner *Greek Athletic Sports* 214–18; Schneider 'Isthmia' 2248–53.
180 The others were the Olympic, Pythian and Nemean games.
181 On the cosmopolitan flavour of the games cf. inscriptions listing competitors from numerous cities: Meritt nos. 14, 15.
182 A board of ten men called the *hellenodikai* assisted the *agonothetes* (cf. Meritt nos. 14, 15). They judged the contests and presented the awards (Kent 30).
183 For all three competitions cf. West no. 86: *agonothete Neroneon Caesareon et Isthmion et Caesareon*. And for a list of events see Meritt no. 14 and Biers and Geagan 'A New List of Victors' 79–93 where, interestingly, musical and literary competitions (Σαλπισταί, Κήρυκες, Ποιηταί, Ἐνκωμιόγραφοι, Αὐληταί, etc.) come before the athletic (Στάδιον, Πένταθλον, Πυγμή, etc.).
184 On the games of AD 51 cf. West no. 82; Kent 31. Broneer 'Pagan Cults' 169 suggests that Paul may have timed his arrival in Corinth to coincide with the Isthmian games in order to preach to large and cosmopolitan crowds.

people in the first century valued most – especially if, as Diogenes maintained, 'men show their real character most clearly at public festivals' (D. Chr. *Or.* 9.1).[185] Examples of those values are displayed vividly in agonistic inscriptions.

First, only victory was esteemed; there was no second or third place. Inscriptions repeatedly acclaim contestants who were πρῶτος πάντων ('first of all') (Moretti no. 59), πρῶτος ἀνθρώπων ('first of men') (Moretti no. 66), πρῶτος τῶν ἀπὸ τῆς οἰκουμένης ('first of those in the inhabited world') (Moretti no. 62) and, most frequently, πρῶτος καὶ μόνος ('first and only') (Moretti, nos. 59, 69, 71, 72 and 75). When Diogenes asked an Isthmian victor why the Corinthians applauded him he boasted: τῶν ἄλλων Ἑλλήνων ταχύτατός εἰμι πάντων ('of the other Greeks I am fastest of all') (D. Chr. *Or.* 9.16; cf. 9.19).[186] Secondly, spectators revered the competitor who maintained his superiority – who won κατὰ τὸ ἑξῆς ('one after another') (Kent no. 272; Hicks no. 609; Moretti nos. 58, 59, 65 and 69) and of whom it could be said πᾶσιν ἄλειπτος ('conquered by no one') (Moretti nos. 71 and 75). Finally, a victor won honour by publicising his feats. Usually this meant posting the number of first places earned: Ἴσθμια δίς . . . Ὀλύμπια τρίς (Moretti no. 62).[187] One Isthmian competitor, G. Ailius Themison, advertised ninety-four victories![188] In short, spectators valued primacy, sustained primacy and the display of primacy.

The games thus reflected in microcosm, and more intensely, the competitive spirit of the first century which we observed above (pp. 23–24). The actor, runner or rhetorician won adulation in the same way as the merchant, banker or tanner – by excelling his rivals. But because the city of Corinth was so immersed in the games it also reflected the competition.[189] Indeed the drive to show oneself better than one's neighbour was perhaps more pronounced in Corinth than anywhere else.

---

[185] Cf. on this last point Pfitzner *Agon Motif* 17.

[186] Lucian *Anach.* 36 adds: 'to be best in one's class' is the goal of all contestants. Further on πρῶτος καὶ μόνος see Robert 'Inscription Agonistique' 105. For athletes boasting in victories, cf. Finley and Pleket *Games* 22, 75.

[187] See also Kent no. 272; Meritt nos. 14, 15; Moretti nos. 59, 62, 69; SEG 29.340 = Michaud 'Chronique' 949; and cf. Finley and Pleket *Games* 74; Gardiner *Athletics* 112.

[188] See Broneer 'Isthmia Excavations' 192–93.

[189] It even erected a statue of Poseidon, its premier deity, in the athletes' sanctuary at Isthmia, thus Broneer 'Pagan Cults' 171.

6   Struggle and conflict

The push to excel bred heavy-handedness and dissension. In the
literature Corinthians are depicted as 'scoundrels' (*Anth. Pal.* 9.284)
and as 'ungracious and not jolly at all' (Alciphron *Ep.* 3.15.2). They
are renowned for their unprincipled pursuit of profit (cf. Apul. *Met.*
10.19, 25)[190] and for creating a city of sordid rich and miserable
poor (Alciphron *Ep.* 3.24.1). Moreover, the city provided a congenial atmosphere for philosophical wrangling, 'crowds of . . .
Sophists . . . shouting and reviling one another . . . their disciples
. . . fighting with one another' (D Chr. *Or.* 8.9) and 'philosophers
wrangling with each other' (Lucian *D. Mort.* 1). Corinth's reputation for ruthlessness and competition was epitomized by its gladi-
atorial contests, the first city in Greece to stage such spectacles (cf.
D. Chr. *Or.* 31.121; Apul. *Met.* 10.18).[191] All this led Alciphron to
conclude: 'surely it is better to lie outstretched, a corpse [in Athens],
than to endure the opulence of the Peloponnesus' (*Ep.* 3.15.4).
While most of these references are framed in the language of satire,
they nevertheless contain an element of truth and hence attest to the
volatile social climate of Corinth.

7   Beauty and eloquence

Given their penchant for self-display it is hardly surprising that the
Corinthians placed a premium on personal appearance and impressive speech, the most noticeable of human traits. The literature
portrays Corinth as a city of beautiful people. Charicles, 'a young
man from Corinth . . . is handsome [and] shows skillful use of
cosmetics' (Lucian *Am.* 9). Charmenion, also a Corinthian, 'strolls
about sleek with curled hair' (Mart. *Ep.* 10.65). Moreover, a handsome lad is implored not to let his 'beauty go to waste in the solitude
(viz. the wilderness)', but to go to Corinth where he will be appreci-
ated and find a bride 'who is young and beautiful' (Lucian *D. Deor.*
20.13). Isthmian athletes set the standard: 'expecting to appear
unclothed before so many people, they try to attain good physical
condition' (Lucian *Anach.* 36). Hence one Menippus is 'well

---

190   In Apuleius' tale we are not to be surprised that money is earned immorally: after
all the setting is Corinth! Thus Mason 'Lucius at Corinth' 160–65.

191   Cf. second-century AD friezes from the Corinthian arena depicting a *venatio*
(men against beasts) in Shear 'Theatre District of Corinth' 452–53; and Stillwell
Corinth: The Theatre 2.87, 95.

endowed with . . . a physique so beautifully proportioned that . . . he resembled a fine . . . athlete' (Philostr. *VA* 4.25).[192] When Diogenes exposed the folly of valuing the physical over the intellect, his message fell on deaf ears (D. Chr. *Or.* 9.15; cf. 8.7–8). The Corinthians, it seems, were simply too enamoured with outward appearances.[193]

Eloquence, too, invited admiration, but not the display of rhetorical precision; rather, it was the ability to project one's personality powerfully on one's hearers. Crowds would gather 'straightaway' to hear 'the wretched sophists around Poseidon's temple, shouting and reviling one another' (D. Chr. *Or.* 8.9–10). Powerful speakers naturally won high office. An example is the second-century figure Lucius Maecius Faustinus, a Corinthian and 'good orator' (ῥήτορα ἀγαθόν), who was a representative of his city in the Panhellenic League (Kent no. 264). We may note as well the orator Poseidonius who was Helladarch and priest (Kent no. 307).[194] The evidence makes it difficult to conceive of a Corinthian leader who was not skilled in speech, so high was the people's regard for imposing oratory.[195]

8 Pleasure

Favorinus described Corinth as 'a city of Aphroditic-type pleasure beyond all that are or ever have been' (πόλιν . . . ἐπαφροδιτοτάτην, D. Chr. *Or.* 37.34). Aristides agreed: 'there is no place where one would rest . . . with more pleasure or enjoyment' (*Or.* 46.24). The absence of sexual restraints surely contributed to these assessments, as Favorinus' turn of phrase attests.[196] But the sensual nature of the

---

[192] Further on the 'excellent beauty' of Corinthians see Apul. *Met.* 10.29; also Alciphron *Fr.* 5.

[193] Cf. Reekmans 'Social Change' 122.

[194] Cf. the third-century AD inscription honouring the Corinthian Nikias for being 'first among orators, pre-eminent as *agonothetes*, having acquired glory in every public office', SEG 18.137; and see Broneer 'Excavations at Isthmia' 324–26.

[195] Cf. MacMullen *Roman Social Relations* 107: 'Great power as a speaker [and] style and taste in one's address' are prerequisites for men of standing. Thus Juvenal 7.145 asks: 'When is eloquence found beneath a shabby coat?' and cf. Petron. *Sat.* 46: 'you have the gift of tongues and . . . make fun of the way we poor talk'.

[196] The famous reference in Strabo 8.6.20 (cf. 12.3.26; D. Chr. *Or.* 8.5; Alciphron *Ep.* 3.24.3) to the thousand prostitutes serving the temple of Aphrodite probably applies to pre-146 BC Corinth (thus Murphy-O'Connor *Corinth* 55–56). Nevertheless, there is ample evidence to impune the morality of the new Corinth. It is no coincidence that Apuleius (ii AD) set his tale of sexual debauchery (*Met.* 10.20–22) in Corinth (see Mason 'Lucius at Corinth' 160–62), nor that Corinth

Corinthian culture ran much deeper. On a sophisticated level Corinth's theatre (seating 18,000),[197] three festivals[198] and a panoply of visual amusements[199] made it the entertainment centre of Greece.[200] More simple is the testimony scratched out on a stone by a workman during a period of rest: 'Alexas and Serapias are lovers of merriment' (φίλοι 'Αλεξᾶς Σαραπίας εὐφροσύνης, Kent no. 361).[201]

The voluptuous atmosphere took its toll on the reputation of Corinthians. In particular, visitors denigrated their knowledge and learning. When the Cynic Demetrius arrived in Corinth he found 'an ignorant fellow reading a book' (Lucian *Ind.* 19). Similarly, the sage Diogenes ministered in Corinth because there 'the fools are the thickest' (D. Chr. *Or.* 8.5).[202] In the opinion of outsiders the sensuality of the city 'stole away the minds of the Corinthians' (Aristid. *Or.* 46.25).[203]

9 Nero

It is worth noting that while the emperor Nero never visited the famous Greek cities of Athens and Sparta, he spent considerable time in Corinth. Suetonius offers the following explanation: 'above all he was carried away by a craze for popularity'; 'he had a longing for immortality and undying fame' (*Nero* 53, 55).[204] These passions

was the setting of Philostratus' (ii AD) story of illicit sex (*VA* 4.25). The city was also a haven for homosexuality: 'the scented sons of Corinth . . . put on perfume and shave their legs to the crotch' (Juv 8.113); they 'smoothe [themselves] with depilatory daily' and their 'tongues lisp' (Mart. *Ep.* 10.65). See also Hertzberg *Geschichte* Griechenlands 82; Dessau *Geschichte* 553; Lenschau 'Korinthos' 1035.

[197] On the main theatre cf. Stillwell *Corinth: The Theatre*; Broneer 'Corinth' 94. A second theatre, the Odeum (seating 3,000), was constructed in the late first century AD (see Broneer *Corinth: The Odeum* 10.143–47). A third, also late first century, was built at Isthmia; cf. Gebhard *Theatre at Isthmia*.

[198] Aristides *Or.* 46.31 calls the Isthmian festival the 'most famous national festival' which 'draws up, surpasses, and again overtakes the rest'.

[199] Cf. D. Chr. *Or.* 8.7; 9.4, 5, 22.

[200] Thus Larsen 'Roman Greece' 472; Wiseman *Ancient Corinthians* 13.

[201] Cf. Ael. *VH* 3.15: 'the Corinthians have been reproached in comedies for being intemperately addicted to wine'. And see Diogenes' discourse against sensual pleasure (cf. D. Chr. *Or.* 8), purposely set, it seems, in Corinth.

[202] Cf. Lucian *Hist. Conscr.* 29: a man who 'had never set foot outside of Corinth . . . is quite ridiculous'; and Alciphron *Ep.* 3.15.2–3: among Corinthians 'you get more tipsy tricks than satisfactions . . . what new tricks they try to introduce . . . they make a man drink while balancing on greased wine-skins'.

[203] Robinson *Ancient Corinth* 21 describes first-century AD Corinth as 'intellectually empty'.

[204] Cf. also Tac. *Ann.* 14.14–15; Suet. *Nero* 25; D. C. 62.20.5, 62.15.2.

were clearly satisfied in Corinth. The Isthmian games provided an opportunity for him to display his chief loves – singing to his own accompaniment on the lyre and chariot racing. More importantly, it gave Achaeans a chance to 'greet his performance with extravagant applause' (Suet. *Nero* 22).[205] Not surprisingly, Nero's ultimate achievement, the restoration of freedom to Achaea, was staged at Corinth where it could win him maximum honour. He ordered 'as many of the inhabitants of the province as possible to come to Corinth' (SIG³ 814 [2–4]). And then, prompting his own acclaim, he gloated: 'Men of Hellas, I give you an unlooked for gift – if indeed anything may not be hoped for from one of my greatness of mind – a gift so great you were incapable of asking for it' (SIG³ 814 [10–13]). Unlike Athens or Sparta, Corinth uniquely satiated Nero's cravings. It provided competition and crowds, but above all it rewarded his self-aggrandisement with adulation and honour.[206]

The appraisal of religion

1   The Cults

As a maritime trading centre Corinth became a collecting ground for the Empire's cults.[207] As such it reflected in miniature the religious character of the Graeco-Roman world at large. We know little of the myths and legends which lie behind Corinthian cults.[208] As in the rest of the Empire, the Corinthians focused on the benefits derived from religion, such as physical healing (cf. D. Chr. *Or.* 8.7)[209] and powerful displays (D. Chr. *Or.* 8.9), not on doctrine.[210]

---

[205] Further on Nero competing in Greece: Suet. *Nero* 25; Lucian *Ner.* 9; and specifically in lyre and song contests: Tac. *Ann.* 14.14; and in chariot races: D. C. 62.15.1.

[206] On Nero's attraction to Corinth see Schneider 'Isthmia' 2253; Warmington *Nero* 113–20; Momigliano 'Nero' 735–37.

[207] In the archaeological and literary sources I find references to as many as thirty-four deities in Corinth; see Paus. 2.1–3; D. Chr. *Or.* 37.11, 33; Lucian *Salt.* 42; Scranton *Corinth: Monuments in the Lower Agora* 1.3.67–73, 147–48; Edwards *Corinth: Coins passim*; Imhoof-Blumer and Gardner *Numismatic Commentary* 10–25, n. 47; Smith 'Egyptian Cults at Corinth' 201–31. For cults at Isthmia cf. Broneer 'Pagan Cults at Isthmia' 169–87; Wiseman *Ancient Corinthians* 50; and at Kenchreai see Scranton, Shaw and Ibrahim *Kenchreai* xvii, 71–77; Finegan *Archaeology* 146.

[208] Thus Broneer 'Hero Cults' 128; Scranton *Corinth: Architecture* 1.2.161.

[209] Cf. the inscription honouring Παιηωνιεῷ Σωτῆρι ('Healing Saviour') (Kent no. 64); and for healing and the Asclepius cult in Corinth see Roebuck *Corinth: The Asklepieion* 14.157–59.

[210] Aristides *Or.* 46.30 refers disdainfully to the 'old and fabulous stories' of Corinthian religion.

They also showed the same, if not greater, tolerance of a multiplicity of cults. The agora alone provided space for the temples of Apollo, Dionysos, Hermes and Aphrodite, a Pantheon and statues of Aphrodite, Apollo, Artemis, Athena, Cybele, Dionysos, Enyo, Hermes, Nemesis, Poseidon, Tyche, Victory and Zeus.[211] In addition, Corinthian coins often bore images of more than one god.[212] And a P. Licinius Priscus Iuventianus donated three sanctuaries, each to different deities: Palaemon, Helios and Demeter and Kore (IG 4.203).[213] The emphasis in Corinth was on harmony, on making one's religion compatible with the rest, not on exclusivity.

2   Religious life

The cults dominated life in Corinth. In particular, temples laid on lavish banquets. Dozens of dining rooms have been exposed on the acropolis in the temenos of Demeter and Kore.[214] Three more such rooms, each with eleven couches, have been uncovered in the Asclepieion.[215] Religion clearly played a central role in the social life of the city.

The cults also supplied the heart of fine culture. The theatre at Isthmia was functionally part of Poseidon's temple. Not only did Poseidon's image appear on tiles throughout the theatre, but the artists of Dionysos (οἱ περὶ τὸν Διόνυσον τεχνῖται, IG 4.558) probably performed there and Nero certainly did, singing a hymn honouring Poseidon and Amphitrite (Lucian *Ner.* 3).[216] Furthermore, the best art – statues of the gods, ornate temples, frescos of deities, etc. – was reserved for religious purposes.

Likewise cult and commerce were interrelated. Temples and shops were frequently located together, and often assisted each other:[217] pilgrims attending the religious festival at Isthmia spent freely on an 'abundance of all wares' (Livy 33.32.2).[218] Conversely,

---

211 See Scranton *Corinth: Monuments of the Lower Agora* 1.3.57–73, 147–48.
212 Cf. coins showing Helios and Poseidon (Edwards no. 53), Zeus and Athena (Edwards no. 18), Dionysos and Kronos (Edwards no. 27), Heracles, Aphrodite and Poseidon (Imhoof-Blumer and Gardner *Numismatic Commentary* 23).
213 Aristid. *Or.* 46.31.   214 Cf. Bookidis 'Sanctuary of Demeter and Kore' 206.
215 See Roebuck *Corinth: The Asklepieion* 14.51–53; Payne 'Archaeology in Greece' 276. These couches, painted red and yellow, were used throughout Roman times.
216 On the religious function of the theatre at Isthmia see Gebhard *Theatre at Isthmia* xiii, 3; on Poseidon's name on tiles of the theatre cf. Broneer 'Excavations at Isthmia, 1959–1961' 10.
217 Thus Scranton *Corinth: Monuments of the Lower Agora* 1.3.153.
218 Cf. Str. 10.5.4: 'the general festival is a kind of commercial affair'.

shops peddled cult items. The *macellum*, for instance, sold temple meat (cf. 1 Corinthians 10:25, and see West nos. 124, 125).[219]

In addition, religion was closely linked to politics. Civic leaders usually served (or had previously served) as cult priests. Examples abound: Philinus was *pontifex* and *duumvir* (Kent no. 155); Laco was imperial priest and *duumvir quinquennalis* (West no. 67); Cornelius Pulcher was high priest of the Hellenes and president of Achaia (Meritt no. 80; IG 4.795); Dinippus was priest of Britannic Victory, curator of grain supply and *duumvir quinquennalis* (Kent nos. 158–63; West nos. 86–90); and Aulus Arrius Proclus was priest of Poseidon, chief engineer and *duumvir* (Kent no. 156).[220]

Moreover, the games were heavily influenced by religion. The Isthmian festival was above all a religious occasion[221] and the *agonothetes* normally possessed cultic titles (cf. West no. 67; Kent nos. 158, 198, 212). Statues of athletes were erected in Poseidon's temple[222] and some of the events had religious meaning, such as the torch race (ἱερά λαμπάς) in which a sacred flame was transferred to an altar with greatest haste, probably to ensure efficacy.[223]

Finally, cult and medicine were fully integrated. Gaius Vibius Euelpistus, a first-century freedman, was both physician and priest of Asclepius (ἰατρὸς καὶ ἱερεὺς τοῦ Ἀσκληπιοῦ).[224] Examples such as this are numerous.[225]

It is clear, then, that religion played a central role in the everyday life of Corinth. People looked to the cults not for a sacred perspective in a secular world, nor even for a retreat from the present world, but for the nucleus of their world – the social, cultural, commercial, political, athletic and medical verities so vital for daily existence. They expected the cults to apply a transcendental stamp of approval to their lives.

---

[219] Cf. Kent no. 127; Cadbury 'Macellum at Corinth' 134–41.

[220] For other examples see Kent nos. 152, 153, 195, 198; IG 4.203; and cf. Bugh 'Roman Corinth' 45–53.

[221] On the temple of Poseidon as the centre of the festival see Broneer *Isthmia: Temple of Poseidon* 1, v, 103.

[222] Thus Paus. 2.1.7: 'within the sanctuary of (Poseidon) stand . . . portrait statues of athletes who have won victories at the Isthmian games'.

[223] Cf. Biers and Geagan 'Victors in the Caesarea' 91–92.

[224] Thus Roebuck *Corinth: The Asklepieion* 14.156–57, nos. 1035, 1134.

[225] On the link between health and science and cult see IGRR 4.520; and Plut. *Mor.* 745A: 'the doctors have Asclepius as their guide'; S. E. *M.* 1.260: 'Asclepius, the founder of our science'; and Str. 8.6.15: 'Asclepius, who is believed to cure diseases of every kind and always has his temple full of the sick'; cf. also Edelstein and Edelstein *Asclepius* 2.139–40.

Summary and conclusion

To sum up, first-century Corinth differed greatly from other Mediterranean cities. Little in the city was more than a century old: traditions were few, the aristocracy fluid, the society open. This suited the populace, mostly ambitious people of ultimately servile descent eager to win respectability and power. In their hands the economy exploded, and at a time when neighbouring cities were in decline. Corinth's location between two land masses facilitated trade and precipitated the emergence of *nouveaux riches* merchants – bankers, toll collectors and fine craftsmen. The Isthmian and Caesarean games and a thriving entertainment industry enhanced the appeal of Corinth, attracting hosts of visitors and swelling city coffers still more. Elegant buildings shot up, exotic goods filled the shops and handsome attire was met at every turn. Corinth had become the envy of the Empire – a city of pleasure, a tribute to human-made splendour, a place where assertiveness and pride reaped great reward. Nero found Corinth much to his liking, spending a winter there in AD 67. And no wonder: it was a city 'inferior in celebrity to no region of the earth' (Pliny *HN* 4.9).

How did first-century Corinthians appraise fellow-humans and religion? On the basis of the foregoing observations the answer would seem to be the same in substance as the one suggested for the Graeco-Roman world at large (see above pp. 19–34). The difference would lie in emphasis. Since the Corinthians were largely of servile descent they possessed, on the whole, *greater* thrust and vigour than people living where freedmen were less dominant. Consequently, they placed a *higher* premium on social prominence and self-display, on personal power and boasting. Likewise, they were *more* inclined to honour success and reward primacy and *more* prone to ridicule the poor and humble. When Corinthians evaluated each other they looked for the same symbols of worth which they prized for themselves – wealth, assertive speech, abusive behaviour, a head carried high – anything which might elevate them above their neighbours.

The same values influenced their perspective of religion. It mattered little who the gods were or what the cults taught. What was important was whether one's needs were being met – whether everyday desires for health, wealth and safety and, more importantly, power and esteem, were being fulfilled. In Corinth, perhaps more than elsewhere, people looked to the cults for satisfaction, and satisfaction as they defined it, as personal exaltation and glory. They wanted religion to confirm and satisfy their yearnings, not challenge to and transform them.

In conclusion, the historical evidence from both the Graeco-Roman world at large and Corinth in particular provides a remarkably uniform picture of the way in which first-century people appraised each other and religion. The picture must of course remain tentative, but even if it is only partly correct we cannot help but be impressed by the subtle force of the social atmosphere which prevailed in Corinth. It must have had a profound impact on all Corinthians, including Paul's young converts. Merely by living in Corinth they would have imbibed – naturally and perhaps subconsciously – many of the perspectives which have been set out in the preceding pages. We must now ask whether these perspectives shed any light on the way in which the Corinthians viewed their apostle Paul.

2

THE SITUATION IN THE CORINTHIAN CHURCH: A BIBLICAL ANALYSIS

We discovered at the outset of our study that the Corinthians are critical of Paul in at least four important respects. They are dismayed by his reticence to boast, by his unimpressive physical appearance, by his inferior speech and by his refusal to take support. We must now ask whether our insights into the culture of first-century Corinth shed any light on these criticisms. But before we do we must gain a more precise understanding of the nature of the criticisms themselves – that is, we must examine carefully what Paul himself reveals about them in the text. Only then will we be able to appreciate how far the criticisms have been prompted by the culture.

Boasting

There can be little doubt that boasting was a matter of great importance in the Corinthian church. The sheer quantity of καυχ-words in 1 and 2 Corinthians alone would suggest that Paul is writing to people for whom boasting is a prized activity.[1] Of special interest is the phrase καυχᾶσθαι δεῖ. It occurs twice in 2 Corinthians (11:30; 12:1) and may well represent a slogan circulating within the church.[2] If so, it confirms our suspicion about Paul's young converts: they are avid exponents of boasting and naturally critical of their apostle's refusal to boast.

What kind of boasting do the Corinthians value? Perhaps the best way to answer this question is to examine the behaviour of Paul's opponents, for it is especially their boasting that the Corinthians find so attractive (cf. 11:18–19). Three passages are particularly relevant.

---

[1] The verb καυχάομαι and its cognates appear thirty-nine times in 1 and 2 Cor., as opposed to only fifteen times elsewhere in Paul.

[2] Thus Betz *Paulus* 72–74, 90.

The boasting of the opponents

I   2 Corinthians 10:12–18

In these verses Paul denounces the kind of boasting which takes pride in the achievements of another. Such boasting, he argues, goes beyond proper bounds (ἡμεῖς δὲ οὐκ εἰς τὰ ἄμετρα καυχησόμεθα, v. 13),[3] infringes on the labours of others (ἐν ἀλλοτρίοις κόποις, v. 15) and takes credit for what is accomplished in another's sphere of influence (ἐν ἀλλοτρίῳ κανόνι εἰς τὰ ἕτοιμα, v. 16).[4] Doubtless Paul is thinking here of the behaviour of his opponents,[5] for not only have they intruded into his field of ministry, the church at Corinth, but they also boast as though that ministry were their own achievement.[6]

In Paul's mind such boasting represents a grave theological misunderstanding (v. 12).[7] Since it is God who 'measures out' a sphere of service and God who prospers a ministry, a minister ought to confine his boasting to what God himself has done (v. 13): he ought to boast only in the Lord (v. 17). By glorying in what amounts to the labours of Paul, the opponents boast beyond the proper limit, beyond a divinely measured sphere of ministry, beyond what God himself has accomplished. They themselves become the measure of their ministry (v. 12), not God, which renders their boasting both unmeasured and empty (v. 18).

The boasting of the opponents is thus characterised by a godless self-commendation which seeks to usurp the achievements of Paul – really the achievements of God – and thus to win for themselves a

---

[3] On taking τὰ ἄμετρα in the sense of 'beyond bounds' cf. Philo *Spec. Leg.* 4.79: 'censure [is] due to every unbounded (πᾶσα ἄμετρος)... impulse... a man [must] set bounds (μέτρα) to his impulses'; see also *Op.* 81; *Leg. All.* 155, 183; *Plant.* 105; Jos. *B.* 4.350; and cf. BAG 45; Furnish 471; Bultmann 195–96.

[4] The word κανών has geographical significance and here means 'a measured area' (so Barrett 268). For an example of this use of the word in the first century see Judge 'Regional *kanon* for requisitioned transport' 36–45; *pace* Käsemann 'Legitimität' 56–61 and Kümmel 209 for whom κανών means a 'standard of judgement'.

[5] Cf., τισιν τῶν ἑαυτοὺς συνιστανόντων in v. 12, a clear reference to the opponents; so Barrett 262; Lietzmann 143.

[6] Cf. Barrett 'Christianity at Corinth' 291–94; Hafemann '"Self-Commendation"' 74–76, 79.

[7] Assuming the longer reading of vv. 12–13. The omission of οὐ συνιᾶσιν ἡμεῖς δέ in the Western tradition (D, F, G, it^ar, d, e, f, g) is probably due to a copyist passing accidently from οὐ to the οὐκ following the four words in question; cf. Bachmann 353 n.1; Kümmel 208–9; Furnish 470–71; *pace* Lietzmann 143, Bultmann 194–95 and Héring 73 who prefer the shorter reading.

status equal to the apostle's. In reality, it gains them no standing at all, for it amounts to boasting in what is not, and can never be, theirs.

2   2 Corinthians 11:12

In this verse Paul implies that the opponents are boasting of the fact that they receive financial support from the Corinthians.[8] The reason for such boasting is set out by Paul in the cryptic telic clause – ἵνα ἐν ᾧ καυχῶνται εὑρεθῶσιν καθὼς καὶ ἡμεῖς. A literal reading of these words would suggest that the opponents want to be like Paul in the matter of their boasting. They want to be viewed as apostles who are worthy of their wage.[9] But this neglects the fact that Paul not only refuses a wage but is belittled for it. It is doubtful whether the opponents really want to be *like him*.

This has prompted the majority of scholars to suggest that what the opponents really want is for Paul to become *like them*, to join them in *their* boasting, and so lend credence to their claim to be apostles of Christ. Such an interpretation would have been better expressed by the words ἵνα ἐν ᾧ καυχῶνται αὐτοί, κἀγὼ εὑρεθῶ.[10] But this view also has its weaknesses. In refusing support Paul actually ignites the displeasure of his converts, which in turn encourages them to embrace those who do take their money, the opponents. This development would doubtless please Paul's rivals and hence curtail any desire on their part for Paul to become *like them*.

This suggests a third interpretation, namely, that v. 12 does not report the desires of the opponents at all, at least not as they would articulate them. Instead it reveals Paul's *own* assessment of their desires. The fact that they are boasting about their support is viewed *by Paul* as an attempt to claim a share of church leadership which belongs exclusively to him. This interpretation would confirm our findings in 10:12–18, that through their boasting the opponents are in effect seeking to elevate themselves to a status equal to Paul.[11]

---

[8] Cf. Windisch 340; Barrett 284–85; Furnish 509; Bultmann 209; Martin 349.

[9] Thus Georgi *Gegner* 235; Lietzmann 148.

[10] So Bultmann 209; Windisch 339–40; Plummer 307–8; Kümmel 211; Barrett 284.

[11] We may thus render v. 12: 'What I am doing I will continue to do, in order to cut off an opportunity from those who *effectively* want an opportunity to become in their boasting just what we already are.'

3   2 Corinthians 11:18

Here Paul accuses his opponents of boasting 'according to the flesh'
(v. 18). The term κατὰ σάρκα is thought by some to signify the
object of the opponents' boasting – namely, their Jewish heritage
(cf. 11:22).[12] But it probably also points to the attitude underlying
their boasting, a brash self-confidence (cf. ἐν ταύτῃ τῇ ὑποστάσει
τῆς καυχήσεως, v. 17).[13] Such 'boastful confidence' represents the
very antithesis of speaking κατὰ κύριον (v. 17). Yet it is precisely
the sort of self-confidence that the Corinthians admire (v. 18),
especially when it begets tyrannical behaviour. They gravitate to
anyone who makes slaves of them, preys upon them, takes advantage of them, puts on airs or strikes them in the face (v. 20).

4   Summary

It is clear from these observations that the boasting of the opponents is impelled by self-confidence and manifested in self-commendation. The goal of such boasting is to achieve personal pre-
eminence, and especially over Paul in the area of his ministry, the
Corinthian church. It thus bears a striking resemblance to the
competitive boasting so prominent in first-century Corinth.
Perhaps, then, the opponents are reflecting the arrogant ways of
their culture, which in turn suggests that the members of the Corinthian church, in paying homage to the opponents, are showing the
same attraction to that culture.

The suggestion becomes more certain when it is noticed that the
Corinthians actually do more than admire the boasting of others.
They indulge in it themselves. We must consider the evidence,
especially as it is set out in 1 Corinthians.

The boasting of the Corinthians

1   1 Corinthians 1:26–29

In this passage Paul reveals that God puts an end to all human

---

[12] *Pace* Windisch 346; Bultmann 213; Lietzmann 149; Plummer 315.
[13] Taking ὑπόστασις to mean 'confidence', not 'venture' or 'plan'; thus Barrett 290;
Hatch *Essays* 88–89; contra Köster 'ὑπόστασις' 583; Harder 'Form' 712; Bultmann 212–13. If τῆς καυχήσεως is an adjectival genitive we may translate the
entire phrase 'in this boastful confidence'.

boasting (v. 29) by conferring his salvation on those who are too foolish, weak, base and contemptible, and hence too humble, to take any credit for their new exalted position in Christ (vv. 27–28). It would seem that Paul is particularly concerned to demonstrate the relevance of this teaching to his young converts in Corinth, as the emphatic sentence in v. 26 makes clear: 'Consider *your* calling, brethren, that not many of *you* are wise, powerful or well-born'. Perhaps his readers are forgetting the lesson implicit in their humble origins and have begun to boast about their exalted position as Christians. This suggestion becomes explicit in 1 Corinthians 4:6b–7.

2   *1 Corinthians 4:6b–7*

Here Paul accuses the Corinthians of becoming puffed up, 'each on behalf of one and against another'.[14] In particular, they are 'boasting in men' (3:21; 4:7), in one leader as opposed to another (cf. 1:12; 3:22). In this way they hope to arrogate to themselves a position of strength and honour (4:10) and so gain supremacy over their neighbour. That the goal of such boasting is indeed supremacy is clear from the ironical question which Paul puts to them in verse 7, τίς γὰρ σε διακρίνει, which translated means, 'Who concedes you any superiority?'[15]

It is obvious from these passages that the Corinthians are not only engaging in boasting, but also doing so in a way not dissimilar to the opponents in 2 Corinthians. They are glorying in themselves in order to assert their supremacy over others. We shall learn more about this boasting if we examine Paul's critique of it.

3   *Paul's appraisal of Corinthian boasting*

Paul brings several accusations against the boasting of his converts. First of all, it represents a complete misapprehension of reality. By boasting as though they were now powerful and wise (1 Corinthians 4:7, 10), the Corinthians effectively forget that they were 'called' from humble origins (1:26). Secondly, it represents a total disregard of Paul's example. He is unable to glory in his position for God has

---

[14] A possible translation of εἰς ὑπὲρ τοῦ ἑνὸς . . . κατὰ τοῦ ἑτέρου cf. Barrett *First Corinthians* 107; Conzelmann *1 Corinthians* 85; Lietzmann 19.

[15] The translation of BAG 184; cf. Barrett *First Corinthians* 107: 'Who makes you different from your neighbour?'

displayed apostles 'last of all' (4:9). This is a point which Paul drives home in 1 Corinthians 3:5–4:5 where he portrays the ministry of apostles figuratively in terms of the farmer, the builder and the steward.[16] If apostles produce steady growth (3:6–9), a firm foundation (3:10–17) and unwavering fidelity (4:1–5), it is not they who deserve the credit, but *God* (cf. 3:5, 7, 9–10; 4:4–6). Consequently, it is absurd for the Corinthians to glory in one leader as opposed to another (4:6c). They must cease their boasting in regard to men (3:21).

Paul elucidates the point still further in 1 Corinthians 4:6 where he exhorts his converts not to go beyond 'what is written' (4:6b). The precise referent of the phrase ἃ γέγραπται has invited much speculation and, unfortunately, we cannot here consider all the interpretations.[17] It must suffice to observe that since this phrase appears throughout Paul as a formula introducing OT citations,[18] it probably refers here to the five scriptural quotations which Paul has already cited in 1 Corinthians 1–3.[19] They are the following:

(i) 'I will destroy the wisdom of the wise, and the cleverness of the clever I will set aside' (1 Corinthians 1:19 = Isaiah 29:14)[20]

(ii) 'Let him who boasts, boast in the Lord' (1:31 = Jeremiah 9:24 [23])[21]

(iii) 'Things which eye has not seen and ear has not heard, and which have not entered the heart of man, all that God has prepared for those who love him' (2:9 = Isaiah 64:4 [3])[22]

(iv) '[He is] the one who catches the wise in their craftiness' (3:19 = Job 5:13)[23]

---

[16] In other words, when Paul says in 4:6, ταῦτα δὲ, ἀδελφοί, μετεσχημάτισα εἰς ἐμαυτὸν καὶ 'Απολλῶν δι' ὑμᾶς, he is referring back to the images of the farmer, builder and steward; cf. McHugh 'Present and Future' 178; Ross '1 Cor. 4:6' 217; Conzelmann *1 Cor.* 85–86.

[17] But for a tidy summary of the views cf. Legault 'Beyond' 227–31.

[18] Cf. Rom 1:20; 2:24; 3:4, 10; 4:17; 8:36; 9:13; etc.

[19] Thus Hooker 'Beyond the Things Which are Written' 128–30.

[20] Here Paul follows the LXX of Isa. 29:14 except where he changes κρύψω to ἀθετήσω.

[21] This represents an abbreviated version of LXX Jer. 9:23; in particular, Paul substitutes ἐν κυρίῳ for ἐν τούτῳ . . . συνίειν καὶ γινώσκειν ὅτι ἐγώ εἰμι κύριος.

[22] This represents a loose citation of LXX Isa. 64:4; see also Isa. 65:16.

[23] The quotation differs markedly in form, but not in meaning, from LXX Job 5:13. Perhaps Paul was using a Greek translation of the OT unknown to us; cf. Barrett *First Corinthians* 94.

(v) 'The Lord knows the reasonings of the wise, that they are useless' (3:20 = Psalms 94 [93]: 11)[24]

A simple glance at these texts will reveal that (i), (iv) and (v) underscore the foolishness of human wisdom before God, whereas (iii) highlights the mystery of God's wisdom before humans. Clearly, Paul is stressing the superiority of God's wisdom to that of humans. It is less clear, however, how his readers may be thought to go 'beyond' this truth. The remaining text, (ii), provides an important clue.

It represents a loose citation of Jeremiah 9:23 (LXX), a verse probably well ingrained in the mind of Paul, a former Pharisee, who doubtless heard it recited regularly in Jewish liturgy – in particular, yearly on the Jewish fast day, the ninth of Ab (*b. Meg.* 31b),[25] triennially as the *haphtarah* on the fourth sabbath of Tisri[26] and yearly on *Rosh Hashanah*, the Jewish New Year (*b. Meg.* 31a).[27] Paul was probably also well acquainted with the context of this verse. Some scholars have even suggested that his teaching in 1 Corinthians 1:26–31 represents an exposition of Jeremiah 9:22–23 (LXX).[28] A comparison of the two passages is instructive:

Jeremiah 9:22–23 (LXX)		*1 Corinthians 1:26–29, 31*
Μὴ καυχάσθω ὁ σοφὸς	v. 26	οὐ πολλοὶ σοφοὶ κατὰ σάρκα . . .
ἐν τῇ σοφίᾳ αὐτοῦ	v. 27	ἀλλὰ τὰ μωρὰ
		τοῦ κόσμου
		ἐξελέξατο ὁ θεὸς
		ἵνα καταισχύνῃ τοὺς σοφοὺς
καὶ μὴ καυχάσθω ὁ ἰσχυρὸς	v. 26	οὐ πολλοὶ δυνατοί . . .
ἐν τῇ ἰσχύι αὐτοῦ	v. 27	καὶ τὰ ἀσθενῆ
		τοῦ κόσμου
		ἐξελέξατο ὁ θεός
		ἵνα καταισχύνῃ τὰ ἰσχυρά

---

24 Here Paul exchanges σοφῶν for the ἀνθρώπων of LXX Ps. 93:11.
25 Though this is on the relatively late authority of Abaye who died in AD 338.
26 So Jacobs 'Triennial Cycle' 256.
27 This time as part of Hannah's song in 1 Sam. 2, though it was probably interpolated from Jer. 9; cf. Thackeray 'Song of Hannah' 183–92.
28 In the same way that Bar. 3:9–4:24 may represent an exposition of Jer. 8:13–9:24 – a suggestion made first by Thackeray *Jewish Worship* 95–100, who also sees a connection between 1 Cor. 1, Jer. 8–9 and Bar. 3–4 (see esp. p. 97; and cf. Hübner 'Der vergessene Baruch' 161–73; Peterson '1 Korinther 1, 18' 98–99). For the view that Jer. 9 may have served as inspiration for 1 Cor. 1:26–31 see Cerfaux 'Vestiges' 524–25, 528–29; Bosch '*Gloriarse*' 127; Héring 12; Barrett 51, 61. Others see a link between Paul's teaching in 1 Cor. 1 and Job 12:17–22 (Hanson 'Book of Job' 251) or Gen. 1:26–28 (Wuellner 'Sociological Implications' 671).

καὶ μὴ καυχάσθω ὁ *πλούσιος*   v. 26   οὐ πολλοὶ *εὐγενεῖς* . . .
ἐν τῷ *πλούτῳ* αὐτοῦ   v. 28   καὶ τὰ ἀγενῆ τοῦ κόσμου
                                              καῖ τὰ ἐξουθενημένα
                                              ἐξελέξατο ὁ θεός
                                              τὰ μὴ ὄντα
                                              ἵνα τὰ ὄντα καταργήσῃ
                              v. 29   ὅπως μὴ καυχήσηται πᾶσα
                                              σάρξ
                                              ἐνώπιον τοῦ θεοῦ . . .

ἀλλ’ ἢ ἐν τούτῳ καυχάσθω   v. 31   ἵνα καθὼς γέγραπται
ὁ καυχώμενος,   ὁ καυχώμενος
συνίειν καὶ γινώσκειν   ἐν *κυρίῳ* καυχάσθω
ὅτι ἐγώ εἰμι *κύριος*

The similarities between the two texts are striking. Both refer to
the wise, powerful and rich or well-born, and both reach the conclusion that humans can boast only in the Lord. Yet they also
diverge at an important point. Whereas Jeremiah simply precludes
human boasting, Paul actually explains why such boasting is
useless. It is because God has put to shame what the world esteems
(cf. vv. 27–28)[29] and so has rendered the world's boasting senseless
(thus v. 29).

It is this insight which unifies the meaning of the OT citations in
1 Corinthians 1–3 and demonstrates in what way the Corinthians
are not to go 'beyond what is written'. The citations teach that while
it is the wisdom of the world to indulge in human boasting there
is a simpler, more perfect kind of wisdom, that of boasting only of
the Lord.[30] Paul enjoins his converts not to go beyond this OT
teaching. Unlike the opponents in 2 Corinthians 10,[31] they must
be 'measured' in their boasting, staying within proper bounds.
In short, they must never exceed the simple boast in the Lord
(1 Corinthians 1:31).

4 Summary

It is clear from these observations that the boasting of the Corinthians is characterised by self-commendation and is calculated to win

[29] Thus taking the thrice repeated genitive phrase τοῦ κόσμου in vv. 27–28 to mean
'in the world's estimation'; so Barrett *First Corinthians* 58.
[30] This is a major theme in the OT: the foolish and the ungodly glory in themselves
(cf. Ps. 52:1; 49:5–6; 94:3; Judg. 7:2; and see *3 Macc.* 2:17); the wise exult in God
(1 Sam. 2:2–3; Ps. 5:11; 34:3; 44:8; Sir. 17:6–8; see also Philo *Leg. All.* 1.52; 3.29–30;
Agr. 173; *Conf.* 127–28); cf. Schreiner 'Jeremia 9, 22. 23' 535–36.
[31] Where in v. 17 Paul, not coincidently, also cites LXX Jer. 9:23.

them a position of prominence among their peers. It is thus the same kind of boasting as that practised by the opponents in 2 Corinthians and the same also as that so apparent in first-century Corinth. Paul vigorously attacks such boasting. It is worldly boasting, running counter to the message of the OT and now, too, to one's position in Christ. Given such an unequivocal denunciation we should never expect to find the apostle himself indulging in such boasting. Yet in 2 Corinthians that is exactly what we do find. We must consider this apparent anomaly.

The boasting of Paul

In 2 Corinthians 11:18 the apostle Paul makes a startling declaration: 'since many boast according to the flesh, I also shall boast'.[32] While conceding that such boasting is 'useless' (οὐ σύμφερον, 12:1) and 'foolish' (ἀφροσύνη, 11:1, 17, 21), his converts have left him no option – by failing to commend him they force him to commend himself (ὑμεῖς με ἠναγκάσατε, 12:11). At first sight it would appear that Paul is endeavouring to boost his self-esteem. He is, in the words of C. H. Dodd, giving himself 'something to be proud of'.[33] Yet this would suggest that his motives are uncharacteristically self-centred. Käsemann is perhaps nearer the mark when he argues that Paul takes up boasting in order to defend his apostleship.[34] Yet even this interpretation falters. It is not primarily in defence of his apostleship that Paul boasts, but, according to him, to build up the Corinthians (12:19). This raises a crucial question: How can an activity which Paul has condemned so vehemently as anti-Christian possibly edify his converts?[35]

Most enquiries into the nature of Paul's boasting tend to focus on its form. H. D. Betz, for example, calls attention to the similarity between Paul's style of boasting and the methods of self-praise employed in hellenistic rhetoric and concludes that Paul must have been drawing sympathetically on such methods.[36] E. A. Judge strongly disagrees. The fact that Paul actually boasts about his

---

[32] What he does not say is that he, too, will boast κατὰ σάρκα.

[33] See Dodd *Studies* 73; cf. 80.

[34] 'Legitimität' 48, 69–70; cf. also Bultmann *Exegetische Probleme* 20.

[35] It is a weakness of the studies of Käsemann ('Legitimität') and Bultmann (*Exegetische Probleme*) that they do not explore the value of Paul's boasting in 2 Cor. 11–12 for the Corinthians themselves.

[36] Betz *Paulus* 74–89.

suffering (cf. 11:22–29) suggests that he is engaging in a careful *reductio ad absurdum* of rhetorical methods.[37] In both of these views we are made to concentrate primarily on the *manner* in which Paul speaks, not on *what* he says, on his style, not on his content. There is of course value in this approach. It certainly expands our appreciation of Paul's rhetorical skills. But by itself it fails to show how those skills actually build up his readers. For an answer to this question we must turn to the *content* of his boasting.

In 2 Corinthians 11:30 Paul announces: 'If I have to boast, I will boast of what pertains to my weakness'. The nature of this 'weakness' has already vividly been set out by Paul in 11:23–29, in the so-called catalogue of woes and sufferings, a list of personal afflictions so horrific that it would have elicited feelings of extreme contempt among his readers. By boasting of such humiliations the apostle would seem to be reveling in his disgrace. The point becomes patently clear in verses 32–33, the odd account of Paul's escape from Damascus. In the first century the highest military award, the *corona muralis*, was reserved for the man first up the wall in the heat of battle.[38] In Paul's moment of danger he was lowered through the wall in a basket! Such an event would have been regarded as profoundly humiliating and certainly not worthy of one's boast. Yet the fact that Paul does glory in it suggests that he is parodying the world's idea of boasting. His boasting is rife with irony.[39]

Yet in another sense it is profoundly straightforward. In his opinion he has no option but to boast about his humiliations and weaknesses (cf. 11:30; 12:5, 9), for it accords with his position in Christ – he *is* weak in Christ (καὶ γὰρ ἡμεῖς ἀσθενοῦμεν ἐν αὐτῷ, 13:4). To boast in any other way would be dishonest (cf. οὐ ψεύδομαι, 11:31).[40] Moreover, by glorying in his weakness he is glorying, not in himself, but in Christ who is his sufficiency in weakness (12:9). In this way Paul maintains the OT standard of boasting only in the Lord (Jeremiah 9:22–23 [LXX]; cf. 1 Corinth-

---

[37] Thus Judge 'Paul's Boasting' 37–50; 'Classical Society' 34–36; 'Socrates' 114; followed by Forbes 'Paul's Boasting' 1–30; and cf. Travis 'Paul's Boasting' 527–32. The position of Judge was partly anticipated by Fridrichsen 'Stil' 25–29; 'Peristasenkatalog' 78–82 who long ago argued that Paul's boasting was meant to be a parody of the *Res Gestae Divi Augusti* (a record of the achievements of Augustus, posted in prominent places).

[38] Cf. Livy 28.48.5: 'The special distinction of a mural crown (*muralis corona*) belonged to the man who had been first to climb the wall'; see also 23.18.7; and Gell. 5.6.16, 19.

[39] So Allo 299; Lietzmann 151.   [40] Cf. Zmijewski *Der Stil* 322–23.

ians 1:31; 2 Corinthians 10:17) – now the standard of those in Christ.

In short, then, Paul's boasting is both deeply ironic and profoundly straightforward. It turns worldly boasting on its head while specifying what is Christian. It is in this way that Paul hopes to edify his converts.

Summary

Boasting is a serious problem in the Corinthian church, perhaps more so than in churches elsewhere. This is due, it would seem, to the influence of secular values and attitudes among Corinthian Christians. They are showing the same obsession with self-exalting behaviour as their pagan counterparts, the same drive to excel the neighbour, the same regard for arrogance and contempt for humility and ultimately the same compulsion to boast. As pertains to boasting they seem to be very much conditioned by their society. Naturally they are critical of Paul for his refusal to boast. In response to this criticism Paul indulges in a kind of boasting which represents the very antithesis of what they admire. He glories in his weakness (11:30; 12:9). In doing so he maintains that he remains true both to the teaching of the OT and to his position in Christ, and in this way builds up the brethren in Christ.

Physical presence

The Corinthians also express their disapproval of Paul's physical appearance. 'His bodily presence' (ἡ παρουσία τοῦ σώματος),[41] they allege, 'is weak' (2 Corinthians 10:10). The precise nature of this weakness has been much disputed. Scholars have suggested variously that it refers to his bodily illness,[42] his unskilled speech,[43] his cowardliness in the face of opposition,[44] his lack of pneumatic power,[45] his handiwork,[46] his reluctance to wield a rod of disci-

---

[41] I.e. what he is when he arrives in the body; so Gundry *Soma* 48; Barrett 260–61; Furnish 479; Lietzmann 142.
[42] So Jervell 'Der schwache Charismatiker' 191–92; cf. Allo *Première épître aux Corinthiens* 24.
[43] Thus Prümm I 581; Strachan 14.   [44] Cf. Windisch 293.
[45] Bultmann *Exegetische Probleme* 24; Schmithals *Gnosis* 168; Käsemann 'Legitimität' 53; Reitzenstein *Mysterienreligionen* 213–14; Wilckens *Weisheit* 46–47.
[46] Cf. Hock *Paul's Ministry* 50–65.

pline,[47] or perhaps a combination of these.[48] An examination of the wider context of 2 Corinthians 10:10 lends precision to the debate.

The charge

First of all, it is instructive to note the full extent of the charge levelled against Paul: 'his letters, they say, are weighty and strong (αἱ ἐπιστολαὶ ... βαρεῖαι καὶ ἰσχυραί) but his bodily presence is weak' (10:10). It would seem that his critics have detected an inconsistency between how Paul comes across in letters and what he is in person. His personal presence, his outward appearance and demeanour, is felt to be comparatively 'weak'. Now we know from our study of the first century that people in antiquity placed a great premium on outward appearance. Epictetus, for example, commended the person who could 'attract the attention of common people by the very appearance of his body' (3.22.88).[49] We also know from the *Acts of Paul and Thekla* that Paul was viewed as 'a man little in stature, bald-headed, with crooked legs, well-born, with eye-brows meeting and a long nose'.[50] Perhaps, then, it was Paul's uninspiring visage which was coming under attack.

Yet the greater context of verse 10 suggests a more searching criticism. The series of contrasts in verses 1–11 is particularly enlightening:

κατὰ πρόσωπον μὲν ταπεινὸς ἐν ὑμῖν	ἀπὼν δὲ θαρρῶ εἰς ὑμᾶς (v. 1)
ἡ παρουσία τοῦ σώματος ἀσθενὴς	αἱ ἐπιστολαὶ ... βαρεῖαι καὶ ἰσχυραί (v. 10)
παρόντες τῷ ἔργῳ	τῷ λόγῳ δι᾽ ἐπιστολῶν ἀπόντες (v. 11)

Taking these antitheses together, we may infer that Paul is being faulted for lacking the sort of *boldness in deed* when present that his more forceful letters have led his readers to expect. The exact nature of this 'boldness' is elucidated in the surrounding verses.

In verse 2 Paul implies that he has been accused of 'walking

---

[47] Oostendorp *Another Jesus* 19–20.   [48] Cf. Barrett 261.
[49] For other refs. cf. Furnish 468.
[50] The citation is from chap. 3 of Lipsius and Bonnet *Acta Apostolorum Apocrypha* I 237. Ramsay *Roman Empire* 381 dates this description of Paul to the first century, but Betz *Paulus* 55 disputes its historical reliability, though conceding it probably corresponds to the attacks of the opponents.

according to the flesh'. Normally this would suggest a moral indictment, such as that he is behaving selfishly or dishonestly.[51] While there may be some truth in this interpretation (as we shall discover below), the context clearly suggests a second way in which to take the term κατὰ σάρκα.

In verse 3 Paul responds to his detractors by conceding that while he may 'walk in the flesh' he by no means 'makes war according to the flesh' (v. 3). Here Paul dramatically changes the terms of the argument by replacing his critics' more placid notion of 'walking' with his own more violent image of 'warring'. The effect is stunning: while he may *walk weakly*, he also *fights strongly*. Indeed his weapons are powerful through God (δυνατὰ τῷ θεῷ),[52] not fleshly (οὐ σαρκικὰ) – so powerful that he is able to tear down every stronghold raised up against the knowledge of God (vv. 4–5). The surprising emphasis here on martial power suggests that Paul is venturing a reply to those who allege that he is unable to project himself with violence of action.[53] We may surmise from this that his *behaviour* in person is thought by some to be 'weak.'

This interpretation is confirmed and elucidated in verse 8. There Paul maintains that he could legitimately boast exceedingly about his authority and not be put to shame. In a parallel affirmation in 13:10 he describes this authority in terms of his readiness to use severity among his converts,[54] in particular to subject them to punishment and discipline (cf. 13:2).[55] The evidence of these two verses helps to fill out the charge levelled against Paul. He is being faulted for his failure to impose himself violently upon the church and, specifically, to mete out punishment and discipline.

Now at first blush such a criticism would seem to be remarkable. Do the Corinthians really want their apostle to wield a heavier stick? Interestingly, the answer would seem to be a resounding 'Yes!' It is precisely such heavy-handedness that they eagerly endorse. They gladly put up with Paul's oppressive rivals, those haughty inter-

---

[51] Thus the view of Georgi *Gegner* 232; Windisch 295; Lietzmann 140; but for other views see the list in Theissen 'Legitimation' 208 n. 2.

[52] The term δυνατὰ τῷ θεῷ is probably not a superlative Hebraism, 'divinely powerful' (as Moule *Idiom* 184; Zerwick *Greek* 56), but a *dativus commodi*, 'powerful on God's behalf' (BDF § 192; Moulton *Grammar* II 443).

[53] Cf. Malherbe 'Paul at War' 170; Furnish 462.

[54] Cf. ἵνα παρὼν μὴ ἀποτόμως χρήσωμαι κατὰ τὴν ἐξουσίαν ἣν ὁ κύριος ἔδωκέν μοι, 13:10.

[55] Cf. Thrall 'Super-Apostles' 54: 'Paul has to defend himself against the charge that he . . . has not dealt firmly with delinquents'; see also Furnish 477.

lopers who enslave them, devour them, take advantage of them, lord it over them and strike them in the face (11:20).[56] Moreover, they responded positively to the strident tone of Paul's own severe letter, reaffirming their support of their apostle (cf. 7:5–13a).[57] Conversely, when he comes to Corinth and refuses to assert himself aggressively among them their support begins to wane. The one who seemed to be so bold in letters now appears in person to be timid and weak (10:10).[58]

It is this last observation which suggests that the term κατὰ σάρκα in 10:2 may also have moral implications. Reading between the lines it would seem that the Corinthians are accusing Paul of duplicity, of pretending to be one thing in letters that he is not in person, of deceiving them into thinking that he is bold and strong when in fact he is timid and meek (2 Corinthians 10:1), of threatening to come with a rod (cf. 1 Corinthians 4:21) when he knows it will be in weakness, fear and trembling (cf. 1 Corinthians 2:3).[59] Their suspicions were only confirmed when Paul reneged on his promise to come to Corinth (cf. 2 Corinthians 1:15–17). He must have something to hide! Perhaps he is afraid that if he visits Corinth he will be exposed as the weak and cowardly person he really is! Maybe he is intentionally concealing his humility! He is duplicitous![60] In charging Paul with walking κατὰ σάρκα the Corinthians thus reveal their disappointment with two related aspects of his character: his weakness and his duplicity (cf. 1:17; 10:2).[61]

The response

Paul's response to his critics is direct and emphatic. 'What we are in word through letters is precisely what we are in deed when present' (10:11). The only difference, he maintains, is that when present his boldness takes an unexpected form. Instead of using severity (13:10) and boasting excessively about his authority (10:8), he spares the rod (cf. 1:23–2:4) and begs his converts not to provoke him to harshness (10:2). In fact he writes the present letter precisely to pave the way for a peaceful visit (13:10). He wants to come in 'humility'

---

[56] Cf. Barrett *Signs* 36: 'the intruders ... have impressed the too impressionable members of the church by their violent and abusive behaviour'.

[57] Cf. Barrett 247, 259–60.   [58] Cf. Watson 'Painful Letter' 342–43.

[59] Cf. Malherbe 'Paul at War' 167–68; Betz *Paulus* 11 n. 38; Reitzenstein *Mysterie-religionen* 212–13; Barrett 249; Plummer 275; Hughes 348.

[60] Cf. Barrett 247.   [61] So apparently Furnish 461.

(10:1) and appear weakest of all (11:29).[62] For in his mind it is only in humility that he reflects the meekness and gentleness of Christ (10:1) and so boldly builds up the Corinthian church (10:8; 13:10).

In order to appreciate the nature of this boldness we must ask how it is that his humility serves to build up his converts. An important clue is to be found in passages where the apostle deals specifically with the theme of punishment.[63] In 2 Corinthians 10:5–6 we read that Paul withholds the use of force until the thoughts of his converts are taken captive for obedience to Christ. Presumably then he will punish, but only his opponents.[64] The same sequence is found in the early chapters of the epistle where, rather than coming with a rod, Paul pens a letter calling for the obedience of his converts (1:23–2:11). On this evidence it would seem that Paul feels he can more successfully foster true obedience by withholding punishment than by unleashing it.

Such a conviction is doubtless due in part to the mixed response which his 'severe letter' produced. On one level the epistle was a great success, prompting the Corinthians to express both a godly sorrow leading to repentance and salvation (7:9–11) and a renewed commitment to their apostle (7:7, 12). Clearly Paul had reason for joy (7:7, 9, 13, 16). Yet on a deeper level he remains troubled. His converts have yet to grasp the full significance of his ministry (cf. 1:13–14, 17; 5:11; 6:11–13; 7:2; 10:1, 7, 10–11; 12:11; 13:3, 5–6). They understand it only in part (cf. καθὼς καὶ ἐπέγνωτε ἡμᾶς ἀπὸ μέρους, 1:14). While they have demonstrated a zeal for him by renouncing the so-called 'offender' (cf. 7:5–13a), it was merely a superficial response to the forcefulness of his letter. As pertains to his meekness and humility, they remain disturbed and unimpressed (10:1).

This probably explains why Paul frets about the strength of his letter (cf. 10:9). It serves only to confirm the Corinthians in a partial, and thus a false, understanding of his ministry. By striking terror in their hearts, he accomplishes only what the opponents do when they behave κατὰ σάρκα (11:18): he engenders a 'worldly sorrow' leading to death (7:10). If he were to exhibit in his person the sort of exalted behaviour which his converts admire in his letters, he would be

---

[62] Cf. on this interpretation of 11:29 Barrett 302.

[63] This is a prominent theme in 2 Cor: cf. 1:23–2:4; 7:8–13a; 10:1–11; 12:19–13:2; 13:10.

[64] Cf. Barrett 253–54; 'Opponents' 239; Furnish 464.

prompting in his congregation, not a 'godly sorrow' (7:9), but a destructive urge to glory in their apostle's human forcefulness. It is clear to Paul that he can use his authority in such a way as to bring down his converts (10:8; 13:10; cf. 7:9) and not build them up.

We can now see why Paul's behaviour in person seems to differ in thrust from the tone of his letters. Knowing that a display of visible force would, far from winning the obedience of his converts, actually prolong their human boasting and lead them ultimately to destruction, he comes to them in a premeditated spirit of meekness and gentleness. That is not to say that he comes without boldness. On the contrary, it is precisely in such 'weakness' that he intends to engage in bold warfare, tearing down strongholds and taking captive the self-exalting attitudes which come into conflict with the knowledge of God (10:3–6). It is through meekness and gentleness that he seeks to win his converts' obedience to Christ.

Of course there is a possibility that his approach will fail. If it becomes clear to Paul that his reluctance to wield a rod has failed to stem the tide of sin among the Corinthians (cf. 12:21) and has not brought every thought captive for obedience to Christ (10:5), then he will have little choice but, on his next visit, to use great severity (13:2). He is resolved to do just that (13:1), even at the risk of causing his converts to exult in his forcefulness.

Summary

It is clear from the foregoing analysis that the Corinthians are eager for Paul to be more assertive in his dealings with the church. They would welcome a heavier hand and applaud more violent behaviour. Here their perspective seems to be shaped by their culture. Indeed in Corinth, perhaps more than elsewhere, people were eager to embrace those who projected themselves with vigour and force. Paul not only rejects this perspective but turns it on its head. He conforms to the meekness and gentleness of Christ, and in this way seeks to build up his converts.

Speech

We have now looked at two areas in which Paul falls short of the expectations of his converts: his boasting and his physical presence. We must turn to a third, his speech.

The charge

1   2 Corinthians 10:10, 11:6

On the evidence of these two verses it becomes clear that the Corinthians are unimpressed with Paul's verbal skills. His speech, they allege, is 'contemptible' (ὁ λόγος ἐξουθενημένος, 10:10) and 'unprofessional' (ἰδιώτης τῷ λόγῳ, 11:6). The precise nature of this charge has been a matter of much debate. Some scholars believe that Paul is being faulted on grounds that his preaching lacks pneumatic power.[65] But this neglects the force of the technical term ἰδιώτης. It is unlikely that Paul would confess to being a 'layman' in *pneumatic* utterance (cf. 1 Corinthians 2:4).[66]

An alternative view is that Paul is being criticised for lacking the skills of a trained rhetorician – he is a 'layman in rhetorical utterance'.[67] This would seem to find confirmation in Paul's own words in 11:5–6, where he maintains that he is not inferior to the most eminent apostles '*even though* my speech is unskilled'.[68] Here he would seem to be conceding that his rhetorical skills are indeed amateurish.

But what rhetorical skills is he felt to lack? Many commentators suggest that it is the finely honed techniques of classical oratory. Sifting through the work of great orators like Philostratus and Quintilian they identify numerous examples of classical irony, metaphor, comparison, etc. which are missing in Paul.[69] Their findings are fascinating, but inconclusive. For it is not necessarily Paul's *use*

---

[65] Thus Reitzenstein *Mysterienreligionen* 214; cited approvingly by Käsemann 'Legitimität' 35 and Lietzmann 142; cf. also Lütgert *Freiheitspredigt* 68; Bultmann *Exegetische Probleme* 24; Georgi *Gegner* 228; Güttgemanns *Apostel* 96; Friedrich 'Gegner' 184; Schmithals *Gnosis* 134, 167 n.1; Rissi *Studien* 17.

[66] So Kümmel 210. On taking the term ἰδιώτης to mean 'layman' or 'unskilled' cf. Lucian *J. Tr.* 27: 'he utterly lacks the courage to speak before a crowd and his language is unskilled' (ἰδιώτης); and Jos. *A.* 2.271: 'I am at a loss to know how I (Moses), a mere layman (ἰδιώτης ἀνήρ), ... can find words to persuade my people'; see also D. Chr. *Or.* 42.3.

[67] So Kümmel 210; Allo 248, 280–81; Héring 80; Plummer 299; Furnish 462, 479, 505; see also Oostendorp *Another Jesus* 11; Munck *Paul* 173; Gemoll 'Xenophonzitat' 28.

[68] The term εἰ δὲ καί in v. 6 introduces a statement of fact; thus Thrall *Particles* 80; Burton *Syntax* § 284.

[69] Thus Forbes 'Self-Praise' 1–30; 'Public Speaker' 11–16; who draws on Judge 'Paul's Boasting' 37; 'Classical Society' 35–36; 'Classical Education' 13; 'Cultural Conformity' 13. Those who take this approach suggest that Paul, far from being ignorant of classical rhetoric, was consciously avoiding it and perhaps even parodying it.

of words – the clever turn of phrase or compelling use of metaphor – which his critics disparage, but his *demeanour* when speaking. At least that is the implication which seems to emerge from the fact that his critics commend his λόγος in letters (τῷ λόγῳ δι' ἐπιστολῶν, 10:11) but repudiate his λόγος in person (ἰδιώτης τῷ λόγῳ, 11:6). Since it is unlikely that the *content* of Paul's λόγος would change from his letters to his speech, it must be his *manner* when speaking which causes the dissension. Perhaps his humble physical presence is affecting his speech.

If so, his critics may well be faulting Paul for refusing to indulge in the imposing and abusive rhetoric which, as we have seen in our historical study, had become so popular in first-century Corinth. This was not the carefully cultivated speech of the academe nor the highly refined speech of classical oratory.[70] It was the 'vulgar rhetoric', a speech characterised by showy and often meaningless monologues in which orators sought to dominate their audience through sheer force of delivery. It was perhaps because Paul eschewed a delivery of this kind that he incurred the ridicule of the Corinthians.

We will learn more about Paul's speech if we examine 1 Corinthians 2:1–5, a passage where he sets out carefully the nature of his preaching.

2 *1 Corinthians 2:1–5*

In verse 4 Paul writes: 'my message and proclamation were not in persuasive words of human wisdom'.[71] The word πειθός occurs only here in the ancient literature but is reminiscent of numerous other πειθ-words in hellenistic rhetoric where the idea of 'persuasion' is especially prominent.[72] This has led many to suggest that Paul is rejecting the persuasive methods and arguments of classical oratory.[73] But this neglects the fact that Paul is addressing a non-intellectual audience and hence people for whom a rejection of

---

[70] Cf. Norden *Kunstprosa* 506–7.

[71] The text here is full of difficulties. We have followed the witness of B, ℵ*, D, 33, *pc*, *vg*ˢᵗ; cf. Conzelmann *1 Cor.* 55; Allo *Première épître aux Corinthiens* 24.

[72] Cf. Demosthenes who praises Lacritus for persuasive speech (λόγους ... πιθανούς, 36.16) and Epictetus who applauds persuasive argument (πιθανολο- γική, 1.8.7); and see Arist. *Rh.* 1.2.10–11; 3.1.3, where 'persuasion' is always the goal of fine speech; and Philostr. *VS* 488, 503, 521 who esteems the sophists Dio Chrysostom, Isocrates and Scopelian for their persuasive charm (πειθώ).

[73] See above nn. 67, 69.

classical speech would scarcely be relevant.[74] A closer look at the text suggests that he is renouncing speech of a different kind.

In verse 1 Paul reminds his converts that when he was present in Corinth he proclaimed the the testimony of God οὐ καθ᾽ ὑπεροχὴν λόγου ἢ σοφίας. The precise meaning of this negative affirmation depends largely on how we take the term ὑπεροχὴ λόγου. Most commentators suggest that Paul is distancing himself from either 'excessive rhetoric'[75] or 'pneumatic utterance'.[76] Yet the word ὑπεροχή simply means 'superiority', which suggests the straightforward translation: 'I have not come in superiority of speech or wisdom'.[77] On this reading, the most we can say with confidence is that Paul is rejecting speech marked by a spirit of pride and arrogance.[78] This assessment is confirmed in an analysis of verse 3, the positive counterpart of verse 1.[79]

Here Paul reminds his readers of his humble demeanour when he was present in Corinth: 'I was with you in weakness and in fear and in much trepidation'. The term φόβος καὶ τρόμος has puzzled scholars. Why was Paul afraid? Did he think his failure in Athens would be repeated in Corinth?[80] Was he sensing a personal inadequacy for the ministry?[81] Was he intimidated by large crowds?[82] Was he anticipating persecution?[83] Certainly each of these possibilities could have provided ample reason to be afraid. Yet there seems to be a more compelling reason.

---

[74] See p. 20, esp. n. 8.
[75] Thus Delling 'ὑπερέχω' 525; Allo *Première épître aux Corinthiens* 23, 25; Lightfoot *Notes* 170; Munck *Paul* 153; Moffatt *First Corinthians* 22–23.
[76] Cf. Baumann *Mitte* 151; Wilckens 'σοφία' 523; Painter 'Πνευματικοί' 241.
[77] Thus BAG 849; cf. an early second-century letter in which a father flatters his son: 'You know that in everything you easily ... hold superiority (ὑπεροχήν) over your brothers' (*CP* 22 [1927] 245, no. 3 [11]); and the command of Josaphat in *Jos. A.* 9.3: 'Take no thought ... of the rank of those who are held to be superior' (ἐν ὑπεροχῇ).
[78] Cf. Schlier *Der Zeit der Kirche* 223–24.
[79] We may note the parallel structures of vv. 1 and 3:
    κἀγὼ   ἐλθὼν πρὸς ὑμᾶς   (v. 1)
    κἀγὼ ... ἐγενόμην πρὸς ὑμᾶς   (v. 3).
[80] Thus Allo *Première épître aux Corinthiens* 24; Robertson-Plummer *First Corinthians* 31; Weiss *Erste Korintherbrief* 47. The idea that Paul's mission to Athens was a failure is inferred from the the derogatory remark of the philosophers in Acts 17:18: 'What would this idle babbler (σπερμολόγος) wish to say?' – another indictment of his speech.
[81] Thus Lightfoot *Notes* 171; Bruce 37; Fascher *Korinther* 115.
[82] So Hartman '1 Cor. 2:1–5' 118.
[83] Cf. Barrett *First Corinthians* 64–65; Glombitza 'Furcht und Zittern' 102; and see Acts 18:9.

In the Septuagint the term φόβος καὶ τρόμος often depicts one's humble response to the awe-inspiring majesty of God. We may note two examples in particular:

> Fear and trembling (φόβος καὶ τρόμος) fall upon them;
> By your (the Lord's) great arm they are motionless as stone
>
> Exodus 15:16 (LXX)

> In that day the Egyptians will be as women in fear
> and trembling (ἐν φόβῳ καὶ ἐν τρόμῳ)
> Because of the appearance of the hand of the Lord
> of Hosts   Isaiah 19:16 (LXX)[84]

Is it possible that Paul has been influenced in his use of φόβος καὶ τρόμος by the LXX? We know from 1 Corinthians 1:17–24 that he views himself as having been entrusted with the word of the cross (vv. 17–18), a word which he regards as the supreme revelation of divine wisdom and power (v. 24).[85] Hence, in the mere outworking of his vocation, in the regular preaching of Christ crucified (2:2), he would have been confronted daily by the awe-inspiring majesty of God – an experience which in the LXX engendered great fear and trembling and which could well now be producing the same in Paul (2:3). Perhaps we should view 1 Corinthians 2:1 and 3 as a neat contrast: 'I did not come in *haughtiness of speech* (v. 1), but in *profound humility and trepidation*' (v. 3). If so, it would confirm that Paul is indeed rejecting the kind of speech which is marked by arrogance – or as he puts it in 4:19b, 'the speech of those who are puffed up' (cf. ὁ λόγος τῶν πεφυσιωμένων).

If we combine this insight with the observations gleaned from 2 Corinthians 10:10 and 11:6 above we can see that Paul is distancing himself from arrogant speech as well as abusive speech. This provides an even firmer basis for supposing that he is rejecting the vulgar rhetoric of his day and not the classical speech of the intellectual elite. It also serves to confirm that the Corinthians are criticising him for not attaining this more popular standard. They want assertiveness and demagoguery, high-falutin rhetoric. He gives them only words of weakness and humility.

---

[84] Cf. also Ps. 2:11; Deut. 2:25; 11:25.
[85] So Wilckens 'Kreuz Christi' 47; Bornkamm *Studien* 92.

3   *Words of wisdom and wisdom of word*

In our discussion of Paul's speech we have thus far passed over the important theme of wisdom. Repeatedly in the first three chapters of 1 Corinthians the apostle brings together the notions of λόγος and σοφία. In particular, he underscores that it is not just any kind of λόγος which he rejects, but λόγος shaped and defined by σοφία – that is, *σοφία λόγου* (1 Corinthians 1:17), ὑπεροχὴ λόγου ἢ *σοφίας* (2:1) and πειθοῖς *σοφίας* λόγοις (2:4). If we are fully to understand what kind of speech he is repudiating we must plumb the nature of the wisdom which shapes it.

The genitive term in 1 Corinthians 2:4 – πειθοῖς σοφίας λόγοις – is instructive. Taken subjectively, it means 'persuasive words directed by wisdom'.[86] This suggests that λόγος draws its persuasive power from σοφία, that wisdom is a technique for persuading the hearer.[87] This has led many commentators to suppose that the wisdom in view here is the σόφια of classical oratory.[88] Yet for reasons enumerated above Paul is probably not thinking of such 'scholastic' wisdom.

A more useful clue may be found in 1 Corinthians 2:5 where the apostle actually gives his reason for rejecting 'persuasive words of wisdom'. He wants to ensure that his converts will not put their trust in the 'wisdom of men'. Here the σοφία which gives shape to λόγος is a wisdom which emanates from humans. An earlier passage underscores this point. In 1 Corinthians 1:17 and 20 Paul appears to renounce the 'wisdom of speech' (v. 17) precisely because it is engendered by the 'wisdom of the world' (v. 20).[89] What is the nature of this worldly and human wisdom? If we are serious about coming to grips with the sort of speech Paul rejects we must seek an answer.

An important assumption has governed the study of 'wisdom' in 1 Corinthians, namely, that Paul uses the word σοφία as a technical term for a well defined system of wisdom in the first century.[90] It is

---

86 So Barrett *First Corinthians* 65.
87 Thus Barrett 'Christianity at Corinth' 278.
88 Thus Robertson-Plummer *First Corinthians* 32–33; Moffatt *First Corinthians* 24; Lightfoot *Notes* 172.
89 Cf. Barrett 'Christianity at Corinth' 278.
90 The fact that Paul uses so many σοφ-words in 1 Cor. 1–3 is thought to confirm this assumption: the noun σοφία occurs sixteen times in these chapters, as opposed to only nine times elsewhere in Paul; the adjective σοφός appears ten times, and only five times elsewhere.

further assumed that the Corinthians are well acquainted with that system[91] – they value it, cultivate it and glory in it;[92] they regard it as a way to God and salvation;[93] they construct a christology from it;[94] and they evaluate Paul's by it.[95] Accordingly, most of what Paul says in 1 Corinthians 1–4 is viewed as a direct and careful attack on this system of wisdom.

On this assumption, it becomes necessary for the prudent interpreter to define σοφία as fully as possible. Unfortunately, the possible definitions are as numerous as they are ingenious. Some have suggested that Paul is opposing the wisdom of Gnosticism;[96] others the wisdom of Greek philosophy;[97] others the wisdom of Hellenistic Judaism;[98] and still others the wisdom of the OT, the rabbis and Qumran.[99] The fact that each of these suggestions can make some sense of Paul's use of σόφια in 1 Corinthians shows the danger of insisting on one in particular. But there is an even greater danger: that of allowing these hypothetical definitions of 'wisdom' to dominate and shape our reading of the passage. One suspects that this error has been committed frequently and, consequently, that insufficient attention has been paid to the scattered clues which Paul himself provides about the nature of σοφία. We must consider those clues.

[91] Cf. Pearson 'Wisdom Speculation' 46: 'the elaborate discussion of "wisdom" . . . shows that it is a major concern of Corinthian Christians'.

[92] Thus Best 'Wisdom of God' 38: the Corinthians are 'elated by their wisdom'; and Barbour 'Wisdom' 60: it is their 'treasured possession'.

[93] Cf. Horsley 'Wisdom of Word' 231: 'These Corinthians had come into an intimate relationship with *sophia* as the means and probably also the content or object of their salvation'; and Funk *Language* 275: 'Quite literally, it (wisdom) is saving knowledge'.

[94] For a sophia christology at Corinth see Wilckens 'σοφία' 519–21; and Knox *Paul* 111–15.

[95] Cf. Pearson 'Wisdom Speculation' 46.

[96] See esp. Wilckens *Weisheit, passim*; 'σοφία' 519–23; and his more recent essay 'Kreuz Christi' 43–81 where he modifies his view of gnosis and wisdom in 1 Cor; cf. also Reitzenstein *Mysterienreligionen, passim*; Bultmann 'γινώσκω' 708–11; *Exegetische Probleme* 4–5; Schmithals *Gnosis, passim*; Schottroff *Glaubende* 170–227; Schlier *Die Zeit der Kirche* 232; Funk *Language* 275; but note the caution of Wilson 'Gnosis at Corinth' 105: 'There are no grounds whatever for seeing any such [gnostic] Sophia-myth in the background to 1 Corinthians'.

[97] Cf. Munck *Paul* 153; Grant 'Wisdom' 51–55; Weiss *Korintherbrief* 23.

[98] Thus the view of Pearson ('Wisdom' 43–66) and Horsley ('Wisdom of Word' 224–39) who argue that the wisdom tradition found in Philo was introduced into the Corinthian church by the Alexandrian Apollos; cf. also Davis *Wisdom, passim*; Knox *Paul* 114; Sellin 'Weisheit' 69–96.

[99] So Ellis 'Wisdom' 82–98; 'Gifts' 128–44; Scroggs 'ΣΟΦΟΣ' 33–55. Still another view is that σοφία spread to Corinth from Paul's own school of wisdom in Ephesus, thus Conzelmann 'Weisheit' 231–44.

In 1 Corinthians 1:25–31 Paul sheds important light on the nature of wisdom by revealing how God assesses it. In short, God regards all human wisdom as folly (v. 25), for it leads to boasting about what the world esteems and hence what God has emptied of all value (vv. 26–29). Such boasting is not only egotistical, it is tantamount to exalting oneself 'in the face of God' (ἐνώπιον τοῦ θεοῦ, v. 29). It is the 'wisdom of men', then, to exult in themselves. A parallel passage, 1 Corinthians 3:18–20, confirms this insight. There the 'wisdom of the world' is manifested in those who exalt themselves by boasting about human leaders.[100] In sum, the wisdom of the world would seem to represent an approach to life in which individuals seek to exalt themselves instead of God.[101] This understanding finds support in the OT passages which Paul cites in 1 Corinthians 1–3 where the word σοφία appears:

(i)   1 Corinthians 1:19 = Isaiah 29:14 (LXX)
       ἀπολῶ τὴν σοφίαν τῶν σοφῶν
       καὶ τὴν σύνεσιν τῶν συνετῶν ἀθετήσω
       I will destroy the wisdom of the wise
       And I will set aside the intelligence of the intelligent

Assuming that Paul has the wider context of Isaiah 29:14 in mind, his citation is especially illuminating. The 'wise' refer to the chief counsellors of the OT king and 'wisdom' to their advice to avert the Assyrian threat by forming alliances with foreign powers (cf. Isaiah 28:14–22; 30:1–5; 31:1–3). It is a wisdom which, in the words of the prophet, trusts in the 'commandments and doctrines of men' (ἐν-τάλματα ἀνθρώπων καὶ διδασκαλίας, Isaiah 29:13) and consequently undermines the true worship of God (μάτην δὲ σέβονταί με, 29:13). It is a man-centred wisdom, which leaves God out of account and incurs his wrath.

(ii)   1 Corinthians 3:19 = Job 5:13 (LXX)
       ὁ δρασσόμενος τοὺς σοφοὺς ἐν τῇ πανουργίᾳ αὐτῶν
       He catches the wise in their own craftiness

Again the context of the OT passage is enlightening. In Job 5 the 'wise' fail to recognise that the Lord is 'sovereign over all' (τὸν πάντων δεσπότην, Job 5:8) and the 'great' and 'glorious' Creator

---

[100] See Munck *Paul* 157: '[the Corinthians] boast about these great names (viz. their leaders), but only to boast about themselves'.

[101] Cf. Barrett *First Corinthians* 52: 'the wisdom spoken of here is a wisdom of this world, a wisdom that leaves God out of account and is man-centred'; 'Christianity at Corinth' 281: 'the σοφία of the rulers is a self-regarding, self-preserving σοφία'; *pace* Best 'Wisdom' 21 who argues that the 'wisdom of men' is simply a false way to God and unrelated to pride or boasting.

(vv. 9–10). They are also ignorant of the fact that he exalts the 'humble' (τὸν ποιοῦντα ταπεινοὺς εἰς ὕψος, v. 11) and brings down the proud and the 'wise' (vv. 12–13). Their wisdom amounts to a haughty refusal to acknowledge God as the mighty Creator.

(iii)   1 Corinthians 3:20 = Psalms 93:11 (LXX)
κύριος γινώσκει τοὺς διαλογισμοὺς τῶν σοφῶν ὅτι εἰσὶν μάταιοι
The Lord knows that the thoughts of the wise are vain

In the context of Psalms 93 the 'thoughts of men'[102] are characterised by arrogance (vv. 3–4) and by a refusal to acknowledge God as Creator (v. 9). Here again the wisdom of men is expressed as an inflated view of one's own importance and a corresponding neglect of the majesty of God.

A common feature of each of these OT contexts is that human wisdom amounts to a way of assessing life which not only leaves God out of account but exalts the individual in his place. This conforms to the kind of wisdom which, as we have seen, Paul is opposing in 1 Corinthians and suggests that if he is drawing on any one 'background' in particular for his understanding of σοφία it is that of the OT. Yet he never explicitly says this; rather, he uses a series of genitive terms to define more closely the kind of σοφία which he opposes in Corinth.

In particular, it is the wisdom τοῦ κόσμου (1:20; 3:19; cf. 1:27, 28; 2:12; 4:13), τῶν ἀνθρώπων (1:25; 2:5), τοῦ αἰῶνος τούτου (2:6; 3:18; cf. 1:20) and τῶν ἀρχόντων τοῦ αἰῶνος τούτου (2:6).[103] Taking these genitive phrases at face value it would seem that Paul is calling attention to a general way of viewing life which arises naturally within this αἰών, from the κόσμος or among ἄνθρωποι – that is, something widely spread and loosely defined, a spirit of the age or an outlook of the time, a sort of habit or fashion of thought which a person might assimilate subconsciously merely by living within a certain society or culture. If we combine this insight with what we have learned about σοφία above it would suggest that in Paul's mind the general outlook of his day – the 'wisdom of the age'

---

[102] The LXX actually reads τοὺς διαλογισμοὺς τῶν ἀνθρώπων.

[103] Scholars who identify σοφία narrowly with gnosticism or hellenistic Judaism or Greek philosophy often fail to reckon with these genitival terms; cf. Horsley's improbable observation: 'these [genitive] phrases are hardly to be taken at face value . . . but are rather polemical references to the heavenly Sophia, the divine agent of creation and salvation' ('Wisdom of Word' 237); and Pearson's: 'the dismissal of Corinthian sophia as "worldly" must be seen as part of Paul's own polemical rhetoric' ('Wisdom' 46).

– is characterised by a proud egocentrism which leaves God out of account.

This picture of the social outlook of first-century Corinth clearly agrees with the earlier findings of our historical analysis. Of all the cities in the Graeco-Roman world, none engendered an atmosphere of self-centredness more striking than Corinth. Energized by upwardly mobile freedmen and their sons, for whom status was an obsession and self-boasting a daily ritual, arrogance and haughtiness were so commonplace that they could easily have been described as the 'wisdom of the age'.

We may now offer a summary of Paul's view of 'wisdom' in I Corinthians 3: (i) the term σοφία seems to be used in a non-technical sense to refer to a general way of assessing life; (ii) the genitive nouns κόσμου, ἀνθρώπων and αἰῶνος τούτου give σοφία its particular thrust – it is the *world's* way of assessing life, *men's* way, etc.; (iii) an examination of I Corinthians 1–3, a brief look at selected OT passages in which σοφία occurs and a reflection on our historical enquiry into first-century Corinth all point to a common conclusion – that the wisdom which Paul opposes in Corinth amounts to a self-regarding outlook in which people exalt themselves in the face of their Creator.

It remains now to ask in what sense the 'wisdom of this age' shaped and influenced the 'speech' which Paul finds so repugnant. The answer would seem to be obvious: 'words of wisdom' are simply a verbal manifestation of the 'wisdom of the world', an audible expression of the proud, self-reliant, God-less outlook of the day.[104] This observation serves to round out our understanding of the kind of speech which Paul rejects. He is opposing the sort of forceful and arrogant speech which springs naturally from the self-regarding wisdom of his day. It is because he fails to indulge in rhetoric of this kind that he incurs the criticism of his converts.

The response

Paul responds to his critics by arguing that while he may indeed be a 'layman in speech' he certainly is not one 'in knowledge' (2 Corinthians 11:6). The specific words here have prompted H. D. Betz to suggest that Paul is drawing a distinction between the form of his speech (λόγος) and the content of his speech (γνῶσις), along the

[104] Cf. Best 'Wisdom' 14.

lines of the ancient debate between the sophists and philosophers. In giving priority to 'knowledge' and hence to the content of his speech Paul seemingly aligns himself with the philosophers, much to the annoyance of his form-conscious critics.[105] Yet it seems unlikely that Paul would draw attention to his 'knowledge' merely to register opposition to the position of sophists.[106]

Elsewhere in his writings the term γνῶσις has a much profounder and broader meaning. For instance, it is used by Paul in 2 Corinthians 10:5 to refer to the 'knowledge *of God*' (γνῶσις τοῦ θεοῦ), a knowledge which, according to 2 Corinthians 4:6, comes to fullest expression in the person of Jesus Christ (cf. φωτισμὸς τῆς γνώσεως τῆς δόξης *τοῦ θεοῦ* ἐν προσώπῳ *Ιησοῦ χριστοῦ*). It is precisely this divine and christocentric knowledge which Paul, in 2 Corinthians 2:14, claims to manifest in his person (τῷ δὲ θεῷ χάρις τῷ . . . τὴν ὀσμὴν τῆς γνώσεως αὐτοῦ φανεροῦντι δι᾽ ἡμῶν), which suggests that he may well be claiming the same thing in the verse we are presently examining: 'in every way I have manifested it (a divine and christocentric knowledge)[107] to you in all things' (ἀλλ᾽ ἐν παντὶ φανερώσαντες ἐν πᾶσιν εἰς ὑμᾶς, 11:6).[108] Hence the kind of knowledge in which Paul is no 'layman' – a knowledge which he manifests in his very person – would seem to be nothing short of the superlative knowledge of God radiating from the person of Jesus Christ.

Clearly for Paul, such a knowledge does far more than represent an alternative to the forms of speech. Indeed, it governs every aspect of his speech. As we have seen, the 'knowledge' of the crucified Christ compels Paul to adopt a manner of speaking which, in terms of both form and content, is characterised by weakness, fear and trembling (1 Corinthians 2:3). That does not mean that his speech lacks thrust. On the contrary, it ensures that his speech will be accompanied by a demonstration of Spirit and power (1 Corinthians 2:4). Herein lies the difference between Paul's speech and that of

---

[105] Thus Betz *Paulus* 59.   [106] Cf. the objection of Barrett 280.

[107] The 'it' is missing from the text; perhaps an αὐτήν was omitted either in transmission or accidently by Paul himself, so Barrett 280.

[108] The syntax of this verse is full of difficulties. The participle φανερώσαντες is probably an epistolary plural (cf. Moule *Idiom* 119; Zerwick *Greek* § 8) and translated as a finite verb (so Moule *Idiom* 180; Zerwick *Greek* § 374; Moulton *Grammar* III 342): 'I have manifested'. I take the term ἐν πᾶσιν to be neuter, 'in all things' (Bachmann 367; Lietzmann 147), not masculine, 'among all [men]' (Bultmann 206; Meyer 324).

contemporary vulgar orators. Their power emerges from the self-imposing wisdom of men. His emanates from the Spirit of God.

Summary

We have seen that the Corinthians object to Paul's speech on the grounds that it fails to measure up to the abusive and arrogant speech of the vulgar orators. We have also observed that such speech reflects the self-regarding atmosphere of the day. Since it is precisely that atmosphere which Paul wishes to reject, it is not surprising that he exhibits a kind of preaching which is marked by weakness, fear and trembling. While this will no doubt disturb his converts, it ought to work for their edification. For in Paul's mind, it is only in humble speech that he manifests the knowledge of the crucified Christ.

Support

There is one more area in which the Corinthians express their dissatisfaction with Paul: the matter of his upkeep. They want to pay Paul for his services in Corinth, but he refuses (2 Corinthians 11:7). He prefers to be self-supporting (2 Corinthians 11:9), working with his hands (1 Corinthians 4:9) and plying his trade as a tent-maker (cf. Acts 18:3). On the other hand, he does take gifts from other churches (2 Corinthians 11:9) and this irritates the Corinthians. They feel slighted by him (12:13) and deceived (cf. 12:16–18). In response Paul asks, 'Have I committed a sin by preaching the gospel to you without charge?' (11:7), and then adds sarcastically, 'Forgive me this wrong!' (12:13) The fact that Paul returns to the matter of his support on three separate occasions (cf. 1 Corinthians 9:3–18; 2 Corinthians 11:7–15; 12:13–18)[109] reveals how sensitive a subject it is in Corinth.

If we are to make sense of this controversy we must answer two questions: (i) Why is it that the Corinthians are dismayed by Paul's refusal of support? (They might well have been relieved!) and (ii) Why in fact does he refuse it?

[109] Cf. also 1 Thess. 2:9.

The charge

The query, Why do the Corinthians object to Paul's refusal of support? has received a number of answers. The main positions are set out as follows.

1 Apostleship

The most popular view is that Paul's refusal of support has prompted the Corinthians to dispute his apostleship. His converts are aware of the dominical teaching that a true disciple is worthy of a wage (cf. Matthew 10:10; Luke 10:7) and of Paul's own respect for that teaching (cf. 1 Corinthians 9:3–14).[110] When he refuses support they naturally wonder whether he is a true apostle and hence whether their church is a true apostolic church. Consequently, they feel inferior to other churches (2 Corinthians 12:13).[111]

This view would seem to find confirmation in Paul's remarks in 2 Corinthians 11:7–11 and 12:13–15. In both passages he makes the extraordinary claim that he is in no way inferior to the superlative apostles and then follows with a vigorous defence of his policy on support (11:5; 12:11).[112] The order of his argument in both places can hardly be accidental. It would seem to indicate that he is defending his apostleship against those who deny it on grounds that he refuses support.[113]

Yet there is one critical factor which might militate against this interpretation – the fact that Paul *does* receive support. From the Macedonians he accepts gifts of money (2 Corinthians 11:9)[114] and from the Corinthians themselves he has received supplies for future travel (cf. 1 Corinthians 16:6; 2 Corinthians 1:16).[115] As pertains to

---

[110] Cf. also *Did.* 11:3–12:2: 'Every apostle must be welcomed . . . assist him as much as you can'.

[111] For this view see Barrett 'Opponents' 245–46; Meeks *Urban Christians* 72; Lüdemann *Paulus* 2.135–36; Dahl *Studies* 33; Bultmann 234; Martin 345, 438; Windisch 397; Wendland 226; Héring 80; Tasker 150; but see Schmithals *Gnosis* 215 n. 2.

[112] Cf. the same pattern in 1 Cor. 9 where Paul asks rhetorically, Do I not have the same authority as οἱ λοιποὶ ἀπόστολοι καὶ οἱ ἀδελφοὶ τοῦ κυρίου καὶ Κηφᾶς? (v. 5), and then proceeds immediately to set out his position on support (vv. 6–18).

[113] So Barrett 'Opponents' 246.

[114] Or, as Caragounis "Οψώνιον" 35–57 argues, 'provisions'.

[115] Taking ὑμεῖς με προπέμψητε in 1 Cor. 16:6 and ὑφ' ὑμῶν προπεμφθῆναι in 2 Cor. 1:16 as technical terms for 'providing goods (namely, food, clothing and money)

support, he clearly qualifies as an apostle, and surely his converts know this. His refusal to take *everything* they offer must be prompting complaints of a different kind – that is, complaints about something other than his 'apostleship'.

If it is true that the Corinthians are not drawing a link between support and 'apostleship' we must ask why Paul himself does, why he twice follows the emphatic assertion that he does not fall short of the superior apostles with a defence of his policy on support. One possibility is that his refusal to take full support is prompting criticism of his leadership in general, not of his apostleship in particular.[116] If that is the case, there could scarcely be a more effective way to silence his critics and defend his policy on support than to claim that his position as a leader remains on a par with the most eminent apostles, the pillar apostles of Jerusalem.[117]

In any case, we are probably safe to conclude that the Corinthians are not objecting to Paul's refusal of support on the grounds that it depreciates his 'apostleship' *per se*.

2   *Hellenistic missionaries*

A few scholars have suggested that the Corinthians are criticising Paul for his failure to measure up to his nearest cultural equivalent, the hellenistic missionary. Such 'missionaries' were usually Cynics or Sophists who were not averse to taking pay for professional services. In fact they often calculated their worth on the basis of the

for one's journey'; cf. Rom. 15:24; 3 John 6; and see Malherbe 'Diotrephes' 230 n. 11; BAG 716; Barrett *First Corinthians* 389; Weiss *Korintherbrief* 383.

116   As we shall see, it was imperative for all *leaders* in antiquity to be well supported financially.

117   On taking οἱ ὑπερλίαν ἀπόστολοι in 2 Cor. 11:5 and 12:11 to refer to the pillar apostles cf. 1 Cor. 9:5 where, in the course of defending his policy on support, Paul compares himself to οἱ λοιποὶ ἀπόστολοι καὶ οἱ ἀδελφοὶ τοῦ κυρίου καὶ Κηφᾶς and see Barrett 'Opponents' 246; 'Christianity at Corinth' 289–91; Käsemann 'Legitimität' 41–46; others take the term οἱ ὑπερλίαν ἀπόστολοι to refer to the opponents, so Bultmann *Exegetische Probleme* 27–30; Munck *Paul* 177–79; Betz *Paulus* 121; McClelland 'Super-Apostles' 82–87; Lietzmann 146; Kümmel 210; Furnish 502–5.

In attempting to identify οἱ ἀπόστολοι scholars have neglected the unusual adverb ὑπερλίαν. It appears only here in the NT and sparingly elsewhere (LSJ mention only two other refs., both in Eustathius [1184.18 and 1396.42], a twelfth-century writer). It is conceivable that Paul himself coined the term, combining a comparative preposition ὑπέρ with a superlative adverb λίαν; cf. BDF § 116.3; 230. A dramatic reading results: [λογίζομαι γὰρ] μηδὲν ὑστερηκέναι τῶν ὑπερλίαν ἀποστόλων: 'I am in no way lower than the utmost apostles'. This represents a powerful reply to those who belittle his leadership.

sort of salary they could command.[118] Presumably Paul's opponents come from this group, for they are keen to use their earnings as a basis for self-boasting (cf. 2 Corinthians 11:12). Next to them, the unsalaried Paul cuts a miserable figure and earns the reproach of his critics.[119]

But this view also has weaknesses. First of all, it lacks clear textual support. Nothing in 2 Corinthians indicates that the Corinthians are actually comparing Paul to hellenistic missionaries. Secondly, there is a considerable amount of historical evidence to suggest that many itinerant Cynics and Sophists actually made a virtue of *declining* support.[120] It could well be argued that Paul *does* fit the mould of the hellenistic missionary.

3   Palestinian charismatics

G. Theissen suggests a third interpretation: namely, that the Corinthians are comparing Paul to a group of itinerant and charismatic preachers from Palestine. These individuals were associates of Jesus and thus careful to observe both the dominical injunction to poverty and the right of support (cf. Mark 9:41). On this criterion Paul seems to be in double violation of the teaching of Jesus. In plying his trade as a tentmaker he both renounces his right to support and pursues material gain. His opponents emerge in fairer light. They dutifully take support and accept their lot among the poor.[121]

This interpretation is open to the same criticism as the last. It has little foundation in the text. Nothing in 2 Corinthians suggests that the Corinthians are particularly conscious of the teaching of Jesus, nor that they are comparing Paul to itinerant preachers from Palestine.[122] Even more telling is the failure of this view to come to grips with Paul's own position. It is not *he* who is guilty of materialistic avarice, but his opponents (cf. 2 Corinthians 11:12, 20). According to the apostle, he subsists in a condition of 'lack' (11:9).

The three views considered thus far have an important feature in

---

[118] On Sophists charging fees cf. Lucian *J. Tr.* 27; *Icar.* 5; *Pisc.* 12; D. Chr. *Or.* 77/78. 35; Philostr. *VS* 519, 591–92.

[119] For this view cf. Georgi *Gegner* 108–11, 188, 237, 239; and see Judge 'Early Christians' 126; 'Classical Society' 32 who believes that Paul would have been perceived and judged as a Sophist.

[120] Cf. the refs. in Betz *Paulus* 108–10. But as we shall see, it was not this virtue nor this kind of philosopher which the Corinthians admired.

[121] Cf. Theissen 'Legitimation' 208–14; and see Agrell *Work* 107–8; Furnish 476–77.

[122] *Pace* Käsemann 'Legitimität' 36; see above pp. 4–7.

common. Each assumes that the Corinthians are comparing Paul to a distinct group of itinerant preachers – apostles, hellenistic missionaries or Palestinian charismatics. Yet, as we have seen, the evidence of 2 Corinthians is not so clear. While it is true that Paul does make reference to rival missionaries he never actually identifies who they are or what they teach. What the text does make clear is that Paul is deeply concerned about the mistaken attitudes of his converts. He is alarmed that they should be embracing secular perspectives on matters such as boasting, physical presence and speech and then using those perspectives to evaluate his performance as a minister of Christ. This would suggest that they might also be using secular perspectives to assess his refusal of support. If so, the key to understanding their criticisms would be found, not in positing hypothetical groups of rival missionaries,[123] but in seeking to discover the prevailing first-century attitudes to matters such as pay, money, wealth, poverty and employment.

4   *The humble handworker*

One attempt to do just that has come, not surprisingly, from those engaged in a sociological analysis of Paul. These scholars argue that the Corinthians are dismayed not so much by Paul's refusal of support as by a dire consequence of that refusal – the fact that he must earn his keep as a tentmaker.[124] His converts are repelled by the thought that he must work with his hands, for in antiquity handwork was regarded as undignified and contemptible. Here the harsh pronouncements of Cicero are typical: 'unbecoming to a gentleman and vulgar are the means of livelihood of all hired workmen whom we pay for mere manual labour . . . for in their case the very wage they receive is a pledge of their slavery' (*Off.* 1.150). Indeed craftsmen are 'the dogs of a city' (*Flac.* 18). We may note as well the verdict of Lucian: 'a labourer toils with his body . . . [and is] personally inconspicuous . . . humble-witted (ταπεινὸς τὴν γνώμην), an insignificant figure in public . . . one of the swarming rabble, ever cringing to the man above . . . a man who has naught

---

123 This is not to deny the influence of the opponents, only that they are Paul's principal opposition; see above pp. 9–11.

124 A leading exponent of this view is Hock *Social Context passim*; 'Paul's Tentmaking' 555–64; cf. also Judge 'Social Identity' 214; 'Radical Critic' 198; Stowers 'Social Status' 71; Malherbe 'Paul at War' 168–69; Furnish 344, 507; Windisch 334; Martin 344; Tasker 151.

but his hands (χειρῶναξ), a man who lives by his hands' (ἀποχει-ροβίωτος, *Somn.* 9 ; cf. also Sen. *Ep.* 88.21 ; Juv. 9.140).

If these sentiments do indeed reflect the dominant ethos of the first century, as members of the sociological school imply,[125] then we should not be surprised to find the Corinthians recoiling at Paul's handwork (cf. κοπιῶμεν ἐργαζόμενοι ταῖς ἰδίαις χερσίν, I Corinthians 4:12); nor to find Paul himself describing his labour as humiliating (ἐμαυτὸν ταπεινῶν, 2 Corinthians 11:7), a source of suffering (1 Corinthians 4:12; 2 Corinthians 11:23b; cf. 1 Thessalonians 2:9) and a symptom of weakness (2 Corinthians 11:30). As a common tradesman, he lacks power and prestige.

Yet this view – the fourth we have considered – suffers from a fundamental flaw. It assumes that literary sources alone provide a full picture of first-century attitudes to work. But that is to neglect the vastly more pertinent record left on stone where a very different story is told. Far from viewing his handwork as a source of embarrassment, the average tradesman was intensely proud of it. How else can we explain the recurring phenomena of tailors, merchants, carpenters, coppersmiths, barbers, corn-dealers, shopkeepers, janitors and many other of the 'despised' handworkers leaving testimony of their work, and many of their place of work, on their tombstones for all posterity to see?[126] Some even paid for funerary reliefs in order to preserve an image of themselves at their work. In Roman Ostia, gravestones depict a butcher surrounded by various cuts of meat and a tool-maker amidst his tools. Similar first-century reliefs depict ship-builders, cutlers, stone-masons, etc.[127] The evidence could be multiplied several times,[128] but there is enough here to demonstrate that the common person's perception of his hand-

---

[125] Cf. as well classical historians Carcopino *Ancient Rome* 66 and Mossé *Ancient World at Work* 28.

[126] On tomb-reliefs cf. a *vestificus* ('tailor', ILS 7427–29); a *mercator* ('merchant', ILS 7516); a *carpentarius* ('carpenter', ILS 7627); an *aerarius* ('coppersmith', ILS 7682–84); a *tonsor* ('barber', ILS 7414; CIL 6.9940); a *frumentarius* ('corn-dealer', ILS 7488, 7533); a *cellarius* ('storekeeper', ILS 7439); an *ostiarus* ('janitor', ILS 7438); a *vestiplicus* ('clothes presser', ILS 7430–31); a *lanarius* ('wool worker', CIL 11.741); a *vilicus* ('farm-overseer', ILS 7367–73); a *marmorarius* ('marble mason', ILS 7539); a *corinthiarius* ('a worker in Corinthian bronze', ILS 7422). For place of work see IG 10.2.291: ἡ συνήθεια τῶν πορφυροβάφων τῆς ὀκτω-καιδεκατῆς ('the profession of purple-dyers on 18th [street]').

[127] For the Ostian reliefs see Meiggs *Roman Ostia*, plate 27; and for other occupations see Gummerus 'Handwerk' 61–126: ship-builders (illus. 14, 15); cutler (illus. 8); stone-mason (illus. 27); carpenter (illus. 31); and coppersmith (illus. 5).

[128] See e.g. ILS 7366–7817 where countless other trades are represented. Hock *Social Context* overlooks this rich mine of information.

work differed markedly from Cicero's or Lucian's or Seneca's. In fact we may conclude that only gentlemen of high education depreciated the trades. The rest, many of whom had moved high up the social ladder and among whom the Corinthian Christians must be numbered, worked the trades and were proud of it.[129] It is highly unlikely, therefore, that the Corinthians objected to Paul's refusal of support on the grounds that it forced him to enter a demeaning profession.

Why then does Paul himself refer to his work in harsh terms? Why does he number it among his sufferings? (1 Corinthians 4:12; 2 Corinthians 11:23b) The answer would seem to lie in the sheer physical strain of his labour. It is noticeable that he draws attention to his *surpassing* toil (ἐν κόποις περισσοτέρως, 2 Corinthians 11:23), his *intense* labour (κόπῳ καὶ μόχθῳ, 11:27) and his *long* hours (νυκτὸς καὶ ἡμέρας ἐργαζόμενοι, 1 Thessalonians 2:9).[130] Yet he always stops short of disparaging work itself. Instead he follows a long line of Jewish tradition by maintaining that while work can be exhausting it is never demeaning.[131] He even commends work to his converts (cf. 1 Thessalonians 4:11).

5   The impoverished leader

Having found the various positions outlined above to be unsatisfactory in explaining Corinthian antipathy to Paul, we turn now to a final interpretation – that by declining support Paul relegates himself to a state of poverty.

In 2 Corinthians 11:7–9 Paul uses bitter irony to reveal the magnitude of Corinthian displeasure – ἢ ἁμαρτίαν ἐποίησα . . . ὅτι δωρεὰν τὸ τοῦ θεοῦ εὐαγγέλιον εὐηγγελισάμην ὑμῖν ('or did I commit a *sin* . . . by preaching the gospel of God to you without

---

129 For this positive view of handwork see Balsdon *Ancient Rome* 135; de Robertis *Lavoro e lavoratori* 34–36; Bolkestein *Wohltätigkeit und Armenpflege* 199, 332; and cf. Petron. *Sat.* 29 where Trimalchio proudly commissions a wall-painting of himself at his work; see also D. Chr. *Or.* 7.124–26.

130 On the rigours of handwork cf. a second-century apprentice who is contracted to labour καθ' ἑκάστην ἡμέραν ἀπὸ ἀν[ατολῆς] ἡλίου μέχρι δύσεως ('each day from the rising of the sun until its setting', P. Oxy. 4.725 [12]; see also P. Oxy. 31.2586 [13–14]; 14.1647 [20–21]).

131 In the OT work is regarded as costly (Gen 3:17–19; 5:29), but honourable (Deut. 11:10–15; 16:14–15). The same tension appears in deutero-canonical literature; cf. Sir. 29:4; 1 Macc. 10:15 and Sir 31:22; 1 Macc. 14:6–15; and in the rabbis see *b. Pesah.* 118a; *b. B. Qam.* 79b; *m. Abot.* 1.10; and for comments see Agrell *Work* 31–32, 45–46, 67.

charge', v. 7). He then proceeds to hint at the reason for their great disappointment. Such a policy is tantamount to a self-imposed humiliation (ἐμαυτὸν ταπεινῶν, v. 7). In particular, it leads to a state of material deprivation, as Paul concedes in verse 9 – 'when present with you and when I was lacking' (καὶ παρὼν πρὸς ὑμᾶς καὶ ὑστερηθείς).[132] We may infer from the tone and content of these verses that it is specifically his material poverty which has touched a raw nerve among his converts and elicited their scorn.

In 2 Corinthians 12:13–14 we find support for this interpretation. Here Paul implies that his converts are eager to share with him of their 'property' (τὰ ὑμῶν)[133] and treasure (cf. θησαυρίζω), which reveals their alarm that he has so little of either. In addition, he concedes that they willingly gravitate to those with material abundance, in particular his prosperous rivals – those who minister for profit (2:17), glory in their support (11:12) and eat the Corinthians out of house and home (11:20). We may surmise from this data that the church in Corinth wants its apostle to display the same tenacity for material gain that his opponents do, and that until he does it will feel inferior to churches whose apostles are financially more sound (12:13). The text thus affirms that it is Paul's impoverished condition that is troubling the Corinthians.

The disappointment over Paul's 'lack' is hardly surprising given the insights of our earlier historical enquiry. We discovered that in the first century material affluence was an important measure of personal worth. Consequently, people placed great value on money and wealth. It was axiomatic that leaders were drawn from the 'financially sound and fit' (εὐπόρου καὶ εὐθετοῦντος) and never from the 'unfit and poor' (ἄθετος καὶ πενιχρός, P. Oxy. 3273).[134] An impoverished leader was a contradiction in terms.[135] Nowhere were these attitudes more prominent than in Corinth, that 'great and wealthy' city (Str. 8.6.23), 'everywhere full of wealth' (Aristid. *Or.* 46.27), 'abounding in luxuries' (Alciphron *Ep.* 3.24.3), whose aggressive citizens were said to 'pride themselves on their wealth'

---

[132] Thus the term ὑστέρημά μου in v. 9 further defines the term ἐμαυτὸν ταπεινῶν in v. 7. The present durative participle παρών, used with the aorist passive participle ὑστερηθείς, indicates that there was indeed a time in Corinth when Paul suffered 'lack'.

[133] On this rendering of τὰ ὑμῶν see Barrett 323.

[134] Cf. Judge *Rank and Status* 14–16.

[135] On wealth as a prerequisite for leadership see Pliny *Ep.* 1.14; Juv. 1.137–40; and cf. Garnsey *Social Status* 79, 208.

(D. Chr. *Or.* 9.8) and to be 'ungracious . . . among their luxuries' (Alciphron *Ep.* 3.15.1). Here, more than elsewhere, wealth was a prerequisite for honour and poverty a badge of disgrace.

It is unlikely that Corinthian Christians escaped this emphasis on materialism. Indeed they themselves seem to have been a prosperous group, at least in comparison to other churches. Paul contrasts their abundance (τὸ ὑμῶν περίσσευμα) with the poverty of Jerusalem Christians (τὸ ἐκείνων ὑστέρημα, 2 Corinthians 8:14), for whom the Corinthians are asked to produce a 'sizeable' offering (ἁδρότης, 8:20). He contrasts them as well with the Macedonians, whom he 'robs' for his mission in Corinth (ἄλλας ἐκκλησίας ἐσύλησα, 11:8), taking from their 'abysmal poverty' (ἡ κατὰ βάθους πτωχεία αὐτῶν, 8:2). The fact that these well-heeled Corinthians are now attacking Paul for his refusal of support would seem to underscore their indebtedness to the materialistic outlook of their day.

6 Summary

This brief review of the social climate brings the conflict between Paul and his converts into sharp relief. In a society where wealth was a sign of status Paul's insistence on remaining poor would naturally offend his converts. Worst of all, it would force them to bear the ignominy of being associated with an impoverished apostle. Paul deepens the wound by entertaining minor gifts from other churches (2 Corinthians 11:9). Not surprisingly, the Corinthians feel inferior and lash out at their apostle – he is acting unjustly (12:13) and without love (11:11; 12:15b).

Some begin to question his motives and to suggest that Paul is making a great show of declining support only, on the sly, to siphon sums of money from the Jerusalem collection (cf. the implication of 2 Corinthians 12:16).[136] Paul emphatically denies such accusations (12:17–18) and steals the initiative by claiming that his policy of refusing support actually works for his converts' exaltation (cf. ἵνα ὑμεῖς ὑψωθῆτε, 11:7). Indeed his self-imposed poverty may be viewed as an act of surpassing love (12:15b; cf. 11:11), a gesture of great personal sacrifice for their good (12:15a). Of course the Corinthians will find this hard to believe. Yet it is precisely here that we must try to understand Paul. Why does he refuse support? And, if it

---

[136] Cf. Georgi *Gegner* 240; Lüdemann *Paulus* 2.135.

is for the sake of the Corinthians, what is his logic? These questions will occupy us in the section which follows.

The response

Paul's motives for declining support have been explained in a variety of ways.

I A review of the interpretations

Some believe that Paul is simply upholding the injunction of his rabbinical education to impart the word of God gratuitously. We may note the words of Hillel: 'He who makes worldly use of the crown (i.e. the Torah) shall perish' (*m. Abot* 1.13); and of Zadok: 'Make them (the words of the Law) not . . . a spade wherewith to dig . . . He who makes profit out of them removes his life from the world' (*m. Abot* 4.5).[137] Others contend that Paul is reflecting the hostility of some Hellenists to charismatic begging. He shares their revulsion and wants to distance himself from such beggary.[138] It is unlikely, however, that either of these traditions, Jewish or Hellenic, explains Paul's motives for declining support, for both would have been superseded in his mind by the 'command' of Jesus to take support – οὕτως καὶ ὁ κύριος διέταξεν τοῖς τὸ εὐαγγέλιον καταγγέλλουσιν ἐκ τοῦ εὐαγγελίου ζῆν (1 Corinthians 9:14). But this complicates matters. How could Paul neglect a dominical injunction?

Some reason that he does so out of a concern for the needy in his congregation. He does not want to burden them with the cost of his upkeep (cf. 2 Corinthians 11:9; 12:13–14, 16).[139] Yet as we have learned from Paul himself, the Corinthians are relatively prosperous and hence well able to care for his material needs (cf. 8:14). Others suggest that he simply wants to avoid the indignity of being dependent on others for his upkeep (cf. 11:10; 1 Corinthians 9:15).[140] Yet

---

[137] Cf. Daube *Rabbinic Judaism* 395–96 who implies that Paul's Jewish-minded converts would have expected him to minister without pay. Further on prohibitions against using the Law for material gain cf. *m. Abot* 1.3; 2.2; and see Moore *Judaism* 2.97.

[138] So Betz *Paulus* 108–9, 115, 117; Hock *Social Context* 44. On scorn for those who 'cultivate philosophy for hire' see Lucian *Nigr.* 25; also *Herm.* 80–81; *Tim.* 56–57; and see Betz *Lukian* 114 n. 3.

[139] So Dungan *Paul* 30–31; Stählin 'ἐγκοπή' 856; Plummer 302.

[140] Thus Bousset *Schriften* 2.116; Weiss *Korintherbrief* 239.

by refusing support he incurs perhaps the greater indignity of poverty and shame.

Another attempt to explain Paul's motive for declining support, and by far the most ingenious, comes from the 'sociological school'. These scholars suggest that Paul is intentionally rejecting a popular convention of his day called contractual friendship. This was the rite of gift-giving whereby a benefactor could place a beneficiary in his debt, obliging him to perform a long line of duties in exchange for the benefaction. To refuse such a gift was to reject the offer of 'friendship' and hence to incur the enmity of the giver. This would explain the hostility between the Corinthians and Paul. By refusing their offer of support he has plunged their relationship into the cauldron of ritual enmity. His motive? He wants to remain free from all social constraints in order to carry out his ministry without obligations.[141]

While this interpretation sheds interesting light on attitudes to giving in antiquity, it is doubtful whether it fully explains Paul's motives for declining support, at least not as he would define those motives. For while Paul does seek what amounts to financial independence, he does not do so in order to be free from social constraints. In his mind he declines support precisely because he is *bound* to his converts in love (cf. 2 Corinthians 12:14–15), because by declining support he hopes to 'win the more' (1 Corinthians 9:19).[142] It would appear that, far from striving for independence, he is abandoning it. In other words, if Paul is in fact seeking independence from the duties of contractual friendship, it is not because he wishes to be free from all social constraints. It is because he wishes to abandon his freedom on his own terms (not on the terms of a benefactor). It is because he wants 'to make himself a slave to all' (ἐλεύθερος γὰρ ὢν ἐκ πάντων πᾶσιν ἐμαυτὸν ἐδούλωσα, 1 Corinthians 9:19).

It seems, then, that none of the views considered above fully answers the question why Paul refuses support. We turn, then, to another possibility.

---

[141] Cf. Judge 'Social Identity' 214; *Rank and Status* 23; 'Classical Education' 12, who draws on the findings of Mott 'Giving and Receiving' 60–65 and is followed by Marshall *Enmity in Corinth* 242–47, 257–58, 397–98 and Furnish 507–8.

[142] He is therefore 'bound' to the Corinthians not in the sense that he becomes a slave to their wishes, but in the sense that he feels constrained to do what is best for them, even if it conflicts with their wishes – as, for example, in the case of his refusal of support.

2   2 Corinthians 11:12

In this verse Paul reveals part of his rationale for refusing support. He wants to remain distinct from those who do take support, his opponents. They revel in support and so conform to the pattern of the secular orators of the day like Peregrinus, whose 'love of glory' impelled him 'to profit by occasions . . . quickly acquiring sudden wealth by imposing himself upon simple folk . . . through whose ministrations he lived in unalloyed prosperity' (Lucian *Peregr.* 1, 13, 16).[143] In Paul's mind such conduct is unbecoming to ministers of Christ. It represents service for profit only (cf. οἱ πολλοὶ καπηλεύοντες τὸν λόγον τοῦ θεοῦ, 2:17)[144] and hence an adulteration of the gospel (cf. δολοῦντες τὸν λόγον τοῦ θεοῦ, 4:2).[145] It is in order to make the worst possible example of his opponents that Paul refuses support.

3   2 Corinthians 11:7–12

Yet Paul does more than make examples of them, for he could have done that merely by accepting support in a humble manner. Instead he adopts the unusual practice of boasting about his refusal of support (cf. v. 10), thus making an example of *himself*.[146] Here Paul is driven by the firm conviction that such a refusal actually serves to exalt his converts (cf. ἵνα ὑμεῖς ὑψωθῆτε, v. 7). Consequently, nothing will shake him from his present course – 'in everything I have kept myself from being a burden to you and will continue to do so' (v. 9), 'this boasting of mine shall not be stopped' (v. 10), 'what I am doing I will continue to do' (v. 12).[147] There can be little doubt that Paul believes his refusal of support will work for the edification of his converts.

---

[143] Cf. also the false prophet Alexander whose 'thigh was bared purposely and showed golden' (Lucian *Alex.* 40); further on avaricious philosophers see Lucian *D. Mort.* 8; Philo *Mos.* 2.212. For the complementary traits of φιλοχρήματος ('love of money') and φιλόδοξος ('love of glory') in wandering orators cf. D. Chr. *Or.* 4.83–84, 133–35; see also Gerhard *Phoenix* 58–59.

[144] In the ancient literature κάπηλοι are associated with tax-gatherers and keepers of brothels (D. Chr. *Or.* 4.98), usurers and promoters of quail fights (Plut. *Mor.* 34D) and those in trades not befitting free men (Philostr. *VA* 7.23).

[145] Cf. Lucian *Herm.* 59 where travelling lecturers are called both κάπηλοι and δόλοι.

[146] Such boasting amounts to glorying in his poverty and shame. That is not egotistical boasting, but boasting only in the Lord; see above pp. 62–64.

[147] According to Pratscher 'Unterhalt' 293, the future tenses of the verbs τηρήσω (v. 9) and ποιήσω (v. 12) suggest an 'unshakable resolve'.

4   2 Corinthians 12:13

Just how this edification takes place may be inferred from 2 Corinthians 12:13. Here Paul asks rhetorically, 'for what is there in regard to which[148] you came lower than[149] the rest of the churches, except that I myself did not burden you?' Some commentators interpret this verse as bitter sarcasm, as though Paul were treating with incredulity the possbility that his refusal of support might promote feelings of inferiority.[150] But the verse can also be interpreted in a straightforward manner. It is possible, for instance, that the Corinthians do indeed feel inferior to other churches.[151] While there is little in the context to indicate which of the two interpretations is correct, our study of first-century attitudes to wealth and money would suggest the latter.

We learned that people in antiquity were skilled in the art of using money for personal advantage. By adorning their cities or guilds or leaders with material splendour they effectively adorned themselves.[152] If Corinthian Christians could maintain their apostle Paul in some measure of self-respect it would clearly enhance their capacity to boast. This probably explains why Paul's refusal of support provokes such a collective outcry. Not only does it deny his converts the opportunity to glory in their own munificence, it also forces them to identify with the poverty of their apostle and hence to feel inferior to churches whose apostles are better maintained.

Ironically, it was probably the expectation of just such an outcry which caused Paul to refuse support. He knew that if he were to accept Corinthian money he would be encouraging his converts to indulge in a kind of self-boasting not dissimilar to the boasting of his rivals and hence patently at odds with his gospel. He could never

---

[148]   Thus Moule's rendering of the relative ὅ (*Idiom* 131) .

[149]   The ὑπέρ here is comparative; so Winer *Grammar* 501.

[150]   Cf. Furnish 556.

[151]   Though not because they sense that Paul regards them as less responsible than other churches, *pace* Dungan *Paul* 39; Barrett 322.

[152]   See above pp. 22–24, 41; and cf. Cic. *Off.* 1.14.44: 'We may observe that a great many people do many things that seem to be inspired more by a spirit of ostentation than by heartfelt kindness; for such people are not really generous but are rather influenced by a sort of ambition to make a show of being open-handed'; and Pliny *Ep.* 1.8.15: 'But when people accompany their generous deeds with words they are thought not to be proud of having performed them, but to be performing them in order to have something to be proud of'; and cf. also Hands *Social Aid* 26: 'In the vast majority of texts and documents relating to gifts in the classical world, it is quite clear that the giver's action is self-regarding'; and see Danker *Benefactor* 436.

be an accomplice in such egotistical boasting. By refusing their support he forced his converts to participate in his humility and thus to conform, albeit unwillingly, to the pattern of Christ. In this way the poverty of Paul might work for his converts' exaltation (11:7).

Now we can see what lies behind Paul's claim that his refusal of support represents an act of supreme love (περισσοτέρως ὑμᾶς ἀγαπῶν, 12:15b; cf. 11:11), the kind of love a parent might lavish on a child (12:14c), the sort of self-giving love which seeks the good of another (cf. ἐγὼ δὲ ἥδιστα δαπανήσω καὶ ἐκδαπανηθήσομαι ὑπὲρ τῶν ψυχῶν ὑμῶν, 12:15a).[153] Paul's rationale is summed up in 2 Corinthians 11:10: 'it is *the truth of Christ within me* that keeps me from stopping this boast of mine' (11:10).[154]

5 Summary

It is clear from these exegetical and historical insights that Paul wishes to overturn the materialistic outlook of his converts. His strategy is to boast about his self-imposed state of poverty. But it is bound to fail. If anything it will probably drive the Corinthians deeper into the fold of the avaricious opponents. For the very outlook which causes Paul to refuse support will probably also cause his converts to ridicule that refusal. What Paul had hoped would clarify their vision will probably only obscure it.

We may now suggest answers to the two questions posed at the outset of this section. (i) It appears that the Corinthians are objecting to Paul's refusal of support on the grounds that it keeps them from boasting in their own generosity and forces them to identify with his poverty. The same reasons seem to motivate Paul's response. (ii) By refusing support he aims to eliminate their self-boasting and encourage their humility. He knows from personal experience that it is only in such humility that his converts might be exalted – 'in having nothing we possess all things' (ὡς μηδὲν ἔχοντες καὶ πάντα κατέχοντες, 2 Corinthians 6:10).

---

[153] Cf. Gutierrez *Paternité* 199.

[154] Taking ἔστιν ἀλήθεια χριστοῦ ἐν ἐμοί literally (and not as an oath formula, as Bultmann *Exegetische Probleme* 138; Windisch 337; Furnish 493) – the truth of Christ is *in* Paul, he actually shares in the poverty and weakness of Christ (cf. 2 Cor. 13:4); cf. Dautzenberg 'Unterhaltsrecht' 225–31; Cerfaux *Paul* 393; Barrett 282. Paul can hardly be accused of violating dominical tradition (cf. above p. 83).

We must now test these findings against Paul's treatment of support in other epistles.

Evidence from other epistles

1   1 Corinthians 9:1–23

In this chapter we find Paul's most extensive treatment of the matter of support. Unfortunately, his argument is not very lucid. He begins by contending vigorously for his right to support, but concludes by waiving that right. Most scholars explain this curious about-face by pointing to the defensive tone of his argument (cf. ἡ ἐμὴ ἀπολογία τοῖς ἐμὲ ἀνακρίνουσίν ἐστιν αὕτη, v. 3). He seems to be defending himself against those who interpret his refusal of support as evidence that he lacks the apostolic right to support and so is not a true apostle. He responds by claiming that he not only possesses that right but can waive it and still be true to his office.[155]

But this interpretation fails to account for some important evidence in the text. (i) The notion of apostleship plays only a small part in his attempt to establish his right to support (cf. vv. 1–2). He bases his argument as well on the common-sense analogies of the soldier, the farmer, the shepherd (v. 7), the ploughman, the thresher (v. 10) and the priest (v. 13) – all of whom, he insists, have the 'right' to profit from their labour. He finds the same principle in the Mosaic Law (vv. 8–10a, citing Deuteronomy 25:4) and in the teaching of Jesus (v. 14; cf. Matthew 10:10; Luke 10:7), and he reminds his readers that they have given other ministers their due reward (v. 12). The point of this rather tedious parade of illustrations would seem to be that he, Paul, also has the right to support, and not just because he is an apostle but because of the universal norm that every person ought to profit from his labour.[156] It would appear that there is insufficient evidence in this chapter to infer that Paul's apostleship specifically is coming under attack.

(ii) Furthermore, it is unlikely that the Corinthians are actively disputing his right to support. The fact that he defends this privilege

---

[155] Cf. Dahl *Studies* 33; Dungan *Paul* 6; Barrett *First Corinthians* 200; Lietzmann 39; Weiss *Korintherbrief* 233–34; Moffatt *First Corinthians* 115; Wolff *Korinther* 19; Robertson-Plummer *First Corinthians* 180–81.

[156] Cf. Schmithals *Gnosis* 215–16 n. 2 who plays down the importance of apostleship in 1 Cor. 9. He contends that vv. 1–3, where apostleship is explicit, are parenthetical and set off sharply from what follows.

in such a pedestrian manner suggests that he is merely reminding his readers of what they already know. We may note the elementary nature of Paul's questions: 'Do we not have a right to take along a believing wife?' (v. 5); 'Or do only Barnabas and I not have a right to refrain from working?' (v. 6); 'If others share the right over you, do we not more?' (v. 12a); 'Do you not know that those performing sacrifices have the right to eat the food of the temple?' (v. 13). Such facile interrogatives are not intended to impart new information, but to underscore what the people take for granted – that ministers have certain inalienable rights.

(iii) Yet they are disputing something (cf. v. 3: ἡ ἐμὴ ἀπολογία τοῖς ἐμὲ ἀνακρίνουσίν). Just what it is the context of 1 Corinthians 9 does not make explicit. Drawing on our insights from 2 Corinthians it is tempting to suppose that the Corinthians are annoyed with Paul's refusal of support on the grounds that it prevents them from boasting in their own generosity. Yet if his converts are so eager to support him, why does he spend so much time defending his right to support?

(iv) Here the greater context of 1 Corinthians 9 provides an important clue. In 1 Corinthians 8 Paul teaches that one ought to put the welfare of the brethren ahead of his own interests. He proceeds to illustrate this principle in 1 Corinthians 9 by drawing on an example from his own experience – he waives his right to support for the sake of the brethren.[157] The matter of waiving one's right is clearly the central thrust of chapter 9, as can be seen from the parallel statements in verses 12 and 15:

ἀλλ' οὐκ ἐχρησάμεθα τῇ ἐξουσίᾳ ταύτῃ   (v. 12)

ἐγὼ δὲ οὐ κέχρημαι οὐδενὶ τούτων   (v. 15)[158]

This means that the issue of support is ancillary to the more fundamental point of waiving a right. Paul elucidates the point further in verses 12–23, where he provides at least six reasons why he is prepared to waive his right to support. He does not want

(a)   to put an obstacle in the way of the gospel of Christ (v. 12d);
(b)   to empty his boast (v. 15c);
(c)   to misuse the stewardship entrusted to him (v. 17b);

rather, he wants

---

[157] Thus Jeremias 'Chiasmus' 156; Didier 'Le salaire' 228–29.
[158] Cf. as well v. 19: being free to use my rights, I freely waive them, that I might save some.

(d)   to receive the reward of preaching for no reward (v. 18);

(e)   to save the souls of some (vv. 19–22);[159]

(f)   to participate in the gospel (v. 23).

Each of these reasons makes perfect sense if we accept the hypothesis that the Corinthians are eager to use their munificence as an
opportunity for personal boasting. On these terms, Paul cannot take
their money. If he did he would be encouraging their self-boasting
and hence putting an obstacle in the path of the gospel (a = v. 12d),
deflecting his converts from the way of salvation (e = vv. 19–22),
abusing his stewardship (c = v. 17b), emptying his boast (b =
v. 15c) and forfeiting his reward (d = v. 18). He would rather
endure affliction (v. 12), even suffer death (v. 15c),[160] and so be
marked out as a fellow-partaker in the gospel (f = v. 23).[161]

There is subtle irony in Paul's teaching here. He is doing more
than merely articulating the principle that one ought to give up a
right for the sake of the brethren. In illustrating that point from his
own experience he reveals that in the matter of his support his
readers *are* the weaker brethren. It is they who will stumble if he
takes their money. The double irony of course is that they will
probably not only miss the point but continue to believe just the
opposite, that in waiving this right he actually does them harm.

To sum up, then, in 1 Corinthians 9 Paul is not primarily defending either his right to support or his apostleship. Instead he is
drawing attention to a right which no one will dispute but which he
refuses to exercise. He wishes to illustrate that the rights of an
individual are not so dear as the welfare of the brethren. But he is
making an additional point as well. By waiving his right to support
he hopes to promote the welfare of the Corinthian brethren by

---

[159] On taking κερδαίνω in vv. 19–22 to mean 'winning over an unbeliever' see Daube
'Κερδαίνω' 109–20.

[160] The depth of Paul's conviction here can be measured by the fact that he repeats
himself in close proximity:

ἀλλ' οὐκ ἐχρησάμεθα τῇ ἐξουσίᾳ ταύτῃ

ἀλλὰ πάντα στέγομεν   (v. 12)

ἐγὼ δὲ οὐ κέχρημαι οὐδενὶ τούτων

καλὸν γάρ μοι μᾶλλον ἀποθανεῖν   (v. 15)

[161] The clause ἵνα συγκοινωνὸς αὐτου (viz. 'the gospel') γένωμαι can mean 'that I
may be a partner with the gospel' (i.e. in the work of salvation; as Orr-Walther
1 Corinthians 243; Robertson-Plummer *First Corinthians* 193), or 'a partner in the
benefits of the gospel' (Barrett *First Corinthians* 216; Bruce 89; BAG 782) or, as
we have rendered it, 'a partner *in* the gospel', i.e. a participant in the sufferings of
Christ.

awakening them to the folly of boasting about their own generosity. This conclusion agrees with our analysis of 2 Corinthians.[162]

2 *1 Thessalonians 2:1–13*

In this passage Paul gives a detailed account of the way in which he behaved when he was in Thessalonica. He touches briefly on his policy on support (v. 9), as well as his attitude to speech (vv. 2–6) and physical demeanour (vv. 7–8) – the very issues which would later come to trouble the Corinthians. In particular, he reminds his readers that he never preached with impurity or deceit (v. 3) and never attempted to win applause from men (vv. 4, 6) through either flattery (v. 5) or abusive behaviour (v. 7).[163] Instead he came as gently as a nurse (v. 7)[164] and manifested through his life the gospel which he preached (v. 8).[165] Such gentleness naturally produced opposition and scorn (v. 2). But no matter: he could rest assured that he had imparted the gospel as a word from God and not from man (v. 13) and thus that he had encouraged his converts to walk in a manner worthy of God (v. 12).

We see in this passage many similarities to 2 Corinthians.[166] Paul rejects a proud and domineering attitude and adopts a spirit of gentleness. Not surprisingly, this has a pronounced effect on his policy on support. He endures 'labour and hardship, working night and day so as not to be a burden to any of you' (v. 9). In this way he hopes to build up his converts (v. 8).

3 *The Macedonians*

Paul makes one noteworthy exception to his policy of refusing support. He allows the brethren in Macedonia to fill up his need when he is in Corinth (2 Corinthians 11:9; Philippians 4:15). Having

---

[162] On the similarity between 1 Cor. 9 and 2 Cor. 11 and 12 cf. Bultmann 'καυχάο-μαι' 652; Lüdemann *Paulus* 2.136; Kümmel 180; and cf. esp. 1 Cor. 9:15 with 2 Cor. 11:10; *pace* Käsemann *Questions* 227.

[163] Since the clause δυνάμενοι ἐν βάρει εἶναι in v. 7 is linked closely to ζητοῦντες ἐξ ἀνθρώπων δόξαν in v. 6, it may be rendered 'to be impressive'. The allusion is primarily to domineering behaviour (cf. βάρυς καὶ ἰσχυρὸς in 2 Cor. 10:10), though perhaps secondarily to Paul's upkeep (see ἐπιβαρῆσαι in v. 9; and cf. 2 Cor. 11:9); so Henneken *Verkündigung* 14–17; Laub *Eschatologische* 79.

[164] On reading ἤπιοι rather than νήπιοι see Metzger *Text* 230–33.

[165] The term οὕτως in v. 8 serves to link his 'gentle' behaviour (v. 7) to the gospel (v. 8); cf. Spicq ''Επιποθεῖν' 194.

[166] Thus Dibelius *Thessalonicher* 9; Laub *Eschatologische* 134.

been so uncompromising with the Corinthians, why does he seem to change his position with the Macedonians? One scholar suggests that it is because Paul loves the Macedonians more than the Corinthians.[167] But Paul not only affirms his love for the Corinthians, he argues that his refusal of support proves that love (2 Corinthians 11:11; 12:15b). Others suggest that Paul has a policy of receiving gifts only from distant donors.[168] But there is no way to test that theory. We simply do not know whether Paul took money from the Macedonians when he was in Macedonia. Still others insist that Paul refuses support in order to distinguish himself from his Corinthian opponents.[169] As we have seen, there is some truth in that view, yet there may be a more fundamental reason for his position with the Macedonians.

It is immediately noticeable that the Macedonians' attitude to giving differs markedly from the Corinthians'. They view their support as an opportunity to participate with Paul in his affliction (συγκοινωνήσαντες μου τῇ θλίψει, Philippians 4:14) and to share in the service of the saints (τὴν κοινωνίαν τῆς διακονίας τῆς εἰς τοὺς ἁγίους, 2 Corinthians 8:4). They give from the depths of their poverty (2 Corinthians 8:2) and beyond their ability (8:3).[170] They beg Paul for the 'favour' of this ministry (τὴν χάριν . . . τῆς διακονίας, 8:4) and thus are conformed to the 'favour' of Christ (τὴν χάριν τοῦ κυρίου ἡμῶν Ἰησοῦ χριστοῦ, 8:9), making themselves poor that others might be made rich (8:9).[171] It is therefore because they have already conformed themselves to the Lord (8:5) that Paul accepts their money. To bring the Corinthians to the same position Paul must *refuse* their support.

Paul's policy on support thus varies according to the spiritual maturity of his converts. In Corinth, where believers are inclined to use their gifts for selfish boasting, Paul chooses to earn his keep as a tentmaker. But in his dealings with the Macedonians he welcomes their support as a fragrant aroma (ὀσμὴν εὐωδίας), an acceptable offering (θυσίαν δεκτήν), well pleasing to God (εὐάρεστον τῷ θεῷ, Philippians 4:18). The criterion in each case is the same. Paul seeks

---

167 Windisch 338.   168 So Caragounis "Ὀψώνιον' 52–53; Dungan *Paul* 32.
169 Cf. Pratscher 'Unterhalt' 294, 298.
170 For Macedonian generosity cf. Phil 4:16: ὅτι καὶ ἐν θεσσαλονίκῃ καὶ ἅπαξ καὶ δὶς εἰς τὴν χρείαν μοι ἐπέμψατε, 'both [when I was] in Thessalonica and more than once [in other places (e.g. in Corinth)] you sent me something towards my needs' – thus the translation of Morris 'καὶ ἅπαξ καὶ δίς' 208.
171 Cf. the same pattern in 8:2: 'and their rock-bottom poverty overflowed in the wealth of their simple-hearted goodness'.

not the gift itself, but the profit which will increase to his converts' account (Philippians 4:17).

Summary

It has become clear in the course of this study that the Corinthians are profoundly embarrassed by Paul's refusal of support. It leaves him in a state of 'lack' and that reflects negatively on them. The stigma of his needy condition was probably especially acute in first-century Corinth where financial prosperity and upward mobility were norms to which all aspired. No doubt this explains why Paul was particularly determined to refuse support in Corinth (cf. ἡ καύχησις αὕτη οὐ φραγήσεται εἰς ἐμὲ ἐν τοῖς κλίμασιν τῆς Ἀχαΐας, 2 Corinthians 11:10). Here, more than elsewhere, he knows that the only way in which to enrich his converts is to encourage them to share in his poverty.

Conclusion

Having completed our textual examination of the criticisms levelled against Paul we are now in a position to draw a few conclusions. A remarkable pattern has emerged. In each of the areas in which the Corinthians find fault with Paul – his boasting, his physical presence, his speech and his support – we have discovered not only that his converts are drawing inspiration from the social outlook of the day but also that Paul responds by adopting a position which represents the exact antithesis of what they would have desired in a religious leader. While the Corinthians will find his position offensive, Paul insists that it actually works for their good. The reason for this fundamental disagreement between Paul and his converts would seem to boil down to a conflict between two opposing perspectives: the worldly outlook of the Corinthians and Paul's own Christ-centred viewpoint. This is a critical observation, for it is precisely out of this conflict that Paul's teaching of power through weakness in 2 Corinthians seems to emerge – that is to say, it is the radical disjunction between the secular prejudices of the Corinthians and his own conception of Christ which spawns his paradoxical description of the Christian ministry.

Having come to grips with what gives rise to Paul's paradoxical language in 2 Corinthians we can now ask, in the second half of our study, what light this sheds on the actual meaning of the language itself.

PART II

Power through weakness: the meaning

3

THE NATURE OF THE CHRISTIAN MINISTRY: THE GLORY OF CHRIST

In the first part of the study we have seen that Paul and the Corinthians disagree fundamentally on how he ought to behave as a minister of Christ. We also discovered that Paul attributes this disagreement to the influence of two sets of radically conflicting values. On the one hand, the Corinthians imbibe the outlook of the world. On the other hand, he is conformed to Christ.

But this is Paul's appraisal of the situation, not the Corinthians'. They would surely object to the idea that their outlook is anything less than fully Christian.[1] In their view the problem is just the reverse. It is not they who have strayed from Christ, but Paul. They look in vain 'for evidence of Christ speaking in him' (2 Corinthians 13:3), and even wonder whether his manner of discharging the ministry is 'of Christ' (2 Corinthians 10:7). What confounds them is how one so unimpressive as Paul can rightly claim to be a minister of the glorious gospel of Jesus Christ.

It is this question which Paul sets out to answer in the extended middle section of 2 Corinthians, namely in 2:14–7:4, and especially in chapter 4, and which evokes his paradoxical teaching of power through weakness. In the next four chapters we shall attempt to unravel his reply.

The glory of Moses

We may begin where Paul himself begins, with his prayer of thanksgiving in 2 Corinthians 2:14:

Thanks be to God[2]
>   who always puts us on *display* (θριαμβεύοντι) in Christ and
>   *manifests* (φανεροῦντι) through us
>   the aroma of his knowledge

---

[1] At one point some even adopted the slogan ἐγὼ χριστοῦ (1 Cor. 1:12).
[2] The emphatic τῷ δὲ θεῷ χάρις is the subject of the following participles.

Here Paul is claiming that his ministry, far from lacking divine attestation, actually possesses it in remarkable degree. Using parallel participles he affirms that God has both led him in a triumphant display,[3] exhibiting him as a captive 'in Christ' (ἐν τῷ χριστῷ, v. 14), and manifested through him 'the fragrance of his knowledge' (τὴν ὀσμὴν τῆς γνώσεως αὐτοῦ, v.14), namely, the 'aroma of Christ' (χριστοῦ εὐωδία, v. 15). In other words, God has displayed Paul in Christ and manifested Christ through Paul. There is thus 'an identity between what is seen in Jesus . . . and what is seen in Paul'.[4] The apostle's teaching here represents a dramatic response to those who query the authenticity of his ministry. He is *God's* display *of Christ*, 'an aroma of Christ to God' (v. 15).

In addition, Paul can marshal more tangible evidence in support of his ministry – the salvation of the Corinthians themselves. As his spiritual children they are at once his letters (ἡ ἐπιστολὴ ἡμῶν ὑμεῖς ἐστε, 3:2) and letters of Christ (ἐστε ἐπιστολὴ χριστοῦ, 3:3), attesting to the validity of his service.[5] He has no need to commend himself as some do by presenting approbatory letters inscribed on parchment (3:1). It is enough that under his ministry the Spirit of the living God has 'inscribed' Christ on their hearts (3:3).[6]

In two very telling ways, then, Paul responds to those who find fault with his ministry: (i) it is *'from God* that we speak *in Christ'* (2:17); and (ii) you yourselves are proof of that, being 'letters of Christ ministered to by us' (3:3).

This dual response is impressive in so far as it represents a forthright reply to those who question the veracity of his ministry. Yet it is unlikely to appease his critics, for it does little to answer the specific charge that a minister of the gospel of Christ ought to appear far more impressive than Paul. They want visible proof that Christ speaks in him (cf. 13:3). Only then will their doubts be

---

[3] The verb θριαμβεύω may be rendered simply 'to display' or 'to manifest' (so Eagen 'Lexical Evidence' 34–62), though the idea of a triumphant display is probably also intended (cf. BAG 860; Allo 43–44; Bruce 187; Héring 18; Kümmel 198; Wendland 176; Williamson 'Triumph' 323–27). Recently Marshall 'ΘΡΙΑΜΒΕΥΕΙΝ' 302–16 has suggested that Paul is identifying himself here with the humiliation of prisoners who are paraded triumphantly by their victorious Roman captors. Hafemann *Suffering* 41–64 has taken it a step farther by arguing that it is God himself who leads Paul triumphantly to the humiliating death of a slave (cf. the language of sacrifice in 2:15–16).

[4] Thus Barrett 100.   [5] Cf. Baird 'Letters of Recommendation' 170–71.

[6] Letters of commendation were widely used in antiquity; see examples in Keyes 'Letter of Introduction' 28–44 and Kim *Letter of Recommendation* Appendix III; and cf. Acts 9:2; 22:5; 1 Cor. 16:15–16; Phil. 4:2–3; 1 Thess. 5:12–13a.

allayed. In 2 Corinthians 3:7–11 Paul attempts to provide such proof. Before examining it we must comment briefly on the complexity of chapter 3 as a whole.

Scholars have invested much time and energy trying to make sense of this chapter. There are basically two difficulties. First, its argument is nearly impossible to follow, hindered at many points by mixed metaphors (writing on stones with ink, v. 3) and puzzling allusions (Moses' fading glory, vv. 7, 13).[7] Most commentators tend to get bogged down in the perplexing details of the text and seldom focus on the broader contours of Paul's thought. If we assume that the apostle's argument begins in 2 Corinthians 2:14, not in 3:1,[8] the issue which dominates Paul's thinking is the integrity of his ministry. What follows in the ensuing verses, and especially in the many contrasts found there,[9] represents a series of attempts to drive home the superiority of that ministry.

The second difficulty is the abrupt introduction of Moses and the old covenant, subjects seemingly ill-suited to a predominantly Gentile audience. Most scholars do not grapple with this problem but merely assume that Paul is responding to the propaganda of his opponents, presumably Jews who are pushing the law and Moses rather than a gospel of grace.[10] On this view, chapter 3 represents Paul's attempt to redress the legalism of his rivals. But this neglects the possibility that Paul might be breaking new ground in his teaching here and not merely responding to the prior arguments of his rivals. It also reads into the Corinthian correspondence a dialectic (law vs. grace) which was spawned and nurtured in the exegesis of two very different epistles, Romans and Galatians.[11]

---

[7] The problem is set out well by Hooker in 'Use of Scripture' 296–97.

[8] *Pace* Richard 'II Cor., III, 1–IV, 6' 340–67; Ulonska 'Die Doxa des Mose' 378–88.

[9] Namely:

> letters written not with ink, but with the Spirit (v. 3)
>> not on tablets of stone, but on tablets of hearts of flesh (v. 3)
>> not of the letter, but of the Spirit (v. 6)
> the letter kills, but the Spirit gives life (v. 6)
> the one is a ministry of death, the other of the Spirit (vv. 7–8)
> the one of condemnation, the other of righteousness (v. 9)
> the one fades, the other remains (v. 11)

[10] See e.g. Schulz 'Die Decke des Moses' 1–30 who suggests that in 2 Cor. 3 Paul is revising the Judeo-Christian midrash of his opponents, a view developed further by Georgi *Gegner* 274–82; cf. also Rissi *Studien* 25–8; Friedrich 'Gegner' 184–85; Ulonska 'Die Doxa des Mose' 378–88; Collange 70–71.

[11] For those reading the anti-Judaising polemic of Romans and Galatians into 2 Cor. 3 cf. Oostendorp *Another Jesus* 35–36; Gunther *Opponents* 63–64, 85–86; Käsemann *Perspectives* 149–55.

In any case, there seems to be a more compelling reason for Paul's interest in Moses and the old covenant. If, as we have suggested, the apostle is trying to defend the integrity of his ministry, his case would surely be strengthened if he could compare it favourably with other ministries. As a former rabbi, he knows of only one comparable 'ministry' and that is the administration of Moses.[12] Hence he compares himself with Moses, employing the familiar rabbinic method of reasoning *a minore ad maius*[13] to assert the superiority of his ministry over its nearest 'rival'.[14]

But we may still wonder: Are Paul's Gentile readers sufficiently familiar with Moses and the old covenant to make sense of this comparison? Or is Paul merely carrying on an 'interior dialogue in his mind'?[15] In answer to that question it is important to note that Moses was not only by far the most widely known Jewish figure in Graeco-Roman antiquity,[16] he was also the most respected.[17] The historian Strabo numbered Moses among 'prophets[18] [who] were held in so much honour that they were deemed worthy to be kings, on the ground that they promulgated to us[19] ordinances and amendments from the gods' (16.2.39).[20] Another historian, the Augustan Pompeius Trogus, described Moses as one 'whose physical beauty commended him as much as the wisdom which he inherited from his father' (Just. *Epit.* 36.2.11). And the first-century literary treatise, *On the Sublime* (Περὶ Ὕψους), declared Moses to be 'no ordinary man' ([Longinus] *Subl.* 9.9).[21]

---

12 This is not to suggest that the rabbis used the word διακονία to describe the work of Moses.
13 See *Mek. Exod.* 20.2.
14 It is Paul, therefore, who initiates the comparison with Moses, not his critics.
15 Thus Hickling 'Sequence of Thought' 386.
16 So Ensslin 'Moses' 361–3; Gager *Moses in Greco-Roman Paganism* 18.
17 This was largely the work of Jewish apologists who argued for the superiority of Moses over Greek philosophers; cf. Aristobulus (second century BC, in Eusebius, *Praep. Evang.* 13.12.1, 13–16), Eupolemus (c. 150 B.C., in *Praep. Evang.* 9.26.1), Artapanus (c. 100 BC, *Praep. Evang.* 9.27) and Josephus (*Ap.* 2.154,168); see also Drage *Homer or Moses?* 15, 45–6, 195, 197; Meeks *Prophet King* 162–63. For the same argument at the beginning of the Christian era cf. Pépin 'Homère-Moïse' 105–22.
18 That is, among the Greek (!) seers Teiresias, Amphiaraeus, Trophonius, Orpheus and Musaeus.
19 The pronoun ἡμῖν here suggests that in Strabo's mind the teachings of Moses were for Greeks too.
20 The text of this citation has been widely attributed to Poseidonius; cf. Norden 'Jahve und Moses' 292–301.
21 To be sure Moses had his detractors, but primarily among those writing from Rome (cf. Quint. 3.7.21; Tac. *Hist.* 5.4–5; Juv. 14.100–4), where distaste for things

Now of course these references are drawn from the intellectual elite and so cannot be held to show definitively that typical Corinthians shared a deep respect for Moses. More representative, however, are the letters of ordinary people, the papyri, and especially the magical papyri. Here we find that Moses is, if anything, better known and more highly esteemed. His name occurs repeatedly in magical recipes and formulae[22] where it ensures the efficacy of charms and the prevention of evil.[23] It appears as well on magical amulets, for similar reasons.[24] The popularity of Moses seems to stem from his unique knowledge of the divine name which he received on Sinai (cf. Exodus 3:14),[25] a knowledge which many believed empowered him to perform his extraordinary deeds (cf. Exodus 7–12).[26] In an age obsessed with magic and the supernatural[27] it is not surprising that Moses attracted so much attention. Indeed no other name in antiquity was more revered for its wonder-working powers.[28]

Semitic had been fostered by the struggle between Jews and the state; so Gager *Moses* III, 132–33.

[22] Cf. Preisendanz 'Laminetta Magica Siciliana' 77: 'The texts of the papyri and amulets . . . used his name (i.e. 'Moses') as an absolute pre-requisite in the marketing of magic'.

[23] Cf. e.g. the title of papyrus no. XIII in PGM: *Holy Book called the Monad or the Eighth Book of Moses concerning the Sacred Name*; and the subtitle: *Secret Holy Book of Moses, called the Eighth or Sacred*. The name 'Moses' rarely occurs in the text of this work, which suggests that its appearance in the title is meant solely to give the work prestige and ensure the efficacy of its charms.

[24] Cf. the stone from Spon with the word Μουση inscribed on it (in De Montfaucon *L'Antiquité expliquée* 2.2.364); and a haematite with αβρασαξ on one side and Μωσην on the other (see Bonner *Magical Amulets* 171).

[25] Cf. papyrus no. XLVI in Kenyon Greek Papyri 68: ἐγώ εἰμι Μουσῆς ὁ προφήτης σου ᾧ παρέδωκας τὰ μυστήρια σου τὰ συντελούμενα Ἰστραήλ . . . τοῦτό ἐστιν σοῦ τὸ ὄνομα τὸ ἀληθινόν ('I am myself Moses your prophet to whom you have given your mysteries which complete Israel . . . this is your true name'); cf. PGM II (126–8); III (158–59); XII (92–94); and see Jos. *A*. 2.276.

[26] Not surprisingly people prayed for this same knowledge; cf. Griffith and Thompson *Demotic Magical Papyrus* 13, col. 5 (13–14): 'reveal yourself (great God seated in fire) to me here today in the fashion of your revelation to Moses which you made upon the mountain'.

[27] Cf. Aune 'Magic' 1519.

[28] Some of the magical papyri cited above are from the third and fourth centuries, but their content probably dates to the first century (so Griffith and Thompson *Demotic Magical Papyrus* 11–13). It is worth noting that Pliny the Elder, a first-century encyclopaedist, refers incidentally to 'another branch of magic, derived from Moses' (*HN* 30.2.11). This demonstrates that the link between Moses and magic had already been established by Pliny's day (for evidence of the same link in the second century cf. Apul. *Apol*. 90). It might be wondered whether papyri and amulets bearing the name of Moses might not be Jewish in origin (so Goodenough *Jewish Symbols* 266) and so of little value in assessing the attitudes of

The literary and papyrological evidence thus points in the same direction: the great lawgiver of the Jews, Moses, was a famous and much honoured personage in the Graeco-Roman world. We are probably safe to conclude, then, that Paul's Gentile readers were well acquainted with Moses – if not with the details of his life, at least with his status as an exalted figure. But may not we conclude much more? As newly initiated members into the people of God, as members now of a tradition which honoured Moses as its most illustrious patriarch,[29] would not their knowledge of him exceed that of their pagan contemporaries? The fact that Paul can write almost incidentally of the law of Moses (1 Corinthians 9:9) and baptism into Moses (1 Corinthians 10:2) would seem to indicate that his readers had much more than a superficial grasp of the lawgiver. In order to discover how much they might have known we must examine the contemporary Jewish teaching about Moses, and especially the broad outlines of such teaching, the sort of things which Paul might naturally have passed on to his Christian congregation.[30]

In contemporary Judaism we find that Moses received even greater acclaim and exaltation than he did in the OT.[31] In Judaism, for example, he was magnified as 'God's chief prophet throughout the earth, the most perfect teacher in the world' (*As. Mos.* 11.6), the one for whom the world was created (*b. Sanh.* 98b), a type of the Messiah (*Qoh. Rab.* I.9; *Ruth Rab.* V.6), the 'greatest and most perfect of men' (Philo *Mos.* 1.1)[32] and sinless (*b. Sabb.* 55b).[33] But these are merely a prelude to greater accolades. He is more than 'a mere man' (*As. Mos.* 11.6); he is 'a man, God' (*Pesiq. Rab. Kah.* XXXII ; cf. *Deut. Rab.* XI.4), 'a divine man' (θεῖος ἀνήρ, Jos. *A.* 3. 180), 'glorious as God' (Sirach 45:2) – indeed it is difficult to tell

Moses

Greeks and Romans. But the boundaries between Judaism, Hellenism and Romanism were, by the first century, fluid and ill-defined (cf. Hengel *Judaism and Hellenism*; Kraabel 'Six Diaspora Synagogues' 89), and thus it is impossible to attribute any one document to a single tradition. Instead the evidence above probably reflects an interplay of all three traditions (thus, commenting specifically on the magical papyri, the conclusion of Dieterich *Abraxas* 70–71; Reitzenstein *Poimandres* 182, 185; Gager *Moses* 156–57).

29 Cf. *Deut. Rab.* XI.3 where Moses is said to 'excel them all' (namely, Adam, Noah, Abraham, Isaac and Jacob); also Jeremias 'Μωυσῆς' 854.
30 Or which Jewish members of the Corinthian church (cf. Acts 18) would naturally teach to Gentile converts.
31 So Jeremias 'Μωυσῆς' 854, 860.
32 Indeed 'the holiest of men ever yet born' (*Mos.* 2.192).
33 R. Simeon, however, dissents, arguing that 'Moses and Aaron too died through their sin' (*b. Sabb.* 55b).

whether he is human or divine (ἀνθρώπινος ἤ θείος, Philo *Mos.* 1.27).[34] This remarkable association of Moses with deity seems to be rooted in his unique encounter with Yahweh on Mount Sinai.[35] There he not only saw what no other mortal had ever seen, the radiating splendour of God's glory,[36] he also came to possess that glory for himself, reflecting it brilliantly on his face.[37] This, more than any other episode in his life, profoundly influenced Jewish exegetes and caused them to wax eloquent on the theme of Moses' glory.[38] It also prompted them to elevate Moses above the other patriarchs,[39] even to the very realm of God. The possibility that Paul's Corinthian converts were unaware of this exalted and glorified vision of Moses is extremely unlikely. It is more reasonable to assume that they had embraced the vision for themselves.

Moses' dramatic meeting with God on Mount Sinai thus left a deep imprint on two traditions: Graeco-Roman and Jewish. Both depicted Moses in exceedingly lofty terms, as a man above men and one to be revered with God/the gods. Doubtless Paul's readers, as beneficiaries of *both* traditions (i.e. as pagans turned Christian), would have held Moses in the loftiest esteem. Indeed it was probably their exalted regard for the lawgiver which led Paul to incorporate Moses into the defence of his ministry in 2 Corinthians 3.[40]

---

[34] Cf. Philo *Quaest. in Ex.* 2.54; *Sac.* 9; *Post.* 28; on the divinity of Moses in Philo see Goodenough *By Light* 224–34.

[35] Cf. *Pesiq. Rab. Kah.* XXXII: 'he was a man in the hour he climbed the mountain, a god in the hour he came down' (cf. *Deut. Rab.* XI.4); and Philo *Mos.* 1.158: 'he was named "god" and "king" (θεὸς καὶ βασιλεύς) . . . [when he] entered . . . into the darkness where God was' (i.e. 'the thick cloud' of Exod. 20:21; see also *Quaest. in Ex.* 2.40). For the link between Moses' ascent and his divinisation cf. Meeks 'Moses as God and King' 355–59, 365.

[36] So Sir 45:2; *Tanch Ki tissa* 121a.

[37] So Exod 34:30: 'When Aaron and all the sons of Israel saw Moses, behold the skin of his face shone'; cf. Philo *Mos.* 2.69–70: 'he descended with a countenance far more beautiful than when he ascended, so that those who saw him were filled with awe and amazement; nor even could their eyes continue to stand the dazzling brightness that flashed from him like the rays of the sun'; see also *Pesiq. Rab. Kah.* 27, 32; *Exod. Rab.* XLVII; *b. Ber.* 7a.

[38] Cf. *Pesiq. R.* 21.6: 'If an opening were to be made in the grave of Moses, the entire world could not endure the light' (so *Tg. Onq. Deut.* 34:7). On identifying Moses' glory with creation light, cf. *b. Sota* 12a; *Exod. Rab.* I.20; on Israel being unable because of its sin to approach Moses in his glory, see *Pesiq. R.* 15.3; *Sifre Num.* 5:3. Cf. further *Deut. Rab.* III.12; and Murmelstein 'Adam' 56.

[39] Cf. *Deut. Rab.* XI.3 where it is argued that Moses is superior to Adam, Noah, Abraham, Isaac and Jacob.

[40] It is therefore unnecessary to view Paul's reference to Moses as a response to those who allege that he falls short of the glory of Moses (*pace* Collange 69–72; Georgi *Gegner* 258–73).

We may now return to the text and examine with greater insight how Paul responds to those who dispute the quality of his ministry. In 2 Corinthians 3:7–11 he argues in a series of contrasts that his ministry, far from being unimpressive, is actually superior to that of Moses.[41] The old covenant is a ministry of death, his is a ministry of the Spirit (v. 7); the old condemns, his confers righteousness (v. 9); the old is passing away, his remains (v. 11). It is tempting to regard these contrasts as careful instruction in the details of two covenants.[42] Yet the flow of the context and the abundant use of the term δόξα and its cognates suggest that the contrasts are meant primarily to illustrate a more fundamental point – that Paul's ministry is much more glorious than Moses'.[43] That is an extraordinary claim, especially since Moses' glory was mediated to him directly by God (Exod 33:18–23; 34:29) and was much too resplendent for the eyes of Israel to behold (Exod 34:30b; here 2 Corinthians 3:7b). It is now precisely that glory which, according to Paul, is not only eclipsed but reduced to nothing by the surpassing splendour of his ministry.[44] The apostle's reply to his critics could scarcely be more potent. His glory exceeds that of the most luminous figure in antiquity. Anyone who belittles the quality of his ministry must be suffering a myopia of the gravest proportions.

[41] Cf. Hooker 'Use of Scripture' 296–97 who suggests that the contrast here is 'not between Law and Gospel, nor between Moses and Christ, but between the ministry of Moses and that of Paul'; see also Davies 'People of Israel' 11; Stockhausen *Glory* 152.

[42] Many scholars (Räisänen *Paul and the Law* 44–6; Prümm 2.1.188–230, esp. 201–3; Käsemann *Perspectives* 147–55; Rissi *Studien* 22–25; Dugandzic *Das 'Ja' Gottes in Christus* 112–20; Cranfield *Romans* 2.853–57; Goudge 28–31) view the contrast between 'letter' and 'spirit' here as the basic theme of the passage, and so read the law-grace antithesis of Galatians and Romans into 2 Cor. 3 (cf. the error especially of Prümm in 'Gal und 2 Kor' 27–72, esp. 30–36; and 'Röm 1–11 und 2 Kor 3' 164–203, esp. 166–71).

[43] The notion of 'glory' is clearly the theme of 3:7–11 (the word δόξα appears at least once in each verse and eight times in total, while δοξάζω occurs twice), and especially the greater glory of Paul's ministry (the term πολλῷ μᾶλλον is repeated in vv. 9 and 11; and cf. v. 8). Cf. Young and Ford *Meaning and Truth* 12–13, 260.

[44] Hence the meaning of the somewhat awkward v. 10: καὶ γὰρ οὐ δεδόξασται τὸ δεδοξασμένον ἐν τούτῳ τῷ μέρει εἵνεκεν τῆς ὑπερβαλλούσης δόξης, which translated means 'for that which stands in glory (i.e., the glory of Moses and the old covenant, a very real and present glory the perfect participle here stressing the lingering effects of a glory bestowed in the past [*pace* Moule *Idiom* 15 who maintains that the 'glory *no longer exists* because it is superseded' (his emphasis)]) does not stand in glory (is, in effect, 'de-glorified') in this case (i.e. in Paul's case) on account of the surpassing greatness of glory' (namely, the glory of the new covenant ministry), i.e., the old glory cannot be seen in the 'shadow' of the new. Thus Paul is not portraying himself merely as a second Moses (*pace* Jones 'Un second Moïse' 36–58), for 'he is *more* than Moses had been' (Bammel 'Paulus, der Moses des Neuen Bundes' 408, my emphasis).

It is clear from this evidence that Paul has crafted his answer to have maximum effect among those who revere Moses and his glory – hence among his *entire* readership! Yet it is equally clear that his gospel remains veiled to many of those same readers (4:3). How can this be? If the glory of Moses prompted the Israelites to shield their eyes because of its unbearable brightness, if the reputation of Moses is now equally luminous in the minds of the Corinthians, how could the allegedly superior glory of Paul be regarded as anything but 'much more' (πολλῷ μᾶλλον) bedazzling? Yet, remarkably, his ministry creates the opposite impression. Many detect no glory at all. It inspires no awe, only pity and revulsion. The fact that he makes the grandiose claims of 2 Corinthians 3:7–11 would only compound the bewilderment. How can he claim to manifest a glorious gospel when his ministry is so dark and uninspiring?

As third parties to this dialogue, we cannot help but wonder at the entirely opposite positions adopted by Paul and his critics. Paul professes to reflect divine glory. His critics not only deny it but claim he is wholly inglorious. Who is right? Whom are we to believe? Or is it possible that both are right? Are there two viable views of Paul and his ministry? indeed two understandings of glory? If so, several questions remain to be answered. What does Paul mean by glory? In what sense is it manifested on/in him? Why do so many miss it? What sort of glory are his critics looking for? Paul attempts to answer these questions in the course of responding to his adversaries in 2 Corinthians 3–4. We must pay close attention to what he says, for his answers contain insights into his paradoxical understanding of the nature of the Christian gospel. We shall begin by looking at his own perception of glory.

The glory of Isaiah

The verse which sheds the most light on Paul's understanding of glory is 2 Corinthians 4:6. Here, at the end of a long exposition on the theme of δόξα, we discover both the source and the nature of his glory. It is worth citing the text verbatim:

ὁ θεὸς ὁ εἰπών ἐκ σκότους φῶς λάμψει,
ὅς[45] ἔλαμψεν ἐν ταῖς καρδίαις ἡμῶν
πρὸς φωτισμὸν τῆς γνώσεως
τῆς δόξης τοῦ θεοῦ

[45] The relative clause here represents an anacoluthon in which ὅς resumes the subject ὁ θεός: 'the God who said . . . has shone in our hearts'.

In this verse Paul maintains that the glory shining in his heart was mediated to him directly by God – 'God . . . shone in our hearts . . . glory'.[46] He also reveals that it is a glory linked very closely to the light of which God was speaking when he said 'Light will shine out of darkness'. Just when and where God uttered this declaration is a matter of dispute. Most scholars believe the words ἐκ σκότους φῶς λάμψει represent a loose citation of the injunction in Genesis 1:3, καὶ εἶπεν ὁ θεός, γενηθήτω φῶς,[47] and hence an affirmation that Paul's glory is related to the light of creation. Yet the term φῶς λάμψει is the future indicative of prophecy and not, like γενηθήτω φῶς, a subjunctive of command.[48] This would suggest that Paul understands his glory as a fulfilment of prophecy and thus as an eschatological light. To explore this possibility further we must discover whether Paul might have known of such a prophecy.

The term φῶς λάμψει is found elsewhere in scripture only in LXX Isaiah 9:1:

> ὁ λαὸς ὁ πορευόμενος ἐν σκότει ἴδετε φῶς μέγα
> οἱ κατοικοῦντες ἐν χώρᾳ καὶ σκιᾷ θανάτου,
> φῶς λάμψει ἐφ᾽ ὑμᾶς

This prophetical oracle describes a day when a great light will illuminate a terrible darkness. In a related passage, LXX Isaiah 4:2, we learn that the source of this light will be God himself (τῇ δὲ ἡμέρᾳ ἐκείνῃ ἐπιλάμψει ὁ θεὸς ἐν βουλῇ μετὰ δόξης ἐπὶ τῆς γῆς). These details comport well with Paul's description of the glory emanating from his heart in 2 Corinthians 4:6 and, together with the exactness of the citation φῶς λάμψει, suggest that he may well have been quoting from LXX Isaiah 9:1.[49]

Other factors seem to confirm this possibility. (i) Since Paul

---

46 ὁ θεός is the subject ('the God who said', thus Furnish 223), not the predicate ('it is the God who said', so Barrett 134; Windisch 139), in agreement with the parallel v. 4 where ὁ θεός is clearly the subject.

47 Thus Allo 103; Barrett 135; Bultmann 111; Furnish 251; Goudge 38; Harris 341; Lietzmann 115; Menzies 29; Plummer 120; Strachan 92; Thrall 138; Wendland 163; Windisch 139–40; Wolff 87–8; and cf. Stanley 'Paul's Interest in Genesis' 247; Stachowiak 'Licht-Finsternis' 390. Jervell *Imago Dei* 173–76, 194–97, 214–18 suggests that the entire passage, 2 Cor. 3:18–4:6, represents a Pauline midrash on Gen. 1.

48 Some copyists (ℵ², C, D², F, G, H, Y, *et al.*) seem to have felt this tension, substituting the optative λάμψαι for the future indicative λάμψει, thereby assimilating the text to the creation account.

49 Cf. Collange 138–39; Martini 'Alcuni temi letterari di 2 Cor. 4:6' 471–72; Richard 'II Cor., III, 1–IV, 6' 359–60; Furnish 223–24; and see Oostendorp *Another Jesus* 48 who believes that Paul is influenced here by the later chapters (40ff.) of Isaiah.

quotes from Isaiah more than any other OT writing it is unlikely that he could have used the rare term φῶς λάμψει without having in mind its usage in LXX Isaiah.[50] (ii) When he quotes from Isaiah in other epistles it is almost always with a view to rebuking spiritual blindness.[51] This is likewise the intent in 2 Corinthians 3–4 (cf. 3:14–15; 4:3). (iii) Paul's frequent use in 2 Corinthians 3–4 of words with visual connotation (e.g. 'light', 'darkness', 'shine', 'blind', 'reveal', 'manifest') parallels a similar abundance of such words in LXX Isaiah.[52] (iv) Finally, and perhaps most tellingly, Paul's concentrated focus on δόξα in 2 Corinthians 3–4 finds a corresponding emphasis in LXX Isaiah.[53]

This last point is worth exploring further. The scribe who rendered Isaiah into Greek employs the term δόξα an extravagant seventy-one times in the course of his translation, as opposed to the mere sixty-five times which it appears in the rest of the prophetical writings.[54] Moreover, he imputes to the term a highly distinctive flavour. Of its occurrences in Isaiah fewer than half translate the word kābôd, the usual Hebrew term for 'glory', compared to a much higher 77 percent in the other prophetical books.[55] In its other uses in LXX Isaiah δόξα renders a wide assortment of Hebrew ideas. It is instructive to consider its range of meaning.

In Isaiah 33:17, the phrase 'Your eyes will see the king in his *beauty*' (meleke beyāpeyô teḥezeynâh 'êneykā) is translated βασιλέα μετὰ *δόξης* ὄψεσθε. In 53:2, 'He has no outward form or *splendour*' (lō' tō'ar lô welō' hādār) is rendered οὐκ ἔστιν εἶδος αὐτῷ οὐδὲ *δόξα*. In 40:6, 'All flesh is like grass, and all its *loveliness* is like the flower of the field' (kāl habāsār ḥāsîr wekāl ḥasedô kesîs haśśādeh) becomes πᾶσα σὰρξ χόρτος καὶ πᾶσα *δόξα* ἀνθρώπου ὡς ἄνθος χόρτου. In 11:3, 'And he will not judge by *what his eyes see*' (welō'

---

[50] Cf. Hickling 'Paul's Reading of Isaiah' 215–23 who figures that 26 per cent of Paul's OT quotations come from Isaiah. I put the number at 28 per cent (twenty-five of eighty-eight), using the Appendix I (A) in Ellis' *Paul's Use of the Old Testament* 150–52 (adding 2 Cor. 4:6 and deleting the references to Ephesians and 1 and 2 Tim.).

[51] Cf. the four contexts of unbelief where citations from Isaiah are clustered: Rom. 2 and 3 (two quotations); 9–11 (eleven); 1 Cor. 1 and 2 (two); 2 Cor. 4–6 (three).

[52] In Isaiah φῶς appears thirty-three times as opposed to thirty-one times in the rest of the prophets; for σκότος the numbers are twenty and thirteen; for λάμπω two and one; for τυφλός ten and two; for ἀνακαλύπτω ten and five; for φανερός three and one.

[53] Cf. Brockington 'Greek Translator of Isaiah and His Interest in ΔΟΞΑ' 26–30.

[54] For δοξάζω the numbers are seventeen and eleven.

[55] δοξάζω translates kābôd a low 30 per cent of the time in Isaiah. The percentage doubles in other prophets.

leᵉmarᵉʾēh ʾēnāyw yišᵉpôt) is rendered οὐ κατὰ τὴν δόξαν κρινεῖ. It is clear from these examples that the word δόξα in LXX Isaiah is used to refer to man's visible, external, and transient beauty. In other passages we learn that it is a 'beauty' which leads to pride. In 10:12, 'the *pomp* of which his eyes are proud' (wᵉʿal tipᵉʾeret rûm ʾēnāyw) is translated τὸ ὕψος τῆς δόξης τῶν ὀφθαλμῶν αὐτοῦ. In 28:1, 'Woe . . . to the fading flower of its *outward beauty*' (hôy . . . ṣîṣ nōbēl ṣᵉbî tipᵉʿarᵉtô), where 'it' refers to Ephraim's 'proud crown' (v. 1), becomes οὐαὶ . . . τὸ ἄνθος τὸ ἐκπεσὸν ἐκ τῆς δόξης. In 17:4, 'the fatness of his *flesh* will become lean' (ûmišᵉman bᵉśārô yērāzeh), where bāśār is understood as 'earthly pomp',[56] is rendered καὶ τὰ πίονα τῆς δόξης αὐτοῦ σεισθήσεται.

In addition, δόξα can be used for human wealth and riches. In 14:11, 'Your *material excellence* has been brought down to Sheol' (hûrad šᵉʾôl gᵉʾônekā hemᵉyat nᵉbāleykā) is rendered κατέβη δὲ εἰς ᾅδου ἡ δόξα σου (cf. 3:18; 22:25; 64:10).

The word δόξα in LXX Isaiah retains many of these same nuances when used of God. In 26:10, 'he (the wicked) does not see the *majesty* of the Lord' (ûbal yirᵉʾeh gēʾût yᵉhwāh) is translated ἵνα μὴ ἴδῃ τὴν δόξαν κυρίου. In 24:14, 'they cry shrilly from the sea the *exaltedness* of God' (bigᵉʾôn yᵉhwāh ṣāhᵃlû mîyām) becomes οἱ δὲ καταλειφθέντες ἐπὶ τῆς γῆς εὐφρανθήσονται ἅμα τῇ δόξῃ κυρίου. In 2:10, 'Enter the rock and hide . . . from the *splendour* of his (Yahweh's) majesty' (bôʾ baṣṣûr wᵉhittāmēn . . . mēhᵃdar gᵉʾônô) is rendered καὶ νῦν εἰσέλθετε εἰς τὰς πέτρας καὶ κρύπτεσθε . . . ἀπὸ τῆς δόξης τῆς ἰσχύος αὐτοῦ (cf. 2:19, 21). In these examples the term δόξα denotes the awesome and visible majesty of God. It can also signify his incredible strength. In 45:24, 'Only in the Lord are righteousness and *strength*' (ʾakᵉ bayhwāh . . . ṣᵉdāqôt wāʾōz) becomes δικαιοσύνη καὶ δόξα πρὸς αὐτὸν ἥξουσιν (cf. 12:2). In 40:26, 'He calls them (stars?) by name, because of the greatness of his *strength* and might' (lᵉkullām bᵉšēm yiqᵉrāʾ mērōb ʾônîm wᵉʾammîṣ) is rendered πάντας ἐπʼ ὀνόματι καλέσει ἀπὸ πολλῆς δόξης καὶ ἐν κράτει ἰσχύος.

It is immediately noticable from the evidence of these passages that the distinctive range of meaning of δόξα in LXX Isaiah bears a striking resemblance to Paul's use of the term in 2 Corinthians 3–4. The apostle is similarly keen to stress the sheer brightness and terrifying splendour of δόξα and in particular to contrast his own

---

[56] So Kittel 'δόξα' 245 n. 35.

superlative glory with the fading radiance of Moses. The remarkable similarity between the two notions of glory suggests that Paul may be doing more than merely citing LXX Isaiah 9:1 in 2 Corinthians 4:6. He could well be drawing on the full exposition of Isaian δόξα throughout his teaching in 2 Corinthians 3–4. We must therefore take a sustained and careful look at the nature of 'glory' in LXX Isaiah, for in doing so we may gain a richer understanding into Paul's own conception of the brightness which has broken forth in his heart.[57]

The plan for the study of Isaiah will be as follows. First, we shall set out the assumptions which will govern our analysis of LXX Isaiah. Secondly, we shall consider how the translator of LXX Isaiah understood the notion of 'glory'. Thirdly, we shall examine the related Isaian themes of light and darkness and assess their contribution to Paul's understanding of 'glory'. Finally, we shall ask how our insights into Isaian 'glory' serve to elucidate Paul's thought in 2 Corinthians 3–4.

Our study proceeds on two assumptions: (i) While the book of Isaiah can be divided into two and possibly three distinct parts written by different authors at different times, there are certain themes which are common to the entire book. One such theme is the notion of glory (along with the related ideas of light and darkness). We shall therefore adopt Paul's unitary approach to the book[58] and examine the term δόξα as it appears in the book *as a whole*.[59] (ii) While LXX Isaiah shows an interest in the political situation in Israel, its principal aim is to expose the spiritual conditions underlying that situation.[60] Our analysis will likewise give priority to the

---

[57] There can be little doubt that Paul relies on the Septuagint version of Isaiah. Of his twenty-five citations from Isaiah, twenty follow the LXX (seven exactly, thirteen vary only slightly), three differ considerably from both the LXX and MT and only two seem to be marginally closer to the MT. Cf. Appendix I (A) in Ellis *Paul's Use of the OT.*

[58] Paul uses the formula Ἡσαίας γὰρ λέγει when citing first (11:10 in Rom. 15:12), second (53:1 in Rom. 10:16) and third (65:1 in Rom. 10:20) Isaiahs.

[59] In his work on canon criticism Childs *Introduction to the Old Testament* 325–38 argues that even if there are separate Isaiahs we must concentrate on the coherence of the book as a whole in its present form. Clements 'The Unity of the Book of Isaiah' 129 agrees, finding 'a measure of connectedness and unity imposed upon the book'. He suggests (in 'Deutero-Isaianic Development of First Isaiah's Themes' 95–113) that the theme of blindness in Isa. 40–55 – a theme closely related to the idea of light and darkness – represents a conscious allusion back to the prophecies of 1–39.

[60] So Thompson *Situation and Theology* 59, 120; cf. Ginsberg *Supernatural in the Prophets* 15–16.

spiritual perspectives of Israel, touching only briefly on the historical and political.

We may begin our study with Isaiah 60:1–3, the most detailed account of the 'glory' which will illuminate Israel's future:[61]

> Be enlightened, be enlightened, O Jerusalem,
> For your light is come,
> Indeed the glory (δόξα) of the Lord is risen upon you.
>
> Behold darkness will cover the earth,
> And gloom [will be] upon the nations.
>
> But the Lord will be manifested upon you,
> And his glory (δόξα) will be seen upon you;
> And the kings will go about in your light,
> And the nations in your brilliancy.

Much in this passage agrees with our observations above. The coming light will be generated by the superlative glory of God (cf. 4:2) and will burst into a world shrouded in darkness (cf. 9:1). What is new here is the seemingly universal scope of the darkness which 'covers the earth' and rests 'upon the nations'. In a parallel passage, Isaiah 59:9, we learn that even Israel falls under its gloom:

> While they (Israel) waited for light,
> darkness came to them;
> While they waited for brightness,
> they walked in confusion.   (cf. 50:10)

The reason for this darkness is not here explicitly revealed. But that there should be darkness at all is surprising in view of the revelation earlier in Isaiah that the glory of God fills the entire earth (6:3). This would suggest that if Israel is mired in darkness it is due not so much to the absence of light as to Israel's inability to see the light. This finds potential confirmation in Isaiah 26:10 where it is written, 'Let the ungodly (ὁ ἀσεβής) be taken away, that they may not see the glory (τὴν δόξαν) of the Lord'. Perhaps Israel's darkness is due to 'ungodliness', an 'ungodliness' which has 'taken Israel away' from the sphere of God's glory. But this is an inference drawn from isolated texts. In accordance with our unitary approach to LXX Isaiah, we must test the hypothesis against the teaching of the book as a whole.

---

[61] All passages cited from LXX Isaiah are my own translations.

In Isaiah 13:11 we read that the sin of the ungodly (οἱ ἀσεβεῖς . . . τὰς ἁμαρτίας αὐτῶν) is identified closely with the 'pride of the haughty' (ὕβρις ὑπερηφάνων). Such haughtiness and pride elsewhere earns the prophet's harshest rebuke, for in his mind they amount to self-exaltation and thus encroachment on ground reserved exclusively for God, the only exalted One (cf. 2:17). Significantly, it is this sort of self-exaltation of which Israel is most guilty. The nation is repeatedly condemned for pride (ὕβρις),[62] arrogance (ὑπερήφανος),[63] loftiness (ὑψηλός),[64] highness (ὕψος)[65] and haughtiness (μετέωρος).[66]

The grave effect of such hubris is that it impairs Israel's perspective of God. Instead of focusing on the work of his hands (5:12b; cf. 22:11), Israel proudly concentrates on its own activity (42:17; cf. 17:8), taking full credit for its own achievements. The irony here is that Israel is itself the Lord's achievement (43:1; 45:8c), 'the clay of the potter' (29:16; cf. 45:9),[67] a nation created specifically by him for his glory (43:7). By neglecting the Lord and cultivating a self-focus (cf. 17:4), Israel effectively denies the most fundamental truth of its existence, namely, its total indebtedness to God. This is an error which the prophetical author underscores with the stinging rhetorical question, 'Will the thing formed say to the one who formed it, "You did not form me!"?' (29:16), 'Will the axe glorify itself without the one who chops with it? Will the saw exalt itself without the one who uses it?' (10:15)

It is clear from these texts that Israel is guilty of far more than merely encroaching on God's domain. It is effectively casting God from his domain. Indeed it is behaving very much like the King of Tyre who, in exalting himself to heaven, usurped the very throne of God (14:13):

> I will ascend into heaven;
> I will set my throne above the stars of heaven;
> I will sit on a lofty mountain, upon the lofty mountains
>   toward the north;
> I will go up above the clouds;
> I will be like the Most High.

---

[62] Cf. 2:2; 9:8; 10:33; 28:1, 3; so also Babylon, 13:3; Moab, 16:6; Tyre, 23:7, 9; the whole earth, 25:11.
[63] Cf. 1:25; 2:12; 29:20.   [64] 2:12; 3:16; 9:9; 10:33–34.
[65] 2:11,17; 10:12; 37:23; on ὑψόω cf. 3:16; 33:23.
[66] 2:12; 5:15   [67] Cf. also Jer. 18:1–6; Sir 33:13; and see Foerster 'κτίζω' 1007

Such egotism is tantamount to claiming *to be* God, a claim which becomes explicit in the words of arrogant Babylon: 'I am, and there is no other' (47:8,10).

Israel, then, has completely misconstrued its position before God and is charged accordingly: 'this people do not understand me' (1:2–3; 44:18);[68] 'Israel does not know me' (1:3; 5:13; 45:5);[69] with an 'exalted heart' (9:9) the people neglect my 'exalted hand' (v.12). The problem is well summed up in Isaiah 26:10: 'O Lord, your arm is exalted, yet they did not know it.' On the basis of this evidence we may conclude that it is ungodliness, and specifically the sin of pride, which has served to blind Israel to the exaltedness of God. Whether it is also pride which submerges Israel in darkness and prevents it from seeing divine *glory*, as suggested in our hypothesis above, remains to be seen.

In this respect it is crucial to note that in LXX Isaiah the exaltedness of God is nearly always synonymous with the glory of God. In fact the translator of LXX Isaiah actually uses the word δόξα to render the Hebrew terms gā'ôn ('exaltedness', 24:14; 26:10) and hādār ('majesty', 2:10, 19, 21). Moreover, in some passages he comes close to equating the glory and the exaltedness of God. For example: in 33:10 the Lord declares 'now I shall be glorified, now I shall be exalted' (νῦν δοξασθήσομαι, νῦν ὑψωθήσομαι);[70] in 6:1 'the Lord sitting on a high and exalted throne' (ἐπὶ θρόνου ὑψηλοῦ καὶ ἐπηρμένου) produces a 'house full of his glory' (πλήρης ὁ οἶκος τῆς δόξης αὐτοῦ);[71] in 12:4 'to proclaim his (the Lord's) glorious works' (τὰ ἔνδοξα αὐτοῦ) is to 'remember that his name is exalted' (ὑψώθη τὸ ὄνομα αὐτοῦ).[72] Because of this link in LXX Isaiah between the exaltedness of God and the glory of God we may conclude that the failure to see one would necessarily imply an

---

68 Further on Israel's lack of σύνεσις cf. 6:9–10; 27:11; 33:19; 40:13–14; 56:11, 59:15.
69 On the absence of γνῶσις in Israel cf. 40:21,28; 42:25; 44:19; 45:20; 48:6–8; 56:10.
70 The MT reads: 'atāh 'ērômām 'atāh 'ennāśē': 'now I will be exalted, now I will be lifted up'.
71 In the Hebrew we read: wā'erʾeh 'eṯ 'aḏōnāy yōšēḇ 'al kisse' rām wᵉniśśā' wᵉšûlāyw mᵉlē'îm 'eṯ hahêḵāl: 'I saw the Lord sitting on a throne, lofty and exalted, with the train of his robe filling the temple'.
72 In the MT we find: hôḏî'û bā'ammîm 'alîôṯāyw hazᵉkîrû kî niśᵉgāb šᵉmû: 'Make known his deeds among the peoples, make [them] remember that his name is exalted'. In each of these examples (in nn. 70 and 71) the translator of the LXX uses the term δόξα to describe the exaltedness of God in the MT (cf. also 40:25–26 and 52:13; and see 4:2 where he adds the notion of exaltation [ὑψῶσαι] to the idea of kāḇôḏ). The translator of LXX Isaiah thus reflects a theology in which the glory of God and the exaltedness of God are identified.

inability to see the other. In missing God's exaltedness Israel naturally misses his glory. Thus our hypothesis stands. Intoxicated by its
own glory Israel is blind to God's.

Yet it would be wrong to suppose that Israel's blindness is simply
a consequence of pride. On the contrary, it is the clear desire of the
proud. At least that is how the translator of LXX Isaiah presents it.
Israel does not want to see light, not divine light. The nation
intentionally hides from God and his glory.[73] It actively rebels
against him[74] – breaking his law,[75] indulging in idolatry,[76] abandoning him[77] and turning away from him.[78] In this it is much
deluded. For by thinking that it can hide from the glory of God and
revel instead in its own glory, Israel 'trusts vainly in a lie' (28:17;
30:12), indeed in 'foolishness' (30:15; 59:4; cf. 45:19). It 'makes
darkness (glorying in itself) light and light (glorying in God) darkness' (5:20).[79] In other words, it seeks glory but only in gloom. The
people of God in LXX Isaiah thus possess an opaque view of
reality.[80] No wonder they are compared to those who have no eyes
(ὡς οὐκ ὑπαρχόντων ὀφθαλμῶν, 49:10), the uncomprehending
blind:

> And who is blind (τυφλός), but my servants,
> And deaf, but the ones who rule over them?
> Indeed, the servants of the Lord have been made blind
>   (ἐτυφλώθησαν).
> You have seen often, but have not taken heed;
> [Your] ears have been opened, but you have not heard
>   42:19–20

---

[73] They avoid the Lord ('Who will know us or what we do?') and engage in hidden
counsel (ἐν κρυφῇ βουλήν, 29:15); and cf. 40:27 where Israel boasts, 'My way is
hidden (ἀπεκρύβη) from God' (see also 44:8); and 33:9–10 where, not wanting 'to
hear the law of God' (v. 9), it implores its prophets, 'Do not announce to us [God's
law] . . . but speak to us . . . a different error' (v. 10).

[74] So 1:2, 25; 63:8.

[75] Thus 1:4–5, 25; 3:8; 5:7, 24; 9:17; 10:6; 13:11; 24:5; 31:6; 33:14; 48:8, 18; 50:1; 53:5;
57:4; 58:1; 59:3, 4, 6, 12; 64:6.

[76] Cf. 2:18; 10:10–11; 30:22; 31:7; 44:9–10, 12–17; 45:20; 46:1; 48:5.

[77] So 1:4; 17:10; 51:13; 57:11.

[78] So 30:2; 31:1; 56:11; 66:3.

[79] Cf. the same error in Job 17:12 (MT): 'They make night into day, saying "The light
is near," in the presence of darkness'; and 1QS 3.3: 'seeking the ways of light he
(the wicked) looks toward darkness'; cf. also Job 5:14; T. Judah 18:6.

[80] Cf. Brueggemann 'Isaiah Tradition' 93: Israel is 'organized against reality, against
God's sovereignty'.

And I have brought forth a blind people (λαὸν τυφλόν);
For [their] eyes are alike blind (τυφλοί),
And those having ears are deaf.   43:8

They have no understanding to perceive,
For they have been blinded so that they cannot see with
    their eyes,
Nor perceive with their heart.   44:18

See how they are all blinded (ἐκτετύφλωνται):
They have not known;
[They are] dumb dogs [that] will not bark;
Dreaming of rest, loving to slumber.   56:10

and note especially,

And he (Yahweh) said, 'Go and say to this people,
Hearing, you will hear and not understand;
Seeing, you will see and not perceive.
For the heart of this people has been dulled,
And they hear with their ears heavily,
And they have shut [their] eyes.'   6:8c–10a[81]

The recurring emphasis here on blindness serves to highlight the
true nature of Israel's problem. Their darkness is not the product of
bad light, but of corrupt vision. In the words of the prophetical
author, it is τὸ ὕψος τῆς δόξης τῶν ὀφθαλμῶν αὐτοῦ ('the highness of the glory of its eyes') which perpetuates Israel's gloom
(10:12).[82]

But the encouraging message of LXX Isaiah is that in spite of its
seemingly intractable blindness Israel has grounds for hope. As the
translator puts it in Isaiah 29:18, a day is coming when 'those in
darkness and those in a fog, the eyes of the blind, will see' (οἱ ἐν τῷ
σκότει καὶ οἱ ἐν τῇ ὁμίχλῃ ὀφθαλμοὶ τυφλῶν βλέψονται).[83] This
relief, however, will not be immediate. First there will be intense

---

[81] Variations of this text are used in both testaments to describe spiritual blindness in
God's people: cf. Isa. 29:10; 64:4; Deut. 29:2–4; Jer. 5:21; Ezek. 12:2; Matt.
13:13–15; Mark 4:12; John 9:39–41; Acts 28:26–27; and esp. Rom. 11:8 and 1 Cor.
2:9.

[82] The words of this verse refer to the 'proud heart' of the 'ruler of the Assyrians', but
they apply to Israel as well — cf. 37:23 where 'the daughter of Jerusalem . . . lifts
up [her] eyes in exaltation (καὶ . . . ἦρας εἰς ὕψος τοὺς ὀφθαλμούς σου) against
the Holy One of Israel'.

[83] So also 35:5; 42:16; 61:1; cf. 35:2; 52:8; 66:18.

suffering, a period of judgement for ungodliness: 'and I (the Lord) will command evils for the whole world, and [will visit] their sins upon the ungodly' (καὶ τοῖς ἀσεβέσιν τὰς ἁμαρτίας αὐτῶν, 13:11).[84] When the prophet asks 'How long, O Lord?' (6:11) will the affliction last, the answer is – 'a little while' (χρόνον μικρόν, 54:7; cf. βραχύ τι, 57:17), long enough for trembling to seize the ungodly (λήψεται τρόμος τοὺς ἀσεβεῖς, 33:14) and for fear to grip the heart of Jacob (26:18; 29:23; 33:14).[85] For in the painful experience of fear and suffering Israel's pride will be crushed. It will be in judgement that Israel will regain a proper humility before God. That is the message of the following passages:

> For Jerusalem is ruined, and Judea is fallen . . .
> Their glory (δόξα) has been humbled (ἐταπεινώθη),
> And the shame of their face stands out against them. 3:8–9

> Behold the Lord, the Lord of hosts, will confound mightily
>   the glorious ones (τοὺς ἐνδόξους),
> And the haughty in pride (οἱ ὑψηλοὶ τῇ ὕβρει) will be
>   crushed,
> And the lofty ones (οἱ ὑψηλοί) will be humbled
>   (ταπεινωθήσονται):
> Indeed the lofty ones will fall by the sword.   10:33–34

> And I (the Lord) will command evils for the whole
>   world . . .
> I will destroy the pride (ὕβριν) of the lawless,
> And humble (ταπεινώσω) the pride of the haughty
>   (ὕβριν ὑπερηφάνων).   13:11

> The earth will be completely laid waste,
> And the earth will be utterly plundered:
> For the mouth of the Lord has spoken these things.

---

[84] Hence judgement is something the ungodly bring upon themselves: it is their sin which prompts the Lord to turn his face (1:15; 8:17; 54:7–8; 59:2; 64:7) and hide his light (13:10; 50:3). Elsewhere, however, the Lord himself 'closes their eyes' and causes their sin, and so initiates their judgement (cf. 29:9–10; and see 6:9–10 in the MT, but in the LXX the harshness of this text is mitigated [cf. Evans 'Isaiah 6:9–10' 415–18]; and also Lam 3:2). Further on judgement of Israel cf. 1:24–26; 3:1–15; 5:24–30; 7:17–25; 9:18–21, etc.

[85] Cf. God instilling fear in the Egyptians (19:16), in the nations (41:4–5) and in 'those from the west' (59:19).

The earth mourns, and the world is ruined;
The lofty ones (οἱ ὑψηλοί) of the earth are mourning.

24:3–4

All our glorious (ἔνδοξα) things have been assailed . . .
You (the Lord) have humbled (ἐταπείνωσας) us
exceedingly.   64:11–12[86]

The humbling of Israel through judgement has the supreme corollary effect of bringing the nation to see that God alone is exalted. Thus 5:15c–16a:

And lofty eyes (οἱ ὀφθαλμοὶ οἱ μετέωροι) will be brought
   low (ταπεινωθήσονται),
And the Lord of hosts will be exalted (ὑψωθήσεται) in
   judgement.

also 2:12, 17b:

For the day of the Lord of hosts[87] [will come] upon all
   who are proud (ὑβριστήν) and haughty (ὑπερήφανον),
   and upon all who are high (ὑψηλόν) and lofty (μετέωρον);
And they shall be brought low (ταπεινωθήσονται) . . .
And the Lord alone will be exalted (ὑψωθήσεται).

In other words divine judgement will serve to open Israel's eyes to its own lowliness before an exalted God.[88] No longer will the people stumble along blindly in search of their own counterfeit glory (cf. 59:10). Instead they will humbly *see* the true glory of God (cf. 35:2–5).

And seeing his glory, they will also reflect it![89] This is the extraordinary revelation of Isaiah 60:1, the verse with which we began our study of Isaian 'glory': 'Shine (φωτίζου), shine (φωτίζου), O Jerusalem, for *your* light (φῶς) is come, the glory (δόξα) of the Lord has risen upon *you*'. We may note as well Isaiah 58:8: 'light will break forth as the morning . . . and the glory of God will clothe *you*' (καὶ ἡ δόξα τοῦ θεοῦ περιστελεῖ σε); and Isaiah 4:2: 'in that day God will shine forth with glory . . . to exalt and glorify (τοῦ ὑψῶσαι

---

[86] Cf. further 5:15; 26:5; see also Prinsloo 'Humiliation, Hubris, Humiliation' 438.
[87] I.e. the day of judgement, when 'the fearful face of the Lord [will] . . . arise to shatter the earth' (2:10).
[88] Cf. Isa. 35:4–5: 'God renders judgement . . . then the eyes of the blind will be opened'.
[89] So Aalen 'Licht und Finsternis' 226.

καὶ δοξάσαι) *the remnant of Israel'.*[90] The people of God will thus come themselves to manifest the eschatological light. In this way their suffering and judgement will work paradoxically for *their* glory![91]

The remarkable nature of this prophecy becomes even more dramatic when we consider the sheer magnitude and the startling effect of this light.[92] According to LXX Isaiah, it will be seven times brighter than the sun (30:26), eclipsing both sun and moon (60:19), and will emanate directly from God himself ('the Lord will be your everlasting light', 60:20).[93] It will precipitate an upheaval greater in scope and power than anything since the first light penetrated the primeval chaos. It will devastate the supposed 'light' of Israel's self-centredness and show it to be the profound darkness that it really is. It will reveal Israel's wisdom to be foolishness,[94] its strength weakness[95] and its truth a lie.[96] Positively, it will foster a radically new understanding of God and of the nation's relation to him.[97] It will demonstrate that he is the Creator,[98] the great 'I am',[99] the only exalted one,[100] and that the people are his creation,[101] his

---

[90] Cf. Isa. 62:2; and *Pesiq. Rab. Kah.* 21: 'The rabbis said: "God spoke to the Israelites: 'My children! . . . my light is your light and your light my light.'"'; also *1 Enoch* 104:2

[91] Cf. Isa. 61:3 where Israel's 'garment of glory' (στολίς δόξης) proceeds from a 'spirit of sorrow' (πνεῦμα ἀκηδίας) see also 44:23; 45:26; 53:4–10; 55:5. Judgement may thus be regarded as Israel's hope (28:17).

[92] Cf. 43:4; 58:10: 60:1–2.   [93] Cf. 2:5; 6:1–3.

[94] Cf. 44:25: 'The Lord . . . will turn the wise back, and make their counsel foolishness'; also 29:14b: 'I (the Lord) will destroy the wisdom of the wise, and will hide the understanding of the prudent'; see also 5:21; 19:11.

[95] So 30:15: 'When you (Israel) trusted in foolish things, your strength (ἡ ἰσχὺς ὑμῶν) became foolish' (ματαία); cf. 1:24; 3:1–2, 25; 5:22; 8:9; 21:17; 22:3.

[96] So 28:15: 'we have made falsehood (ψεῦδος) our hope'; 44:20: 'there is a lie (ψεῦδος) in my right hand'; 48:1: 'hear O house of Jacob . . . who swear by the name of the Lord . . . but not with truth' (ἀληθείας); 59:4: 'no one . . . judges truly (ἀληθινή), they trust in vanities' (ματαίοις); 59:14–15: 'truth (ἡ ἀλήθεια) is consumed in their ways . . . and truth (ἡ ἀλήθεια) has been taken away'. On trusting vainly in falsehood cf. 28:17; 30:12.

[97] See 29:24; 41:20; 43:10; 52:13, 15; 53:11; cf. 11:2; on a new γνῶσις cf. 52:6; 58:12; also 11:9 (on φῶς γνώσεως cf. Hos. 10:12; *T. Levi* 4:3; 18:3; 1QS 11:3); and cf. Seeligmann *Septuagint Version of Isaiah* 108 who suggests that in LXX Isaiah φῶς is synonymous with γνῶσις θεοῦ.

[98] So 17:7; 37:16; 42:5; 45:7–8, 11–12, 18; 48:13; cf. Harner 'Creation Faith in Deutero-Isaiah' 298–306.

[99] Cf. 43:10: 'Be my witnesses . . . that you may know and believe and understand that I am' (ἐγώ εἰμι); so 41:4; 45:19.

[100] See 2:17; 42:28; 45:21; 48:11; on there being no God besides the one, true God cf. 40:18; 43:11; 44:6–8; 45:5–6, 14, 18, 21–22; 46:5, 9.

[101] 43:1, 7; 44:2, 21, 24; 51:13; 54:5.

clay.[102] Never again will Israel pursue its old self-serving ways,[103] but will in fear seek the vastly different ways of its Maker[104] – trusting him,[105] not men,[106] glorifying him[107] (indeed making him its glory),[108] not itself.[109] No wonder the prophetical author describes the arrival of this light as a time of new creation.[110] The advent of God's glory will reverse the folly of humankind, making crooked things straight and turning darkness back into light (42:16).[111]

On the basis of this evidence it is not difficult to see how this future light came to be regarded as salvation[112] and how God, as the

---

[102] 29:16; 64:8.

[103] As in 40:27; 42:24; 53:6; 56:11; 59:7–8, 14; 63:17; 65:2; 66:3.

[104] Cf. 58:2: 'They (Israel) [will] seek me by day, and desire to know my ways'; and 42:16: 'I (the Lord) will cause them (Israel) to tread paths which they have not known'; on seeking God cf. 65:10; 51:1; 55:6; and his ways: 2:3; 64:5; and see 48:17; on turning and repenting: 46:8.

[105] See 10:20; 12:2; 17:7; 26:3–4; 41:20; 50:10; cf. 1:26. Thompson *Situation and Theology* 53 (cf. 120) rightly calls faith in the Lord 'the cardinal issue for Isaiah'.

[106] As in 32:3; 36:7–9; on trusting Egypt in particular: 30:3; or horses and chariots: 31:1; cf. 30:16.

[107] 24:14–15; 25:1; 42:12; 49:3; 60:7; 63:14.   [108] Thus 12:2.

[109] Cf. 3:18–26; 10:15; 23:9; and see 17:4.

[110] The word καινός figures prominently in Isaianic descriptions of the end times; cf. 42:9; 43:19; 48:6–8; 62:2; see also 65:17.

[111] It is worth noting that in Jer. 4:22–23 the sin of Israel causes Jeremiah to lament that the earth has become tōhû wābōhû, a clear allusion to the sinister nothingness of the beginning (Gen. 1:2). In Isaiah, too (in 34:11; 45:18–19 [cf. Clements *Isaiah* 274]), the evil of Israel engenders a condition of tōhû and bōhû (cf. Ps. 82:5; also *Gen. Rab.* II.3; XXXIII.1; and note Reisel 'Isaiah 43:7 and 45:7' 75), plunging the earth back into the bleakness of its original chaos (cf. *4 Ezra* 7:11,30; and see Foerster 'κτίζω' 1013). Only a new creation, indeed a 're-creating' light, can lift the gloom and make crooked things straight (cf. Schwantes *Schöpfung und Endzeit* 33–37). Such a renewal was the object of much speculation in later Judaism and so would have been a subject with which Paul was familiar. On a new creation in general cf. *1 Enoch* 45:4–5: 'I (God) shall transform heaven and make it a blessing of *light* forever'; 72:1: '[there will be] a new creation which abides forever'; 91:1: 'a new heaven will appear and . . . *shine* forever sevenfold'; also *Jub.* 1:29; 4:26; *2 Bar.* 32:6; 44:11–12, 15; 57:2; *4 Ezra* 7:75; *Sib. Or.* 5:273, 476–83; *T. Dan.* 5:12; *Midr. Ps.* 50.1; *Gen. Rab.* II.5 (and cf. Isa. 11 [esp. vv. 6–9]; 65:17; 66:22); on a future light cf. *1 Enoch* 1:8; 58:3–6; 92:4–5; 96:3; *Sib. Or.* 3:282–85, 787; 5:482–83; *Midr. Ps.* 22:11; 27:1–6 (cf. Dan. 12:3; Amos 5:18, 20; Hab. 3:11; Zech. 14:6; Tob. 13:11; Bar. 5:9); see Aalen *Licht und Finsternis* 318; and on the creative energy of God's glory cf. *Cant. Rab.* I.3.3: 'he who has brought a man under the wings of Shekinah (the divine glory), to him it is reckoned as if [God] had created, formed and moulded him'.

[112] Cf. Olley *Septuagint of Isaiah* 50; Aalen *Licht und Finsternis* 65, 93; on the coming salvation of Israel cf. 25:9; 33:22; 35:4; 37:20, 35; 38:20; 43:3; 45:17; 46:4, 13; 48:20; 49:26; 51:14; 52:7; 56:1; 60:16; 63:4–5, 8–9; and see esp. 10:22; 31:5; 37:32; 38:11; 40:5; 60:6 where the translator of the LXX actually adds σωτηρία/σωτήριον to the Hebrew text, revealing his distinctive interest in soteriology.

source of this light, was heralded as saviour,[113] redeemer[114] and ideal king.[115] We may note in particular Isaiah 59:20, 60:1 and 60:6, verses which comprise a single context and in which the ideas of light and deliverance are closely related:

> And the *Deliverer* will come for the sake of Zion
> (καὶ ἥξει ἕνεκεν Σιὼν ὁ ῥυόμενος)
>
> Your *light* is come . . . the glory of the Lord is upon you
> (ἥκει γάρ σου τὸ φῶς . . . ἡ δόξα Κυρίου)
>
> And [you] will proclaim the *salvation* of the Lord
> (καὶ τὸ σωτήριον κυρίου εὐαγγελιοῦνται)[116]

The terms of this salvation are consistent with what we learned above. It will be available to anyone who turns to God ('turn [ἐπιστράφητε] to me and you will be saved', 45:22)[117] and hence anyone who has eyes to see the exalted glory of Yahweh and approaches him in humility ('the humble [οἱ ταπεινοί] of the people will be saved', 14:32).[118] But it is also clear that Israel will not exhibit this kind of saving humility until it first experiences extreme affliction.[119] We thus come to a remarkable paradox in the teaching of LXX Isaiah, that the salvation of Israel will be effected through judgement;[120] and to the extent that Israel serves as a 'lamp of God's

---

[113] So 12:2; 17:10; 43:11; 45:15, 21; 62:11; 63:8.

[114] Cf. 41:14; 43:1, 14; 44:23–24; 62:12; 63:9; on God as 'deliverer' see 47:4; 48:17, 20; 49:7, 26; 50:2; 52:9; 54:5, 8; 63:5, 16.

[115] So 6:5; 9:1–7 (on this passage see Thompson 'Isaiah's Ideal King' 79–88; and cf. Knierim 'The Vocation of Isaiah' 53–54); 11:1–5.

[116] Cf. as well 40:5: 'And the glory (δόξα) of the Lord will be seen, and all flesh will see the salvation (τὸ σωτήριον) of God'; 12:2: 'for the Lord is my glory (δόξα) and my praise, and he has become my salvation' (σωτηρία); 44:23: 'for God has redeemed (ἐλυτρώσατο) Jacob, and Israel will be glorified' (δοξασθήσεται); and 46:13: 'I (God) have given salvation (σωτηρία) in Zion to Israel for glory' (δόξασμα). The link between 'glory' and 'salvation' is another distinctive feature of LXX Isaiah; cf. Brockington 'Greek Translator of Isaiah and His Interest in ΔΟΞΑ' 30–32.

[117] Cf. 55:7.

[118] Cf. 66:2: 'and whom will I look upon but the humble and meek and the one who trembles [at] my words'. On humble trust as a condition for salvation cf. 10:20: 'In that day . . . the saved of Jacob will no longer trust in [men], but . . . in the holy God of Israel'; and 20:6: 'Behold we trusted [in men] . . . how now shall we be saved?'; see also 25:9.

[119] See above pp. 120–22.

[120] See 30:15: 'When you . . . moan [because of affliction], then you will be saved'; and cf. 33:2: 'our salvation was in a time of affliction' (θλίψεως); 9:13: 'and the people did not turn until they were smitten'; 35:4: 'God renders judgement . . . then he will come and save us'; and 63:8–9: 'and he (the Lord) became to them (Israel) salvation from all their affliction' (θλίψεως).

salvation' to other nations,[121] the redemption of the entire world will come through judgement.[122] This grim reality is appropriately called the Lord's 'strange task', his 'alien work' (28:21), for who would have expected him to exalt his people through such bitter humiliation or to glorify them through such terrible darkness?[123] Yet it is precisely this paradox which undergirds the teaching of LXX Isaiah and, in particular, which lies at the heart of the verse which launched our study of Isaian glory – 'Those dwelling in the region [and] darkness of death, a light will shine upon you' (9:1).

If we are right in thinking that Paul is drawing broadly on the theme of glory in LXX Isaiah when he writes 2 Corinthians 3–4, his response to those who question the character of his ministry could hardly be more dramatic. The light which is shining in his heart (2 Corinthians 4:6) is none other than the unapproachable splendour of God's own glory, a brilliance surpassing that of the sun and a brightness not seen since creation. Indeed it is the long awaited light of the eschaton, heralding a new creation and commencing the day of salvation. As such it is a paradoxical glory, visible only to those whose pride has been shattered through judgement, a judgement precipitated by the re-creating energy of this very light.

It may be wondered whether Paul's readers in Corinth are able to appreciate the full magnitude of this glory. Are they sufficiently versed in the themes of LXX Isaiah to plumb below the surface of Paul's brief allusion to the prophet in 2 Corinthians 4:6 and grasp his deeper understanding of glory? The presence of Jewish settlers in Roman Corinth (cf. Acts 18:1, 4; Philo *Leg. Gai.* 281–82) and the corresponding probability that Jewish and proselyte converts made up a portion of Paul's congregation would seem to augur in favour of the view that some would have been able to apprehend his profound OT reference to LXX Isaiah. Indeed, it is even possible that gentile Christians would have understood, for doubtless Paul had instructed them on a theme so important as glory and from a source so strategic in the development of that theme as LXX Isaiah.

---

121 Thus τὸ σωτήριόν μου ὡς λαμπὰς, 62:1; cf. also 42:6–7 where Israel is described as 'a light (φῶς) to the nations, to open the eyes of the blind' (τυφλῶν); and see 49:6; 66:19; and Hempel 'Lichtsymbolik' 366; Aalen *Licht und Finsternis* 202–24.
122 Cf. 51:4–5: 'My (the Lord's) judgement [will be] for a light of the nations . . . a light of my salvation'; see also 52:9–10.
123 Cf. also God strengthening man through weakness: 35:3; 40:29; 41:17; 49:13; 57:15; 60:22; 61:1, 3; and see Sanders *Torah and Canon* 70–71. The crushing of Israel through judgement is thus part of the process of creating Israel anew.

We may conclude, then, that by drawing on LXX Isaiah Paul hopes to overwhelm his congregation with the fathomless dimensions of glory attending his ministry. Not only is it a light more brilliant than that of Moses and more powerful than that of creation, it is also the great eschatological glory foretold in the prophets and destined to consummate history by reversing the proud ways of humankind. The light radiating in his heart could scarcely be more pregnant with meaning.[124]

The glory of Christ

Yet the apostle Paul does see a more profound level of meaning to his glory. In 2 Corinthians 4:4 and 6, verses with parallel structures, we discover even more striking details about the nature of his glory. We must examine the two texts side by side:

v. 4	*v. 6*
ὁ θεὸς	ὁ θεὸς
τοῦ αἰῶνος τούτου	ὁ εἰπών ἐκ σκότους φῶς λάμψει
ἐτύφλωσεν	ὃς ἔλαμψεν
τὰ νοήματα τῶν ἀπίστων	ἐν ταῖς καρδίαις ἡμῶν
εἰς τὸ μὴ αὐγάσαι	πρὸς
τὸν φωτισμὸν τοῦ εὐαγγελίου	φωτισμὸν τῆς γνώσεως
τῆς δόξης τοῦ χριστοῦ	τῆς δόξης τοῦ θεοῦ
ὅς ἐστιν εἰκὼν θεοῦ	ἐν προσώπῳ Ἰησοῦ χριστοῦ

The initial words of these verses suggest that Paul is contrasting the activities of two very different gods. One cloaks the world in a veil of darkness (v. 4). The other beams his light into people's hearts (v. 6). One is identified as the god *of this age*; the other as the God *who said light will shine out of darkness* (note the first pair of italicised terms above). These qualifying phrases are so dissimilar as to suggest a breakdown in the parallelism. Yet on reflection it seems that Paul has actually constructed a neat antithesis. The god of this age perpetuates gloom; the God of a new age shines a great light. Since we now know this light to be the eschatological glory promised in Isaiah, we may conclude that the glory emanating from

---

[124] The reason why we tend to miss the link between 2 Cor. 4:6 and Isaiah, and especially the connection between Paul's view of glory and that of the translator of LXX Isaiah, is probably because we are accustomed to working with either our Hebrew Bibles or our English translations of Hebrew Bibles, and not with the LXX.

Paul's heart represents the light of the new aeon breaking into the old.

In the latter half of verses 4 and 6 Paul brings his understanding of eschatological light to a striking denouement. Drawing our insights again from the parallel structure of the two verses, we can see that Paul forges a close union between the glory of God and the gospel of Christ. He identifies the 'light of the knowledge of the glory of God' with the 'light of the gospel of the glory of Christ' (note the second pair of italicised terms above). The eschatological light promised in Isaiah would thus seem to receive its consummate fulfilment in the gospel of Christ. Hence Paul makes the remarkable assertion that the glory which was beamed into his heart is that which appeared initially and with stunning effect on the face of Jesus Christ (v. 6).[125]

Just how Paul came to identify the light of Isaiah with Christ is difficult to say. It was certainly an expectation of later Judaism that the arrival of a future Messiah would be accompanied by heavenly glory, and specifically by the eschatological glory promised in Isaiah. In *Pesiq. R.* 36.2 we read: 'Behold [the Messiah's] light which rises upon you, as is said "Arise, shine, for thy light is come, and the glory of the Lord is risen upon you" (Isa. 60:1) . . . Then they shall walk, all of them, by the light of the Messiah . . . as is said "And the nations shall walk at thy light" (Isa. 60:3)'.[126] Moreover, the rabbis awaited a Messiah who would manifest the light of creation.[127] But we do not know for sure whether Paul was acquainted with this rabbinic speculation. Others suggest that his insight into the divine light of Christ would have come from his encounter with the glorified Jesus on the Damascus Road, an incident recorded in the book of the Acts (chapter 9) and to which an allusion may be found in 2 Corinthians 4:6.[128] In any case, what

125 Thus reading ἐν προσώπῳ Ἰησοῦ χριστοῦ (A, B and 33 omit Ἰησοῦ, reading only χριστοῦ; but p[46], ℵ, C, H read Ἰησοῦ χριστοῦ and D, F, G, 0243 χριστοῦ Ἰησοῦ, making the latter two the stronger readings).

126 See further *Pesiq. R.* 36.1; 37.1; *T. Levi* 18:3–4 (a Christian passage?); *T. Ben.* 11.2; *Sib. Or.* 3:785–87; *Gen. Rab.* III.6; XII.6; *Num. Rab.* XIII.12; *Cant. Rab.* I.6; *Midr. Ps.* 27:1; 36:6; and see Michel 'Licht des Messias' 41–42; Aalen *Licht und Finsternis* 265–66, 304–5.

127 Cf. *b. Hag.* 12a; *Gen. Rab.* III.6; XXI.6; XLII.3; *Exod. Rab.* XXXV.1; *Lev. Rab.* XI.7; *Midr. Ps.* 27:1; 97:11; *Pesiq. R.* 23.6.

128 Some scholars see in the phrase ὁ θεὸς . . . ἔλαμψεν ἐν ταῖς καρδίαις ἡμῶν a reference to Paul's conversion experience on the Damascus road; thus Kim *Paul's Gospel* 7: 'the aorist ἔλαμψεν refers back to . . . the moment of the Damascus event'; see also Bruce 196; Plummer 120; Goudge 38; Strachan 92; Hughes 133–34; contra Collange 140; Windisch 140.

is important is that Paul ultimately did come to see that the glory of the future (the eschatological light of LXX Isaiah) came to stunning expression in 'the light of the gospel of the glory of Christ' (v. 4), a light which now radiated incandescently from his own ministry.

We can now see that it would have been difficult for Paul to fashion a more compelling reply to those who disparage his ministry for lacking splendour (cf. 2 Corinthians 10:7; 13:3). Not only does the glory of his ministry far surpass the light of the exalted Moses, it also represents the light of the new age and the new creation, indeed the explosive eschatological light which adorned the face of Christ himself. It is thus a glory which sets Paul on the threshold of something mighty and new, a re-creation of cataclysmic proportions, an age in which the people of God will be redeemed from the present darkness, a time when the long awaited light of the eschaton, now the light of the gospel of the glory of Christ, emanates dynamically from the ministry of Paul.

Having come to grips with Paul's understanding of glory we must now enquire about the Corinthians'. Why do they fail to perceive a splendour so overwhelming? Their view of glory must differ markedly from Paul's. But in what way? Fortunately, the apostle himself provides sufficient hints for us to be able to answer these questions. While those hints certainly reflect his personal bias, it will not hinder our enquiry. For it is in reply to the Corinthian problem as he assesses it that Paul formulates his paradoxical description of the Christian ministry in terms of power through weakness.

4

THE NATURE OF THE CHRISTIAN
MINISTRY: THE SHAME OF THE CROSS

So far we have seen that the apostle Paul views his ministry in exceedingly glorious terms. We have yet to discover why his critics do not. An important clue may be found in 2 Corinthians 4:3: 'our gospel is veiled . . . among those who are perishing'.[1] According to Paul, a veil lies over the eyes of his critics, hiding from their view the glory of his ministry and consigning them to destruction. In this chapter we shall seek to unravel the precise nature of this veil.

A useful place to start is with Paul's own pre-conversion blindness. It is no secret that the apostle himself was once veiled to the glory of the Christian gospel. On a number of occasions he concedes that he was both an enemy of Jesus and a persecutor of the church (cf. Galatians 1:13; 1 Corinthians 15:9; Philippians 2:6).[2] It was only when his heart was penetrated by divine light that the veil was lifted and his eyes were opened to the truth about Christ. If we can discover what it was that once darkened Paul's heart, perhaps we shall be able to appreciate the nature of the veil which now blinds the Corinthians.

The law

It would seem that Paul's initial hostility to Christians was the result of his intense devotion to the law of God. In a rare autobiographical reflection, Paul sums up his former life in Judaism by sandwiching the words 'as to zeal a persecutor of the church' between 'as to the law a Pharisee' and 'as to the righteousness which is in the law found blameless' (Philippians 3:5–6). The implication of these verses is that

---

[1] Bain '2 Cor. iv. 3–4' 380 suggests that ἐν τοῖς ἀπολλυμένοις here is neuter – the gospel is veiled 'by things that are perishing' (cf. Höpel '2 Cor. iv. 3–4' 428). But this is unlikely in view of the clearly masculine reading in the parallel passage of 2 Cor. 2:15.

[2] See also Acts 8:1–3; 9:4; 22:7–8; 26:9–15; and cf. 1 Tim. 1:13.

it was Paul's zealousness for the law which prompted him to persecute Christians. What was it about the law that engendered such hostility?

The curse of the law

Many scholars believe that an answer may be found in Paul's own later Christian teaching that Christ had incurred the curse of the law. By citing in Galatians 3:13 the words of LXX Deuteronomy 21:23 (κεκατηραμένος ὑπὸ θεοῦ πᾶς κρεμάμενος ἐπὶ ζύλου),[3] Paul reveals his conviction that the law pronounced a negative verdict on the way in which Christ died, his execution by crucifixion. This would explain his early hostility to Christians. When they worshipped the crucified Jesus and attributed to him the exalted title of κύριος (cf. 1 Corinthians 12:3; Romans 10:9; Philippians 2:11)[4] – a title which probably had associations with the tetragrammaton yhwh – the pharisaic Paul would have been profoundly scandalised by their blasphemy and quick to mete out stiff retribution.

Some commentators, however, reject this line of interpretation and argue that it is wrong to use Galatians 3:13 as a basis for Paul's pre-Christian attitude to Jesus. As a Pharisee, it simply would not have occurred to Paul to apply the curse of Deuteronomy to Christ, for in its OT context the curse fell on those who were killed by means other than crucifixion and whose *corpses* were posthumously hanged on trees (cf. Deuteronomy 21:22–23: 'if a man . . . is put to death, and you hang him on a tree, his corpse shall not hang all night on the tree . . . for he who is hanged is accursed of God').[5] For Paul to have used this text against Jesus would have meant extending its meaning to include one whose death was actually caused by hanging on a tree.[6]

---

[3] In Gal 3:13 Paul actually writes ἐπικατάρατος πᾶς ὁ κρεμάμενος ἐπὶ ξύλου, substituting the verbal adjective ἐπικατάρατος (which he probably borrowed from Deut. 27:26 [cf. Gal. 3:10]) for the participle κεκατηραμένος, and omitting ὑπὸ θεοῦ, possibly to avoid the idea that Christ was accursed by God.

[4] The pharisee Paul would doubtless have heard the early Christian confession Κύριος Ἰησοῦς (1 Cor. 12:3; cf. Thrall 'Pauline Christology' 308).

[5] So Lindars *Apologetic* 233; Dupont 'The Conversion of Paul' 187–88; Fredriksen 'Paul and Augustine' 11–13; Tuckett 'Deuteronomy 21, 23' 345–50. Cf. Josh 10:26, where it is specifically *dead* men who are hanged on trees, and usually those who had been stoned (cf. *m. Sanh.* 6.4).

[6] The sort of extension which early Christians *did* make: cf. Acts 5:30 where Jesus is described as one ὃν ὑμεῖς διεχειρίσασθε κρεμάσαντες ἐπὶ ζύλου (cf. 10:39) – a

But this argument neglects recent discoveries which indicate that an 'extended' meaning was already present in some sectors of early Judaism. For instance, the covenanters at Qumran seem to have envisioned a link between the curse of Deuteronomy and crucifixion. In the pesher of Nahum we read of one called 'the Lion of Wrath [who discovered a crime punishable by] death in the Seekers-after-Smooth-Things, whom he hanged as *live men* (yiṭ‘leh ᵃnāšîm ḥayyîm) [on a tree]' (4QpNah 1.6–9). Scholars generally agree that the 'Lion of Wrath' is a reference to Alexander Janneus,[7] the Sadducean high priest who in 88 BC crucified eight hundred Pharisees, the 'Seekers-after-Smooth-Things'.[8] The pesher goes on to say: 'of those hanged *alive* on a tree (kî lᵉṭālûy ḥay 'al hā'ēṣ) (Scripture) re[ads]: "Behold, I am against [you], say[s Yahweh of Hosts]"'. This quotation seems to be a clear reference to the curse of Deuteronomy 21:23[9] and hence evidence that at least one strand of early Jewish tradition applied the curse of Deuteronomy to crucifixion.[10]

The covenanters of Qumran were not alone in this application. In Philo we read that Moses 'ordered manslayers to be crucified'[11] and 'buried in the earth before the sun goes down' (*Spec. Leg.* 3.151–52). The reference to a quick burial suggests that Philo was aware of Deuteronomy 21:23 and its injunction to provide rapid interments for the cursed bodies of those who had died on trees ('his corpse shall not hang all night on the tree, but you shall surely bury him on the same day ... so that you not defile your land'). Philo, too, appears to have seen a link between Deuteronomy and crucifixion.

It would seem that by Paul's day there was a clear precedent for applying the curse of Deuteronomy 21 to one who had been executed on a cross. We may safely conclude, then, that it was indeed

---

clear reference to καὶ κρεμάσητε αὐτὸν ἐπὶ ξύλου of Deut. 21:22 (LXX); so Haenchen *Acts* 251.

[7] So Allegro 'History of the Qumran Sect' 92; Yadin 'Pesher Nahum' 1–12.

[8] On identifying the 'Seekers-after-Smooth-Things' with Pharisees cf. Jos. *A.* 13.410; Amoussine 'Péshèr de Nahum' 392–94. For the grisly incident itself see Jos. *A.* 13.380–81, 410–11; *B.* 1.92–7, 113.

[9] So Fitzmyer 'Crucifixion' 507; Wilcox 'Upon the Tree' 88.

[10] Also noteworthy is 11QTemple 64.9–12: 'if a man has committed a crime punishable by death ... you shall hang him ... on the tree and he shall die' (wtlytmh ... 'wtw 'l h'ṣ wymwt). Here again one is hanged alive on a tree, dying as a result. The scroll adds: 'for what is hanged upon the tree is accursed by God and men' – a clear reference to Deuteronomy 21 and thus a link between curse and cross.

[11] The word is actually ἀνασκολοπίζω, which may be rendered 'to impale' (LSJ 120); but since Philo uses it elsewhere with προσηλόω, 'to nail up' (*Som.* 2.213; *Post.* 61), it probably means 'to crucify'; cf. Bruce *Galatians* 164–65.

the law of God, and probably its negative verdict on the way in which Jesus had died, his execution by crucifixion, which prompted Paul's early opposition to Christians.[12]

The veil of the law

But there is a puzzling incongruity here. While the law was held to pronounce a curse on Jesus, it ought also to have pronounced a blessing. For in Jewish thinking the law represented the earthly repository of divine glory. We may note in particular the many references in Judaism to the δόξα νόμου (Bar 4:1–3 [LXX]) and the φῶς νόμου (Psalms 118:130 [LXX]; Proverbs 6:23 [LXX]; *Ps. Sol.* 18:4 ; *2 Bar.* 46:2–3; *T. Levi* 14:4 , 19:1 ; *Sifre Num.* 6:25).[13] When the divine glory suddenly appeared in the earthly figure of Jesus a student of scripture like Paul ought to have concluded that this Jesus was not only compatible with the law but also, in some sense, its fulfilment. He radiated the law's glory! That of course *was* Paul's conclusion when he was confronted personally by the divine light in the face of Jesus – this Jesus was the τέλος νόμου (Rom 10:4), the one in whom the law was consummated and to whom it must always have pointed.[14] What is astonishing is that the law did not reveal this to Paul earlier. Indeed, far from identifying Christ as the Lord of glory, it incited Paul to persecute Christians.

We can now appreciate the magnitude of Paul's confession in 2 Corinthians 4:6 that the revelation of divine glory in the face of Jesus Christ came as an 'illumination of knowledge'.[15] Formerly it

---

[12] This is the conclusion – after a careful analysis of the meaning of Deut 21:22–23 in first-century Judaism – of O. Betz 'Probleme des Prozesses Jezu' 603–11, and more briefly of Kuhn 'Jesus als Gekreuzigter' 33–34; cf. also Räisänen *Paul and the Law* 251.

[13] Further on the law bringing light to Israel cf. Ps. 19:8; Sir. 45:17; Bar. 4:1–2; 4QMess ar; *2 Bar.* 17:4; 38:1–2; *Deut. Rab.* VII.3; on darkness without the law see Sir. 32:15–16; *4 Ezra* 14:20–21; on the 'lamp' of the law cf. *2 Bar.* 59:2, 77:13–16; *Pesiq. R.* 8.5; on the study of Torah brightening one's countenance see *Lev. Rab.* XIX.1; *Qoh. Rab.* VIII.4; *Pesiq. R.* 36.1; *Pesiq. Rab. Kah.* 4; cf. also Aalen *'Licht' und 'Finsternis'* 191–95; Davies *Paul* 148. See Rom. 9:4 where Israel possesses both 'glory (δόξα) . . . and the giving of the law' (νομοθεσία).

[14] On the view that at his conversion Paul realised that Jesus Christ was the 'end of the law' cf. Stuhlmacher 'Das Ende des Gesetzes' 30; Kim *Paul's Gospel* 3–4, 126, 307–8; Dunn 'Light to the Gentiles' 257.

[15] Cf. φωτισμὸν τῆς γνώσεως in 2 Cor. 4:6, where the word φωτισμός can mean simply 'light' (cf. LXX Job. 3:9; Ps. 26:1; 43:4; 77:14; 89:8: 138:11) or with the epexegetical genitive τῆς γνώσεως (cf. Barrett 134) a light which consists of knowledge, hence an 'illumination'.

would have been unthinkable to associate divine glory with one whom the law had cursed. Now, as a young convert, Paul must have puzzled long and hard over how his devotion to the law could have led him to oppose one who so completely fulfilled the law. How could a devout exponent of the law have been so blinded to Jesus Christ? It will be important to discover how the apostle answers this question, for it could well shed light on what he sees as the present blindness of the Corinthians.

The failure of the law

Some scholars doubt whether Paul ever answers the question. E. P. Sanders, for example, maintains that Paul never explains how or why the law failed but merely condemns it broadly for not being Christ.[16] Yet this neglects the fact that in Paul's mind there was something vastly more insidious about the law than its not being Christ – namely, its failure to reveal Christ. The great tragedy of Paul's pre-conversion experience, a tragedy which he never forgets nor allows his readers to forget, is that he was not merely ignorant of Christ but also actively hostile to Christ, indeed a persecutor of Christians (cf. 1 Corinthians 15:9; Galatians 1:13; Philippians 3:6) – and that this was in some sense the result of his devotion to the law.[17] We must turn to Paul's critique of the law.

In 2 Corinthians 3:12–18 the apostle laments that Israel is unable to see divine glory and suggests that its blindness is due to a hardness of mind: 'their minds were hardened, for until this very day at the reading of the old covenant the same veil remains unlifted' (v. 14). The cause of this hardening is not here revealed; there is no subject for the passive verb ἐπωρώθη. But in Romans 11:7–8, another text dealing with Israel's hardness and the only other place where Paul uses the verb πωρόω, a subject is given – namely, God:

And the rest [of Israel] were hardened (ἐπωρώθησαν);
    just as it is written,
    'God gave them a spirit of stupor,

---

16 Thus *PPJ* 551, 552: 'what went wrong with the law is that it is not Christ'; 'what Paul finds wrong in Judaism [is that] it is not Christianity'; and *PLJP* 47: 'what he (Paul) finds wrong in Judaism is that it lacks Christ'; see also van Dülmen *Theologie des Gesetzes* 178–79.
17 Cf. Gal. 1:13–14 where Paul's persecution of the church is bound closely to τὴν ἐμὴν ἀναστροφήν ποτε ἐν τῷ Ἰουδαϊσμῷ; and Phil 3:6, where it is linked to κατὰ δικαιοσύνην τὴν ἐν νόμῳ γενόμενος ἄμεμπτος.

Eyes to see not and ears to hear not,
Down to this very day'

In these verses Paul is quoting from two texts in the Septuagint,
Isaiah 29:10 and Deuteronomy 29:3, each of which also ascribes
Israel's hardness to the Lord. This would suggest that the verb
ἐπωρώθησαν in Romans 11:7 is meant to be taken as a divine
passive.[18] Perhaps the verb ἐπωρώθη in 2 Corinthians 3:14 is meant
to be interpreted similarly, for there Paul also seems to have Deuteronomy 29:3 in mind, citing the LXX phrase ἕως τῆς ἡμέρας
ταύτης in both 3:14 and 15.[19] If so, the failure of the law to reveal
divine glory is doubtless the result of a veil which God himself has
placed over Israel's heart.

The idea that Israel's blindness is the product of divine hardening
might at first seem to be in conflict with what Paul says later in the
same context, that it is 'the god of this age,' namely Satan, who
blinds the minds of unbelievers (2 Corinthians 4:4). Yet elsewhere
Paul implies that God sometimes accomplishes his work through the
activity of Satan (cf. 2 Corinthians 12:7; 1 Corinthians 5:5).

At least on one level, then, the blindness which afflicts Israel is the
work of God himself. This would explain why a divine revelation is
necessary – in Paul's case a shaft of divine light – to root out the
spiritual darkness (cf. 2 Corinthians 4:6). Yet we must not neglect
the countervailing suggestion that the act of unveiling also depends
on human action. In 2 Corinthians 3:16 we read that 'the veil is
taken away whenever *one turns to the Lord*'. This would indicate
that there is a sense in which Israel itself must act to remove the veil.
There must be, then, a second level on which Paul addresses the
question, How did the law fail? – namely, the human level. We turn
now to two passages which approach the question from a specifically anthropocentric perspective.

In Philippians 3:2–9 the apostle reflects on his early life in
Judaism[20] and contrasts it sharply with his present existence in
Christ. As a Pharisee he placed confidence in the flesh, now he
boasts in Christ (v. 3); formerly he sought prestige for himself, now
he loses honour for Christ's sake (v. 7); once he pursued his own
righteousness through law, now he seeks the righteousness of God

---

[18] Thus Cranfield *Romans* 2. 549; Michel *Römer* 342.
[19] The citations are loose: in v. 14 he writes ἄχρι γὰρ τῆς σήμερον ἡμέρας and in
v. 15 ἀλλ᾿ ἕως σήμερον; cf. Rom. 11:8 (a verbatim citation of LXX Deut 29:3)
ἕως τῆς σήμερον ἡμέρας.
[20] Cf. the past tense ἦν in v. 7.

through Christ (v. 9). It is obvious that Paul is contrasting a former
life in which his focus was squarely on himself to a present existence
in which his eyes are firmly on Christ. He was formerly too self-
absorbed to give proper honour to Christ.[21] If we ask why this was
so his answer would seem to be that the law itself encouraged such
self-absorption. It was zeal for ancestral traditions which prompted
him to be obsessed with his rising status in Judaism (cf. Galatians
1:14). It was his quest to be found blameless before the law which led
him to regard the righteousness of God as though it were his own
(Phil 3:6, 9). It was his zeal for the law which led him to put
confidence in the flesh (πεποίθησις ἐν σαρκί, 3:4) and not boast in
Christ (καύχησις ἐν χριστῷ Ἰησοῦ, Philippians 3:3).

In the light of the attention paid recently to Paul's critique of the
law it is perhaps wise to spell out more carefully exactly what he is
and is not saying about the law. On the one hand, he is not faulting
the law for encouraging salvation by merit and self-effort,[22] nor
merely for failing to be 'worth anything in comparison with . . .
Christ',[23] nor primarily for engendering national righteousness and
pride.[24] Instead he is faulting the law for causing people to be proud
of what they have received – their righteousness, their Jewish standing, even their individual accomplishments (Phil 3:5–6) – and hence
to act as though they had not received, as though, in Paul's own
self-incriminating words, τὴν ἐκ θεοῦ δικαιοσύνην were really ἐμὴν
δικαιοσύνην (3:9).[25] This is very different from saying with the
traditional view that the law led Paul to think that he could earn his
own righteousness. As a good Jew he knew he could not.[26] It is
rather to suggest that the law, by encouraging Paul to be proud of
the righteousness which he knew intellectually came from God,
effectively led him to regard that righteousness as his own.[27]

---

[21] The contrast between self-centredness and Christ-centredness is brought out
clearly in v. 7: ἅτινα ἦν μοι κέρδη, ταῦτα ἥγημαι διὰ τὸν χριστὸν ζημίαν.

[22] The view of Bultmann *Theology* 1. 261–65; (cf. Hübner *Law* 15, 18, 152), rightly
criticised by Sanders *PPJ* 481–82.

[23] Sanders' *PPJ* 500 own position (cf. Räisänen *Paul and the Law* 168, 174).

[24] Though the corporate pride of Israel was certainly part of the problem fostered by
the law; on this view cf. Wright 'Paul of History' 65; and Dunn 'New Perspective
on Paul' 95–122; 'Works of the Law' 523–42.

[25] Cf. the similar problem (though without the stimulus of law) in 1 Cor. 4:6–7,
where Paul reminds the Corinthians that what they are they owe to God (cf. 1 Cor.
1:30).

[26] Here Sanders' point is well taken.

[27] Thus to deny that the fault of the law was to inspire meritorious righteousness is
not also to deny that the law engendered personal pride and boasting, a distinction
Sanders *PLJP* 44 fails to make.

The lesson is similar in Romans 9:30–10:12. Here Paul laments the performance of his people, the Jews, under law. They have pursued a law of righteousness, but never attained it (9:31), expressed a zeal for God, but without understanding (10:2). Their problem is well summed up in 9:32a – they have sought righteousness οὐκ ἐκ πίστεως ἀλλ᾿ ὡς ἐξ ἔργων (9:32a). That is to say, as 10:3 makes clear, their pursuit of righteousness has not been marked by humble submission to God (οὐκ ὑπετάγησαν [10:3c] = οὐκ ἐκ πίστεως [9:32a]).[28] Instead they have become arrogant and proud, *as though* they were establishing 'their own righteousness' (τὴν ἰδίαν δικαιοσύνην ζητοῦντες [10:3b] = ὡς ἐξ ἔργων [9:32a]).[29] Israel's zeal for the law has thus caused it to commit the very error acknowledged personally by Paul in Philippians 3, the sin of revelling in its righteousness as though it were its own accomplishment. This is a grave offence, for it amounts to using for its own honour a righteousness which was meant for God's.[30]

The last time we encountered Israel usurping the honour of God in this way was in our study of Isaiah.[31] There we learned that in exalting itself Israel necessarily lost sight of the exaltedness of God. Now in Romans 10 we discover a similar idea. In seeking to exhibit its own righteousness Israel naturally misses the righteousness of God (Rom 10:3).[32] But there is another consequence of Israel's pride: namely, that it also misses God's Messiah, Jesus Christ, 'the end of the law for righteousness to all who believe' (v. 4). The two-fold nature of Israel's blindness is underscored in verses 6–8. Speaking metaphorically, Paul compares his compatriots to those

---

[28] The frequent use of πίστις in Phil. 3 and Rom. 9–10 is instructive. It denotes humble trust in God.

[29] The contrast here between 'God's righteousness' and 'their own righteousness' is thus explained by the phrase τῇ δικαιοσύνῃ τοῦ θεοῦ οὐκ ὑπετάγησαν: by failing to seek righteousness in a *humble* and *submissive* manner, Israel arrived at its own righteousness, not God's, and hence no righteousness at all (cf. Rom. 9:31: 'Israel, pursuing a law of righteousness, did not attain [that] law [of righteousness]'). *Pace* Sanders *PLJP* 37–38.

[30] Commenting on Rom. 9:30–10:13, Sanders *PLJP* 37 maintains that 'Israel's failure is not that it does not obey the law in the correct way, but that it does not have faith in Christ'; their problem is not anthropological, but christological (cf. Räisänen *Paul and the Law* 168–69). But this is to pose a false dichotomy. Israel's law-inspired pride and its lack of faith in Christ are, as we have seen, different sides of the same coin: anthropology and christology are intertwined.

[31] See above pp. 117–120.

[32] Of course in Isaiah Israel's blindness was due to disobedience to the law (cf. Isa. 42:24), whereas in Rom. 10 it is due to self-righteous obedience. In both cases pride serves as the basis of blindness.

who search for righteousness in the heights of heaven (v. 6) and in the depths of the abyss (v. 7), unaware that it is immediately before them in the gospel which he preaches, the gospel of the right-eousness of Christ (v. 8).

These verses also disclose the reason for Israel's blindness. In citing the injunction 'Do not say in your heart ... "Who shall ascend into heaven?" ... "Who shall descend into the pit?"' (10:6–7), Paul lifts the first six words – μὴ εἴπῃς ἐν τῇ καρδίᾳ σου – directly from LXX Deuteronomy 8:17 and 9:4, verses which in their original contexts serve to warn Israel against pride and boasting.[33] By quoting these words here Paul reveals his conviction that the warning against egotism is just as pertinent to contemporary Israel. His fellow-countrymen have become proud, and it is because of their pride that they are unable to see the righteousness of Christ in their midst.

This may help to explain what Paul sees as the blindness of his rivals in 2 Corinthians. If the opponents are of Jewish extraction and possibly even schooled in the teachings of Judaism, as Paul seems to imply in 2 Corinthians 11:22, they could well be afflicted (he would think) by the same veil which blinded the pharisaic Paul before his conversion. In their zeal to uphold the law they may have been smitten by the very pride which blinded Paul to the great end and goal of the law, namely, the glory of God in the face of Jesus Christ. Naturally, as self-proclaimed servants of Christ (cf. 2 Corinthians 1:23), they would reject such a suggestion and eagerly affirm the proposition that divine glory now appears pre-eminently in Jesus. But for Paul their affirmation would lack substance. Their law-engendered pride has caused them to miss the peculiar sort of glory which radiates from the exalted Christ.

It will be helpful now to summarise our findings. Both the phari-saic Paul and first-century Israel, and perhaps even his present opponents, suffered (the apostle would think) from an acute insen-sitivity to divine glory. In particular, they were veiled to the true identity of Jesus Christ. According to Paul, such blindness was linked directly to an intense devotion to the law. His own zeal for the Torah had promulgated in him an irresistible urge to exalt himself, the sort of urge which, as we have seen in our study of LXX Isaiah, always blinds one to the exaltedness and glory of God. It was thus a law-engendered pride which veiled Paul to the glory of Christ.

---

[33] So Cranfield *Romans* 2. 523.

It would require a divinely-inspired revelation to eradicate that veil, in particular, a shaft of heavenly light beamed into his heart. Only then would he be empowered to see what he had hitherto missed, the divine glory in the face of Jesus Christ.

To understand the nature of this veil still further we must consider how exactly the divine light served to open Paul's eyes.

The Messiah

In 2 Corinthians 3:14 Paul explains how one comes to see the glory of the Lord: '[the veil] is removed in Christ'. If we take the emphatic dative term ἐν χριστῷ in an inclusive and titular sense we may translate: 'the veil is abolished in solidarity with the Messiah'.[34] In principle, first-century Israel would have been eager to link its destiny to a Messiah, an anointed one of God. But it would have rebelled vigorously at the thought of solidarity with Jesus Christ. That was because Jesus singularly failed to accomplish what Israel expected of one appointed by God. It will be helpful to examine the nature of Israel's expectations.

Future expectations: the glory of a new age

We know that the principal expectation of many first-century Jews was that of a coming new age. They eagerly awaited a time when God would re-assert his rule over the earth and restore his people to the position of honour they enjoyed in the days of David.[35] Naturally they longed to share in the glory of such an age and they prayed fervently for its arrival (cf. the first-century Kaddish prayer: 'May he establish his kingdom in your lifetime and in your days'[36]). There may also have been a lesser expectation of an individual whom God would appoint to help in the inauguration of that age.[37] This person

---

[34] Taking ἐν χριστῷ locatively, see Wright *Colossians* 47, 63.

[35] The Jewish literature, especially apocalyptic, is filled with speculation about a coming age. On the future reign of God see Dan. 2:44; 4:17, 25, 32; *Sib. Or.* 3:47–48, 175–79; *As. Mos.* 10:1; 1QM 6:6; *Ps. Sol.* 17:3; on the subjugation of enemies: *Ps. Sol.* 17:24–25; *Jub.* 23:30; *1 Enoch* 71:14–17; on the glory of the new kingdom: *1 Enoch* 62:2; 91.7–16; *4 Ezra* 7:112; on the new age generally: *1 Enoch* 47:1–4; 96:8; *2 Enoch* 50:2; 61:2; 66:6; *Jub.* 1:22–25, 27, 29; *4 Ezra* 6:9; 7:47, 113; 8:1; and for discussion see Rowland *Open Heaven* 156–76.

[36] The citation is reproduced in Jeremias *New Testament Theology* 198.

[37] Cf. *Ps. Sol.* 17–18; *2 Bar.* 70:1–10; *4 Ezra* 12:32–34; on the glory of the Elect One see *1 Enoch* 45:3–4; cf *Ps. Sol.* 17:31. But the important point, stressed by Harvey

would, according to a few reports, assist in the overthrow of foreign oppressors and in the restoration of Israel to its former eminence.[38] He would personify the nation's fondest aspirations.

It is doubtless these expectations which explain the reticence of many to accept Jesus the Christ. How could he be God's appointed when he so completely failed to inaugurate the new age? Far from manifesting divine glory, he seemed to bear a divine curse. Far from purging the nation of pagan domination, he succumbed to a pagan cross. The latter detail would have been especially repugnant to first-century Israel. Still fresh on its mind was the bitter memory of mass crucifixions of Jews under the repressive regimes of the Seleucid king Antiochus Epiphanes IV in 175 BC[39] and the Roman general Varus in 4 BC.[40] It was precisely this kind of barbarity that a representative of God would avenge. To suggest that a Messiah had endured a similar fate was not only intolerable but made a mockery of Jewish expectations. It effectively nailed those expectations to a cross. No self-respecting Jew could accept such a Messiah.[41]

Jesus 77–79, 136, 145, is that the new age took priority in Jewish minds over a person appointed by God to bring it.

[38] On the glory which Israel would receive in the new age cf. Dan. 12:3; Bar. 5:1, 3; 1QS 4:7–8; CD 3:20; 1QH 17:15; *1 Enoch* 5:7–9; 38:2, 4; 50:1–5; 58:3–6; 62:14–16; 96:3; 104:2; *2 Enoch* 22:8–9; *3 Enoch* 12:1–2; *Jub.* 1:29; *2 Bar.* 15:8; 51:3, 5, 10; 54:15–16, 21; *Sib. Or.* 3:282; *4 Ezra* 7:96–8; 8:51; *T. Levi* 18:9; *Mart. Isa.* 7:25; 9:9; *Midr. Ps.* 27:1.

[39] For the poignant account see Josephus *A.* 12.256: '[the Jews] were whipped, their bodies were mutilated, and while still alive and breathing, they were crucified (ἀνεσταυροῦντο), while their wives and their sons . . . were strangled, the children being made to hang from the necks of their crucified parents'. In the words of the author of *The Assumption of Moses*, this was 'a visitation and wrath such as had not befallen [the Jews] from the beginning' (8:1). Cf. the report of 'Antiochus' slaughter of the Jews' in 1 Macc. 1:48, 60, 61.

[40] Cf. again Josephus *B.* 2.75: 'Varus now detached part of his army to scour the country in search of the [Jewish] authors of the insurrection, many of whom were brought in . . . , the most culpable [of whom], in number about two thousand, he crucified' (ἀνεσταύρωσεν; cf. Jos. *A.* 17.295; also *As. Mos.* 6:9).

Crucifixion of the Jews continued under Cumanus in AD 48–52 (Jos. *A.* 20.129; *B.* 2.241), Felix in AD 54 ('of those whom he crucified [ἀνασταυρωθέντων] . . . the number was incalculable', Jos. *B.* 2.253), Florus in AD 66 ('many of the peaceful [Jewish] citizens were arrested and . . . scourged and then crucified . . . , the total number of that day's victims . . . amounted to about 3,600', Jos. *B.* 2.306–7; cf. 2.308) and, finally, Titus in AD 70 ('[Jewish rebels] were accordingly scourged and subjected to torture of every description, before being killed, and then crucified (ἀνεσταυροῦντο) . . . , and so great was their number that space could not be found for the crosses or crosses for the bodies', Jos. *B.* 5.449–51; cf. 5.289).

[41] Israel thus rejected Jesus not because he failed to conform to a set of well defined 'messianic expectations' – there probably were no such expectations – but because God did not inaugurate a powerful and glorious new age while Jesus was alive.

If the Jewish notion of a Messiah was more developed than what we have just suggested, if for example the people of Israel were looking specifically for a royal Messiah from the line of David, then their reasons for resisting Jesus would have been all the more formidable.[42] Such a figure would, like David, represent the nation in an inclusive manner.[43] What would be true of him would be true of them.[44] To suggest that Jesus was the Davidic heir would require far more than accepting that he merely personified the nation's aspirations. It would mean acknowledging that he summed up the nation in himself – that in his death the whole nation had effectively died. No one in his right mind would willingly embrace such a Messiah. In order to escape the indignity and the curse of his cross Jesus would have been rejected out of hand.

This brief assessment of the expectations of Israel receives potent support from the pen of Paul in Romans 9:32–33, where he suggests that Israel has 'stumbled over' its Messiah:[45]

> As it is written,
> 'Behold I am laying in Zion a stone of stumbling
>   and a rock of offence
> And the one who believes in it [or him] shall not
>   be ashamed' (v. 33)

This verse represents a skilful conflation of two passages from the Septuagint, Isaiah 8:14a and Isaiah 28:16. The structure and content of Paul's words derive basically from Isaiah 28:16, except at one crucial point where he replaces the 'precious corner stone' of 28:16 with the 'stone of stumbling' of 8:14a.[46] For Jews familiar with the OT Paul's point would have been inescapable. They have mistaken the costly foundation stone, their Messiah, for a stone of stumbling. They have regarded what was laid up in Zion for their good as a rock for their offence.

But there is a profound irony in Israel's antipathy to Jesus. The

---

[42] On the evidence for a Davidic Messiah in the inter-Testamental period cf. *Ps. Sol.* 17:21–32; *Shemoneh Esreh* 15 (Bab. rec.) and 14 (Pal. rec; though see Harvey *Jesus* 128); 4QPBless; 4Q 161; also 4QFlor 1:11–12; cf. Vermes *Jesus the Jew* 130–34; and Horbury 'Messianic Associations' 39–40.

[43] Cf. 2 Sam 19:12–13 where David refers to Israel as '*my* bone and *my* flesh' (see also 2 Sam. 5:1; 1 Chr. 11:1); and 2 Sam. 20:1 where the rebellious Sheba asserts that 'we have no portion *in David*, nor do we have inheritance *in the son of Jesse*.' These passages suggest that David was regarded as Israel's inclusive representative.

[44] Cf. Wright *Messiah* 11–13; Caird 'Paul's Theology' 738.

[45] Cf. Barrett *Romans* 194; Michel *Römer* 322; Lagrange *Romains* 250.

[46] Cf. the analysis of Paul's use of Isaiah here by Evans 'Romans 9–11' 563–66.

very 'Messiah' who causes them to stumble is, according to Paul, the only one through whom they can regain their sight. This, we may recall, is the message of 2 Corinthians 3:14. It is in solidarity with Jesus the Messiah that the veil can be removed. We are now in a position to understand the inner logic of this unveiling.

Future salvation: the shame of the cross

In our study of Isaiah we learned that the pride of Israel would one day be crushed in a humiliating judgement. We also discovered that such a judgement would have the supreme corollary effect of opening Israel's eyes to the exalted glory of God. It is worth noting that Paul refers to the death of Christ as a divine judgement on sin. 'God . . . judged (κατέκρινεν) sin[47] in the flesh [of his son]' (Rom 8:3). This suggests that the apostle sees a connection between the death of Jesus and the judgement foretold in Isaiah. If so, such a link would have had a devastating effect on religious Jews of the first century. It would have meant not only that their Messiah had suffered the curse of crucifixion, but also that in Jesus, the inclusive Messiah, they *themselves* had been judged and subjected to the shame of crucifixion. By participating in the judgement pronounced on the representative Christ they would have been profoundly humbled. But as we learned in our study of LXX Isaiah, that was precisely the intent of the coming judgement – it was meant so to humble God's people that they would forget about their own glory and focus exclusively on his.

In Paul's mind the promises of Isaiah find striking fulfilment in Jesus Christ. It is Christ who brings salvation through judgement, who crushes Israel's pride and renews its humility, who opens Israel's eyes to the glory of the Lord, who re-creates the people according to God's image, who accomplishes God's 'strange task' and 'alien work' (Isa. 28:21). The eschatological light has arrived – in Jesus Christ – and so is a paradoxical light. Instead of bringing judgement and radiating salvation through a dazzling display of force and splendour, it accomplishes its dramatic work through the humility of a shameful cross.

It is perhaps the very profundity of this paradox which enables us to reconcile the two apparently incongruous reasons for Israel's

---

[47] Presumably this includes Israel's sin; so Wright *Messiah* 154–55; Cranfield *Romans* 1. 382).

blindness examined earlier in the chapter: divine hardening and human pride. Perhaps God is seen by Paul as having achieved the hardening of Israel by choosing to manifest his glory precisely where Israel, in its pride, would refuse to see it. In that way it could be ensured that when Israel did come to see the glory it would be on God's terms – when Israel had been humbled sufficiently to see the glory in the ignominy of the cross.

Just how this glory served to illuminate Paul personally is recorded in 2 Corinthians. According to the apostle's own admission, he once viewed Christ κατὰ σάρκα (2 Corinthians 5:16) – that is, according to self-seeking desires aroused by the law. Like his fellow countrymen, he had been awaiting a new age in which God would restore the nation of Israel to its former grandeur and eminence. But the revelation of divine glory put an end to such self-regarding ambitions. It made Paul see that an anointed one had come in the person of the crucified Jesus and that in this inclusive Messiah all had died (εἷς ὑπὲρ πάντων ἀπέθανεν, ἄρα οἱ πάντες ἀπέθανον, 2 Corinthians 5:14). This proved to be a radical 'illumination of knowledge' (4:6), for it meant that he, Paul, had himself been crucified with Christ, together with his self-centred passions and desires (cf. Galatians 5:24: οἱ δὲ τοῦ χριστοῦ Ἰησοῦ τὴν σάρκα ἐσταύρωσαν σὺν τοῖς παθήμασιν καὶ ταῖς ἐπιθυμίαις). In Christ he had therefore become a new creature, the old things passed away, new things had come (2 Corinthians 5:17). He no longer sought his own advantage, but lived for him who died and rose for him (5:14). He was reconciled to God (5:18–19). Profoundly humbled, he could now see the Lord's glory (4:6).

Conclusion

We may now return to the question posed at the outset of this chapter, Why, in Paul's view, are his critics veiled to his glory? Perhaps it is because they have been smitten by the same veil which once darkened the heart of the pre-Christian Paul – the veil of self-exaltation and pride. If the church in Corinth included a contingent of Jewish or proselyte converts, many could have been influenced by the same sort of Jewish environment which, with its intense devotion to the law and its lofty eschatological expectations, had engendered pride in Paul and erected his veil. In addition, Gentile Christians would not have been immune to such a veil, for they were party to a Graeco-Roman milieu which, as we saw in our historical study of chapter two, was every bit as egocentric as anything the pharisaic Paul had encountered. Could it be, then, that Jew and Gentile alike were imbibing a self-regarding outlook? And is it possible that the opponents were exploiting this outlook in order to win the favour of Corinthian Christians? We will test the hypothesis in the next chapter.

5

THE PATTERN OF THE CHRISTIAN
MINISTRY: GLORY THROUGH SHAME

In the last two chapters we have examined Paul's verdict on those
who fail to appreciate the superlative glory of his ministry. In a
word, a veil has darkened their vision (2 Corinthians 4:3). This
could well be the veil of self-exaltation and pride, like Paul's own
veil before his conversion. To test this theory we must discover two
things: how divine glory is actually manifested in Paul and how such
a manifestation would have been viewed by those enmeshed in the
environment of first-century Corinth. In the first half of the chapter
we shall consider Paul's understanding of how his glory works out
in practice. In the second half we shall consider how his converts
interpret that glory. By finding answers to these questions we shall
be in a position to make sense of Paul's paradoxical teaching of
power through weakness.

Transformed into the image of the cross

We may begin by considering Paul's own description of the glory
manifested in his ministry. The most illuminating text is 2 Corinthians
3:18:

> ἡμεῖς δὲ πάντες ἀνακεκαλυμμένῳ προσώπῳ τὴν δόξαν
> κυρίου κατοπτριζόμενοι τὴν αὐτὴν εἰκόνα μετα-
> μορφούμεθα ἀπὸ δόξης εἰς δόξαν, καθάπερ ἀπὸ κυρίου
> πνεύματος.

This verse presents many interpretive difficulties, each of which
must be resolved before the text as a whole can be understood.

First is the meaning of the participial phrase ἀνακεκαλυμμένῳ
προσώπῳ. The word ἀνακαλύπτω is used once elsewhere in the NT,
notably four verses earlier in 2 Corinthians 3:14 where Paul employs
it to explain why Israel fails to see the glory of the Lord – it is

βεψαυσε 'τηε ϑειλ . . . ρεμαινσ υνλιφτεδ (μένει μὴ ἀνακαλυπτόμε-νον).[1] He then prescribes a remedy for such a veil: 'it is abolished in Christ' (v. 14). The logic of this unveiling was examined in the last chapter. The one who is 'in Christ', who shares in the judgement pronounced on the crucified Messiah, is so humbled and divested of pride that he is able to see the exalted glory of the Lord. By using the perfect participle ἀνακεκαλυμμένῳ of himself in verse 18, Paul directs our attention to the moment of *his* 'unveiling', his co-crucifixion with Christ, and discloses the principal ongoing result of that mutual death, clarity of vision.

This interpretation of ἀνακεκαλυμμένῳ in turn sheds light on the meaning of the second participle κατοπτριζόμενοι.[2] Commentators have long debated whether this word should be translated 'reflecting as a mirror does'[3] or 'beholding as in a mirror'.[4] Our understanding of ἀνακεκαλυμμένῳ would suggest the latter. Uppermost in Paul's mind is the fact that the veil is gone and he can now see. The opening words of verse 18, ἡμεῖς δὲ πάντες, seem to confirm this interpretation. They serve to contrast Paul (and his fellow believers) with Israel, his unveiled face with Israel's veiled heart, his ability to see with Israel's blindness (cf. 3:14–15).[5] Hence the first half of 2 Corinthians 3:18 affirms what we discovered in the last chapter, that in dying with Christ one is enabled to see the glory of the Lord.

When we turn to the latter half of the verse we break new ground in our study, and in the area which concerns us most – how the divine glory is manifested in Paul. The verse may be paraphrased as

---

[1] Hence the translation of Barrett 120, Furnish 209 and Windisch 122 who take the neuter participle with κάλυμμα. The alternative is to regard μὴ ἀνακαλυπτόμενον as absolute (cf. BDF § 424): 'the veil remains, it not being revealed that . . . ' (so Allo 91; Collange 98–99).

[2] A *hapaxlegomenon* in the NT, though see ἔσοπτρον in 1 Cor. 13:12 and Jas 1:23.

[3] Thus Dupont 'Le chrétien, miroir de la gloire divine' 392–411; van Unnik 'With Unveiled Face' 167–8; Caird 'Everything to Everyone' 392; Allo 96; Plummer 105–6.

[4] Cf. Hugedé *La métaphore du miroir* 20–24; Wilckens *Weisheit* 74; Collange 116–18; Furnish 214; Wolff 77; Windisch 128; Kümmel 200. Bultmann 93–97 (cf. Hughes 119 n. 19) translates κατοπτρίζω, 'to see', without reference to a mirror; but see Philo *Leg. All.* 3.101, where a mirror is clearly implied (so Brooke 98). Wright 'Reflected Glory' 145 argues that the mirror in which Christians see the reflected glory of the Lord is not Jesus Christ, but one another.

[5] So Barrett 124–25; Furnish 213, 239; Bultmann 93–94. Others argue that Paul's use of πρόσωπον in 3:18 suggests that the contrast is between Paul and Moses (cf. 3:13): the 'face' of Moses is veiled whereas Paul's is not (so Plummer 105–6). The most likely solution is that Paul intends 'a double contrast', with both Israel and Moses (so Windisch 127).

follows: Since we behold with unveiled face the glory of the Lord we are being transformed into the same image.[6] The expression τὴν αὐτὴν εἰκόνα is surprising here. We would have expected τὴν αὐτὴν δόξαν, since (i) the adjective τὴν αὐτὴν clearly refers back to the term τὴν δόξαν κυρίου[7] and (ii) the word δόξα has already appeared some eight times in the context (in 3:7–11). Why does Paul suddenly shift to εἰκών?[8] Moreover, what does he mean by the phrase 'transformed into the same image'? Here a detailed look at the verb μεταμορφόω is instructive.

Transformation

Many scholars believe that Paul has borrowed this term from the hellenistic mystery religions where transformation into the image of the gods was a prominent theme.[9] Others suggest that the apostle is indebted more to Jewish backgrounds, and especially to the recurring apocalyptic idea that one day the elect will be transformed. We read in *2 Bar.* 51 , for example, that '[the elect] will be transformed into the light of their beauty' (v. 3), 'they will be changed into the splendour of angels' (v. 5), 'they will be changed into . . . the splendour of glory' (v. 10).[10] Rather than choose between these two traditions, perhaps we should view Paul as borrowing from both, drawing the word μεταμορφόω itself from the hellenistic milieu but filling it with Jewish meaning. Regardless of origin, however, we cannot be confident of the term's meaning until we have examined its usage elsewhere in Paul.

In the entire pauline corpus the word μεταμορφόω occurs elsewhere only in Romans 12:2. There Paul exhorts his readers to be 'transformed by the renewing of the mind' (μεταμορφοῦσθε τῇ

---

[6] The participles ἀνακεκαλυμμένῳ and κατοπτριζόμενοι are subordinated causally to the main verb μεταμορφούμεθα, and τὴν αὐτὴν εἰκόνα points to both the manner and the goal of the transformation (Robertson *Grammar* 486, 530).

[7] Cf. Lambrecht 'Transformation' 243–46.

[8] We are assuming here that 'image' and 'glory' are not identical; cf. de Lacey 'Form of God' 56, 62; *pace* Larsson *Christus als Vorbild* 280–81.

[9] Cf. an initiate into the cult of Isis at Corinth named Lucius who, on seeing the brilliant light of the gods, began to shine himself (Apul. *Met.* 11.23–24). On the hellenistic derivation of μεταμορφόω see Behm 'μεταμορφόω' 763–67; Reitzenstein *Mysterienreligionen* 158–9, 208–9; Lietzmann 113–4; Windisch 129.

[10] Cf. also *1 Enoch* 50:1; 58:3–6; 62:16; 108:11–14; *2 Bar.* 48:49; 54:15; and see Furnish 240–41. Further on the future glory of the elect see above p. 140, n. 38. For the motif of being transformed through sight at Qumran cf. Fitzmyer 'Glory' 640–44.

ἀνακαινώσει τοῦ νοὸς). Transformation thus appears to consist of a change of one's mind. The precise nature of this change is perhaps hinted at in Colossians 3:10, a verse roughly parallel to Romans 12:2, in which the new self is said to be renewed according to the image of God (τὸν ἀνακαινούμενον εἰς ἐπίγνωσιν κατ' εἰκόνα τοῦ κτίσαντος). This bears a striking resemblance to 2 Corinthians 3:18, where the apostle implies that the goal of his transformation is to reflect τὴν αὐτὴν εἰκόνα, that is, the image of the Lord. Taken together, the three verses – 2 Corinthians 3:18, Romans 12:2 and Colossians 3:10 – manifest a common thread, namely that transformation entails a remoulding of a person, especially of a person's mind, according to the image of God. We must learn more about Paul's understanding of the divine image.

Adam and Christ

It is natural to suppose that Paul derived his notion of God's image from Genesis 1:26 where it is reported that God created man κατ' εἰκόνα ἡμετέραν καὶ καθ' ὁμοίωσιν (LXX).[11] These words have been much interpreted, but probably mean no more than what they explicitly say, that man was created in 'a relation of likeness to God'.[12] Later the rabbis, doubtless reflecting on what God is like, added a second dimension to God's image, that of glory. We see this in the rabbinic picture of Adam. As one created in God's likeness, Adam manifested superlative glory.[13] When R. Bana'ah 'came to the cave of Adam,[14] a voice came forth from heaven saying "Thou hast beholden the likeness of my likeness"' – an experience which prompted R. Bana'ah to declare, 'I have discerned his [Adam's] two heels, and they were like two orbs of the sun' (*b. B. Bat.* 58a).[15] We may compare the view of R. Levi: 'The ball of Adam's heel outshone the sun ... how much more the beauty of

---

11 Jervell *Imago Dei* 173–76 views Paul's teaching on εἰκών in 2 Cor. 3:18–4:6 as a midrash on Gen 1:27; cf. Spicq *Dieu et l'homme* 188; Dahl 'Christ, Creation and the Church' 435; Black 'Second Adam' 174. On an allusion to Gen. 1 in Col. 3:10 cf. Scroggs *Last Adam* 69.

12 So Barr 'Image of God in the Book of Genesis' 24. The word ὁμοίωσις in Gen. 1:26 thus defines and limits the meaning of the first term εἰκών — to be created in God's image is to be 'like' God in some sense (cf. de Lacey 'Image' 11–12).

13 So Jervell *Imago Dei* 100–101; see esp. his references to *Tanch Pikude* 2 and *Deut. Rab.* XI.3.

14 I.e. the cave of Machpelah where according to tradition Adam and Eve were buried.

15 Further on the link in Adam between God's image and glory cf. *Gen. Rab.* XXII.2

his face' (*Qoh. Rab.* VIII.1.2; cf. *Lev. Rab.* XX.2; *Pesiq. Rab. Kah.* 36b).[16]

As long as Adam remained in God's presence he reflected God's glory.[17] When he sinned and was expelled from the Garden of Eden the glory departed.[18] This suggests that, in sinning, Adam fell from his relation of likeness to God and that the divine image was in some sense effaced. The rabbis, however, never explicitly say this.[19] What they do affirm is that the glory returned at the giving of the law, appearing pre-eminently on the face of Moses after he had been in God's presence.[20] But his glory also faded, when Israel sinned.[21] The rabbis now look for yet a third visitation of glory when it will appear on the face of one who will perfectly reflect the divine likeness, the Messiah.[22]

This matrix of Jewish ideas regarding the divine image, while comparatively late in document form, probably reflects an exegesis current in the first century AD. It certainly reflects an exegesis known to Paul, for he repeatedly combines the notions of 'image' and 'glory' and usually in contexts where Adam is at least implicit.[23] Yet the apostle goes beyond rabbinic teaching in at least one important sense. He attempts to show why sin causes the glory to fade and the image to wane.

[16] The earliest reference to Adam's glory is perhaps Sir. 49:16 (LXX) where it is said that Shem, Seth and Adam ἐδοξάσθησαν. For 'all the glory of Adam' in the scrolls of Qumran cf. 1QS 4:23; CD 3:20; 1QH 17:15. See further *2 Enoch* 30:11; *Gen. Rab.* XXII.12; *Num. Rab.* XIII.3; *Mek. Exod.* 20:11; *Cave of Treasures*, fol. 5a, col. 1 (Budge 52–55)

[17] Cf. *3 Enoch* 5:3 *Num. Rab.* XIII.2.

[18] Cf. *Gen. Rab.* XI.2: '[God] deprived him (Adam) of his splendour and expelled him from the Garden of Eden'. On Adam's sin leading to expulsion from God's presence and consequent loss of glory see *Apoc. Mos.* 20:2; 21:6; *3 Bar.* 4:16; *Pesiq. R.* XXIII.6; *Gen. Rab.* XII.6; XVII.8; XIX.7; XLII.3; *Num. Rab.* XII.6; XIII.12; *Qoh. Rab.* V.1.1. On the darkness of Adam: *2 Bar.* 18:2; *Pirqe R. El.* 14.

[19] Though see *Deut. Rab.* XI.3: 'Adam said to Moses: "I am greater than you because I have been created in the image of God" . . . Moses replied to him: "I am far superior to you, for the honour which was given to you (that of being created in God's image?) has been taken away'; cf. Wis. 2:23–24.

[20] On Moses regaining the glory which Adam lost cf. *2 Bar.* 17:4–18:2; *Gen. Rab.* XIX.7; *Num. Rab.* XIII.2; *Cant. Rab.* V.1.1; also Murmelstein 'Adam' 55–56; Scroggs *Last Adam* 53. Further on the glory of Moses see below pp. 106–9; and Jervell *Imago Dei* 45, 115–18.

[21] On Israel's sin resembling Adam's cf. *Num. Rab.* XVI.24; *b.Yebam.* 103b.

[22] On the Messiah restoring what Adam lost cf. *2 Bar.* 73–74; *Gen. Rab.* XII.6; *Exod. Rab.* XXX.3; further on the glory of the Messiah see p. 128, esp. nn. 126, 127.

[23] Cf. e.g. the passage we are presently studying, 2 Cor. 3:18–4:6 and also Rom. 1:21–23 (which we will consider next); and see Rom. 8:29–30; 1 Cor. 11:7; 15:40–49; Phil. 2:6–11 (where μορφὴ θεοῦ is used for εἰκὼν τοῦ θεοῦ).

In Romans 1:23 Paul reveals the following about sinful people: 'they exchange the glory of the incorruptible God for the likeness of an image of corruptible man' (ἤλλαξαν τὴν δόξαν τοῦ ἀφθάρτου θεοῦ ἐν[24] ὁμοιώματι εἰκόνος φθαρτοῦ ἀνθρώπου). These words probably represent an allusion to LXX Psalms 105:20 – 'they exchanged their glory for the likeness of a calf' (ἠλλάξαντο τὴν δόξαν αὐτῶν ἐν ὁμοιώματι μόσχου) – and thus to Israel's worship of idols.[25] By substituting his own phrase 'the likeness of the image of corruptible man' for 'the likeness of a calf' in Psalms 105 Paul is making the penetrating point that the people of his day are worshipping, not idols, but *man*. Or more precisely, they are making idols of *themselves*, and hence, effectively, of God's image.[26] This represents a flagrant misuse of the divine likeness. It is to use for human glory what was meant for God's. It is to exchange God's glory for a corrupted image. It is to turn what was meant to reflect God's likeness – namely themselves – into a darkened image.

We are probably right to see behind Paul's teaching here an implicit reference to the story of Adam.[27] We know from Genesis 3 that Adam abused the image of God. Instead of reflecting the divine likeness he tried to become like God, knowing good and evil.[28] Ironically, in his quest to achieve divine status he became less like God.[29] The details of Adam's experience seem to coalesce neatly with Paul's instruction in Romans 1 and thus doubtless serve as the backdrop for his teaching that self-exaltation is patently not the way in which to manifest the divine likeness.

When the apostle remarks in 2 Corinthians 4:4 that his critics have been blinded to 'the light of the gospel of the glory of Christ *who is the image of God*' (τὸν φωτισμὸν τοῦ εὐαγγελίου τῆς δόξης τοῦ χριστοῦ, ὅς ἐστιν εἰκὼν τοῦ θεοῦ), he demonstrates how the divine likeness *is* to be manifested. It comes to perfect expression in the gospel of Christ. What this gospel entails is set out perhaps most vividly in Philippians 2:6–8. There we learn that even though Christ existed in the form of God – enjoying a relation

---

[24] Here ἐν means 'for'; so BDF § 179.2.
[25] So Lagrange *Romains* 26; Käsemann *Romans* 45.
[26] The word εἰκών here has a double meaning. In worshipping themselves people make idols of God's image; cf. Wedderburn 'Adam in Paul's Letter to the Romans' 417–19.
[27] Thus Hooker 'Adam in Romans I' 297–306.
[28] Barrett *First Adam to Last* 12–13.
[29] I.e., according to the rabbis, he lost divine glory.

of likeness to God[30] – he did not regard equality with God as something to be exploited for his own aggrandisement.[31] Rather, he viewed it as a call to take on the form of a slave, indeed to die a slave's death on a cross.[32] In short, Christ dramatically rejected the course taken by Adam, that of grasping after his own advantage, and chose instead the path of self-negation. In doing so he did not empty himself of the divine likeness. He perfectly expressed it.[33]

We thus find in Paul two very different ways of using God's image. One is the way of Adam, the other the way of Christ. One is self-grasping, the other self-giving. One depreciates the image, the other manifests it fully. Before his conversion Paul was unwittingly a follower of Adam, self-regarding and self-grasping. When the light of God penetrated his heart his eyes were opened to the truth about Jesus Christ, indeed the truth about God's image. He discovered that the divine likeness was manifested pre-eminently in the self-emptying death of the crucified Christ. This caused a *transformation of his mind* and forced him to concede that his own self-centredness had made a mockery of the divine image. His mind was thus renewed according to the image of God.

It was precisely this sort of reconciliation to the divine image which was envisaged in LXX Isaiah. The arrival of eschatological light was to prompt a transformation in human hearts: arrogance would be replaced by humility, egocentricity by theocentricity. The glory of God would thus inaugurate a new age of salvation. Doubtless it was the conviction that this glory had indeed arrived that prompted Paul to declare in 2 Corinthians 6:2 – drawing his words directly from LXX Isaiah[34] – '*Now* is the acceptable time, *now* is the day of salvation'. By sharing in the judgement of the cross Paul's mind had been purged of adamic pride and refashioned according to the self-giving image of God.

We may now make sense of the phrase τὴν αὐτὴν εἰκόνα μεταμορφούμεθα. By using the word εἰκών instead of δόξα Paul seems to be drawing attention to the visible character, the salient image, of

---

[30] Thus taking the phrase ὃς ἐν μορφῇ θεοῦ ὑπάρχων (v. 6) causally (with Moule 'Manhood of Jesus' 97), and μορφὴ θεοῦ (v. 6) as nearly equivalent to εἰκὼν θεοῦ (so Martin *Carmen Christi* 99–120).

[31] Thus interpreting ἁρπαγμός in v. 6 to mean 'the act of snatching', and especially snatching for personal gain; cf. Moule 'Further Reflexions on Philippians 2:5–11' 266–68, 271–76; Hoover 'Harpagmos Enigma' 118; Wright 'ἁρπαγμός' 339–44.

[32] Thus the interpretation of Wright 'Adam in Pauline Christology' 379–81.

[33] Cf. Hooker 'Philippians 2:6–11' 163–64.

[34] Namely, LXX Isa 49:8.

Jesus Christ. He is underscoring the fact that Christ, in his resolve to live for God's glory and not his own and in his act of consummate self-sacrifice on the cross, demonstrates not only what God is like but also, dramatically, what humans ought to be like. They ought to manifest the same self-emptying character which Christ displayed on the cross. They ought to be 'transformed into the same image'.

Accordingly, they ought also to radiate his glory. Since the terms τὴν αὐτὴν δόξαν and τὴν αὐτὴν εἰκόνα in 2 Corinthians 3:18 are almost interchangeable, the one who manifests 'the same image' will also radiate 'the same glory'. Hence Paul describes his transformation as one in which he comes to reflect increasing increments of divine glory (cf. ἀπὸ δόξης εἰς δόξαν).[35]

We may now venture a partial response to the first question posed at the outset of this chapter, How is the glory of God actually manifested in the ministry of Paul? It is manifested paradoxically, in self-emptying humility.[36]

The ministry and the cross

The apostle lends specificity to this humility in 2 Corinthians 4. In verse 1 Paul declares that he will not lose heart (οὐκ ἐγκακοῦμεν, a term repeated in v. 16).[37] Along with similar expressions of resolve in the near context (cf. 2:14; 3:4, 12; 5:6, 8), we may infer that there must be good reasons why Paul might lose heart. Foremost among them is probably the constant threat of physical persecution (cf. 4:8–9; 6:4–10).[38] Paul makes no attempt to conceal this threat and even discloses that on one occasion it was so terrifying that he despaired of life itself (cf. 1:8). But he also affirms that in the midst of such humiliation he always receives mercy (ἠλεήθημεν, 2 Corinthians 4:1),[39] and thus the strength to carry out his duty as a minister of Christ.

---

35 Cf. 2 Cor. 4:17.
36 The paradox here is not total, in the sense that humility *is* glory (*pace* Spencer 'Irony' 357); rather, humility is *the place where* divine glory is revealed – glory is manifested *through* humility (thus Schrage 'Leid' 168; Lambrecht 'Nekrosis of Jesus' 131, see refs. in n. 51). See the discussion below pp. 164–69.
37 The reading ἐγκακοῦμεν (p[46], ℵ, A, B, D, etc.) is to be preferred over ἐκκακοῦμεν (C, Ψ, etc.) and may be translated 'to lose heart' (BAG 240; Plummer 110), 'to become discouraged' (Allo 98; Héring 29), 'to shrink back' (Furnish 217), not 'to become negligent' (Windisch 132) or 'to find distasteful' (as though Paul were denying that he finds the ministry distasteful, cf. Baumert *Täglich sterben* 318–46).
38 So Collange 128; Bruce 194; Harris 340.
39 Thus the term καθὼς ἠλεήθημεν refers not to Paul's conversion (*pace* Lietzmann 115; Windisch 131; Bultmann 102; Plummer 110) or his call (Kim *Origin* 11, 26

Paul summarises that duty in 2 Corinthians 4:5. It is to proclaim 'Jesus Christ as κύριος and ourselves as your δοῦλοι'. The first half of this proclamation is unsurprising. The confession Κύριος Ἰησοῦς was probably a standard formula in the Christian worship of Paul's day and may well have formed the nucleus of the Christian message (cf. 1 Corinthians 12:3; Romans 10:9; see also Philippians 2:11; 3:8). What is striking is the second half of the proclamation, 'and ourselves as your slaves'. The phrase represents a second object of the main verb κηρύσσομεν and indicates that an important part of Paul's message was his own humble service.[40]

This unusual truth, without parallel in Paul, can perhaps be elucidated by noting the similarity between this verse and 1 Corinthians 1:23. In 2 Corinthians 4 Paul writes 'we preach . . . Jesus Christ as Lord' (κηρύσσομεν . . . Ἰησοῦν χριστὸν κύριον). In 1 Corinthians 1 he says 'we preach Christ as crucified' (κηρύσσομεν χριστὸν ἐσταυρωμένον). This suggests that in Paul's mind there is a unity between preaching Jesus as *Lord* and proclaiming Christ as *crucified*. Indeed, as the apostle underscores in another epistle, it is precisely in dying the death of a slave (δοῦλος) on a cross that Jesus demonstrates what it means to be Lord (κύριος, Philippians 2:5–11). At the heart of the kerygma thus lies a paradox which draws together two seemingly contradictory features about Christ, his humility and his lordship.[41]

This explains why Paul can actually preach himself as δοῦλους ὑμῶν. The gospel which he preaches is being worked out in his life. He is being transformed into the likeness of Jesus Christ, a likeness which, as we have seen, comes to expression pre-eminently in self-giving service. Paul's behaviour among the Corinthians thus embodies the message he is proclaiming. His 'service' is indivisible from his preaching. He must, 'because of Jesus' (διὰ Ἰησοῦν, 4:5),[42] preach himself as δοῦλους ὑμῶν.

Here, then, are at least two ways in which Paul's humility works out in practice: in his willingness to submit to suffering and in his service to others. We may now be more precise about the way in which divine glory works out in the ministry of the apostle Paul. It

---

n. 5, 288 n. 4; Furnish 217), but the mercy he receives amidst the rigours of ministry (cf. Barrett 127).

[40] Cf. Bultmann 110.

[41] Cf. Mark 10:42–45 where Jesus teaches that whoever wishes to rule (κατα-κυριεύειν) must become πάντων δοῦλος. This applies especially to the Son of Man who will establish his authority by giving his life as a ransom for many.

[42] Not 'for Jesus' sake' (as Furnish 223, 250; Bultmann 109).

works out in the same way in which it did in Christ – in humble suffering and sacrificial service.

Blinded to the glory of the cross

Yet it is precisely for this reason that his critics fail to appreciate his glory. They regard his humility as incompatible with his alleged glory and hence as proof of his failure as a minister of Christ. This brings us to the second question posed at the outset of this chapter, How do the Corinthians interpret Paul's glory? Why do they fail to appreciate it? Paul ventures a reply in 2 Corinthians 4:4 by suggesting that their eyes have been blinded by 'the god of this age'. The unusual mention of a foreign deity is thought by most commentators to be a reference to Satan.[43] Yet few go on to ask how it is that Satan could have concealed what ought to have been so obvious, the superlative glory of Paul's ministry. We take up this question in what follows.

The god of this age

An important clue may be found in Paul's distinctive use of the word νόημα. The term appears five times in 2 Corinthians (as opposed to only once elsewhere)[44] and nearly always in reference to the work of Satan. It is the mind (τὰ νοήματα) which Satan blinds to the glory of Paul's ministry (4:4). Furthermore, as the serpent once deceived Eve, so he now corrupts the minds of the Corinthians (τὰ νοήματα ὑμῶν) by undermining their single-hearted loyalty[45] and purity of devotion[46] to Christ (11:3).[47] He carries out his sinister work through deputies (cf. οἱ διάκονοι αὐτοῦ in 11:15, where

---

43 Furnish 220; Barrett 130–31; Martin 78; and cf. *Mart. Isa.* 10.11; but see Müllensiefen 'Satan' 295–98 who regards ὁ θεὸς τοῦ αἰῶνος τούτου as a reference to God.
44 Cf. Phil. 4:7.
45 On interpreting ἁπλότης in 2 Cor. 11:3 as 'undivided loyalty' cf. Col. 4:22; Eph. 6:5; *T. Iss.* 7:7; *T. Levi* 13:1; and see Malherbe 'Simplicity or Singleness?' 119–29.
46 Thus reading καὶ τῆς ἁγνότητος in 2 Cor. 11:3 according to p[46], ℵ*, B, F, G, etc., and regarding its omission in ℵ[2], H, C, etc. as a scribal oversight, since the last six letters of ἁπλότητος and ἁγνότητος are the same (cf. Allo 275–76; Prümm I 594; Furnish 487; *pace* Barrett 270 n. 1 who omits the phrase).
47 The similarity of structure between 2 Cor. 4:4 and 11:3 –
     ὁ θεὸς τοῦ αἰῶνος τούτου ἐτύφλωσεν τὰ νοήματα τῶν ἀπίστων
     ὡς ὁ ὄφις ἐξηπάτησεν Εὕαν . . . φθαρῇ τὰ νοήματα ὑμῶν
     – suggests that a common point is being made in each verse.

αὐτοῦ refers to Satan, 11:14), namely rival missionaries who undercut the apostle's ministry.[48] Whereas Paul labours to present his converts as chaste virgins to one husband,[49] Jesus Christ (11:2), his rivals effectively subvert that union by preaching what amounts to 'another Jesus' (ἄλλος Ἰησοῦς, 11:4). It is thus a confusion about Jesus which Satan and his deputies are fomenting in Corinth.

1 Another Jesus

We must examine the nature of this confusion and in particular the identity of ἄλλος Ἰησοῦς. Most scholars look for a clue in the preaching of Paul's opponents. Some point to the fact that Paul also accuses his rivals of preaching εὐαγγέλιον ἕτερον (cf. 11:4), presumably the law-centred 'gospel' of Palestinian Christianity. Such nomism would be incompatible with Paul's understanding of the gospel of Jesus and hence evoke his charge that the opponents preach ἄλλον Ἰησοῦν.[50] Others give priority to the fact that the opponents also preach πνεῦμα ἕτερον (11:4). Doubtless they are 'spiritualists', gnostics, who preach Jesus as a heavenly being.[51] That would be at variance with the more earthly Jesus of Paul and explain his conviction that they preach 'another Jesus'.[52]

It is immediately clear that neither of these interpretations seeks to understand ἄλλος Ἰησοῦς on its own terms. Both interpret it in the light of either εὐαγγέλιον ἕτερον or πνεῦμα ἕτερον. It is partly for this reason that Georgi has suggested a third interpretation, that the opponents are hellenistic Jews who regard the earthly Jesus as a θεῖος ἀνήρ, in contrast to the more human and humble Jesus of Paul.[53] While this proposal does attempt to make sense of ἄλλος Ἰησοῦς in its own right, it suffers from the fundamental weakness mentioned above in the Introduction that nowhere in 2 Corinthians

---

[48] Thus taking the singular term ὁ ἐρχόμενος in 2 Cor. 11:4 generically to refer to several opponents (cf. the plural τινας, 10:2; οἱ τοιοῦτοι, 11:13; and see Bultmann 203–4; Plummer 296; *pace* Barrett 275; Bachmann 365).

[49] Here the ἑνί is emphatic.

[50] Many draw a comparison with ἕτερον εὐαγγέλιον in Gal. 1:6; so Schlatter 633; Oostendorp *Another Jesus* 7, 58; Bachmann 363; Plummer 296; Goudge 102; and see Borse *Galaterbriefes* 84–91. The weakness of this view is that there is no evidence in 2 Cor. for the error of legalism; the word νόμος does not even appear. See the discussion above p. 5.

[51] So Lütgert *Freiheitspredigt* 66–68; Schmithals *Gnosis* 57–59, 124–28; Bultmann 204–5.

[52] Thus Schmithals *Gnosis* 126–27.

[53] *Gegner* 286; cf. Schütz *Apostolic Authority* 177.

is there a hint that the opponents consciously view themselves as *divine* men. Rather, they regard themselves as mortals, needing letters of recommendation.[54] It would seem, then, that none of the various attempts to identify Paul's opponents fully explicates the meaning of the term ἄλλος Ἰησοῦς.[55]

There is good reason for this. As we observed at the outset of our study, we know disappointingly little about Paul's rivals and thus little about what distinguishes their Jesus from his.[56] Yet the apostle does provide one enticing, though often unnoticed, insight into the opponents' understanding of Jesus. When he stresses in 2 Corinthians 11:4 that his preaching differs from that of his rivals, the precise phrase he employs is revealing: the opponents preach 'another Jesus *whom we did not preach*' (εἰ μὲν γὰρ ὁ ἐρχόμενος ἄλλον Ἰησοῦν κηρύσσει ὃν οὐκ ἐκηρύξαμεν). The last three words in the Greek here are reminiscent of Paul's earlier positive affirmation in 2 Corinthians 4:5: 'We preach ... Jesus Christ *as Lord*' (κηρύσσομεν . . . Ἰησοῦν χριστὸν *κύριον*). A quick comparison of the two statements would suggest that while the opponents may well be preaching Jesus, it is not Jesus as Paul preaches him, not Jesus *as Lord*. As we have seen, preaching 'Jesus as Lord' makes certain moral requirements on the one who is doing the preaching; in particular, it makes one a 'servant of all' (ἑαυτοὺς δὲ δούλους ὑμῶν, 4:5).[57] If the opponents are preaching ἄλλον Ἰησοῦν, then perhaps it is because their Jesus is not making the same moral requirements on them as he does on Paul, that is to say, not producing in them the same servant-like humility.[58]

This would seem to be the implication of the opening words of 2 Corinthians 4:5, 'We do not preach ourselves' (οὐ γὰρ ἑαυτοὺς κηρύσσομεν). The emphatic ἑαυτούς here suggests that Paul is conducting an oblique polemic against those who *do* preach them-

---

[54] See above pp. 8–9.

[55] Käsemann's interpretation of ἄλλος Ἰσοῦς is somewhat idiosyncratic. He believes that, since the opponents were closely allied to the pillar apostles in Jerusalem, their Jesus was more personal than Paul's – they had witnessed Jesus first-hand, κατὰ σάρκα (5:16; 'Legitimität' 49; cf. Lietzmann 125–26). But this view fails to do justice to the adjective ἄλλος: it is difficult to see how Paul's Jesus would have *differed* from Käsemann's Jesus κατὰ σάρκα.

[56] Cf. Hickling 'Second Epistle to the Corinthians' 287: 'we must be content to remain largely in ignorance of the doctrinal position or tendencies of Paul's rivals'.

[57] Cf. our exegesis above on pp. 152–54.

[58] Cf. Barrett 'Opponents' 242.

selves.[59] In 2 Corinthians 11:18 and 20 the apostle becomes explicit. His rivals not only boast about themselves (πολλοὶ καυχῶνται κατὰ σάρκα, v. 18) but also make the Corinthians *their* 'slaves' (εἴ τις ὑμᾶς καταδουλοῖ). Far from being humble servants, the opponents actually exploit, take advantage of, assume airs over and insult members of the Corinthian church (v. 20).[60] It is clear that in Paul's mind the opponents are patently not proclaiming Jesus as *Lord*. By their self-exalting behaviour they are effectively preaching ἄλλον Ἰησοῦν.

No wonder Paul likens his rivals to 'hucksters' (κάπηλοι, 2 Corinthians 2:17), the competitive merchants of the first century who sacrifice the integrity of their product for personal gain.[61] By promoting their own interests,[62] the opponents adulterate the word of God (cf. οἱ πολλοὶ καπηλεύοντες τὸν λόγον τοῦ θεοῦ, 2:17; δολοῦντες τὸν λόγον τοῦ θεοῦ, 4:2).[63] Their self-regarding ambitions represent the exact antithesis of the self-giving gospel of Christ.[64] For this reason, Paul unleashes his most scathing invective on the intruders at Corinth. They are false apostles, workers of deceit, ministers of Satan (11:13–15).

The irony of course is that the opponents claim to be just the opposite – apostles of Christ and ministers of righteousness (cf. 11:13, 15). Yet for Paul this is an inversion of the truth. What his opponents regard as worthy of praise – competitive boasting and aggressive behaviour – he condemns. What they deplore as ignoble and base – humility and meekness – he esteems. In Paul's thinking, their error arises from a false understanding of the cross. They have ignored its offensiveness and bypassed its shame. They have shown little interest in a Jesus of humility, a gospel of suffering or a Spirit who affirms that Jesus is Lord (cf. 1 Corinthians 12:3). They proclaim ἄλλον Ἰησοῦν, εὐαγγέλιον ἕτερον, πνεῦμα ἕτερον.

---

[59] So Collange 136; Bachmann 190–91; *pace* Windisch 138, Barrett 133 and Plummer 118 who argue that Paul is *defending* himself against accusations that he preaches himself.

[60] The rendering of the terms κατεσθίω (BAG 423), λαμβάνω (Furnish 497), ἐπαίρω (Barrett 291) and εἰς πρόσωπον δέρω (Windisch 347).

[61] Cf. D. Chr. *Or.* 31.37, where 'tradesmen (κάπηλοι) cheat in their measures [and] ... depend upon base gain'. On sophists and philosophers peddling wisdom (σοφίαν καπηλεύειν) for profit cf. Philostr. *VA* 1.13; D. Chr. *Or.* 8.9.

[62] Thus the meaning of περιπατεῖν ἐν πανουργίᾳ in 2 Cor. 4:2 (Barrett 128; Plummer 111); cf. κατὰ σάρκα περιπατεῖν in 2 Cor. 10:2 and ἐν σοφίᾳ σαρκικῇ ἀναστρέφειν in 2 Cor. 1:12.

[63] In Luc. *Herm.* 59 both words appear: philosophers are likened to merchants (οἱ κάπηλοι) who adulterate (δολώσαντες) their product for sordid gain.

[64] Cf. Wolff 8.

We can now appreciate why Paul should be so alarmed that his converts are actually 'putting up' with the opponents (2 Corinthians 11:4)[65] and accepting them 'gladly' (ἡδέως, 11:19). It shows that the Corinthians themselves have become confused about the identity of Jesus. In response to this situation Paul spends little time attacking the opponents. Instead, he endeavours to reclaim the minds (πᾶν νόημα) of his converts by taking them captive for obedience to Christ (10:5).

On the basis of this analysis we may draw a few further conclusions about Paul's opponents. While Paul seems to identify his rivals as 'Hebrews', 'Israelites' and 'descendants of Abraham' (11:22), it is not clear how much we should infer from these titles. It would be tempting to use the appellations to extrapolate a full-blown portrait of the opponents – their origin, their identity, their teaching. But the fact that Paul never fills out the meaning of these terms serves to caution us against doing so ourselves.

What he does provide is a series of candid insights into the *behaviour* of the opponents. According to Paul, they exemplify everything in terms of competitive boasting and assertiveness that his congregation eagerly looks for but fails to find in him. The opponents are opportunists who are exploiting the self-exalting tastes of the Corinthians to win places of honour and esteem for themselves within the church. Their approach to 'ministry' speaks volumes of their 'Jesus'. It suggests to Paul that their grasp of Jesus is not only gravely inadequate, but almost non-existent. Their doctrine is not just unsound, it is empty. They use the name 'Jesus' and claim to be his ministers, but only as a means by which to advance their own interests. Such recklessness in 'the service of Christ' earns Paul's most damning rebuke. They are servants of Satan (11:14-15).

The opponents were successful in Corinth because they were able to cater to the self-exalting perspectives already in place when they arrived. They did not create those perspectives. They merely exploited them. To be sure their machinations caused the situation to deteriorate sharply, and Paul is deeply concerned about the deleterious effect of his rivals. But in his mind the opponents are not the primary agents of the christological confusion in the Corinthian church.

---

[65] Reading ἀνέχεσθε (p[46], B, D*, 33) and thus a statement of fact, rather than the hypothetical ἀνείχεσθε (p[34], ℵ, D[2], G), following Barrett 270 n. 2; Windisch 326; Lietzmann 146; Kümmel 210.

2 Another wisdom

According to Paul, the primary agent is Satan, the 'god of this age' (2 Corinthians 4:4). The genitive term here, τοῦ αἰῶνος τούτου, is instructive. It receives no elaboration in the near context, but in 1 Corinthians 1–3, where it is used frequently to qualify the word σοφία, it signifies the proud and self-seeking wisdom of the age (cf. 1:20; 2:6, 8; 3:18). Doubtless it is used similarly in 2 Corinthians 4:4, serving to draw our attention to the general intellectual climate of the day, the social atmosphere of the first century, the sort of competitive and self-serving outlook which, as we have seen, the Corinthians would have imbibed as naturally as the air they breathed.[66] It is this outlook which Paul attributes to Satan. It is this outlook which is blinding people to Christ.[67]

It is not difficult to imagine how this blinding might have happened. It would have been natural for first-century Corinthians to regard Christ κατὰ σάρκα, according to the self-centred passions of their day, as the agent by which their desires might be fulfilled. They had grown accustomed to projecting their ambitions onto religion. As we saw earlier, the cults in Corinth catered scrupulously to the requirements of the worshipper. Rarely did religion make difficult demands, rarely did it call for personal sacrifice. Instead it confirmed an individual in the pursuit of happiness and satisfaction – exalting him, seldom challenging him. Even the provision of sal-

---

[66] See our historical analysis above pp. 37–49, 77–8.

[67] Traditionally scholars have attributed the blindness to an 'enthusiastic' view of Christ. In particular, they have suggested that the error in Corinth is an over-realized eschatology in which the Corinthians, thinking the resurrection had already occurred (1 Cor. 15:12), regard the blessings of the eschaton as a present reality (1 Cor. 4:8). Cf. the formative article by Schniewind 'Leugner der Auferstehung' 110–39; and see further Barrett *First Corinthians* 109, 347–48; Conzelmann *1 Corinthians* 85–89; Bruce 49–50, 144; Käsemann *Questions* 125–26; Kümmel 192; Becker *Auferstehung* 69–76; Grant *Introduction* 204; Wilson 'Resurrection' 90–107. But this is to suggest (i) that the error at Corinth is being articulated as ἀνάστασιν ἤδη γεγονέναι when in fact Paul represents it as ἀνάστασις νεκρῶν οὐκ ἔστιν (1 Cor. 15:12) and (ii) that the late and isolated heresy of Hymenaeus and Philetus in 2 Tim. 2:18 can be read into the situation in Corinth.

Others attribute the 'enthusiasm' to an avid interest in the Spirit. As 'spiritual people' (1 Cor. 2:15; 3:1) the Corinthians are naturally filled, rich and kings (1 Cor. 4:8). Cf. Wedderburn 'Denial of the Resurrection' 234–35, 238–39; Thiselton 'Realized Eschatology' 510–26. Yet in Paul's thinking it is not spirituality which prompts Corinthian 'enthusiasm', but 'fleshliness' – he cannot speak to them as ὡς πνευματικοῖς ἀλλ' ὡς σαρκίνοις (1 Cor. 3:1).

vation, a universal feature among first-century cults, was conceived in terms of personal health, wealth and happiness.[68]

What would have prevented the recently converted Corinthians from approaching their new life in Christ with the same set of expectations with which they once approached their pagan worship? They were recent initiates into a religion of surpassing glory and power, the very things which people of their day cherished. How reasonable, then, to expect to share in that glory. How natural to regard Christ as the source of all blessing. How plausible to view his lordship as the fountain of individual wealth and his exalted position as the source of personal honour and esteem.[69]

Indeed such assumptions would have been entirely correct, to a degree. There *was* great glory in Christ. Yet, as we have seen, there was also a more austere implication to life in him. The Corinthians were now under the sign of his cross and hence called to an existence of personal self-emptying. The fact that they were opting for comfort and ease would seem to indicate that they had missed this implication, that they had set aside the supreme scandal of crucifixion for a more pleasing and sentimental view of Christ, that they were assimilating the cross to their own worldly and self-exalting expectations, expectations which represented the exact antithesis of the message of Christ crucified.

By failing to submit to the word of the cross, indeed by enslaving it for their own advancement, the Corinthians demonstrated the same sort of arrogance and pride which, as we have seen, was present at different times in Adam (when he sinned), in Israel (as depicted in Isaiah) and in Paul (before his conversion). In each of those cases the sin of pride served to confuse minds and blind people to the glory of the Lord. We should not now be surprised if the Corinthians, too, have difficulty detecting the Lord's glory. Their self-regarding attitudes, inspired and sustained by Satan himself, would naturally lead them to look for the kind of glory which the world esteems but which is at odds with the cruciform glory manifested in their apostle.[70]

---

[68] This paragraph recapitulates the findings of our study of religion in first-century Corinth, see above pp. 25–34, 50–3.

[69] Cf. Hooker 'Interchange in Christ and Ethics' 11.

[70] It is worth noting that pride and arrogance may have continued to plague the Corinthian church long after Paul passed from the scene. This we might infer from the fact that in 1 Clement, a letter addressed to the church in Corinth round AD 96 (cf. Lightfoot *Apostolic* 1:1:346–58), or perhaps as early as AD 70 (Robinson *Redating* 327–35), we find repeated exhortations to humility, the noun ταπεινο-

We may further surmise that the opponents, by personifying the self-assertive spirit of the age, demonstrated that they, too, had assimilated the prevailing Graeco-Roman outlook of their day, despite their seemingly Jewish roots (cf. 11:22). This should occasion no surprise, for by the first century the lines dividing cultures and creeds had become fluid.

The glory of the cross

It may be wondered why Paul does not endeavour more earnestly to publish the nature and scope of his glory. We find an answer in 2 Corinthians 12:6. He restrains himself in order to 'spare' the Corinthians.[71] He could quite truthfully boast of revelations and visions – and hence of a wealth of evidence illustrating the glory of his ministry – but in doing so he would be encouraging his display-conscious converts to impute to his account what in fact belongs to God.[72] It is to keep them from going 'beyond' (ὑπέρ) what they see in him and hear from him – namely, his humility and suffering – that he refuses to dramatise his glory.[73]

The preposition ὑπέρ here serves to convey the same truth which the ὑπέρ did in 1 Corinthians 4:6. Just as the Corinthians are not to go 'beyond' the meaning of the OT citations compiled in 1 Corinthians 1–3,[74] neither are they to go 'beyond' what they see and hear in Paul – in both cases, beyond a simple boast in the Lord. The problem in each context is that the Corinthians are showing a desire to boast about the achievements of people, in the one case, the merits of rival leaders, in the other, Paul's revelations and visions. But for Paul the vital truth is that any achievement worth glorying in belongs to the Lord and hence any boasting must, by definition, be exclusively in him (cf. 1 Corinthians 1:29 and 31).

φροσύνη and related words occurring no less than thirty-one times (cf. ταπεινο-φροσύνη [21:8; 30:8; 31:4; 44:3; 56:1 and 58:2]; ταπεινοφρονεῖν [2:1; 13:1, 3; 16:1-2, 17; 17:2; 19:1; 30:3; 38:2; 48:6 and 62:2]; ταπεινόφρων [19:1; 38:2]; ταπείνωσις [16:7; 53:2; 55:6]; ταπεινοῦν [18:8, 17; 59:3]; ταπεινός [30:2; 55:6; 59:3-4]). I am indebted to Dr. M. B. Thompson for these references.

71 Thus translating φείδομαι, 'I spare', conforming to its usage in 2 Cor. 1:23 and 13:2; so Barrett 312; *pace* Furnish 527 who translates 'I decline'.

72 On the commercial use of the term λογίζεσθαι εἰς cf. P.Fay. 21(9): 'I now give orders generally with regard to all payments actually made or credited to (λογι-ζομένων εἰς) the government'; see also Dit. *Or.* 2.595 (12); P.Flor. 2.123 (7).

73 So Barrett 'Opponents' 244–45; Georgi *Gegner* 228; Windisch 381; Bultmann 225–26.

74 For this interpretation of 1 Cor. 4:6 see above pp. 59–61.

It is for this reason that Paul is content to remain a mystery, a living parable, hidden in Christ (cf. Colossians 3:3), intelligible only to those with eyes to see and ears to hear, those enlightened by the Spirit (2 Corinthians 3:18). To adopt another course, in particular to parade his visions and revelations in such a way as to cause people to think they were his achievement, would be to obviate the work of the Spirit and usurp the honour of God. It would be to encourage a worldly-minded trust in him, the apostle, rather than in God (cf. 1 Corinthians 2:5). It would be to hinder his converts from seeing the truth about Christ, namely, that true glory, the glory of the Lord, is manifested pre-eminently in the shame of a cross.

Conclusion

For three chapters now we have been considering Paul's response in 2 Corinthians 3–4 to those who find it difficult to understand how a minister of the glorious gospel can suffer such ignominy and shame. The essence of Paul's reply is as startling as it is simple. It is precisely his humility which authenticates his status as a minister of the glorious gospel of Christ.

This means that in criticising Paul's humble appearance the Corinthians betray an ignorance of his gospel (2 Corinthians 4:3). In asking for evidence that Christ speaks in him (2 Corinthians 13:3) they place a question-mark over their faith (2 Corinthians 13:5). They demonstrate that they are still fleshly, still babes in Christ, still clutching after the milk of the word, not the meat (1 Corinthians 3:1–2).[75] Above all, they show that the self-centred outlook of their pagan neighbours has made a deeper impression on them than the radically divergent message of the cross.

In Paul's mind the problem boils down to a difference of christology. There is discord in Corinth on the matter of what it means to be 'in Christ'. For many, influenced by the wisdom of the day, it means championing a Christ who confers a showy status and honour. For Paul, drawing inspiration from the cross, it means conforming to a Jesus of humility and shame. On the one hand, few see anything impressive in the ministry of the humble Paul. On the other hand, Paul sees nothing impressive apart from humility. For the Corinthians, this represents an opaque paradox. For Paul, it is the mystery of Christian ministry.

---

[75] Cf. Hooker '1 Cor. 3:2' 19–22.

In response to their criticism Paul has little option but to try to explicate the paradox for them. Accordingly, he commends *himself* to the conscience of his readers, calling attention to the very humility which they disdain (2 Corinthians 4:2).[76] His aim is not principally to defend himself or even his ministry but rather to edify and restore his wayward converts (2 Corinthians 12:19; 13:9). Since he embodies in himself the truth about Christ (τῇ φανερώσει τῆς ἀληθείας συνιστάνοντες ἑαυτούς, 2 Corinthians 4:2) he regards their assessment of him as a telling indication of their spiritual condition. Paul hopes they will judge him accurately (ἐλπίζω δὲ ὅτι γνώσεσθε ὅτι ἡμεῖς οὐκ ἐσμὲν ἀδόκιμοι, 2 Corinthians 13:6; and see 2 Corinthians 1:13; 5:11), for if they do so they will proceed towards salvation and life, but if not towards perdition and death (2 Corinthians 2:15–16; 4:3).[77] He never ventures to identify who is and is not in the process of being saved. He merely poses an implicit question: Do you see that my ministry bears the glorious imprint of the cross?

---

[76] Cf. Thrall 'Pauline Use of ΣΥΝΕΙΔΗΣΙΣ' 123, 125.

[77] Cf. Munck *Paul* 191–92: 'again and again the thought is expressed that although the Corinthians are in the way of salvation, the way of perdition lies close by it'.

6

THE PATTERN OF THE CHRISTIAN
MINISTRY: POWER THROUGH WEAKNESS

Having examined the variety of factors which gave rise to Paul's paradoxical description of the Christian ministry, we are now in a position to make sense of the description itself. In particular, we can plumb the logic underlying the apostle's conviction that it is only in human weakness that the power of God *can* be manifested. Paul's exposition of this paradox reaches a climax in 2 Corinthians 4:7–18. We shall examine the passage exegetically and at some length.

2 Corinthians 4:7

In verse 7 we find both a summary of Paul's understanding of his ministry and the thesis of the entire paragraph beginning in verse 7 and ending in verse 15. The text bears quoting in full:

ἔχομεν δὲ τὸν θησαυρὸν τοῦτον ἐν ὀστρακίνοις σκεύεσιν,
ἵνα ἡ ὑπερβολὴ τῆς δυνάμεως ᾖ τοῦ θεοῦ καὶ μὴ ἐξ ἡμῶν.

It is immediately noticeable that the apostle is depicting his ministry in terms of a paradoxical image: a 'treasure' housed in an 'earthen vessel'. We must determine the meaning of these terms.

The phrase ἔχομεν δὲ τὸν θησαυρὸν τοῦτον has puzzled commentators. Does 'this treasure' refer to the glorious gospel (cf. vv. 3, 4),[1] the apostolic ministry (3:7–9; 4:1)[2] or the 'knowledge of the glory of God'? (v. 6)[3] The parallel phrase in 4:1, ἔχοντες τὴν διακονίαν ταύτην, would suggest that it is the apostolic ministry which is in view,[4] yet elsewhere Paul describes that ministry in terms of proclaiming the gospel of the glory of God (cf. 3:18; 4:4, 6). Perhaps, then, the 'treasure' is a combination of all these things – the ministry of the gospel of the glory of God.[5]

---

[1] So Lietzmann 115. [2] Bultmann 114. [3] Allo 113; Plummer 126.
[4] Cf. Rissi *Studien* 45. [5] Cf. Furnish 279.

The term ὀστράκινα σκεύη has sparked even more debate.[6] Some regard it as a gnostic metaphor for the contemptible nature of the human body.[7] Others point to its affinities with the language of Cynic-Stoic diatribe where humans are portrayed as weak and perishable vessels (cf. Sen. *Dial.* 6.11.3 ; Cic. *Tusc.* 1.52).[8] Still others take it as a reference to ancient wrestlers who, in covering their bodies with oil and dust, resembled fragile clay pots.[9] Finally, others see a parallel in the scrolls of Qumran where mortal men are portrayed as vessels of clay (cf. 1QS 11.22; 1QH 1.21–22; 3.20–21; 4.29; 10.5; 11.3; 12.24–31; 13.15–16).[10] It is difficult to say which, if any, of these interpretations is correct. What is significant is that each regards the 'earthen vessel' as a metaphor for human weakness.

Many believe Paul is using the term ὀστράκινα σκεύη to illustrate his *own* weakness. In doing so he establishes a neat contrast between himself and the superlative *power* of God in the latter half of verse 7.[11] If this is the case, it would make sense to suppose that Paul is borrowing his metaphor specifically from the OT, especially from passages where clay pots are depicted as weak and prone to shatter (cf. σκεῦος ἀπολωλός, LXX Psalms 30:13; σύντριμμα ἀγγείου ὀστρακίνου, LXX Isaiah 30:14).

But others suggest that the term ὀστράκινα σκεύη implies cheapness, not weakness. On this view, Paul is contrasting himself with the inestimable *worth* of the 'treasure' in the first half of verse 7. This interpretation finds support in LXX Lamentations 4:2 where the precious sons of Zion, who were once equal in value with gold (οἱ ἐπηρμένοι ἐν χρυσίῳ), are now counted as cheap earthen jars (ἀγγεῖον ὀστράκινον).[12]

The obvious question at this point is whether we must actually decide between these two views. Or is it possible that the term ὀστράκινα σκεύη in 2 Corinthians 4:7 can imply both weakness *and* cheapness? The two ideas certainly appear together in the OT. In LXX Leviticus 6:21 and 15:12 temple priests are enjoined to shatter unclean earthen vessels (σκεῦος ὀστράκινον) while preserving those made of bronze or wood. The implication is clear: earthen

---

[6] Cf. 2 Tim. 2:20, the only other occurrence of ὀστράκινος in the NT (also used with σκεῦος).

[7] Thus Schmithals *Gnosis* 150–52.   [8] See Dupont *ΣΥΝ ΧΡΙΣΤΩΙ* 120–24.

[9] Thus Spicq 'L'image sportive' 216–17.

[10] See Salguerro 'El Dualismo Qumranico y San Pablo' 559–60; Braun *Qumran und das Neue Testament* 199.

[11] Cf. Dupont *ΣΥΝ ΧΡΙΣΤΩΙ* 121–22; Allo 113; Héring 32.

[12] Thus the view of Barrett 137–38; Bachmann 194–96.

vessels are *both* weak *and* inferior, fragile *and* expendable.[13] Perhaps Paul has chosen the metaphor precisely because it can bear two meanings, because it forms a tidy contrast in verse 7 with both the 'treasure' and the 'power of God'. If so it would serve as a nice 'hinge' in his argument, shifting the focus away from the *glory* of the gospel (the subject of 3:7–4:6) towards the *power* of the gospel (the subject in 4:8–18). It would also provide a two-fold expression of the paradox of his ministry: the glorious gospel is borne about by those who are comparatively inferior, the powerful gospel by those who are weak.[14]

Having suggested possible meanings for the two metaphors, we may now examine the rest of the verse. The treasure, Paul maintains, is housed in earthen vessels 'in order that the surpassing greatness of power may be of God and not of us' (ἵνα ἡ ὑπερβολὴ τῆς δυνάμεως ᾖ τοῦ θεοῦ καὶ μὴ ἐξ ἡμῶν). Most commentators render the verb ᾖ here as though Paul meant to write φανερωθῇ or φανῇ or εὑρεθῇ.[15] On this view, he is arguing that his weakness serves to highlight – to make visible – God's strength.[16] But this interpretation fails to reckon with why Paul actually wrote ᾖ, especially when he could easily have written φανερωθῇ, the latter appearing twice in the near context (vv. 10, 11). Is it possible that Paul means exactly what he says, that it is only in weakness that the power may *be* of God, that his weakness in some sense actually serves as the grounds for divine power?[17]

A helpful commentary on this verse is found in 2 Corinthians 12:1–10.[18] There Paul reveals that he has received from God both superlative[19] revelations and a thorn in the flesh (12:1–7).[20] The thorn, he acknowledges, was given to humble him,[21] to prevent him

---

13 The dual character of clay pots would not be lost on Corinthian readers. On the terra-cotta industry in first-century Corinth see Davidson *Corinth: Minor Objects* 64.

14 Collange 146 rightly cautions against taking this paradox to mean that the Christian minister is in some sense dishonourable — after all he bears a glorious treasure; cf. Martin 85.

15 So Barrett 138; Furnish 254; Bultmann 115; Martin 85; Héring 32; Plummer 127; Harris 342.

16 Cf. Güttgemanns *Apostel* 112–19 who speaks of an 'Epiphanie' of power.

17 Thus Collange 147; Bachmann 196–97.

18 Cf. Rood 'Le Christ comme *ΔΥΝΑΜΙΣ ΘΕΟΥ*', 105 who also sees a link between 2 Cor. 4:7 and 12:1–10; and see Windisch 391.

19 The word is ὑπερβολή, the same as in 2 Cor. 4:7.

20 The identity of the σκόλοψ is a much discussed, though ultimately insoluble, problem. For a survey of recent views see Furnish 547–50.

21 I.e., ἵνα με κολαφίζῃ, 'that it might batter me' or 'knock me about'.

from boasting on the basis of his revelations (v. 7). This humility in turn served a supremely exalted function: it became the necessary pre-condition for the indwelling power of Christ (v. 9). In other words, *the very existence* of Christ's power in Paul was conditioned on the apostle's prior humility and weakness.[22] This would confirm the literal sense of 2 Corinthians 4:7, that it is only in Paul's weakness that the power may *be* of God.

There is interesting logic behind this insight. Had Paul not been humbled by the thorn in the flesh he would have been tempted to boast of his divine visions as though they were his own achievement. He would have used them to exalt himself (the implication of ἵνα μὴ ὑπεραίρωμαι, which appears twice in 12:7).[23] But this would have amounted to denying God's role as agent in the visions. Indeed it would have been tantamount to usurping that role for himself.[24] On this basis, the power could hardly have been 'of God', but rather 'of Paul' (cf. ἐξ ἡμῶν, in 4:7). In other words, where there is pride and arrogance there cannot, by definition, be divine power.

This principle is enunciated repeatedly in the OT. Those who enjoyed the most dramatic manifestations of divine power were often those of the greatest humility – men such as Abraham ('I am but dust and ashes' [Gen 18:7]), Moses ('Who am I that I should go to Pharaoh' [Exodus 3:11]), Gideon ('My family is the least in Manasseh, and I am the youngest in my father's house' [Judges 6:15]) and David ('I am a poor man and lightly esteemed' [1 Samuel 18:23]). It is axiomatic in the OT that God 'dwells with the contrite and lowly of spirit' (Isa 57:15), 'looks to the humble' (66:22) and 'is near the broken hearted' (Ps 34:18).[25] Where there is humility there, too, will be the power of God.

The principle is carried over into Judaism. The rabbis taught that it was with humble men that God was pleased to dwell. This was especially true in the cases of Abraham (*Num. Rab.* XIII.3), Moses (*Lev. Rab.* I.5), Joseph (*Exod. Rab.* I.7) and Saul (*Pesiq. Rab. Kah.*

---

22 Cf. Dunn *Jesus and the Spirit* 329–30.
23 The second occurrence of ἵνα μὴ ὑπεραίρωμαι is omitted in manuscripts A, D, F and G. The verb may be rendered as a reflexive middle, 'that I not exalt myself', like ὑπεραιρόμενος in 2 Thess 2:4 (on the latter see Bruce *1 & 2 Thessalonians* 168).
24 Cf. *Tanch. B.* 12b: 'the proud . . . raise themselves and deify themselves'; Philo *Virt.* 172: 'the arrogant man . . . holds himself . . . to be neither man nor demigod, but wholly divine'.
25 Cf. also 1 Sam. 2:8; 2 Sam. 22:28; Job 5:11; Ps. 137[138]:6; 147:6; Prov. 3:34; 11:2; 15:33; 18:12; 29:23; Isa. 25:4; 49:13; 61:1; Ezek. 17:24; Zeph. 2:3; Jdt. 9:11; Sir. 3:20; 11:1.

5.44a). Of these, Moses was particularly esteemed for his closeness to God. 'What brought him this distinction?' R. Jose asked. 'His humility',[26] was his reply, to which he added, '"Now the man Moses was very humble" (Numbers 12:3)'[27] and 'whosoever is humble will cause the Shekinah to dwell with man on earth' (*Mek. Exod.* 20:15–19, *Bahodesh* 9; cf. *b. Ned.* 38a).[28] The notion of God dwelling with the humble appears in an especially striking light in *Cant. Rab.* I.2.3 where the word of God, the Torah, is said to dwell in the one who makes himself like an earthenware vessel (cf. *Sifre Deut.* 48 [on 11:22]). The idea is remarkably similar to 2 Corinthians 4:7.[29]

From these examples we can see that Paul would have learned from his Jewish background what was later reinforced by the thorn in the flesh, that the power of God comes to dwell in the humble. Yet his most vivid instruction in this truth would have come from the cross of Christ itself. There, in the most humiliating of all forms of execution, Paul discovered the surpassing power of God (cf. 1 Corinthians 1:23–24). Moreover, he realised that it was especially in the cross that the power of God *could* dwell. Had it appeared in some other place arrogant humans would have been tempted to usurp it for themselves and to treat it as an object of personal boasting. In the first century the cross was simply too repugnant to be exploited for personal gain.

From several quarters, then, Paul became convinced that there were two mutually exclusive options available to people: the way of human arrogance and the way of divine power. This conviction is revealed perhaps most clearly in his warning to his converts at the end of 1 Corinthians 4: 'I will come quickly, if the Lord wills, and I will find out, not the words of those who are puffed up, but the power' (v. 19). This warning underscores the antithetical relationship between human pride and true power. If there is to be a demonstration of the surpassing power of God it will be in human

---

26 I.e. his 'nyn, which literally means 'meekness' or 'submissiveness' (so Jastrow 1094).

27 More precisely in the MT: 'Now the man Moses was very humble, more than any man who was on the face of the earth'.

28 The converse is also true: God cannot dwell with the proud and arrogant (*b. Sota* 4b-5a).

29 For other examples in Judaism of God rewarding the humble with his presence cf. *T. Reuben* 6:10; *b.'Erub.* 13b, 54a; *Ta'an.* 7a; *Sota* 5a; *Lev. Rab.* I.5; VII.2; *Num. Rab.* IV.20; *Tanh. B.* 43a; see also 1QH 4:8; 5:15–16; Philo *Spec. Leg.* 1.265; *Post.* 136; *Congr.* 107; and for a discussion cf. Maher 'Humility in Rabbinic Literature' 25–43; Moore *Judaism* II 273–75; Grundmann 'ταπεινός' 12–15.

self-negation (hence the message of 2 Corinthians 4:7). As Paul put it in 2 Corinthians 12:10, 'it is when I am weak that I am strong'.

We thus come to see in a preliminary fashion the logic underpinning Paul's paradoxical understanding of the Christian ministry. To the question, Why *must* the glory of God be revealed in human shame? the apostle answers, It is because only in shame can there *be* a demonstration of divine power. To explore the meaning of this paradox further we must move on to verses 8–12.

2 Corinthians 4:8 and 9

In these two verses Paul presents a series of four parallel antitheses:

> ἐν παντὶ
> θλιβόμενοι   ἀλλ' οὐ   στενοχωρούμενοι,
> ἀπορούμενοι   ἀλλ' οὐκ ἐξαπορούμενοι,   (v. 8)
> διωκόμενοι   ἀλλ' οὐκ ἐγκαταλειπόμενοι,
> καταβαλλόμενοι ἀλλ' οὐκ ἀπολλύμενοι   (v. 9)

which may be translated as follows:

> in every way[30] we are[31]
> hard pressed,[32]   but not crushed;
> perplexed,[33]   but not despairing;[34]
> persecuted,[35]   but not forsaken;[36]
> struck down,   but not destroyed.

The antitheses would seem to be illustrating a pattern inherent in Paul's sufferings.

Such lists of suffering were commonplace in antiquity, especially in Cynic-Stoic diatribe. Of particular interest is Plutarch's (*Mor.* 1057E) description of the sage who

---

[30] ἐν παντί probably applies to all four contrasts, and is to be translated modally, not temporally; cf. 2 Cor. 7:5.

[31] The participles which follow are absolute and thus probably not connected to the main verb ἔχομεν in v. 7; so Barrett 138.

[32] I.e. 'afflicted' (BAG 362).

[33] I.e. at a loss as to how to act; cf. Gal. 4:20; Furnish 254

[34] I.e. 'perplexed to the final degree'; thus the force of the perfective ἐκ-; see Robertson *Grammar* 596.

[35] Though some translate 'pursued', seeing here an allusion to the sport of wrestling – hence 'pursued, but not overtaken' (Spicq 'L'image sportive' 215; cf. Héring 31; Plummer 129).

[36] I.e. 'not forsaken *by God*'; on this meaning of ἐγκαταλείπω in the LXX cf. Gen. 28:15; Deut. 31:6, 8; 1 Chr. 28:20; Ps. 15:10; 36:25, 28; Sir. 2:10.

ἐγκλειόμενος	οὐ κωλύεται
κατακρημνιζόμενος	οὐκ ἀναγκάζεται
στρεβλούμενος	οὐ βασανίζεται
πηρούμενος	οὐ βλάπτεται

when confined	is not impeded,
when flung down a precipice	is not under compulsion,
when on the rack	is not put to the torture,
when mutilated	is not injured.

Similarly, Epictetus portrays the true Stoic as one 'who though sick is happy, though in danger is happy, though dying is happy, though condemned to exile is happy, though in disrepute is happy' (2.19.24).[37] Because of the similarities between these lists and Paul's in 2 Corinthians 4:8 and 9 many scholars conclude that the apostle is drawing on the forms of Cynic-Stoic diatribe.[38]

Others, however, believe that he was more influenced by comparable lists in apocalyptic Judaism.[39] We may note, for instance, the lament of the righteous in *1 Enoch* 103:9–15: 'In the days of our toil, we have surely suffered hardships and have experienced every trouble; we have faced many evil things and have become consumed; we have died and become few'; and in *2 Enoch* 66:6 : 'Walk, my children, in long-suffering, in meekness, in affliction, in distress . . . in weakness, in derision, in assaults, in temptation, in deprivation, in nakedness'.[40]

Whether or not Paul was indeed making use of the lists of Stoicism or apocalyptic Judaism – or, as one scholar suggests, of both, along with the similar lists of Josephus, the Mishnah and Nag Hammadi[41] – is impossible to say. And even if we could say, it is unlikely that it would shed much light on the meaning of 2 Corinthians 4:8–9.[42] What is clear is that the pathos of these verses derives more from the acute anxieties of personal experience than from any

---

[37] Cf. also Sen. *Ep.* 71.26; *Dial.* 2.10.4; Philo *Spec. Leg.* 3.6.

[38] Thus Bultmann *Stil der paulinischen Predigt* 71–72, 76, 80; Liechtenhan 'Ueberwindung des Leides bei Paulus' 376–77; Fridrichsen 'Paulus und die Stoa' 27–31; Dupont *ΣΥΝ ΧΡΙΣΤΩΙ* 117–19; Kümmel 201; Windisch 143.

[39] Cf. Schrage 'Leid, Kreuz und Eschaton' 143–46; Furnish 282.

[40] Cf. also 1QH 9.6–7.   [41] So Hodgson 'Tribulation Lists' 59–80.

[42] On differences of meaning between Paul and the Stoics see Fridrichsen 'Paulus und die Stoa' 30; Sevenster *Paul and Seneca* 159; Schrage 'Leid, Kreuz und Eschaton' 150–54; Dupont *ΣΥΝ ΧΡΙΣΤΩΙ* 119; between Paul and apocalyptic Judaism see Furnish 282–83.

literary form.[43] The important matter is to determine the nat
the experiences which gave rise to Paul's antitheses.

That is not an easy task using verses 8 and 9 alone, for here Paul
describes his experience in general terms – 'hard pressed', 'perplexed', etc. Fortunately, other pauline lists are more specific. In
2 Corinthians 6:5, for example, he defines his 'afflictions', 'hardships'
and 'distresses' (6:4) more precisely in terms of 'beatings', 'imprison-
ments', 'tumults', 'labours', 'sleeplessness' and 'hunger'. He adds in
2 Corinthians 11:23–27 that he has five times received the thirty-nine
lashes, thrice been beaten with rods, once stoned, thrice ship-
wrecked, often been in danger from rivers, robbers, Jews and
Gentiles, frequently threatened in cities and in the wilderness, on the
sea and among false brethren, often hungry and thirsty, cold and
exposed.[44] It is probably the cumulative weight of these physical
afflictions which underlies Paul's comments in 4:8 and 9.

But verses 8 and 9 represent more than a mere catalogue of
suffering. They comprise a series of antitheses in which Paul seeks to
give a remarkable interpretation to his suffering. The two participles
in each antithesis are joined by the particle οὐκ (rather than the
customary μή) which indicates that Paul is emphatic about this
interpretation – 'we are hard pressed, but *by no means* crushed'.[45]
The emphasis here suggests that Paul is anticipating those who will
dispute his interpretation.[46] He responds in advance by arguing that
while he may indeed be hard pressed, perplexed, persecuted and
struck down no one should infer – as some will be inclined to infer –
that he is also crushed, despairing, forsaken and destroyed. Indeed
one ought to infer just the opposite: that he is *by no means* crushed,
despairing, etc. That is because – as we saw in verse 7 – it is precisely
when he is weak and suffering, when he is 'hard pressed' and
'perplexed', that the power of God springs to action and preserves
him from ultimate crushing and despair.[47]

Verses 8 and 9 thus reveal that the power of verse 7 is an active
and a purposeful power. It always prevents Paul's suffering from
running its full course. No matter how grim the situation may
become, and the catalogue of woes in 2 Corinthians 11:23–33

---

[43] So Lambrecht 'Nekrosis of Jesus' 124; Collange 149.
[44] Cf. also the lists in 2 Cor. 12:10; 1 Cor. 4:11–13; Rom. 8:35; Phil. 4:12; see as well
2 Cor. 1:8–9.
[45] So Robertson *Grammar* 1137–38; Allo 113.
[46] And not merely his opponents (as Georgi *Gegner* 244), but also his converts.
[47] Cf. Bultmann 116; Barrett 139.

suggests that it can become very grim indeed, it never reaches the point where the apostle succumbs to ultimate defeat and despair. In Paul's mind this is a tribute to the surpassing excellence of God's power working in him.

2 Corinthians 4:10 and 11

In verses 10 and 11 Paul sharpens the antitheses of verses 8 and 9 to show that his suffering conforms to the pattern of Christ.[48] He 'carries about in the body the dying of Jesus' (v. 10a). He is 'delivered over to death because of Jesus' (v. 11a). It could well be argued that these two statements, more than any other in Paul, form the nucleus of the apostle's understanding of the Christian ministry. To make sense of their profound message two unusual features must be explicated: (i) the interchange of the words νέκρωσις and θάνατος; and (ii) the use of the simple name Ἰησοῦς.

Normally when Paul speaks of death he employs the word θάνατος (cf. 2 Corinthians 4:11 and 12).[49] The fact that he uses νέκρωσις in verse 10a suggests that he is thinking of a process of dying, a putting to death, rather than the final condition of death.[50] This in turn serves to clarify the unusual occurrence of the single name 'Jesus' – a feature repeated six times in this chapter alone (4:5, 10 [2], 11 [2], 14).[51] Scholars are quick to point out that Paul is probably not focusing here on the historical Jesus *as opposed to* the Christ of faith. This dialectic simply would not have occurred to him.[52] Yet he may still be referring to the human life of Jesus, and ultimately his dying on the cross. Indeed the phrase ἡ νέκρωσις τοῦ Ἰησοῦ would suggest that he is thinking of the excruciating suffering of just that dying.[53]

---

48 Thus Schrage 'Leid, Kreuz und Eschaton' 168.
49 Cf. also 2 Cor. 1:9, 10; 2:16; 3:7; 4:12; 7:10; 11:23.
50 In the medical jargon of the second century the term νέκρωσις denoted a withering away of the body and was used in parallel to γάγγραινα ('an eating sore which slowly mortifies the body') and σφάκελος ('mortification'); see Aret. *SA* 2.10.4; Gal. 18(1).156K. For this meaning of νέκρωσις in 2 Cor. 4:10 cf. Lambrecht 'Nekrosis of Jesus' 120; Barrett 139–40; Wolff 92; Bruce 197; Windisch 145; Meyer 495–96; Plummer 129; Strachan 94; *pace* Collange 155 and Güttgemanns *Apostel* 114–17 who point to Paul's other use of νέκρωσις in Rom. 4:19 where it simply means death.
51 Elsewhere in Paul the simple name 'Jesus' appears only nine times (Rom. 3:26; 8:11; 1 Cor. 12:3; 2 Cor. 11:4; Gal. 6:17; Phil. 2:10; 1 Thess. 1:10; 4:14 [2]).
52 Cf. Kramer *Christ* 200.
53 Cf. Collange 155; Lambrecht 'Nekrosis of Jesus' 124–25; Rissi *Studien* 49; Stanley *Resurrection* 135.

By claiming to carry about 'the dying of Jesus' Paul is thus making the remarkable assertion that he endures the same sufferings which marked the cross of Jesus.[54] Moreover, he endures such suffering unceasingly, as the emphatic adverb πάντοτε (v. 10; cf. ἀεί in v. 11) and the present tense of the participle περιφέροντες make clear.[55] He also endures it physically, 'in the body' (v. 10), 'in our mortal flesh' (v. 11).[56] In short, Paul experiences – continually and physically – the sufferings of the cross. His affliction is an extension of Christ's.

That is why he can assert so boldly elsewhere that 'the sufferings of Christ are *ours* in abundance' (2 Corinthians 1:5), that he 'suffers *with* Christ' (Romans 8:17) and, most graphically, that he bears in his body the 'scars of Jesus' (τὰ στίγματα τοῦ Ἰησοῦ, Galatians 6:17).[57] What it does not explain is the extent to which his suffering is *actually* Christ's. In what sense does Paul manifest the scars *of Jesus*? What does he really mean by carrying about in his body the dying *of Jesus*? Our answer to these questions will proceed in four parts.

A sharing in a heritage of righteous suffering

Of particular interest is the famous text in Colossians 1:24 where either Paul or an amanuensis makes the remarkable claim that he fills up 'what is lacking in the afflictions of Christ' (τὰ ὑστερήματα τῶν θλίψεων τοῦ χριστοῦ). These words have long puzzled scholars. Do they imply that there is a deficiency in the efficacious suffering of Christ?[58] Most respond with a resounding 'No!',[59] though seldom for the obvious reason that the notion of efficacy is completely absent from the context.[60]

Modern scholars have tended to focus on the phrase αἱ θλίψεις τοῦ χριστοῦ and have suggested that it refers to the 'messianic woes' of the last times.[61] It is these 'woes' which Paul is filling

---

54 Cf. Proudfoot 'Realistic Participation?' 155.
55 Cf. 1 Cor. 15:31: *καθ᾽ ἡμέραν ἀποθνήσκω*.
56 Here the words σῶμα and σάρξ are used interchangeably; cf. Rissi *Studien* 48–49; Furnish 256; Barrett 141; Kümmel 201–2.
57 On this rendering of στίγμα cf. BAG 776; Bruce *Galatians* 276.
58 The view of Windisch *Paulus und Christus* 236–50.
59 Thus Moule *Colossians* 75; Lohse *Colossians* 69.
60 For criticism of those who approach this text with pre-conceived notions about the efficacy of Christ's death cf. Hooker 'Interchange and Suffering' 81.
61 Cf. ḥblw šl mšyḥ, 'the travail of the Messiah', in *Mek. Exod.* 16:25, 29; *b. Sab.* 118a; *Pesah.* 118a.

up.[62] But that is to find the basis of Paul's suffering in a set number of apocalyptic afflictions and not, as the apostle himself seems to maintain, in Christ himself (It is *because of Jesus* that we are constantly delivered over to death', 2 Corinthians 4:11). Moreover, it is to assume that Paul's suffering is peculiarly eschatological, and hence characteristically the product of the last times. But that neglects the fact that the righteous have always suffered and that the affliction of Paul probably represents just one more episode in a long line of tragic suffering, a heritage which will need 'completing' as long as the present evil age persists.[63]

In filling up the afflictions of Christ, then, Paul embarks on something which is neither new nor exclusively eschatological but rather typical of the experience of God's people throughout the ages.[64] Interestingly, in Romans 8:36 he describes his experience of suffering in the same terms which the ancient psalmist used to describe his affliction: 'we are being put to death all day long' (Psalms 44:22).[65] The long succession of righteous suffering represents a legacy which began in the distant past and which continues even now in the afflictions of Christ. To the question, What does it mean to carry about the dying of Jesus? we can offer at least a partial response. It means sharing in and filling up a heritage of righteous suffering.

A sharing in the weakness of the cross

But of course the afflictions of Christ represent more than the typical sufferings of history. According to Paul, they mark the denouement of history. The dying of Jesus is archetypal. Henceforth all righteous suffering will bear a specifically christological imprint.

This is the thrust of Paul's teaching in 2 Corinthians 13 where he uses the language of incorporation to underscore that his suffering is uniquely and ultimately like Christ's. 'He (Christ) was crucified because of weakness . . . we also are weak in him' (v. 4).[66] From earlier observations we know that to be weak in Christ means to

---

[62] Cf. O'Brien *Colossians* 78–79; Zeilinger *Erstgeborene der Schöpfung* 82–94.

[63] Thus Dunn *Jesus and the Spirit* 332.

[64] In the Psalms (LXX) the term θλῖψις occurs thirty-six times, and always in reference to the people of God. This suggests that epigrams such as that found in LXX Ps. 33: 20 (= *4 Macc.* 18:15), 'many are αἱ θλίψεις of the righteous', represent a timeless truth.

[65] On this interpretation of Rom. 8:36 see Cranfield *Romans* 1.440.

[66] A few manuscripts (ℵ, A, F) read σὺν αὐτῷ, rather than ἐν αὐτῷ (B, D, C, 0243).

share in his un-self-striving, self-negating, servant-like, God-centred faith. Here Paul enunciates the related teaching that it is precisely 'because of'[67] such weakness that Christ was crucified. In other words, it was the 'weakness' of humble faith that provoked the self-exalting of this world to afflict Christ with ridicule and scorn, and ultimately crucifixion. Accordingly, those who are 'weak in him' can expect their humble faith to precipitate a suffering like his.[68]

We may now respond further to the question, In what sense does Paul carry about the dying of Jesus? In the sense that he reflects in his person the weakness and humility of Christ and so must endure the same – if not exactly in substance at least in principle – sort of ridicule and scorn, and even physical abuse, which Jesus himself experienced in his dying on the cross.[69]

A sharing in the demise of the present age

It is important to observe that Paul did not regard suffering as an end in itself. He was intent on a higher purpose – that of manifesting the life of Jesus in his body (the phrase ἵνα καὶ ἡ ζωὴ τοῦ Ἰησοῦ φανερωθῇ appears in both verses 10b and 11b). Just what this 'life of Jesus' entails is not immediately clear, and needs our attention.

We gain an important insight into its meaning in 2 Corinthians 13:4 where Paul discloses that Christ 'was crucified because of weakness, but lives through the power of God'. Here 'life' clearly represents the overthrow of the old power of death. This would suggest that in so far as Paul 'manifests' in his body the 'life of Jesus'

---

[67] On taking ἐκ in this verse causally cf. BAG 234 3–4; Robertson *Grammar* 598; Moulton *Grammar* III 260.

[68] On the inevitability of the humble being made to suffer we may compare the plottings of the wicked against the righteous in Wis 2:

> Let us lie in wait for the righteous man, because he is
>   inconvenient to us and opposes our actions . . .
> He became to us a reproof of our thoughts;
>   the very sight of him is a burden to us,
>   because his manner of life is unlike that of others,
>   and his ways are strange . . .
> Let us test him with insult and torture . . .
> Let us condemn him to a shameful death   (vv. 12, 15, 19–20).

We may also note Plato *Rep.* 361E: 'the just man will be thrown into prison, scourged and racked, will have his eyes burned out, and, after every kind of torment, be crucified'.

[69] Cf. Kamlah 'Wie beurteilt Paulus sein Leiden?' 232; Dunn *Jesus and the Spirit* 335; Lambrecht 'Nekrosis of Jesus' 137–38.

he possesses a resurrection power which not only vanquishes death but also represents the overthrow of the old order. Put succinctly, Paul possesses the power of a new age.

We have already seen one way in which this power works out in Paul's own experience. In 2 Corinthians 4:8 and 9 we discovered that even though the apostle comes face to face with the powers of death and incurs the brutalities of those who owe their allegiance to the present evil age he has no cause ultimately to fear such malefactors. The power residing in him exceeds that of the old order. He may be hard pressed and experience the 'dying of Jesus' in his body but that only serves to ensure that the 'life of Jesus' will also become operative in his mortal flesh, preserving him from being crushed and rebuffing the otherwise indomitable power of death. The 'life of Jesus' within him thus makes Paul an agent of something new and epochal.[70]

The great irony is that it is precisely in submitting to the suffering meted out by the powers of the old age that Paul is able to repulse those very powers (verses 8–9). Living as he does at the intersection of two ages he endures the 'dyings' of the old in order to receive the 'life' of the new (verses 10–11). This remarkable fact is underscored by the telic ἵνα's and emphatic καί's in 2 Corinthians 4:10 and 11. He 'carries about the dying of Jesus . . . *in order that* the life of Jesus *also* . . . might be manifested'. He 'is . . . delivered over to death . . . *in order that* the life of Jesus *also* might be manifested'. Incidently, the teaching here is similar to Philippians 3:10, a text closely related to 2 Corinthians 4:10–11, where the apostle affirms that he knows '*both* the power of [Christ's] resurrection *and* the fellowship of his suffering'.[71]

We thus find in 2 Corinthians 4:10 and 11 a dramatic exposition of the principle enunciated in 2 Corinthians 4:7 and illustrated in verses 8 and 9. It is in human weakness that the superlative power of God springs to action, bringing 'life' out of 'death' and a new age from the old.

---

[70] The phrase ἡ ζωὴ τοῦ Ἰησοῦ in vv. 10 and 11 thus denotes present, not future, power – i.e. 'life' which occurs ἐν τῇ θνητῇ σαρκί (v. 11); so Nielsen 'Paulus Verwendung des Begriffes Δύναμις' 150–51; Schrage 'Leid, Kreuz und Eschaton' 169; Bultmann 121; Collange 156; *pace* Barrett 140; Lietzmann 116–17.

[71] Cf. Hooker *Pauline Pieces* 91: 'for [Paul] death and resurrection . . . are superimposed'.

A sharing in the paradox of new life

But the 'life of Jesus' does more than merely counteract the power of death. Since it is a present manifestation of resurrection life, it serves to empower an entirely new way of existence.[72] Paul sums it up well in 2 Corinthians 5:15 and 17: those who have this resurrection life (οἱ ζῶντες)[73] no longer live for themselves but for him who died and rose for them. They become new creatures, the old self-indulgent ways pass away, new self-sacrificing ones come.[74] The 'life of Jesus' thus enables Paul to sustain an existence of self-emptying humility. Ironically, it is precisely such humility that evokes the scorn and ridicule of the world and issues in Paul having to carry about in his body the 'dying of Jesus.' Consequently, we can see why Paul views his ministry in such paradoxical terms – 'we who live (οἱ ζῶντες) are constantly being delivered over to death' (εἰς θάνατον παραδιδόμεθα, 2 Corinthians 4:11) – for, in his experience, to live is to die.

Yet to die is also truly to live. Or, as Paul himself puts it, 'as dying, yet behold, we are living' (ὡς ἀποθνήσκοντες καὶ ἰδοὺ ζῶμεν, 2 Corinthians 6:9). This paradox may be elucidated in a variety of ways. It is in being conformed to the death of Christ that one takes on the divine likeness, the image of the new Adam and the true Man, and so discovers what it means to be truly human. It is in being delivered over to death for Christ's sake that one is transformed from one level of glory to another and so advances towards the ultimate goal of true spiritual maturity (2 Corinthians 3:18; 4:11). It is by boasting of human weakness that one comes increasingly to manifest in one's person the perfect power of Christ (cf. ἡ γὰρ δύναμις ἐν ἀσθενείᾳ τελεῖται, 2 Corinthians 12:9). It is in succumbing willingly to the consequences of humble faith – in particular, the sufferings of Christ – that one discovers what it means fully to live.[75]

There is thus a supreme purpose in carrying about the dying of

---

[72] Cf. Furnish 256: the 'life of Jesus' refers to 'the power of his resurrection life' (also 284).

[73] Namely, those who have risen with Christ (cf. 2 Cor. 5:14); see Furnish 311.

[74] Cf. Rom. 6:10 and 11 where 'life' is defined in terms of dying to sin and living to God.

[75] The idea of gaining true life through dying is nowhere expressed more clearly than in the words attributed to Jesus in Mark 8 (here roughly paraphrased): 'whoever wishes to save his life must lose it for my sake and the gospel's – by denying himself and taking up the cross' (vv. 34 and 35). On the similarities between 2 Cor. 4:10–11 and Mark 8 cf. Bruce 197.

Jesus – namely, to turn back the forces of death and to open up a whole new way of life. Just as human weakness is a prerequisite for divine power (2 Corinthians 4:7), so carrying about the dying of Jesus precedes a manifestation of the image, the glory, the new age and the fulness of life of Jesus Christ (2 Corinthians 4:10–11).

It is worth noting that according to Paul it is not just apostles who share in the dying and life of Jesus, but all who are in Christ. It is this paradox which reveals the essence of what it means to be a Christian. We may note that in 2 Corinthians 1:4–6 Paul applies a different form of the same paradox to his *converts*. By participating in the sufferings of Christ they also receive his comfort.[76]

2 Corinthians 4:12 and 15

The apostle moves on quickly to show how the 'life of Jesus' in him redounds to the benefit of others. In verse 12 he writes, 'death works in us, but life in *you*'.[77] These words represent an interesting departure from the message of verses 10 and 11, where the recipient of both the dying and the life of Jesus was Paul himself. Here it is the Corinthians who receive 'life'. What this means in practical terms is elucidated in 2 Corinthians 1:6 where Paul reveals that his suffering (viz. his 'dying') works for the Corinthians' *salvation*. The message is similar in 2 Corinthians 13:9: his weakness works for their *restoration* (κατάρτισις). In some way, then, Paul's suffering serves to commute life and salvation to his readers.[78]

The message of verse 12 is expanded and elaborated in verse 15: 'all things (especially his 'dying') are for your sake,[79] that grace, which is multiplying the thanksgiving of the majority, may abound to the glory of God'.[80] The 'life' of verse 12 is defined more closely here in verse 15 as a maturing church which brings glory to God.[81]

---

76 On 2 Cor. 4:10–11 applying to all Christians see Kamlah 'Leiden' 227, 231; Tannehill *Dying and Rising* 86–7; Dunn *Jesus and the Spirit* 327; Lambrecht 'Nekrosis of Jesus' 142–43; Furnish 283; Bultmann 118; Thrall 140–41; and cf. Hooker 'Interchange in Christ' 360–61.

77 The opening ὥστε shows that v. 12 flows as a direct consequence from the message of vv. 10 and 11; so Furnish 257.

78 For this view of 2 Cor. 4:12 see Hooker *Pauline Pieces* 82.

79 Cf. 2 Cor. 12:19: τὰ δὲ πάντα, ἀγαπητοί, ὑπὲρ τῆς ὑμῶν οἰκοδομῆς.

80 The syntax of this verse is jumbled. We have taken the participle πλεονάσασα as transitive, with τὴν εὐχαριστίαν as its object, and the verb περισσεύω as intransitive.

81 Thus interpreting διὰ τῶν πλειόνων as 'the majority' in the Corinthian congregation (cf. 2 Cor. 2:6; 9:2; Barrett 144–45) and not as an 'increasing number' of converts (as Furnish 260; Lietzmann 116).

We thus arrive at a compelling answer to the question, Why *must* glory be revealed in shame? Because only in shame will the power of God spring into action, effecting the demise of the powers of this age, spreading life and power to more and more people, transforming them into the image and glory of the Lord and causing thanksgiving to abound to the honour of God.

2 Corinthians 4:13

The opening words of this verse, ἔχοντες δὲ τὸ αὐτὸ πνεῦμα τῆς πίστεως, are reminiscent of other introductory statements in the near context. For the fifth time in two chapters Paul begins a new section with a form of the verb ἔχω, a particle of transition and an intensifying demonstrative.

πεποίθησιν δὲ τοιαύτην ἔχομεν	(3:4)
ἔχοντες οὖν τοιαύτην *ἐλπίδα*	(3:12)
διὰ τοῦτο, ἔχοντες τὴν *διακονίαν* ταύτην	(4:1)
ἔχομεν δὲ τὸν *θησαυρὸν* τοῦτον	(4:7)

In each of these cases the noun receiving the emphasis (see the italicised words) serves to remind the reader of the theme of the preceeding verses. This would also seem to be true of the nominal term stressed in verse 13, τὸ πνεῦμα τῆς πίστεως. It sums up the theme of verses 7–12.[82]

If this is so, then the most difficult interpretive problem of this verse, the meaning of the demonstrative αὐτό, has already received an important clue. Commentators have debated vigorously over whether this term refers to the 'same' faith as the psalmist who is cited in the latter half of verse 13[83] or the 'same' faith as Paul's Corinthian readers.[84] On our reckoning it refers to neither, but points instead to the pattern of life which Paul has just enunciated in verses 7–12 – his carrying about the dying and the life of Jesus (v. 10), his being delivered over to death for Jesus' sake so that others may live (vv. 11–12) – a pattern of life which is summed up now in the term 'this *very* spirit of faith'.[85]

---

[82] Cf. Rissi *Studien* 58–59; *pace* Baumert *Täglich sterben* 83 who links v. 13 to v. 12a only.
[83] Thus Collange 162; Barrett 142; Bultmann 123; Furnish 258; Meyer 499; Martin 89.
[84] Cf. Strachan 96; Schlatter 535; Baumert *Täglich sterben* 83–84.
[85] Cf. Rissi *Studien* 59.

This suggestion leads to three further observations. (i) The faith which Paul manifests in his affliction must be the same faith which Jesus himself demonstrated in his suffering.[86] (ii) Since it is the Spirit who conforms Paul to the image of Christ (cf. 2 Corinthians 3:18), it must also be the Spirit who produces Paul's Christ-shaped faith – thus we can read 'Spirit' (with a capital 'S').[87] (iii) In criticising Paul for his humility and suffering the Corinthians demonstrate that they may lack this 'Spirit of faith', which helps to explain Paul's injunction in 2 Corinthians 13:5 that they should examine their own πίστις.

The phrase, ἔχοντες δὲ τὸ αὐτὸ πνεῦμα τῆς πίστεως, also serves to introduce the matter of Paul's preaching – 'having this very Spirit of faith . . . we also speak'.[88] Clearly, it is faith which moves Paul to preach.[89] In this he is taking up the mantle of the psalmist, quoting verbatim the words of LXX Psalms 115:1, 'I believed, therefore I spoke' (ἐπίστευσα, διὸ ἐλάλησα). The entire psalm is of relevance to Paul.[90] Its author laments the horrific nature of his affliction (LXX Psalms 114:3, 8), and yet because of the firmness of his faith he continues to speak, even though he knows it will mean further suffering.[91] The same reality would seem to be etched in Paul's mind. In spite of his affliction, he, too, will speak; his faith compels him to do so – a faith borne of the conviction that in carrying about

---

86 Thus while the term τὸ αὐτὸ πνεῦμα τῆς πίστεως may be translated demonstratively ('this very spirit of faith'), gathering up the ideas of vv. 7–12, it may also refer to the faith of Jesus implicit in those verses; cf. Hooker 'Interchange and Suffering' 78–79.

87 Cf. Rissi *Studien* 59; Collange 162; Furnish 258; and see 1 Cor. 12:9; *pace* Hughes 147 and Bultmann 123 who take πνεῦμα here as a reference to the human spirit.

88 The relation of the word πίστις (occurring here with its cognates three times) to λαλεῖν (occurring twice) is clearly the emphasis of v. 13; so Collange 161.

89 Thus taking the verb λαλεῖν as a technical term for preaching (cf. Siber *Mit Christus leben* 70; *pace* Murphy-O'Connor 'Faith' 547; see 1 Cor. 3:1; 2 Cor. 2:17; Phil. 1:14; 1 Thess. 2:2, 4, 16).

90 Some commentators (e.g. Barrett 143) think Paul is citing LXX Ps. 115:1 atomistically and not drawing on the surrounding context. Yet LXX Ps. 115 formed part of a larger collection of psalms (LXX 112–117; MT 113–118), the so-called Egyptian Hallel, which were sung as a unit every Passover – LXX 112–113:8 before the evening meal and LXX 113:9–117 after (cf. Allen *Psalms* 99–100; Kraus *Psalmen* 951). The psalms would have been very familiar to Paul, which suggests that in quoting LXX Ps. 115:1 it would have been hard for him not to be contemplating its context; cf. Rissi *Studien* 59; Baumert *Täglich sterben* 87; Qwarnström 'Paulinsk skriftanvändning' 148–53; Young and Ford *Meaning and Truth* 64–67; Hanson *Paradox of the Cross* 52–53; Allo 116; Plummer 133.

91 Thus LXX 115:1: ἐπίστευσα, διὸ ἐλάλησα, ἐγὼ δὲ ἐταπεινώθην σφόδρα ('I believed, therefore I spoke; and I was greatly humbled' – i.e., made to endure further affliction).

the dying of Jesus the life of Jesus will also spring powerfully to work in his ministry.

In Paul's case persecution seems actually to fortify his faith. In 2 Corinthians 1:8 and 9 we read that when Paul was in Asia his suffering became so intense that he despaired of life itself. This prompted him to put his entire confidence in God.[92] Faith thus initiates a remarkable cycle in Paul. By faith Paul preaches the gospel, which in turn brings affliction, which then produces in him greater faith, which in turn creates greater boldness of speech, which then provokes additional affliction. For the minister of Christ, the pattern of believing – speaking – suffering is inescapable and perpetual.[93]

2 Corinthians 4:14

In verse 14 Paul elaborates the content of his faith. He has faith that the God who raised the Lord Jesus will also raise him together with Jesus.[94] This hope of a future resurrection has a profound impact on Paul's earthly existence.[95] It is partly because he believes in a future resurrection of the dead that he is presently willing to carry about in his body the dying of Jesus (4:10–11). It is because he trusts in a future exaltation that he submits now to the condition of a 'slave' (4:5). It is because he looks forward to a future heavenly life that he is willing to die daily (1 Corinthians 15:30). It is because he anticipates reigning with Christ in the future that he can speak so boldly in the present (2 Corinthians 4:13). Without faith in a future resurrection Paul's present suffering would be not only intolerable, but also meaningless (1 Corinthians 15:30–32). He would, on his own admission, be a man most to be pitied (1 Corinthians 15:17–19).

But it is precisely this faith in a future resurrection which some of the Corinthians seem to lack (cf. 1 Corinthians 15:12: πῶς λέγουσιν ἐν ὑμῖν τινες ὅτι ἀνάστασις νεκρῶν οὐκ ἔστιν). Whether this was due to a generally pessimistic view of life after death[96] or a belief

---

[92] The perfect construction πεποιθότες ἐπί can be translated as 'trust in' or 'rely on' (cf. Furnish 114).

[93] Interestingly, Collange 162 regards πίστις as 'the key to our passage (2:147:4)'.

[94] Cf. Siber *Mit Christus leben* 71.

[95] There can be little doubt that Paul is referring here to a future resurrection (cf. the future tense of the verb ἐγερεῖ; thus Siber *Mit Christus leben* 71–75; Barrett 143; *pace* Baumert *Täglich sterben* 90–91 who argues that Paul is referring to a present resurrection.

[96] We may note MacMullen's (*Paganism* 53–57) appraisal of first-century views to life after death: 'assurances of immortality prove unexpectedly hard to find in the

only in the immortality of the soul (as opposed to the resurrection of the body),[97] their scepticism on this matter doubtless contributed to their carefree approach to life. Without such a future hope they would have had little incentive to follow the example of their apostle and 'die daily' (1 Corinthians 15:30). How much more sensible to adopt the popular dictum 'Let us eat and drink, for tomorrow we die' (1 Corinthians 15:32).[98]

This evidence suggests to Paul that the resurrection of Jesus is just as important as his death in determining the moral character of Christians. If the Lord Jesus did not rise from the dead, then Christian existence as Paul knows it would cease to exist.[99]

2 Corinthians 4:16–18

But for Paul resurrection was not just a future hope. It was a present reality.[100] This is the implication of verses 16–17 where he claims that his 'inner man is being renewed day by day' (v.16)[101] and that 'an eternal weight of glory' is presently accumulating in his account (v. 17). The term ἔσω ἡμῶν probably does not refer to the inward part of man, the soul, as opposed to the outward flesh, for Paul seems to have had little interest in that kind of psychological dualism.[102] Rather, it refers to the *entire* person. The day by day renewal of the 'inner man' may be identified with the progressive transformation of the 'new man' into the image of Christ and thus with the ongoing manifestation of increasing increments of glory (cf.

---

evidence. Even the longing for it is not much attested' (here p. 53); see above pp. 27–9; but see Meeks *Urban Christians* 181–82.

97 Cf. Wedderburn 'Hellenistic Christian Traditions' 347–49, 'Hellenistic Mystery-Cults' 825–26 who maintains that the idea of bodily resurrection would have been exceedingly difficult for hellenistic Christians to understand; see also Lietzmann 209; Robertson-Plummer *First Corinthians* 329.

98 Contrary to Furnish 286, the problems of 1 Cor. 15 do seem to be in the back of Paul's mind in 2 Cor. 4:14.

99 Cf. the dramatic assessment of Rissi *Studien* 60: '*In der Auferweckungshoffnung findet die ganze Argumentation des Paulus ihr Ziel. Ohne sie würde alles, was Paulus sagt und lebt, sinnlos*' ('*In the hope of resurrection the entire argument of Paul finds its objective. Without it everything Paul says and does would be meaningless*'; his emphasis); cf. Barrett *First Corinthians* 365–68.

100 On the *present* experience of future resurrection cf. Hooker *Pauline Pieces* 91–92.

101 The term ἡμέρᾳ καὶ ἡμέρᾳ is probably not a Hebraism for yôm yôm and translated 'every day' or 'daily' (as e.g. BDF § 200.1; Moulton *Grammar* III 243; Martin 91; cf. Furnish 262), but a phrase denoting a progressive, 'day *by* day' renewal (cf. ἀπὸ δόξης εἰς δόξαν in 3:18; and see Barrett 145).

102 Cf. Barrett 146; Martin 91–92; *pace* Feuillet 'Mort du Christ' 501.

2 Corinthians 3:18; Colossians 3:10).[103] By coming to reflect the person and glory of Christ, Paul is reaping eternal glory now.

What makes this revelation especially striking is that elsewhere the apostle speaks of conformity to Christ as a future event. In Philippians 3:21, for example, he maintains that the transformation of his humble body into conformity with the exalted and glorified body of Christ is something which *awaits* the arrival of a Saviour, the Lord Jesus Christ. In 2 Corinthians 4:16 and 17 this transformation has already begun.[104]

Yet one would hardly know it by looking at Paul. His outward appearance is so unimpressive that it causes his converts to wonder whether he possesses any glory at all. But again Paul reverses their logic. It is precisely because his outer man is decaying[105] that his inner man is being renewed day by day (v. 16). His outer afflictions serve to multiply the glory of his inner man (v. 17). His critics fail to see this increasing weight of glory because it is accumulating in his heart (v. 6),[106] a place hidden to their externally-minded outlook.

The apostle is himself amazed by the sheer quantity of his glory. In an exuberant and nearly untranslatable phrase Paul maintains that there is working within him καθ' ὑπερβολὴν εἰς ὑπερβολὴν αἰώνιον βάρος δόξης, an unimaginably brilliant and profoundly weighty glory. It is so weighty that it makes the trials of his present affliction seem light by comparison.[107] This is a remarkable affirmation, for earlier in the epistle Paul bemoaned the overwhelming 'heaviness' of his afflictions. He used the very terms there to describe his sufferings that he now uses to describe his glory: 'we were weighed down surpassingly and beyond our strength' (καθ' ὑπερβολὴν ὑπὲρ δύναμιν ἐβαρήθημεν, 2 Corinthians 1:8). The affliction which once felt like a lethal weight round his neck now seems weightless in comparison to his eternal load of glory.

So great is the glory that Paul almost forgets his affliction. Indeed

---

[103] On the link between this verse, transformation in 3:18 and renewal in Col. 3:10 (where see the verb ἀνακαινόω) cf. Furnish 289–90; and see above pp. 147–48.

[104] It is of course a transformation which will be *completed* in the future — an idea Paul develops at length in 2 Cor. 5:1–10, where he longs for the day when he will finally exchange his decaying mortal body for a glorious heavenly dwelling.

[105] Here we may identify the term ὁ ἔξω ἡμῶν ἄνθρωπος with ἡ θνητὴ σάρξ ἡμῶν in 2 Cor. 4:11, and thus with the physical body which is constantly being delivered over to death because of Jesus; thus Furnish 289; Gundry *SOMA* 136–37.

[106] Cf. Wright 'Reflected Glory' 150.

[107] Thus 'our momentary lightness of affliction' (τὸ παραυτίκα ἐλαφρὸν τῆς θλίψεως ἡμῶν, v. 17).

he fixes his gaze on what cannot be seen (v. 18),[108] his inner glory, not his outer affliction (4:17), his inward renewal, not his external decay (4:16), the new age, not the old (4:18), resurrection life, not present dying (4:10, 11), the weighty, not the trifling (4:17), the eternal, not the temporal (4:18), the heavenly, not the earthly (5:1–2). In short, he adopts a perspective of faith, of walking by faith and not by sight (διὰ πίστεως γὰρ περιπατοῦμεν, οὐ διὰ εἴδους, 5:7), of trusting that, for the present eschatological moment, glory really does come to expression through affliction.

Sadly for Paul, it is precisely this perspective which some of his converts lack. As he reveals in 2 Corinthians 10:7, they look at things κατὰ πρόσωπον – that is to say, according to what is immediately before them.[109] Their perspective is superficial. We may note Paul's liberal use, in 2 Corinthians 2:14–4:18, of words, which have visual connotations[110] – θριαμβεύω (2:14); φανερόω (2:14; 3:3; 4:10 [2], 11); δόξα (3:7 [2], 8, 9 [2], 10, 11 [2], 18 [3]; 4:4, 6, 17); πρόσωπον (3:7 [2], 13, 18; 4:6); ἀτενίζω (3:7, 13); δοξάζω (3:10 [2]); κάλυμμα (3:13, 14, 15, 16); ἀνακαλύπτω (3:14, 18); κατοπτρίζομαι (3:18); κρυπτός (4:2); φανέρωσις (4:2); καλύπτω (4:3 [2]); τυφλόω (4:4); αὐγάζω (4:4); φωτισμός (4:4, 6); σκότος (4:6); φῶς (4:6); λάμπω (4:6 [2]); σκοπέω (4:18); βλέπω (4:18 [4]) – words which doubtless were chosen for their usefulness in correcting the display-conscious perspective of the Corinthian church.[111] By filling these terms with new meaning Paul hopes to teach his converts that the correct outlook, the perspective of faith, does not fix its gaze on what can be seen, the counterfeit glory of outward displays, but on what cannot be seen, the authentic glory of the heart.[112]

---

108 On this paradox see Michaelis 'ὁράω' 349–50.

109 The entire clause reads: τὰ κατὰ πρόσωπον βλέπετε. The second person plural βλέπετε may be either imperative (so Lietzmann 141; Windisch 300; Barrett 255–56; Allo 276; Héring 71; Meyer 290) or indicative, and, if indicative, a statement (so Plummer 279; Goudge 96) or a question (Bultmann 189). Since in the NT the imperatival βλέπετε *always* stands first in its clause (in Paul see 1 Cor. 1:26; 8:9; 10:18; 16:10; Gal. 5:15; Phil. 3:2; Col. 2:8; 4:17) and the indicatival βλέπετε *always* elsewhere (cf. Matt. 11:4; 13:17; 24:2; etc.), we should translate βλέπετε in 2 Cor. 10:7 as a simple statement.

110 cf. Collange 126.

111 The frequent use of πρόσωπον in 2 Cor. (1:11; 2:10; 3:7, 13, 18; 4:6; 5:12; 8:24; 10:1, 7; 11:20) is probably also indicative of Paul's concern with the superficial perspective of the Corinthians.

112 For evidence of a wrong, faithless perspective cf. 2 Cor. 5:12, where some are reported to be boasting in appearance (τοὺς ἐν προσώπῳ καυχωμένους) and not in the hidden things of the heart (καὶ μὴ ἐν καρδίᾳ); see also LXX 1 Sam. 16:7:

Here again Paul draws inspiration from his gospel. In the cro
Christ he discovered not only that divine power had been manifested in human weakness, but also that it took eyes of humility,
eyes of faith, to detect that power. It required an outlook which
itself had been moulded by the cross – a cross-shaped faith which
focused on the unseen, not the seen.

Summary

A close examination of Paul's teaching in 2 Corinthians 4:7–18,
especially in the light of the situation which seemed to have
prompted it, a clash between the worldly outlook of the Corinthians
and the apostle's own cross-centred perspective, puts us in a position to make sense of Paul's otherwise confusing and seemingly
contradictory description of his ministry. The things which the
Corinthians find so objectionable about their apostle – his failure to
boast, his timid personal presence, his amateurish speech, his refusal
of support – all represent deliberate attempts by Paul to remain
humble before an exalted God. His critics, buoyed by the self-
exalting culture in which they live, naturally lament his resolve.
Indeed they regard it as a sign of 'weakness'. Paul accepts this
caricature but adds the stunning qualification that it is precisely in
such 'weakness' – in his mind, such humble faith – that true power,
the power of God, becomes effective in his ministry.

The inspiration for this conviction comes from the cross of Christ
itself, where the principle of power working in what the world
regards as a place of abject weakness receives its most striking
manifestation. As a minister of Christ, the same principle must
operate in Paul. He, too, must appear hopelessly 'weak'. He, too,
must suffer because of weakness. Indeed he labours on the brink of
total ruin, hard pressed, despairing, persecuted, struck down – yet
precisely because he does, because he carries about in his body the
dying of Jesus, the life of Jesus springs to action, rescuing his mortal
flesh from ultimate destruction, commuting life and hope to increasing numbers of people and channelling the power of the new age
into the gloom of the old.

The glory emanating from Paul's ministry could thus scarcely be
more brilliant. Still, many miss it. They fail to see the splendour of

'A person sees what is outward (εἰς πρόσωπον), but God sees what is within
(εἰς καρδίαν).'

the new life in Christ irrupting in the hearts of those formerly engulfed in darkness. That is because the new life comes to expression in the humility of faith, a trait viewed with scorn by those absorbed in the self-exalting outlook of their day. Far from seeing the glory of Paul's ministry, the radiance of new life spreading to more and more people, they see only 'weakness'. It is clear that the Corinthian church is still plagued by the secular outlook. Some of its members imbibe it. The opponents, seeking to win for themselves a position of honour and esteem, ruthlessly exploit it.

The apostle Paul has little choice but to resort to the language of paradox. As a servant of Christ, he is bound by the pattern inherent in the central object of his religion, the cross of his Lord – an object which not only marks the intersection of two ages, but does so by virtue of the fact that it represents the supreme example of what happens when the outlooks of the two ages, godless egotism and humble faith, converge. The apostle accepts his position at the centre of this convergence and affirms to his bewildered converts that it is only in his cruciform weakness and suffering that there can be a demonstration of divine power.

CONCLUSION

The purpose of this book has been to make sense of Paul's paradoxical teaching in 2 Corinthians and in particular of his description of his ministry in terms of two seemingly contradictory, yet overlapping, experiences – of power manifested through weakness, of glory revealed in shame, of life working through death. We may now briefly summarise our findings and draw a few conclusions.

In the first part of the study we discovered that before we could understand the meaning of Paul's teaching we had first to identify the situation which gave rise to it. This meant coming to grips with the nature of the criticisms levelled against Paul, for it was in response to those criticisms that the apostle imparted his paradoxical instruction.

We learned, first of all, that the Corinthians were evaluating Paul according to the self-exalting standards of their secular environment. They wanted him to be proud and assertive, to boast of his personal exploits, to employ powerful speech, to draw comfort from financial security – in a word, to embody the self-regarding aspirations of their culture. By making these demands on Paul they demonstrated that they were assimilating their idea of a minister of Christ to the egocentric norms of their society. Not surprisingly, they were dismayed by Paul's humility – or, as they put it, his 'weakness' – and it caused them to wonder whether he was really a minister of the exalted Christ. The so-called 'opponents' exploited this already tense situation, infiltrating the congregation which Paul had planted, presenting themselves as models of the sort of aggressiveness and self-boasting which the Corinthians admired and winning for themselves accolades of honour and positions of importance within the Corinthian church.

We saw, secondly, that in responding to his critics Paul felt he had little choice but to turn their logic on its head. It was precisely his 'weakness' which not only affirmed his position as a minister of

Christ but also ensured that his labours would be accompanied by divine power. As a minister of Christ, he had no alternative but to renounce the self-exalting tendencies of his world.

Thus, by the end of the first half of our study, it was evident that the Corinthian church was embroiled in a conflict between two opposing viewpoints: the worldly outlook of the Corinthians and Paul's own Christ-centred perspective, the so-called 'wisdom of this age' and the 'wisdom of God'. This was an important observation, for it was precisely this conflict which seems to have evoked Paul's paradoxical teaching of power through weakness.

In the second part of the book we examined the paradoxes themselves, focusing our attention on 2 Corinthians 3–4, where the antitheses of power through weakness, glory through shame and life through death emerge in an especially striking light.

We considered, first of all, Paul's understanding of the nature of his ministry. Contrary to the accusations of his critics, he regarded his ministry as exceedingly glorious. It surpassed in splendour the dazzling brightness which adorned the face of Moses. It harnessed the creative light of Genesis 1 and reproduced it as the stunning glory of the eschaton. As such, it represented everything in terms of ineffable majesty that his critics could possibly have wanted in a minister of Christ. Yet, surprisingly, they failed to see it. In Paul's mind, it suggested that their vision was defective. It also revealed that there was something unusual about his glory.

Indeed for all its alleged brightness, the apostle's glory was not accessible to the naked eye. According to Paul, it was a paradoxical glory – a heavenly light which appeared in a terrestrial being named Jesus, an unearthly beauty manifested in the ugliness of an execution. It was thus the 'strange' and 'alien' glory anticipated by LXX Isaiah, a light revealed in the darkness of death, a splendour manifested in the most appalling object of antiquity – a cross. The ancients had no category for such a paradoxical glory. They looked for glory in great displays of human power – imposing oratory, a large and loose wallet, a domineering personality. Even Paul himself, before his conversion and while still influenced by the assumptions of his age, refused to believe that glory, and especially the glory of heaven, could be found in the curse of crucifixion.

It was only when God shone his light in Paul's heart that the apostle accepted by faith what his eyes had failed to see: the glory of God in the face of a crucified man. It proved to be a stunning revelation. It forced him to concede that the new age, the long awaited eschaton, had been inaugurated by an individual and through an event which made a mockery of the self-regarding aspirations he had cultivated so ardently. Shattered were his dreams of personal glory. Obliterated were his hopes of worldly greatness. Now he was compelled to identify with the most repugnant incident in antiquity, a hitherto unthinkable anomaly – a crucified Messiah! It was as though he himself had been crucified with Christ. Radically humbled, emptied of self, reduced to humble faith, he was, in his own words, made 'weak' in Christ.

But that did not mean he was weak in practice. According to Paul, it was only his critics, inspired by the self-exalting outlook of the day, who regarded his humility as 'weakness'. In the revelation which he received from God, he had discovered something very different – that it was precisely in the radical self-abnegation of the crucified Messiah that the power of God had come to its mightiest expression. It was in human weakness that God had chosen to manifest his illimitable power. The implication for Paul was clear. Insofar as he was conformed to the humility of Christ he, too, became a fitting vessel for the expression of divine power. The power of God was thus manifested in Paul in the same way in which it was expressed in Jesus: in cross-shaped humility.

But, as the apostle has made clear, this is the kind of humility which the world, and especially the world of first-century Corinth, abominates. The proud of this age will always regard the self-negation of God's true servants as both contemptible and a mortal threat to their own self-seeking outlook. It should not be surprising, then, if such 'weakness' is made to endure ridicule and abuse, and indeed the apostle himself suffered terrible affliction – in his mind, the same kind of affliction which Christ, in his 'weakness', also suffered. It is for this reason that Paul can make the astonishing assertion that he carries about in his body the dying of Jesus. Yet this serves merely as the pre-condition for an even more remarkable claim: that by enduring the dying of Jesus Paul also manifests the life of Jesus in his mortal flesh.

Hence the apostle guides us to the paradoxical – yet now more intelligible – conclusion that it is only in cruciform sufferings like his that the Lord can perform his powerful work, introducing glory into an age of darkness, salvation into a world of despair, a new age within the old and life and power to more and more people. The fruit of Paul's ministry could scarcely be more powerful and glorious. But, as he himself makes clear, it is a glory and a power manifested in 'weakness'.

As a minister of the gospel of the crucified Christ, and as one called to serve in an age dominated by a self-exalting outlook, the apostle Paul has little option but to respond to his worldly critics: 'When I am weak, then I am strong.'

APPENDIX

It is the assumption of this monograph that chapters 10–13 of
2 Corinthians represent a separate epistle written shortly after
chapters 1–9. This is the position of Barrett 18–21; "Ο 'ΑΔΙΚΗΣΑΣ'
156–57; 'Titus' 8–14; Thrall 'Second Thanksgiving' 121–22; Munck
Paul 169–71; Buck 'Collection' 9–29; Pherigo 'Paul' 341–50; Batey
'Paul's Interaction' 139–46; Windisch 17–20; Bruce 170–72; Furnish
35–41; Martin xli–xlvi. Others, however, identify chapters 10–13
with the painful letter of 2:3–4, 9; 7:8, 12, and thus with a letter
composed *before* chapters 1–9 (see Hausrath *Vier-Capitelbrief*
302–14, Watson 'Painful Letter' 324–46 and Strachan xvi–xx; and cf.
Weiss *Earliest Christianity* 323–57 [esp. 349, 357], Vielhauer
Geschichte 150–55 and Bultmann 23, who include 2:14–6:13 and
7:2–4 with 10–13 as part of the painful letter; and Bornkamm
'Vorgeschichte' 162–94, Georgi *Gegner* 25–29 and Marxen *Introduction* 77–82, who identify 10–13 with the painful letter but regard
2:14–6:13 and 7:2–4 as an earlier, and 1:1–2:23 and 7:5–8:24 as a
later, epistle). Still others contend for the full literary integrity of
2 Corinthians (thus Bates 'Integrity' 56–59; Stephenson 'Partition
Theories' 639–46; Allo l–lvi; Hughes xxi–xxxv; Kümmel *Introduction*
287–93; Lietzmann 139; Wendland 7; Tasker 23–25; Harris 303–6;
Menzies xxxiv–xxxvii).

There are good reasons for identifying 10–13 with a separate
letter written shortly after 1–9: (i) the sharp difference of tone
between 1–9 and 10–13 suggests that they are not parts of the same
letter; (ii) it is unlikely that 10–13 represents the earlier, painful
letter, since (a) it makes no mention of the one who had wronged
Paul (cf. 2:3–11; 7:8–12; and Munck *Paul* 170; Furnish 37), (b) given
its harsh content it could scarcely have been dispatched with a word
of commendation (cf. 7:14; and Barrett 'Titus' 9–10), (c) it seems
itself to refer to the earlier painful letter (cf. 10:1, 10) and (d) it
mentions in 12:17–18 a *past* visit by Titus which is still *future* in 8:18

(cf. Barrett 19–21; 'Titus' 12; but see Watson 'Painful Letter' 332–35); (iii) in chapters 8 and 9 Paul is not yet aware of the suspicion of some in 12:14–18 that he is guilty of deceit in administering the collection (cf. Furnish 38); and (iv) in taking 10–13 to be later than 1–9 we do not need to assume that Titus was 'disastrously mistaken' (Watson 'Painful Letter' 332) in giving his favourable report on the progress of the Corinthians (cf. 7:6–16), only that he rightly conveyed news of their outward obedience.

It is also the assumption of this monograph that chapters 1–9 represent a unity (see the arguments of Watson 'Painful Letter' 335–39 and Thrall 'Second Thanksgiving' 101–21) and that they contemplate the same situation as chapters 10–13, though an earlier stage within it (thus Georgi *Gegner* 24; Barrett 'Opponents' 236).

SELECT BIBLIOGRAPHY

Primary sources

(Abbreviations of primary sources follow established usage: for Classical literature see LSJ and *OCD*, for Jewish material see *JBL* 95 [1976] 335–38 and for Philo and Josephus see LCL)

Acta Apostolorum Apocrypha, ed. R. A. Lipsius and M. Bonnet, 3 vols. Hildesheim: Georg Olms Verlagsbuchhandlung, 1959.
Aelianus, ed. A. F. Scholfield, 3 vols., LCL, 1958– .
Alciphron, eds. A. R. Benner and F. H. Fobes, LCL, 1962.
The Apocrypha and Pseudepigrapha of the Old Testament in English, Vol. 1, *Apocrypha*, ed. R. H. Charles. Oxford: The Clarendon Press, 1913.
Appian, *Roman History*, ed. H. White, 4 vols., LCL, 1912– .
Apuleius, ed. G. F. Hildebrand, 2 vols. Leipzig: Sumtibus C. Cnoblochii, 1842.
Aretaeus, ed. K. Hude, Berlin: Aedibus Academiae Scientiarum, 1958.
Aristides, *Opera Omnia*, ed. W. Dindorf, 3 vols. Leipzig: G. Reimer, 1829.
Aristotle, *Rhetorica ad Alexandrum*, ed. H. Rackham, LCL, 1965.
Artemidorus Daldianus, *Onirocrita*, ed. R. A. Pack. Leipzig: B. G. Teubner, 1963.
Athenaeus, *The Deipnosophists*, ed. C. B. Gulick, 7 vols., LCL, 1927– .
Augustine, *The City of God against the Pagans*, ed. G. E. McCracken *et al.*, 7 vols., LCL, 1966– .
The Babylonian Talmud, ed. I. Epstein. 18 vols. London: The Soncino Press, 1961.
Biblia Hebraica Stuttgartensia, eds. K. Elliger and W. Rudolph. Stuttgart: Deutsche Bibelstiftung, 1967/77.
The Book of the Cave of the Treasures, ed. E. A. W. Budge. London: The Religious Tract Society, 1927.
Brunet de Presle, W. *Notices et extraits des papyrus grecs du musée du Louvre et de la bibliothèque impériale* xviii (2), Paris, 1865.
Calabi-Limentani, I. *Epigrafia Latina*. Milano: Istituto Editoriale Cisalpino, 1968.
Cicero, *Letters to His Friends*, ed. W. G. Williams, 3 vols., LCL, 1965– .
Tusculan Disputations, ed. J. E. King, LCL, 1966.
The Collection of Ancient Greek Inscriptions in the British Museum, eds. C. T. Newton, E. L. Hicks *et al.* 4 pts. Oxford: The Clarendon Press, 1874– .

Corpus Inscriptionum Graecarum, ed. A. Boeckhius. 4 vols. Berlin: G. Reimer, 1828– .
Corpus Inscriptionum Latinarum, ed. T. Mommsen *et al.* 14 pts. Berlin: G. Reimer, 1863– .
The Dead Sea Scrolls in English, ed. G. Vermes, 2nd ed. Harmondsworth: Penguin Books Ltd., 1962.
The Digest of Justinian, eds. T. Mommsen and P. Krueger, 4 vols. Philadelphia: University of Pennsylvania Press, 1985.
Dio Cassius, *Roman History*, ed. E. Cary, 9 vols., LCL, 1914–27.
Dio Chrysostom, *Discourses*, eds. J. W. Cahoon and H. Lamar Crosby, 5 vols., LCL, 1932– .
Diodorus Siculus, ed. C. H. Oldfather *et al.*, 12 vols., LCL, 1968– .
Edwards, K. M. *Corinth: Coins 1896–1929*. Vol. 6. Cambridge, Mass.: ASCSA, 1933.
Epictetus, ed. W. A. Oldfather., 2 vols., LCL, 1926– .
Eusebius Pamphilus, *La Préparation Évangélique*. 3 vols. Sources Chrétiennes 206, 215, 228. Paris: Les Éditions du Cerf, 1974–74.
Galenus, *On the Natural Faculties*, ed. J. Brock, LCL, 1963.
Gellius, Aulus, *The Attic Nights*, ed. J. C. Rolfe, 3 vols. LCL, 1967– .
Greek Papyri in the British Museum, eds. F. G. Kenyon and H. I. Bell. 5 vols. London: Oxford University Press, 1893– .
Grenfell, B. P., Hunt, A. S. and Hogarth, D. G. *Fayûm Towns and their Papyri*. London: Egypt – Exploration Fund, Graeco-Roman Branch, 3, 1900.
Griffith, F. L. and Thompson, H. *The Demotic Magical Papyrus of London and Leiden*. Vol. 1. London: H. Grevel and Co., 1904.
The Hebrew-English Edition of the Babylonian Talmud, eds. H. Freedman and I. Epstein, 20 vols. to date. London: The Soncino Press, 1969– .
Horace, *The Odes and Epodes*, ed. C. E. Bennett, LCL, 1968.
Inscriptiones Graecae, ed. A. Kirchhoff *et al.* 14 vols. Berlin: G. Reimer, 1873– .
Inscriptiones Graecae ad Res Romanas Pertinentes, ed. R. Cagnat *et al.* 3 vols. Paris: Ernest Leroux, Éditeur, 1911.
Inscriptiones Latinae Selectae, ed. H. Dessau. 3 vols. Berlin: Weidmann, 1902– .
Josephus, ed. H. St J. Thackeray *et al.*, 9 vols., LCL 1926– .
Juvenal, ed. G. G. Ramsay, LCL, 1969.
Kaibel, G. *Epigrammata Graeca*. Berlin: G. Reimer, 1878.
Kent, J. H. *Corinth: The Inscriptions 1926–1950*. Vol. 8, pt. 3. Princeton, N.J.: ASCSA, 1966.
Lane, E. *Corpus Monumentorum Religionis dei Menis*. Vol. 1. Leiden: E. J. Brill, 1971.
Le Bas, P. and Waddington, W. H. *Voyage archéologique en Grèce et en Asie Mineure*. 5 vols. Paris, 1847– .
Lightfoot, J. B. *The Apostolic Fathers*. Part 1. *S. Clement of Rome*. Vol. 1. London: MacMillan and Co. 1890.
Livy, ed. B. O. Foster *et al.*, 14 vols., LCL, 1913.
Lucan, ed. J. D. Duff, LCL, 1969.
Lucian, ed. A. M. Harmon *et al.*, 8 vols., LCL, 1968– .

Martial, *Epigrams*, ed. W. C. A. Ker, 2 vols., LCL, 1919– .
Mekilta de-Rabbi Ishmael, ed. J. Z. Lauterbach, 3 vols. Philadelphia: The Jewish Publication Society of America, 1933–35.
Meritt, B. D. *Corinth: Greek Inscriptions 1896–1927*. Vol. 8, pt. 1. Cambridge, Mass.: ASCSA, 1931.
The Midrash on Psalms, ed. W. G. Braude, 2 vols. New Haven: Yale University Press, 1959.
Midrash Rabbah, eds. H. Freedman and M. Simon. 10 vols. London: The Soncino Press, 1939.
Midrash Sifre on Numbers, ed. P. P. Levertoff. London: S.P.C.K., 1926.
Midrasch Tanchuma, ed. S. Buber, 4 vols. Wilna: Wittwe und Gebrüder, 1885.
The Mishnah, ed. H. Danby. Oxford: Oxford University Press, 1933.
Moretti, L. *Inscrizioni Agonistiche Greche*. Rome: Angelo Signorelli, 1953.
Novum Testamentum Graece, eds. E. Nestle and K. Aland, 26th ed. Stuttgart: Deutsche Bibelstiftung, 1979.
The Old Testament Pseudepigrapha: Vol. 1, *Apocalyptic Literature & Testaments*; Vol 2, *Expansions of the 'Old Testament' and Legends, Wisdom and Philosophical Literature, Prayers, Psalms and Odes, Fragments of Lost Judeo-Hellenistic Works*, ed. J. H. Charlesworth. London: Darton, Longman & Todd, 1983–85.
Orientis Graecae Inscriptiones Selectae. Ed. W. Dittenberger. 2 vols. Leipzig, 1903–5.
Origen, *Contra Celsum*, ed. H. Chadwick. Cambridge: Cambridge University Press, 1953.
Ovid, *Fasti*, ed. J. G. Frazer, LCL, 1969.
Metamorphoses, ed. F. T. Miller, 2 vols., LCL, 1966– .
Oxyrhynchus Papyri, eds. B. P. Grenfell, A. S. Hunt *et al.* 51 vols. London: The Egyptian Exploration Fund, 1898– .
Papiri Fiorentini, documenti pubblici e privati dell'età romana e bizantina. Vol. 1. Ed. G. Vitelli. Milano, 1906. Vol. 2. Ed. D. Comparetti, 1908–11. Vol. 3. Ed. G. Vitelli, 1915.
Pausanias, *Description of Greece*, ed. W. H. S. Jones *et al.*, 5 vols., LCL, 1918.
Pesikta Rabbati, ed. W. C. Braude, 2 vols. New Haven and London: Yale University Press, 1968.
Petronius, eds. M. Heseltine and E. H. Warmington, LCL, 1975.
Philo, eds. F. H. Colson and G. H. Whitaker, 12 vols., LCL, 1929– .
Philostratus, *The Life of Apollonius of Tyana*, ed. F. C. Conybeare, 2 vols., LCL, 1912.
The Lives of the Sophists, ed. W. C. Wright, LCL, 1921.
Plato, *The Republic*, ed. P. Shorey, 2 vols. LCL, 1953.
Pliny the Elder, *Natural History*, ed. H. Rackham *et al.*, 10 vols., LCL, 1938– .
Pliny the Younger, *Letters*, ed. W. Melmoth, 2 vols., LCL, 1915– .
Plutarch, *Lives*, ed. B. Perrin, 11 vols., LCL, 1914– .
Moralia, ed. F. C. Babbit *et al.*, 15 vols., LCL, 1927– .
Preisendanz, K. *Papyri Graecae Magicae*. 2 vols. Berlin: B. G. Teubner, 1928–31.

Quintilian, ed. H. E. Butler, 4 vols. LCL, 1969– .
Seneca, *Letters*, ed. R. M. Gummere, 2 vols. LCL, 1925– .
    Moral Essays (Dialogues), ed. J. W. Basore, 3 vols., 1970– .
Septuaginta, ed. A. Rahlfs. Stuttgart: Deutsche Bibelgesellschaft, 1935.
Sextus Empiricus, ed. R. B. Bury, 4 vols., LCL, 1967– .
Siphre ad Deuteronomium, ed. L. Finkelstein. Berlin: Jüdischer Kultusbund
    in Deutschland E. V. Abteilung Verlag, 1939.
Statius, ed. J. H. Mozley, 2 vols., LCL 1928– .
Strabo, *Geography*, ed. H. L. Jones, 8 vols., LCL, 1917– .
Suetonius, ed. J. C. Rolfe, 2 vols., LCL 1913.
Supplementum Epigraphicum Graecum., ed. J. J. E. Hondius. Leiden: A. W.
    Sijthoff, 1923– .
Sylloge Inscriptionum Graecarum, ed. W. Dittenberger. 3rd ed. 4 vols.
    Leipzig: A. S. Hirzel, 1915– .
Tacitus, ed. W. Peterson *et al.*, 5 vols., LCL, 1914– .
Le Talmud de Jérusalem, ed. M. Schwab, 6 vols. Paris: G.–P. Maisonneuve
    et C$^{ie.}$, 1960.
The Targums of Onkelos and Jonathan ben Uzziel on the Pentateuch, ed.
    J. W. Etheridge, 2 vols. London: Longman, Green and Roberts,
    1862–65.
Tatianus, *Oratio ad Graecos*, ed. M. Whittaker. Oxford: The Clarendon
    Press, 1982.
The Temple Scroll, ed. Y. Yadin, 3 vols. Jerusalem: The Israel Exploration
    Society, 1977–83.
Die Texte aus Qumran. Hebräisch und Deutsch, ed. E. Lohse. Darmstadt:
    Wissenschaftliche Buchgesellschaft, 1981.
The Tosefta, ed. J. Neusner, 6 vols. New York: KTAV Publishing House
    Inc., 1979– .
Trypho, *Grammatici Alexandrini Fragmenta*, ed. A. de Velsen, Amsterdam:
    Verlag Adolf M. Hakkert, 1965.
Vettius Valens, ed. G. Kroll. Berlin: Weidmann, 1908.
Vidman, L. *Sylloge inscriptionum religionis Isiacae et Serapiacae*. Berlin:
    Walter de Gruyter, 1969.
West, A. B. *Corinth: Latin Inscriptions 1896–1927*. Vol. 8, pt. 2. Cambridge,
    Mass.: ASCSA, 1931.
Wünsche, A. *Bibliotheca rabbinica. Eine Sammlung alter Midraschim*. 12
    vols. Leipzig: Otto Schulze, 1880–85.

Commentaries on 2 Corinthians

(Cited in the text by author only)

Allo. E. B. *Seconde épître aux Corinthiens*. 2nd ed. Paris: Études bibliques,
    1956.
Bachmann, P. *Der Zweite Brief des Paulus an die Korinther*. 1st and 2nd. ed.
    Kommentar zum Neuen Testament, VIII. Ed. Th. Zahn. Leipzig:
    Deichert, 1909.
Barrett, C. K. *The Second Epistle to the Corinthians*. Black's New Testa-
    ment Commentaries. London: Adam and Charles Black, 1973.
Boor, W. de. *Der zweite Brief an die Korinther*. 4th ed. Wuppertaler

Studienbibel. Wuppertal: Grand Rapids, Mich.: Zondervan Publishing House, 1976.

Bruce, F. F. *1 and 2 Corinthians*. New Century Bible. London: Oliphants, 1971.

Bultmann, R. *Der zweite Brief an die Korinther*. Ed. E. Dinkler. Kritisch-exegetischer Kommentar über das Neue Testament. Göttingen: Vandenhoeck & Ruprecht, 1976.

Collange, J. F. *Énigmes de la deuxième éptre aux Corinthiens, Étude exégétique de 2 Cor. 2:14–7:4*. Society for New Testament Studies Monograph Series 18. Cambridge: Cambridge University Press, 1972.

Furnish, V. P. *II Corinthians*. The Anchor Bible. Garden City, N.Y.: Doubleday & Co., Inc., 1984.

Goudge, H. L. *The Second Epistle to the Corinthians*. Westminster Commentaries. London: Methuen & Co., Ltd., 1927.

Harris, M. J. '2 Corinthians', In *The Expositor's Bible Commentary,* ed. F. E. Gaebelein. Vol 10. Grand Rapids, Mich.: Zondervan Publishing House, 1976.

Héring, J. *The Second Epistle of St. Paul to the Corinthians*. Tr. A. W. Heathcote and P. J. Allcock. London: The Epworth Press, 1967.

Hughes, P. E. *Paul's Second Epistle to the Corinthians*. London: Marshall, Morgan & Scott, 1962.

Kümmel, W. G. Supplemental notes to Lietzmann's *An die Korinther I, II*, pp. 165–214. Handbuch zum Neuen Testament 9. Tübingen: J. C. B. Mohr (Paul Siebeck), 1969.

Lietzmann, H. *An die Korinther I, II*. 4th ed. Handbuch zum Neuen Testament 9. Tübingen: J. C. B. Mohr (Paul Siebeck), 1969.

Martin, R. P. *2 Corinthians*. Word Biblical Commentary 40. Waco, Texas: Word Books, Publisher, 1986.

Menzies, A. *The Second Epistle of the Apostle Paul to the Corinthians*. Cambridge Greek New Testament Commentary. Cambridge: Cambridge University Press, 1912.

Meyer, H. A. W. *Handbuch über den zweiten Brief an die Korinther*. 6th ed. Ed. G. Heinrici. Göttingen: Vandenhoeck & Ruprecht, 1883.

Plummer, A. *A Critical and Exegetical Commentary on the Second Epistle of St. Paul to the Corinthians*. The International Critical Commentary on the Holy Scriptures of the Old and New Testaments. Edinburgh: T & T Clark, 1915.

Prümm, K. *Diakonia Pneumatos. Der zweite Korintherbrief als Zugang zur apostolischen Botschaft. Auslegung und Theologie*. 2 vols. Rome-Freiburg-Vienna: Herder, 1960–67.

Schlatter, A. *Paulus, der Bote Jesu. Eine Deutung seiner Briefe an die Korinther*. 4th ed. Repr. 1969. Stuttgart: Calwer Verlag, 1934.

Strachan, R. H. *The Second Epistle of Paul to the Corinthians*. The Moffatt New Testament Commentary. London: Hodder and Stoughton, 1935.

Tasker, R. V. G. *The Second Epistle of Paul to the Corinthians*. The Tyndale New Testament Commentaries. London: The Tyndale Press, 1958.

Thrall, M. E. *The First and Second Letters of Paul to the Corinthians*. The Cambridge Bible Commentary. Cambridge: Cambridge University Press, 1965.

Wendland, H.-D. *Die Briefe an die Korinther*. Repr. of 13th ed. [1968]. Das Neue Testament Deutsch 7. Göttingen: Vandenhoeck & Ruprecht, 1972.
Windisch, H. *Der zweite Korintherbrief*. 9th ed. Kritisch-exegetischer Kommentar über das Neue Testament. Göttingen: Vandenhoeck & Ruprecht, 1924.
Wolff, C. *Der zweite Brief des Paulus an die Korinther*. Theologischer Handkommentar zum Neuen Testament 8. Berlin: Evangelische Verlagsanstalt, 1989.

Other books and articles

(Cited in the text by author and short title)

Aalen, S. *Die Begriffe 'Licht' und 'Finsternis' im Alten Testament, im Spätjudentum und im Rabbinismus*. Oslo: I Kommisjon Hos Jacob Dybwad, 1951.
Agrell, G. *Work, Toil and Sustenance: An Examination of the View of Work in the New Testament*. Lund: Håkan Ohlssons, 1976.
Allegro, J. M. 'Further Light on the History of the Qumran Sect' *JBL* 75 (1956) 89–95.
Allen, L. C. *Psalms 101–150*. Word Biblical Commentary 21. Waco, Texas: Word Books, Publisher, 1983.
Allo, E. B. *Première Épître aux Corinthiens*. 2nd ed. Études bibliques. Paris: J. Gabalda et Cⁱᵉ, 1956.
Amoussine, J. 'Éphraïm et Manassé dans le Péshèr de Nahum (4 Qp Nahum)' *RevQ* 4 (1963–64) 389–96.
Armstrong, A. H. 'Greek Philosophy and Christianity'. In *The Legacy of Greece: A New Appraisal*, pp. 347–75. Ed. M. I. Finley. Oxford: The Clarendon Press, 1981.
Aune, D. E. 'Magic in Early Christianity' *ANRW* II, 23/2 (1980) 1507–57.
Bain, J. A. '2 Cor. iv.3–4' *ExpT* 18 (1907) 380.
Baird, W. R. 'Letters of Recommendation: A Study of 2 Cor 3:1–3' *JBL* 80 (1961) 166–72.
Balsdon, J. P. V. D. *Life and Leisure in Ancient Rome*. London: The Bodley Head, 1969.
Bammel, E. 'Paulus, der Moses des Neuen Bundes' *Theologia* (1983) 399–408.
Barbour, R. S. 'Wisdom and the Cross in 1 Corinthians 1 and 2'. In *Theologia Crucis–Signum Crucis: Festschrift für Erich Dinkler zum 70. Geburtstag*, pp. 57–72. Eds. C. Andresen and G. Klein. Tübingen: J. C. B. Mohr (Paul Siebeck), 1979.
Barnett, P. W. 'Opposition in Corinth' *JSNT* 22 (1984) 3–17.
Barr, J. 'The Image of God in the Book of Genesis–A Study in Terminology' *BJRL* 51 (1968) 11–26.
Barrett, C. K. *A Commentary on the Epistle to the Romans*. Black's New Testament Commentaries. London: Adam & Charles Black, 1957.
    From First Adam to Last: A Study in Pauline Theology. London: Adam & Charles Black, 1962.
    'Christianity at Corinth' *BJRL* 46 (1964) 269–97.

A Commentary on the First Epistle to the Corinthians. Black's New Testament Commentaries. London: Adam & Charles Black, 1968.

'Titus'. In *Neotestamentica et Semitica, Studies in Honour of Matthew Black*, pp. 1–14. Eds. E. E. Ellis and M. Wilcox. Edinburgh: T. & T. Clark, 1969.

The Signs of an Apostle. London: Epworth Press, 1970.

"Ο 'ΑΔΙΚΗΣΑΣ (2. Cor 7, 12)'. In *Verborum Veritas, Festschrift für Gustav Stählin*, pp. 149–57. Eds. O. Böcher and K. Haacker. Wuppertal: Rolf Brockhaus, 1970.

'ΨΕΥΔΑΠΟΣΤΟΛΟΙ (2 Cor 11.13)'. In *Mélanges Bibliques en Hommage au R. P. Béda Rigaux*, pp. 377–96. Eds. A. Descamps and A. de Halleux. Gembloux: Duculot, 1970.

'Paul's Opponents in II Corinthians' *NTS* 17 (1971) 233–54.

'Boasting (καυχᾶσθαι, κτλ.) in the Pauline Epistles' In *L'Apôtre Paul: Personnalité, Style et Conception du Ministère*, pp. 363–38. Ed. A. Vanhoye. Leuven: Leuven University Press, 1986.

Barton, S. C. and Horsley, G. H. R. 'A Hellenistic Cult Group and the New Testament' *JAC* 24 (1981) 7–41.

Bates, W. H. 'The Integrity of II Corinthians' *NTS* 12 (1965) 56–59.

Batey, R. 'Paul's Interaction with the Corinthians' *JBL* 84 (1965) 139–46.

Bauer, W. *A Greek-English Lexicon of the New Testament and Other Early Christian Literature.* Trans. and adapted by W. F. Arndt and F. W. Gingrich. 2nd ed. Revised and augmented by F. W. Gingrich and F. W. Danker. Chicago: University of Chicago Press, 1979.

Baumann, R. *Mitte und Norm des Christlichen.* Münster: Verlag Aschendorff, 1968.

Baumert, N. *Täglich sterben und auferstehen. Der Literalsinn von 2 Kor 4, 12–5, 10.* Studien zum Alten und Neuen Testament 34. München: Kösel-Verlag, 1973.

Baur, F. C. *Paulus, der Apostel Jesu Christi. Sein Leben und Wirken, seine Briefe und seine Lehre. Ein Beitrag zu einer kritischen Geschichte des Urchristenthums.* Stuttgart: Verlag von Becher & Müller, 1845.

Becker, J. *Auferstehung der Toten im Urchristentum.* Stuttgarter Bibelstudien 82. Stuttgart: Verlag Katholisches Bibelwerk, 1976.

Behm, J. 'μεταμορφόω' *TWNT* 4 (1942) 762–67.

Berger, K. 'Die impliziten Gegner. Zur Methode des Erschliessens von 'Gegnern' in neutestamentlichen Texten'. In *Kirche: Festschrift für Günther Bornkamm zum 75. Geburtstag*, pp. 372–400. Eds. D. Lührmann and G. Strecker. Tübingen: J. C. B. Mohr (Paul Siebeck), 1980.

Best, E. 'The Power and the Wisdom of God. I Corinthians I. 18–25'. In *Paolo, A Una Chiesa Divisa (1 Co 1–4)*, pp. 9–39. Ed. L. De Lorenzi. Roma: Edizioni Abbazia di S. Paolo, 1980.

'Paul's Apostolic Authority–?' *JSNT* 27 (1986) 3–25.

Betz, H. D. *Lukian von Samosata und das Neue Testament: Religionsgeschichtliche und paränetische Parallelen. Ein Beitrag zum Corpus Hellenisticum Novi Testamenti.* Texte und Untersuchungen 76. Berlin: Akademie–Verlag, 1961.

Der Apostel Paulus und die sokratische Tradition. Eine exegetische Unter-

suchung zu seiner 'Apologie' 2 Korinther 10–13. Beiträge zur histor-
ischen Theologie 45. Tübingen: J. C. B. Mohr (Paul Siebeck), 1972.

'Gottmensch II' *RAC* 12 (1983) 234–311.

'The Problem of Apocalyptic Genre in Greek and Hellenistic Literature:
The Case of the Oracle of Trophonius'. In *Apocalypticism in the
Mediterranean World and the Near East,* pp. 577–97. Ed. D. Hellholm.
Tübingen: J. C. B. Mohr (Paul Siebeck), 1983.

Betz, O. 'Probleme des Prozesses Jezu' *ANRW* 2.25.1 (1982) 565–647.

Bieder, W. 'Paulus und seine Gegner in Korinth' *TZ* 17 (1961) 319–33.

Biers, W. R. and Geagan D. J. 'A New List of Victors in the Caesarea at
Isthmia' *Hesp* 39 (1970) 79–93.

Black, M. 'The Pauline Doctrine of the Second Adam' *SJT* 7 (1954) 170–79.

Blass, F. and Debrunner, A. *A Greek Grammar of the New Testament and
Other Early Christian Literature.* Translation and revision of the
ninth–tenth German edition by R. W. Funk. Cambridge, Eng.: Cambridge University Press, 1961.

Bolkestein, H. *Wohltätigkeit und Armenpflege im vorchristlichen Altertum.*
Utrecht: A. Oosthoek, 1939.

Boman, T. *Hebrew Thought Compared with Greek.* Tr. J. L. Moreau,
London: S. C. M. Press, 1960.

Bonhöffer, A. *Epiket und das Neue Testament.* Giessen: Töpelmann, 1911.

Bonner, C. 'Magical Amulets' *HTR* 39 (1946) 25–53.

Studies in Magical Amulets. Ann Arbor, Mich.: The University of
Michigan Press, 1950.

Bookidis, N. 'The Sanctuary of Demeter and Kore in Corinth: Excavations
1970–1972' *AJA* 77 (1973) 206–7.

Bornkamm, G. *Studien zu Antike und Urchristentum.* Munich: Chr. Kaiser
Verlag, 1963.

Paul. New York: Harper and Row, 1971.

'Die Vorgeschichte des sogenannten Zweiten Korintherbriefes',
pp. 162–94. In *Gesammelte Aufsätze,* IV. Beiträge zur evangelischen
Theologie 53. Munich: Chr. Kaiser Verlag, 1971.

Borse, U. *Der Standort des Galaterbriefes.* Bonner Biblische Beiträge. Köln:
Hanstein Verlag GMBH, 1972.

Bosch, J. S. *'Gloriarse' segun San Pablo.* Rome: Biblical Institute Press,
1970.

Bousset, W. *Die Schriften des Neuen Testaments.* Vol. 2. Göttingen: Vandenhoeck & Ruprecht, 1917.

Bowersock, G. W. *Augustus and the Greek World.* Oxford: Oxford University Press, 1965.

Greek Sophists in the Roman Empire. Oxford: The Clarendon Press, 1969.

Braun, H. *Qumran und das Neue Testament.* 2 Vols. Tübingen: J. C. B.
Mohr (Paul Siebeck), 1966.

Gesammelte Studien zum Neuen Testament und seiner Umwelt. 2nd ed.
Tübingen: J. C. B. Mohr (Paul Siebeck), 1967.

Brockington, L. H. 'The Greek Translator of Isaiah and His Interest in
ΔΟΞΑ' *VT* 1 (1951) 23–32.

Broneer, O. 'Excavations in the Odeum at Corinth, 1928' *AJA* 32 (1928)
447–73.

Corinth: Terracotta Lamps. Vol. 4, pt. 2. Cambridge, Mass.: ASCSA, 1930.

Corinth: The Odeum. Vol. 10. Cambridge, Mass.: ASCSA, 1932.

'Hero Cults in the Corinthian Agora' *Hesp* 11 (1942) 128–61.

'Investigations at Corinth, 1946–1947' *Hesp* 16 (1947) 233–47.

'Corinth: Center of St. Paul's Missionary Work in Greece' *BA* 14 (1951) 78–96.

'Isthmia Excavations, 1952' *Hesp* 22 (1953) 182–95.

Corinth: The South Stoa and Its Roman Successors. Vol. 1, pt. 4. Princeton: ASCSA, 1954.

'Excavations at Isthmia' *Hesp* 28 (1959) 298–343.

'Excavations at Isthmia, 1959–1961' *Hesp* 31 (1962) 1–25.

Isthmia: The Temple of Poseidon. Vol. 1. Princeton, N.J.: ASCSA, 1971.

'Paul and the Pagan Cults at Isthmia' *HTR* 64 (1971) 169–87.

Isthmia: Terracotta Lamps. Vol. 3. Princeton, N.J.: ASCSA, 1977.

Brooke, A. E. Review of *A Manual Greek Lexicon of the New Testament*, by G. Abbott–Smith. *JTS* o.s. 24 (1923) 97–98.

Bruce, F. F. 'The New Testament and Classical Studies' *NTS* 22 (1976) 229–42.

The Epistle of Paul to the Galatians: A Commentary on the Greek Text. The New International Greek Testament Commentary. Exeter: The Paternoster Press, 1982.

1 & 2 Thessalonians. Word Biblical Commentary 45. Waco, Texas: Word Books, Publisher, 1982.

Brueggemann, W. 'Unity and Dynamic in the Isaiah Tradition' *JSOT* 29 (1984) 89–107.

Buck, C. H. 'The Collection for the Saints' *HTR* 43 (1950) 1–29.

Bugh, G. R. 'An Emendation to the Prosopography of Roman Corinth' *Hesp* 48 (1979) 45–53.

Bultmann, R. *Der Stil der paulinischen Predigt und die kynisch-stoische Diatribe.* Göttingen: Vandenhoeck & Ruprecht, 1910.

'γινώσκω' *TWNT* 1 (1933) 688–719.

'εὐφραίνω' *TWNT* 2 (1935) 770–73.

'καυχάομαι' *TWNT* 3 (1938) 646–54.

Exegetische Probleme des zweiten Korintherbriefes. Zu 2. Kor 5,1–5; 5, 11–6,10; 10–13; 12,21. Uppsala: Wretmans Boktryckeri, 1947.

Theology of the New Testament. 2 vols. Tr. K. Grobel. London: S.C.M. Press Ltd., 1952–55.

Burford, A. *Craftsmen in Greek and Roman Society.* London: Thames and Hudson, 1972.

Burton, E. DeW. *Syntax of the Moods and Tenses in New Testament Greek.* 3rd. ed. Repr. 1973. Edinburgh: T. & T. Clark, 1898.

Cadbury, H. J. 'Erastus of Corinth' *JBL* 50 (1931) 42–58.

'The Macellum of Corinth' *JBL* 53 (1934) 133–41.

Caird, G. B. 'The New Testament Conception of Doxa.' D. Phil. dissertation. Oxford University, 1944.

'Everything to Everyone' *Int* 13 (1959) 387–99.

'Paul's Theology'. In *Dictionary of the Bible*, pp. 736–42. 2nd ed. Ed.

J. Hastings. Revised by F. C. Grant and H. H. Rowley. Edinburgh: T. & T. Clark, 1963.

Paul's Letters from Prison. New Clarendon Bible. Oxford: Oxford University Press, 1976.

Caragounis, C. ''Οψώνιον: A Reconsideration of Its Meaning' *NT* 16 (1974) 35–57.

Carcopino, J. *Daily Life in Ancient Rome: The People and the City at the Height of the Empire*. Ed. H. T. Rowell. Tr. E. O. Lorimer. London: Routledge & Kegan Paul, 1941.

Cartledge, P. and Spawforth, A. *Hellenistic And Roman Sparta: A Tale of Two Cities,* London: Routledge, 1989.

Castrèn, P. *Ordo Populusque Pompeianus*. Rome: Bardi Editore, 1975.

Cerfaux, L. 'Vestiges d'un florilège dans 1 Cor. 1.18–3.24?' *RHE* 27 (1931) 521–34.

Recueil Lucien Cerfaux. Études d'Exégèse et d'Histoire Religieuse. Vol 2. Gembloux: Éditions J. Duculot, S. A., 1954.

Christ in the Theology of St. Paul. Trs. G. Webb and A. Walker. Edinburgh and London: Thomas Nelson and Sons Ltd., 1959.

Childs, B. S. *Introduction to the Old Testament as Scripture*. London: S.C.M. Press Ltd., 1979.

Clarke, A. D. 'Another Corinthian Erastus Inscription' *TB* 42 (1991) 146-51.

Clements, R. E. *Isaiah 1–39*. New Century Bible Commentary. London: Marshall, Morgan & Scott Publishers Ltd., 1980.

'The Unity of the Book of Isaiah' *Int* 36 (1982) 117–29.

'Beyond Tradition–History: Deutero–Isaianic Development of First Isaiah's Themes' *JSOT* 31 (1985) 95–113.

Clines, D. J. A. 'The Image of God in Man' *TB* 19 (1968) 53–103.

Collange, J.-F. *The Epistle of Saint Paul to the Philippians*. Trans. A. W. Heathcote. London: Epworth Press, 1979.

Conzelmann, H. 'Paulus und die Weisheit' *NTS* 12 (1966) 231–44.

'φῶς κτλ' *TWNT* 9 (1973) 302–49.

1 Corinthians. Tr. J. W. Leitch. Hermenia. Philadelphia: Fortress Press, 1975.

Cramer, F. H. *Astrology in Roman Law and Politics*. Philadelphia: Memoirs of the American Philosophical Society 37, 1954.

Cranfield, C. E. B. *A Critical and Exegetical Commentary on the Epistle to the Romans*. 2 vols. International Critical Commentary. Edinburgh: T. & T. Clark Ltd., 1975, 1979.

Crook, J. *Law and Life of Rome*. Ithaca, N.Y.: Cornell University Press, 1967.

Cullmann, O. *Die Christologie des Neuen Testaments*. Tübingen: J. C. B. Mohr (Paul Siebeck), 1957.

Cumont, F. *Les religions orientales dans le paganisme romain*. Paris: Ernest Leroux, Éditeur, 1929.

Dahl, N. A. 'Christ, Creation and the Church'. In *The Background of the New Testament and Its Eschatology*, pp. 422–43. Eds. W. D. Davies and D. Daube. Cambridge, Eng.: Cambridge University Press, 1956.

Studies in Paul: Theology for the Early Christian Mission. Minneapolis: Augsburg Publishing House, 1977.

Dahood, M. J. 'Two Pauline Quotations from the Old Testament' *CBQ* 17 (1955) 19–24.

Danker, F. W. *Benefactor: Epigraphic Study of a Graeco–Roman and New Testament Semantic Field*. St Louis: Clayton, 1982.

Daube, D. 'κερδαίνω as a Missionary Term' *HTR* 40 (1947) 109–20.

The New Testament and Rabbinic Judaism. London: The Athlone Press, 1956.

Dautzenberg, G. 'Der Verzicht auf das apostolische Unterhaltsrecht. Eine exegetische Untersuchung zu 1 Kor 9' *Bib* 50 (1969) 212–32.

Davidson, G. R. *Corinth: The Minor Objects*. Vol. 12. Princeton, N.J.: ASCSA, 1952.

Davies, W. D. *Paul and Rabbinic Judaism: Some Rabbinic Elements in Pauline Theology*. London: S.P.C.K., 1955.

'Paul and the People of Israel' *NTS* 24 (1978) 4–39.

Davis, J. A. 'Wisdom and the Spirit: An Investigation of 1 Corinthians 1.18–3.20 against the Background of Jewish Sapiential Tradition in the Hellenistic–Roman Period.' Ph.D. dissertation, Nottingham University, 1982.

Day, J. 'Agriculture in the Life of Pompeii' *YCS* 3 (1932) 167–208.

Deissmann, A. *Light from the Ancient East*. Tr. L. R. M. Strachan. London: Hodder and Stoughton, 1927.

Delling, G. 'ὑπερέχω' *TWNT* 8 (1969) 523–25.

Demargne, J. 'Fouilles à Lato en Crète 1899–1900 (1)' *BCH* 27 (1903) 206–32.

De Montfaucon, B. *L'Antiquité expliquée*. Vol. 2, pt. 2. Paris, 1719.

Den Boer, W. *Private Morality in Greece and Rome: Some Historical Aspects*. Leiden: E. J. Brill, 1979.

'"Tapeinos" in Pagan and Christian Terminology'. In *Tria Corda: Scritti in onore di Arnaldo Momigliano*, pp. 143–62. Ed. E. Gabba. Como: Edizioni New Press, 1983.

Dessau, H. *Geschichte der römischen Kaiserzeit*. Vol. 2. Berlin: Weidmannsche Buchhandlung, 1930.

Dibelius, M. *An die Thessalonicher, an die Philipper*. Handbuch zum Neuen Testament 11. Tübingen: J. C. B. Mohr (Paul Siebeck), 1925.

Didier, B. 'Le salaire de désintéressement' *RSR* 43 (1955) 228–51.

Dieterich, A. *Abraxas*. Leipzig: B. G. Teubner, 1891.

Dihle, A. 'Antike Höflichkeit und christliche Demut' *SIFC* 26 (1952) 169–90.

'Demut' *RAC* 3 (1957) 735–78.

'Ethik' *RAC* 6 (1966) 646–796.

Dill, S. *Roman Society from Nero to Marcus Aurelius*. London: MacMillan and Co., 1904.

Dinkler, E. 'Korintherbriefe' *RGG³*. Vol. 4 (1960) cols. 17–24.

Dodd, C. H. *New Testament Studies*. Manchester: Manchester University Press, 1953.

Dodds, E. R. *The Greeks and the Irrational*. Berkeley and Los Angeles: University of California Press, 1951.

Pagan and Christian in an Age of Anxiety: Some Aspects of Religious Experience from Marcus Aurelius to Constantine. Cambridge, Eng.: Cambridge University Press, 1965.

Drage, A. J. *Homer or Moses? Early Christian Interpretations of the History of Culture*. Hermeneutische Untersuchungen zur Theologie 26. Tübingen: J. C. B. Mohr (Paul Siebeck), 1989.

Dudley, D. R. *Urbs Roma*. Aberdeen: Phaidon Press, 1967.

Duff, A. M. *Freedmen in the Early Roman Empire*. Cambridge, Eng.: W. Heffer and Sons Ltd., 1958.

Dugandzic, I. *Das 'Ja' Gottes in Christus. Eine Studie zur Bedeutung des Alten Testaments für das Christusverständnis des Paulus*. Würzburg: Echter Verlag, 1977.

Dülmen, A. van *Die Theologie des Gesetzes bei Paulus*. Stuttgarter Biblische Monographien 5. Stuttgart: Verlag Katholisches Bibelwerk, 1968.

Dungan, D. L. *The Sayings of Jesus in the Churches of Paul: The Use of the Synoptic Tradition in the Regulation of Early Church Life*. Oxford: Basil Blackwell, 1971.

Dunn, J. D. G. '2 Corinthians III. 17—"the Lord is the Spirit"' *JTS* n.s. 21 (1970) 309–20.

Jesus and the Spirit: A Study of the Religious and Charismatic Experience of Jesus and the First Christians as Reflected in the New Testament. London: S.C.M. Press Ltd., 1975.

'The New Perspective on Paul' *BJRL* 65 (1983) 95–122.

'Works of the Law and the Curse of the Law (Galatians 3. 10–14)' *NTS* 31 (1985) 523–42.

'"A Light to the Gentiles": The Significance of the Damascus Road Christophany for Paul' In *The Glory of Christ in the New Testament: Studies in Christology*, pp. 251–66. Eds. L. D. Hurst and N. T. Wright. Oxford: Clarendon Press, 1987.

Dupont, J. 'Le chrétien, miroir de la grâce divine, d'après 2 Cor. 3: 18' *RB* 56 (1949) 392–411.

ΣΥΝ ΧΡΙΣΤΩΙ. L'union avec le Christ suivant St Paul. 1ère partie: 'avec le Christ' dans le vie future. Bruges: Éditions de l'Abbaye de Saint-André, 1952.

'The Conversion of Paul, and Its Influence on His Understanding of Salvation by Faith'. In *Apostolic History and the Gospel: Biblical and Historical Essays presented to F. F. Bruce on his 60th Birthday*, pp. 176–94. Eds. W. W. Gasque and R. P. Martin. Exeter: The Paternoster Press, 1970.

Eagen, R. B. 'Lexical Evidence on Two Pauline Passages' *NT* 19 (1977) 34–62.

Edelstein, E. J. and Edelstein, L. *Asclepius: A Collection and Interpretation of the Testimonies*. 2 vols. Baltimore: The Johns Hopkins Press, 1945.

Edwards, K. M. *Corinth: Coins 1896–1929*. Vol. 3. Cambridge, Mass.: ASCSA, 1933.

Elderkin, G. W. 'Two Curse Inscriptions' *Hesp* 6 (1937) 382–95.

Elliger, W. *Paulus in Griechenland. Philippi, Thessaloniki, Athen, Korinth*. Stuttgart: Verlag Katholisches Bibelwerk, 1978.

Ellis, E. E. *Paul's Use of the Old Testament*. London: Oliver and Boyd, 1957.

'"Spiritual" Gifts in the Pauline Community' *NTS* 20 (1974) 128–44.

'"Wisdom" and "Knowledge" in 1 Corinthians' *TB* 25 (1974) 82–98.

'Paul and His Opponents: Trends in the Research'. In *Christianity, Judaism and Other Greco-Roman Cults: Studies for Morton Smith at Sixty*, pp. 264–98. Pt. 1. Ed. J. Neusner. Leiden: E. J. Brill, 1975.

Engels, D. *Roman Corinth: An Alternative Model for the Classical City*. Chicago: The University of Chicago Press, 1990.

Ensslin, W. 'Moses' *PW* 16.1 (1933) 361–63.

Erbse, H. 'Plutarchs Schrift Περί δεισιδαιμονίας' *Hermes* 80 (1952) 296–314.

Evans, C. A. 'The Text of Isaiah 6:9–10' *ZAW* 94 (1982) 415–18.

'Paul and the Hermeneutics of "True Prophecy": A Study of Romans 9–11' *Bib* 65 (1984) 560–70.

Fahy, T. 'St. Paul's "Boasting" and "Weakness"' *ITQ* 31 (1964) 214–27.

Fantham, E. 'Imitation and Decline: Rhetorical Theory and Practice in the First Century after Christ' *CP* 73 (1978) 102–16.

Fascher, E. 'Die Korintherbriefe und die Gnosis'. In *Gnosis und Neues Testament. Studien aus Religionswissenschaft und Theologie*, pp. 281–91. Ed. K.-W. Tröger. Berlin: Evangelische Verlagsanstalt, 1973.

Der erste Brief des Paulus an die Korinther: Erster Teil: Einführung und Auslegung der Kapitel 1–7. Berlin: Evangelische Verlagsanstalt, 1980.

Ferguson, J. *The Religions of the Roman Empire*. London: Thames and Hudson, 1970.

Feuillet, A. 'Mort du Christ et mort du Chrétien d'après les épîtres pauliniennes' *RB* 66 (1959) 481–513.

Le Christ, Sagesse de Dieu. D'après les épîtres pauliniennes. Paris: J. Gabalda et Cie Éditeurs, 1966.

Finegan, J. *The Archaeology of the New Testament: The Mediterranean World of the Early Christian Apostles*. London: Croom Helm, 1981.

Finley, M. I. *The Ancient Economy*. London: Chatto and Windus, 1973.

and Pleket, H. W. *The Olympic Games: The First Thousand Years*. London: Chatto and Windus, 1976.

Fischel, H. A. 'Martyr and Prophet' *JQR* n.s. 38 (1946–47) 265–80.

Fitzmyer, J. A. 'Crucifixion in Ancient Palestine, Qumran Literature, and the New Testament' *CBQ* 40 (1978) 493–513.

'Glory Reflected on the Face of Christ (2 Cor 3:7—4:6) and a Palestinian Jewish Motif' *TS* 42 (1981) 630–44.

Foerster, W. 'κτίζω' *TWNT* 3 (1938) 999–1034.

Forbes, C. '"Unaccustomed as I Am": St Paul the Public Speaker in Corinth' *BH* 19 (1983) 11–16.

'Comparison, Self-Praise and Irony: Paul's Boasting and the Conventions of Hellenistic Rhetoric' *NTS* 32 (1986) 1–30.

Fredriksen, P. 'Paul and Augustine: Conversion Narratives, Orthodox Traditions, and the Retrospective Self' *JTS* 37 (1986) 3–34.

Fridrichsen, A. 'Zum Stil des paulinischen Peristasenkatologs 2 Cor. 11:23ff.' *SO* 7 (1928) 25–29.

'Peristasenkatalog und *res gestae*. Nachtrag zu 2 Cor 11:23ff.' *SO* 8 (1929) 78–82.

'Zum Thema Paulus und die Stoa. Eine stoische Stilparallele zu 2 Kor 4:8ff.' *CN* 9 (1944) 27–31.

Friedländer, L. *Roman Life and Manners under the Early Empire*. 4 vols. Tr. L. A. Magnus. London: George Routledge and Sons Ltd., 1908–   .

Friedrich, G. 'Die Gegner des Paulus im 2. Korintherbrief'. In *Abraham unser Vater: Juden und Christen im Gespräch über die Bibel: Festschrift für Otto Michel*, pp. 181–215. Eds. O. Betz, M. Hengel and P. Schmidt. Leiden/Köln: E. J. Brill, 1963.

Früchtel, L. 'Attizismus' *RAC* 1 (1950) 899–902.

Funk, R. W. 'Word and Word in I Corinthians 2:6–16'. In *Language, Hermeneutic, and Word of God: The Problem of Language in the New Testament and Contemporary Theology*, pp. 275–305. New York: Harper & Row, Publishers, 1966.

Gager, J. G. 'Religion and Social Class in the Early Roman Empire'. In *Early Church History*, pp. 99–120. Eds. S. Benko and J. J. O'Rourke. London: Oliphants, Marshall, Morgan and Scott, 1971.

Moses in Greco-Roman Paganism. Society of Biblical Literature Monograph Series 16. Nashville and New York: Abingdon Press, 1972.

'Review of R. M. Grant *Early Christianity and Society*, A. J. Malherbe *Social Aspects of Early Christianity* and G. Theissen *Studien zur Soziologie des Urchristentums*' *RSR* 5 (1979) 174–80.

Gardiner, E. N. *Greek Athletic Sports and Festivals*. London: MacMillan and Co., Ltd., 1910.

Athletics of the Ancient World. Oxford: The Clarendon Press, 1930.

Garnsey, P. *Social Status and Legal Privilege in the Roman Empire*. Oxford: The Clarendon Press, 1970.

Geagan, D. J. 'Roman Athens: Some Aspects of Life and Culture I. 86 B.C.—A.D. 267' *ANRW* II, 7/1 (1979) 371–437.

'Tiberius Claudius Novius, the Hoplite Generalship and the Epimeleteia of the Free City of Athens' *AJP* 100 (1979) 278–87.

Gebhard, E. R. *The Theatre at Isthmia*. Chicago: The University of Chicago Press, 1973.

Gemoll, W. 'Ein Xenophonzitat bei dem Apostel Paulus' *PhilW* 52 (1938) 28.

Georgi, D. *Die Gegner des Paulus im 2. Korintherbrief. Studien zur religiösen Propaganda in der Spätantike*. Wissenschaftliche Monographien zum Alten und Neuen Testament. Neukirchen-Vluyn: Neukirchener Verlag, 1964.

'Socioeconomic Reasons for the "Divine Man" as a Propagandistic Pattern'. In *Aspects of Religious Propaganda in Judaism and Early Christianity*, pp. 27–42. Ed. E. S. Fiorenza. Notre Dame: University of Notre Dame Press, 1976.

Gerhard, G. A. *Phoenix von Kolophon*. Leipzig: B. G. Teubner, 1909.

Gigon, O. *Die antike Kultur und das Christentum*. Gütersloh: Gütersloher Verlagshaus Gerd Mohn, 1966.

Gill, D. W. J. 'Corinth: A Roman Colony in Achaea' *BZ* 37 (1993) 259–264.

'In Search of the Social Élite in the Corinthian Church' *TB* 44 (1993) 323–337.

Ginsberg, H. L. *The Supernatural in the Prophets*. Hebrew Union College Press, 1978.

Giversen, S. 'Der Gnostizismus und die Mysterienreligionen'. In *Handbuch der Religionsgeschichte*, pp. 255–99. Vol. 3. Eds. J. P. Asmussen, J. Laessøe and C. Colpe. Göttingen: Vandenhoeck and Ruprecht, 1975.

Glombitza, O. 'Mit Furcht und Zittern: zum Verständnis von Philip. II 12' *NT* 2 (1959) 100–6.

Glover, T. R. *Paul of Tarsus*. London: S. C. M. Press Ltd., 1925.

Goodenough, E. R. *Jewish Symbols in the Greco-Roman Period*. Vol. 2. Kingsport, Tenn.: Kingsport Press, 1953.

By Light, Light: The Mystic Gospel of Hellenistic Judaism. Amsterdam: Philo Press, 1969.

Gordon, M. L. 'The Freedman's Son in Municipal Life' *JRS* 21 (1931) 65–77.

Gordon, R. L. 'Mithraism and Roman Society: Social Factors in the Explanation of Religious Change in the Roman Empire' *Religion* 2 (1972) 92–121.

Graf, F. *Eleusis und die orphische Dichtung Athens in vorhellenistischer Zeit*. Religionsgeschichtliche Versuche und Vorarbeiten 33. Berlin: Walter de Gruyter, 1974.

Grant, F. C. *Roman Hellenism and the New Testament*. Edinburgh and London: Oliver and Boyd, 1962.

Grant, R. M. 'The Wisdom of the Corinthians'. In *The Joy of Study: Papers on New Testament and Related Subjects Presented to Honor Frederick Clifton Grant*, pp. 51–55. Ed. S. E. Johnson. New York: The MacMillan Co., 1951.

A Historical Introduction to the New Testament. London: Collins, 1963.

Early Christianity and Society: Seven Studies. London: Collins, 1978.

Grundmann, W. 'ταπεινός' *TWNT* 8 (1969) 1–27.

Gülzow, H. 'Soziale Gegebenheiten der altkirchlichen Mission'. In *Die Alte Kirche*, pp. 189–226. Vol. 1. Eds. H. Grohnes and U. W. Knorr. Munich: Chr Kaiser Verlag, 1974.

Gummerus, H. 'Darstellungen aus dem Handwerk auf römischen Grab- und Votivsteinen' *JKI* 28 (1913) 61–126.

Gundry, R. H. *Soma in Biblical Theology, with Emphasis on Pauline Anthropology*. Society for New Testament Studies Monograph Series 29. Cambridge, Eng.: Cambridge University Press, 1976.

Gunther, J. J. *St. Paul's Opponents and Their Background: A Study of Apocalyptic and Jewish Sectarian Teachings*. Supplements Novum Testamentum 35. Leiden: E. J. Brill, 1973.

Gutbrod, W. 'Ἰσραήλ' *TWNT* 3 (1938) 370–94.

Gutierrez, P. *La Paternité Spirituelle selon Saint Paul*. Librairie Lecoffre. Paris: J. Gabalda et Cⁱᵉ. Éditeurs, 1968.

Güttgemanns, E. *Der leidende Apostel und sein Herr. Studien zur paulinischen Christologie*. Göttingen: Vandenhoeck & Ruprecht, 1966.

Haenchen, E. *The Acts of the Apostles: A Commentary*. Oxford: Basil Blackwell, 1971.

Hafemann, S. J. *Suffering and the Spirit: An Exegetical Study of II Cor. 2:14—3:3 within the Context of the Corinthian Correspondence*. Wissenschaftliche Untersuchungen zum Neuen Testament 19. Tübingen: J. C. B. Mohr (Paul Siebeck), 1986.

'"Self-Commendation" and Apostolic Legitimacy in 2 Corinthians: A Pauline Dialectic?' *NTS* 36 (1990) 66–8.

Hammond, N. G. L. and Scullard, H. H. (eds). *The Oxford Classical Dictionary.* 2nd ed. Oxford: The Clarendon Press, 1970.

Hands, A. R. *Charities and Social Aid in Greece and Rome.* London: Thames and Hudson, 1968.

Hanson, A. T. *The Paradox of the Cross in the Thought of St Paul.* Journal for the Study of the New Testament Supplement Series 17. Sheffield: Sheffield Academic Press, 1987.

Hanson, J. S. 'Dreams and Visions in the Greco-Roman World and Early Christianity' *ANRW* II, 23/2 (1980) 1395–1427.

Hanson, R. P. C. 'St. Paul's Quotations of the Book of Job' *Theology* 53 (1950) 250–53.

Harada, M. 'Paul's Weakness: A Study in Pauline Polemics (II Corinthians 10–13)' Ph.D. dissertation, Boston University, 1968.

Harder, G. 'Form' *TNIDNTT* 1 (1975) 710–14.

Harner, Ph. B. 'Creation Faith in Deutero–Isaiah' *VT* 17 (1967) 298–306.

Harris, J. M. 'Coins Found at Corinth' *Hesp* 10 (1941) 143–62.

Hartman, L. 'Some Remarks on 1 Cor. 2:1–5' *SEÅ* 39 (1974) 109–20.

Harvey, A. E. 'The Opposition to Paul'. In *Studia Evangelica*, pp. 319–32. Vol. 4. Ed. F. L. Cross. Berlin: Akademie-Verlag, 1968.

Jesus and the Constraints of History. London: Gerald Duckwork & Co., 1982.

Hatch, E. *Essays in Biblical Greek.* Oxford: The Clarendon Press, 1889.

Hausrath, A. *Der Vier–Capitelbrief des Paulus an die Korinther.* Heidelberg: Bassermann, 1870.

Hempel, J. 'Die Lichtsymbolik im Alten Testament' *SG* 13 (1960) 352–68.

Hengel, M. *Judaism and Hellenism: Studies in their Encounter in Palestine during the Early Hellenistic Period.* 2 vols. S.C.M. Press Ltd.,1974.

Property and Riches in the Early Church: Aspects of a Social History of Early Christianity. London: S.C.M. Press Ltd., 1974.

Crucifixion in the Ancient World and the Folly of the Message of the Cross. London: S. C. M. Press Ltd., 1977.

Henneken, B. *Verkündigung und Prophetie im Ersten Thessalonicherbrief. Ein Beitrag zur Theologie des Wortes Gottes.* Stuttgarter Bibelstudien 29. Stuttgart: Verlag Katholisches Bibelwerk, 1969.

Hertzberg, G. F. *Die Geschichte Griechenlands unter der Herrschaft der Römer.* Halle: Verlag der Buchhandlung des Waisenhauses, 1868.

Hickling, C. J. A. 'Is the Second Epistle to the Corinthians a Source for Early Church History?' *ZNW* 66 (1975) 284–87.

'The Sequence of Thought in II Corinthians, Chapter Three' *NTS* 21 (1975) 380–95.

'Paul's Reading of Isaiah'. In *Studia Biblica 1978 III. Papers on Paul and Other New Testament Authors*, pp. 215–23. Ed. E. A. Livingstone. Journal for the Study of the New Testament Supplement Series, 3. Sheffield: JSOT Press, 1980.

Hill, B. H. *Corinth: The Springs.* Vol. 1, pt. 6. Princeton, N.J.: ASCSA, 1964.

Hock, R. F. 'Paul's Tentmaking and the Problem of His Social Class' *JBL* 97 (1978) 555–64.

The Social Context of Paul's Ministry: Tentmaking and Apostleship. Philadelphia: Fortress Press, 1980.

Hodgson, R. 'Paul the Apostle and First Century Tribulation Lists' *ZNW* 74 (1983) 59–80.

Holladay, C. H. *Theios Aner in Hellenistic–Judaism: A Critique of the Use of This Category in New Testament Christology.* Society of Biblical Literature Dissertation Series 40. Missoula, Montana: Scholars Press, 1977.

Holmberg, B. *Paul and Power: The Structure of Authority in the Primitive Church as Reflected in the Pauline Epistles.* Lund: CWK Gleerup, 1978.

Hooker, M. D. 'Adam in Romans I' *NTS* 6 (1960) 297–306.

'"Beyond the Things Which Are Written": An Examination of I Cor iv. 6' *NTS* 10 (1963) 127–32.

'"Hard Sayings": 1 Corinthians 3:2' *Theology* 69 (1966) 19–22.

'Interchange in Christ' *JTS* 22 (1971) 349–61.

'Philippians 2:6–11' In *Jesus und Paulus. Festschrift für Werner Georg Kümmel zum 70. Geburtstag*, pp. 151–64. Eds. E. E. Ellis and E. Grässer. Göttingen: Vandenhoeck & Ruprecht, 1975.

Pauline Pieces. London: Epworth Press, 1979.

'Beyond the Things That Are Written? St Paul's Use of Scripture' *NTS* 27 (1980) 295–309.

'Interchange and Suffering'. In *Suffering and Martyrdom in the New Testament: Studies presented to G. M. Styler by the Cambridge New Testament Seminar*, pp. 70–83. Eds. W. Horbury and B. McNeil. Cambridge Eng: Cambridge University Press, 1981.

'Interchange in Christ and Ethics' *JSNT* 25 (1985) 3–17.

Hoover, R. W. 'The Harpagmos Enigma: A Philological Solution' *HTR* 64 (1971) 95–119.

Höpel, H. '2 Cor. 4:3–4' *ExpT* 18 (1907) 428.

Hopkins, K. 'Elite Mobility in the Roman Empire' *P&P* 32 (1965) 12–26.

Conquerors and Slaves. Vol. 1. Cambridge, Eng.: Cambridge University Press, 1978.

Horsley, G. H. R. 'The trial of bishop Phileas' *NDIEC* (1982) no. 106, 185–91.

Horsley, R. A. 'Wisdom of Word and Words of Wisdom in Corinth' *CBQ* 39 (1977) 224–39.

'"How Can Some of You Say There is No Resurrection of the Dead?" Spiritual Elitism in Corinth' *NT* 20 (1979) 203–31.

Hübner, H. *Law in Paul's Thought.* Tr. J. C. G. Grieg. Ed. J. Riches. Edinburgh: T. & T. Clark, 1984.

'Der vergessene Baruch. Zur Baruch–Rezeption des Paulus in 1 Kor 1, 18–31' *SNTU* 9 (1984) 161–73.

Hugedé, N. *La métaphore du miroir dans les épîtres de Saint Paul aux Corinthiens.* Neuchâtel and Paris: Delachaux et Niestlé, 1957.

Imhoof-Blumer, F. W. and Gardner, P. *Ancient Coins Illustrating Lost Masterpieces of Greek Art: A Numismatic Commentary on Pausanias.* Chicago: Argonaut, Inc., 1964.

Jacobs, J. 'Triennial Cycle'. In *The Jewish Encyclopedia*, pp. 254–57. Ed. Isidore Singer. New York: Funk and Wagnalls Company, 1906.

Jastrow, M. A *Dictionary of the Targumim, the Talmud Babli and Yerushalmi, and the Midrashic Literature*. New York and Berlin: Verlag Choreb, 1926.

Jeremias, J. 'Μωυσῆς' *TWNT* 4 (1942) 852–78.

'Chiasmus in den Paulusbriefen' *ZNW* 49 (1958) 145–56.

New Testament Theology: The Proclamation of Jesus. Tr. J. Bowden. New York: Charles Scribner's Sons, 1971.

Jervell, J. *Imago Dei. Gen 1, 26f. im Spätjudentum, in der Gnosis und in den paulinischen Briefen.* Göttingen: Vandenhoeck & Ruprecht, 1960.

'Der schwache Charismatiker'. In *Rechtfertigung. Festschrift für Ernst Käsemann zum 70. Gebrutstag*, pp. 185–98. Eds. J. Friedrich, W. Pöhlmann and P. Stuhlmacher. Tübingen: J. C. B. Mohr (Paul Siebeck), 1976.

Jewett, R. 'Enthusiastic Radicalism and the Thessalonian Correspondence'. *The Society of Biblical Literature One Hundred Eighth Annual Meeting Book of Seminar Papers*, pp. 181–232. Vol. 1. Ed. L. C. McGaughy. Society of Biblical Literature, 1972.

Jones, A. H. M. *The Greek City from Alexander to Justinian.* Oxford: The Clarendon Press, 1940.

Jones, C. P. 'The Reliability of Philostratus'. In *Approaches to the Second Sophistic*, pp. 11–16. Ed. G. W. Bowersock. University Park, Penn.: Science Press, 1974.

The Roman World of Dio Chrysostom. Cambridge, Mass.: Harvard University Press, 1978.

Jones, P. 'L'Apôtre Paul. Un second Moïse pour la Communauté de la nouvelle Alliance. Une Etude sur l'Autorité apostolique paulinienne' *Foi et Vie* 75 (1976) 36–58.

Judge, E. A. 'The Early Christians as a Scholastic Community' *JRH* (1960) 4–15, 125–37.

'Paul's Boasting in Relation to Contemporary Professional Practice' *ABR* 16 (1968) 37–50.

'St. Paul and Classical Society' *JAC* 15 (1972) 19–36.

'"Antike und Christentum": Some Recent Work from Cologne' *Prudentia* 5 (1973) 1–13.

'St Paul and Socrates' *Interchange* 14 (1973) 106–16.

'St. Paul as a Radical Critic of Society' *Interchange* 16 (1974) 191–203.

'"Antike und Christentum": Towards a Definition of the Field: A Bibliographical Survey' *ANRW* 2.23.1 (1979) 4–58.

'The Social Identity of the First Christians: A Question of Method in Religious History' *JRH* 11 (1980) 201–17.

'The regional *kanon* for requisitioned transport'. In *New Documents Illustrating Early Christianity: A Review of the Greek Inscriptions and Papyri published in 1976*, pp. 36–45. Ed. G. H. R. Horsley. North Ryde, Australia: Macquarie University, 1981.

Rank and Status in the World of the Caesars and St Paul. Christchurch, New Zealand: Whitcoulls Limited, 1982.

'The Reaction against Classical Education in the New Testament' *JCE* 77 (1983) 7–14.

'Cultural Conformity and Innovation in Paul: Some Clues from Contemporary Documents' *TB* 35 (1984) 3–24.

Kahrstedt, U. *Das wirtschaftliche Gesicht Griechenlands in der Kaiserzeit.* Bern: Bernae Aedibus A. Francke, 1954.

Kamlah, E. 'Wie beurteilt Paulus sein Leiden? Ein Beitrag zur Untersuchung seiner Denkstruktur' *ZNW* 54 (1963) 217–32.

Kapelrud, A. S. 'The Main Concern of Second Isaiah' *VT* 32 (1982) 50–58.

Kardara, C. 'Dyeing and Weaving Works at Isthmia' *AJA* 65 (1961) 261–66.

Käsemann, E. 'Die Legitimität des Apostels: Eine Untersuchung zu II Korinther 10–13' *ZNW* 41 (1942) 33–71.

New Testament Questions of Today. London: S.C.M. Press Ltd., 1969.

Perspectives on Paul. London: S.C.M. Press Ltd., 1971.

Commentary on Romans. London: S.C.M. Press Ltd., 1980.

Keck, L. E. 'On the Ethos of Early Christians' *JAAR* 42 (1974) 435–52.

Kee, D. 'Who Were the "Super-Apostles" of 2 Corinthians 10–13' *RestQ* 23 (1980) 65–76.

Kennedy, G. *The Art of Rhetoric in the Roman World: 300 B.C.–A.D. 300.* Princeton, N.J.: Princeton University Press, 1972.

Keyes, C. W. 'The Greek Letter of Introduction' *AJP* 56 (1935) 28–48.

Kim, C.-H. *The Familiar Letter of Recommendation.* Society of Biblical Literature Dissertation Series 4. Missoula, Mont. and Chico, Calif.: Scholars Press, 1972.

Kim, S. *The Origin of Paul's Gospel.* Wissenschaftliche Untersuchungen zum Neuen Testament 4. Tübingen: J. C. B. Mohr (Paul Siebeck), 1981.

Kittel, G. 'δόξα' *TWNT* 2 (1935) 235–40, 245–58.

Klaiber, W. 'Archäologie und Neues Testament' *ZNW* 72 (1981) 195–215.

Kleinknecht, K. T. *Der leidende Gerechtfertigte. Die alttestamentlich-jüdische Tradition vom "leidenden Gerechten" und ihre Rezeption bei Paulus.* Wissenschaftliche Untersuchungen zum Neuen Testament, 2. Reihe, 13. Tübingen: J. C. B. Mohr (Paul Siebeck), 1984.

Knierim, R. 'The Vocation of Isaiah' *VT* 18 (1968) 47–68.

Knox, W. L. *St Paul and the Church of the Gentiles.* Cambridge, Eng.: Cambridge University Press, 1939.

Kolb, F. 'Zur Statussymbolik im antiken Rom' *Chiron* 7 (1977) 239–59.

Kolenkow, A. B. 'Relationships between Miracle and Prophecy in the Greco–Roman World and Early Christianity' *ANRW* II, 23/2 (1980) 1470–1506.

Kos, M. S. 'A Latin Epitaph of a Roman Legionary from Corinth' *JRS* 68 (1978) 22–25.

Köster, H. 'ὑπόστασις' *TWNT* 8 (1969) 571–88.

Einführung in das Neue Testament im Rahmen der Religionsgeschichte und Kulturgeschichte der hellenistischen und römischen Zeit. Berlin: Walter de Gruyter, 1980.

Kraabel, A. T. 'The Social Systems of Six Diaspora Synagogues' In *The Ancient Synagogue: The State of Research.* Ed. J. Gutmann. Brown Judaic Studies 22. Chico: Scholars Press, 1981.

Kramer, W. *Christ, Lord, Son of God.* Tr. B. Hardy. Studies in Biblical Theology 5. Naperville, Illinois: Allenson, 1966.

Kraus, H.-J. *Psalmen.* Vol. 2. Biblischer Kommentar Altes Testament 15. Neukirchen-Vluyn: Neukirchener Verlag, 1961/1978.

Kreissig, H. 'Zur sozialen Zusammensetzung der frühchristlichen Gemeinden im ersten Jahrhundert u.Z.' *Eirene* 6 (1967) 91–100.

Kuhn, H.-W. 'Der irdische Jesus bei Paulus als traditionsgeschichtliches und theologisches Problem' *ZTK* 67 (1970) 295–320.

'Jesus als Gekreuzigter in der früchristlichen Verkündigung bis zur Mitte des 2. Jahrhunderts' *ZTK* 72 (1975) 1–46.

Kümmel, W. G. *Introduction to the New Testament.* London: S.C.M. Press, Ltd., 1975.

Lacey, D. R. de 'The Form of God in the Likeness of Men: A Study in Pauline Christology'. Ph.D. dissertation, Cambridge University 1974.

'Image and Incarnation in Pauline Christology – A Search for Origins' *TB* 30 (1979) 3–28.

Lagrange, M.-J. *Saint Paul Épitre aux Romains.* Études bibliques. Paris: J. Gabalda et Cⁱᵉ, Éditeurs, 1950.

Lambrecht, J. 'Transformation in 2 Cor 3, 18' *Bib* 64 (1983) 243–54.

'The Nekrosis of Jesus: Ministry and Suffering in 2 Cor 4,7–15' In *L'Apôtre Paul: Personnalité, Style et Conception du Ministère*, pp. 120–43. Ed. A. Vanhoye. Leuven: Leuven University Press, 1986.

Larsen, J. A. O. 'Roman Greece'. In *An Economic Survey of Ancient Rome*, pp. 259–498. Vol. 4. Ed. T. Frank. Baltimore: The Johns Hopkins Press, 1938.

Larsson, E. *Christus als Vorbild. Eine Untersuchung zu den paulinischen Tauf- und Eikontexten.* Acta Seminarii Neotestamentici Upsaliensis 23. Uppsala: Almqvist & Wiksells, 1962.

Lattimore, R. *Themes on Greek and Latin Epitaphs.* Urbana: The University of Illinois Press, 1962.

Laub, F. *Eschatologische Verkündigung und Lebensgestaltung nach Paulus. Eine Untersuchung zum Wirken des Apostels beim Aufbau der Gemeinde in Thessalonike.* Regensburg: Verlag Friedrich Pustet, 1973.

Launey, M. 'Le verger d' Héraklès à Thasos' *BCH* 61 (1937) 380–409.

Legault, A. 'Beyond the Things which are Written (I Cor. iv.6)' *NTS* 18 (1971) 227–31.

Lenschau, T. 'Korinthos' *PWSup* 4 (1924) 991–1036.

Liddell, H. G. and Scott, R. *A Greek–English Lexicon.* Revised and augmented by H. S. Jones, with the assistance of R. McKenzie. Oxford: The Clarendon Press, 1940.

Liechtenhan, K. 'Die Überwindung des Leidens bei Paulus und in der zeitgenössischen Stoa' *ZTK* 3 (1922) 368–99.

Lightfoot, J. B. *Notes on Epistles of St Paul from Unpublished Commentaries.* London: MacMillan and Co., 1895.

Lim, T. H. '"Not in Persuasive Words of Wisdom, But in the Demonstration of the Spirit and Power"' *NT* 29 (1987) 137–49.

Lindars, B. *New Testament Apologetic: The Doctrinal Significance of the Old Testament Quotations.* London: S.C.M. Press Ltd., 1961.

Lohse, E. *Colossians and Philemon.* Trs. W. R. Poehlmann and R. J. Karris. Hermeneia. Philadelphia: Fortress Press, 1971.

Lüdemann, G. *Paulus, der Heidenapostel.* Vol. 2. *Antipaulinismus im frühen Christentum.* Göttingen: Vandenhoeck & Ruprecht, 1983.
Lührmann, D. *Das Offenbarungsverständnis bei Paulus in paulinischen Gemeinden.* Wissenschaftliche Monographien zum Alten und Neuen Testament. Neukirchen-Vluyn: Neukirchener Verlag, 1965.
Lütgert, W. *Freiheitspredigt und Schwarmgeister in Korinth. Ein Beitrag zur Charakteristik der Christuspartei.* Gütersloh: Bertelsmann, 1908.
MacMullen, R. *Enemies of the Roman Order: Treason, Unrest, and Alienation in the Empire.* Cambridge, Mass.: Harvard University Press, 1967.
'Market-Days in the Roman Empire' *Phoenix* 24 (1970) 333–41.
'Social History in Astrology' *AS* 2 (1971) 105–16.
Roman Social Relations: 50 B.C.–A.D. 284. London and New Haven: Yale University Press, 1974.
Roman Government's Response to Crisis: A.D. 235–337. New Haven: Yale University Press, 1976.
'Women in Public in the Roman Empire' *Hist* 29 (1980) 208–18.
Paganism in the Roman Empire. New Haven and London: Yale University Press, 1981.
'Conversion: A Historian's View' *The Second Century* 5 (1985/86) 67–81.
Maher, M. 'Humble of Heart: The Virtue of Humility in Rabbinic Literature' *Milltown Studies* 11 (1983) 25–43.
Malherbe, A. J. 'Through the Eye of the Needle: Simplicity or Singleness?' *RestQ* 5 (1961) 119–29.
'"Gentle as a Nurse": The Cynic Background to I Thess ii' *NT* 12 (1970) 203–17.
'The Inhospitality of Diotrephes'. In *God's Christ and His People: Studies in Honour of Nils Alstrup Dahl*, pp. 222–32. Eds. J. Jervell and W. A. Meeks. Oslo: Universitetsforlaget, 1977.
Social Aspects of Early Christianity. Baton Rouge, Louisiana: Louisiana State University Press, 1977.
'Antisthenes and Odysseus, and Paul at War' *HTR* 76 (1983) 143–73.
Markus, R. A. *Christianity in the Roman World.* London: Thames and Hudson, 1974.
Marshall, P. 'A Metaphor of Social Shame: ΘΡΙΑΜΒΕΥΕΙΝ in 2 Cor 2:14' *NT* 25 (1983) 302–17.
Enmity in Corinth: Social Conventions in Paul's Relations with the Corinthians. Wissenschaftliche Untersuchungen zum Neuen Testament 23. Tübingen: J. C. B. Mohr (Paul Siebeck), 1987.
Martin, R. P. *Carmen Christi: Philippians ii. 5–11 in Recent Interpretation and in the Setting of Early Christian Worship.* Society for New Testament Studies Monograph Series 4. Cambridge, Eng.: Cambridge University Press, 1967.
Martini, C. M. 'Alcuni temi letterari di 2 Cor 4:6 e i racconti della conversione di San Paolo negli Atti'. In *Studiorum Paulinorum Congressus Internationalis Catholicus 1961*, pp. 461–74. Vol. 1. Analecta Biblica 17–18. Romae: E. Pontificio Instituto Biblico, 1963.
Marxen, W. *Introduction to the New Testament: An Approach to Its Problems.* Tr. G. Buswell. Oxford: Basil Blackwell, 1968.

Mason, H. J. 'Lucius at Corinth' *Phoenix* 25 (1971) 160–65.

Mattusch, C. C. 'Bronze- and Ironworking in the Area of the Athenian Agora' *Hesp* 46 (1977) 340–79.

'Corinthian Metalworking: The Forum Area' *Hesp* 46 (1977) 380–89.

McClelland, S. E. '"Super-Apostles, Servants of Christ, Servants of Satan": A Response' *JSNT* 14 (1982) 82–87.

McDonald, J. I. H. 'Paul and the Preaching Ministry: A reconsideration of 2 Cor. 2:14–17 in its context' *JSNT* 17 (1983) 35–50.

McHugh, J. 'Present and Future in the Life of the Community (I Cor 4, 6–13 in the context of I Cor 4, 6–21)'. In *Paolo: A una Chiesa Divisa (I Co 1–4)*, pp. 177–88. Ed. L. De Lorenzi. Roma: Edizioni Abbazia di S. Paolo, 1980.

Meeks, W. A. *The Prophet–King. Moses Traditions and the Johannine Christology*. Supplementary volumes to NT 14. Leiden: E. J. Brill, 1967.

'Moses as God and King'. In *Religions in Antiquity: Essays in Memory of Erwin Ramsdell Goodenough*, pp. 354–71. Ed. J. Neusner. Supplementary volumes to Numen 14. Leiden: E. J. Brill, 1970.

'The Urban Environment of Pauline Christianity'. In *Seminar Papers: Society of Biblical Literature*, pp. 113–23. Ed. P. J. Achtemeier. Chico, Calif.: Scholars Press, 1980.

The First Urban Christians: The Social World of the Apostle Paul. New Haven and London: Yale University Press, 1983.

Meiggs, R. *Roman Ostia*. Oxford: The Clarendon Press, 1960.

Metzger, B. *The Text of the New Testament: Its Transmission, Corruption, and Restoration*. Oxford: The Clarendon Press, 1964.

A Textual Commentary on the Greek New Testament. London: United Bible Societies, 1971.

Michaelis, W. 'ὁράω' *TWNT* 5 (1954) 315–81.

Michaud, J.-P. 'Chronique des fouilles et découvertes archéologiques en Grèce' *BCH* 94 (1970) 883–1164.

Michel, O. *Der Brief an die Römer*. Kritisch–exegetischer Kommentar. Göttingen: Vandenhoeck & Ruprecht, 1955.

'Das Licht des Messias'. In *Donum Gentilicium*, pp. 41–42. Eds. C. K. Barrett, E. Bammel and W. D. Davies. Oxford: Oxford University Press, 1978.

Miller, J. M. 'In the "Image" and "Likeness" of God' *JBL* 91 (1972) 289–304.

Miller, S. G. 'A Mosaic Floor from a Roman Villa at Anaploga' *Hesp* 41 (1972) 332–54.

Moffatt, J. *The First Epistle of Paul to the Corinthians*. London: Hodder and Stoughton, 1938.

Momigliano, A. 'Nero'. In *CAH*. Vol 10: *The Augustan Empire 44 B.C.–A.D. 70*, pp. 702–42. Cambridge, Eng.: Cambridge University Press, 1934.

Claudius: the Emperor and His Achievement. Tr. W. Hogarth. Cambridge, Eng.: Heffer, 1961.

Moore, G. F. *Judaism in the First Centuries of the Christian Era: The Age of the Tannaim*. 2 vols., Cambridge, Mass.: Harvard University Press, 1927.

Morris, L. 'Καὶ ἅπαξ καὶ δίς' *NT* 1 (1956) 205–8.
Mossé, C. *The Ancient World at Work*. Tr. J. Lloyd. London: Chatto & Windus, 1969.
Mott, S. C. 'The Power of Giving and Receiving: Reciprocity in Hellenistic Benevolence'. In *Current Issues in Biblical and Patristic Interpretation*, pp. 60–72. Ed. G. F. Hawthorne. Grand Rapids, Michigan: Eerdmans Publishing House, 1975.
Moule, C. F. D. *An Idiom Book of New Testament Greek*. Cambridge, Eng.: Cambridge University Press, 1953.
 The Epistles of Paul the Apostle to the Colossians and to Philemon. Cambridge Greek Testament Commentary. Cambridge, Eng.: Cambridge University Press, 1957.
 'Further Reflexions on Philippians 2:5–11'. In *Apostolic History and the Gospel: Biblical and Historical Essays presented to F. F. Bruce on his 60th Birthday*, pp. 264–76. Eds. W. W. Gasque and R. P. Martin. Exeter: The Paternoster Press, 1970.
 'The Manhood of Jesus in the New Testament'. In *Christ, Faith and History: Cambridge Studies in Christology*, pp. 95–110. Eds. S. W. Sykes and J. P. Clayton. Cambridge, Eng.: Cambridge University Press, 1972.
 '2 Cor 3, 18b'. In *Neues Testament und Geschichte. Historisches Geschehen und Deutung im Neuen Testament. Oscar Cullmann zum 70. Geburtstag*, pp. 231–37. Eds. H. Baltensweiler and B. Reicke. Zurich: Theologischer Verlag, 1972.
 'The Distinctiveness of Christ' *Theology* 76 (1973) 562–72.
Moulton, J. H. *A Grammar of New Testament Greek*. Vol. I. *Prolegomena*. Edinburgh: T. & T. Clark, 1906. Vol. II *Accidence and Word-Formation*. By Moulton and W. F. Howard, 1929. Vol. III *Syntax*. By N. Turner, 1963. Vol. IV *Style*. By N. Turner, 1976.
Müllensiefen, W. 'Satan der θεὸς τοῦ αἰῶνος τούτου, 2 Kor. 4, 4?' *TSK* 95 (1924) 295–98.
Munck, J. *Paul and the Salvation of Mankind*. London: S.C.M. Press Ltd., 1959.
Murmelstein, B. 'Adam, ein Beitrag zur Messiaslehre' *WZKM* 35 (1928) 242–75 and 36 (1929) 51–86.
Murphy–O'Connor, J. 'Corinthian Bronze' *RB* 90 (1983) 23–36.
 St. Paul's Corinth: Texts and Archaeology. Wilmington, Del.: Michael Glazier, Inc., 1983.
 'The Corinth that Saint Paul Saw' *BA* 47 (1984) 147–59.
 'Faith and Resurrection in 2 Cor 4:13–14' *RB* 95 (1988) 543–50.
Nielsen, H. K. 'Paulus' Verwendung des Begriffes Δύναμις. Eine Replik zur Kreuzestheologie'. In *Die paulinische Literatur und Theologie*, pp. 137–58. Ed. S. Pedersen. Teologiske Studier 7. Aarhus and Göttingen: Aros and Vandenhoeck & Ruprecht, 1980.
Nilsson, M. P. 'Problems of the History of Greek Religion in the Hellenistic and Roman Age' *HTR* 36 (1943) 251–75.
 The Dionysiac Mysteries of the Hellenistic and Roman Age. Lund: CWK Gleerup, 1957.

Geschichte der griechischen Religion. Vol. 2. München: C. H. Beck'sche Verlagsbuchhandlung, 1961.

Nock, A. D. 'Studies in the Graeco–Roman Beliefs of the Empire' *JHS* 45 (1925) 84–101 (= *Essays on Religion and the Ancient World*, pp. 33–48. Vol 1. Ed. Z. Stewart. Oxford: The Clarendon Press, 1972).

'Greek Magical Papyri' *JEA* 15 (1929) 219–35 (= *Essays on Religion and the Ancient World*, pp. 176–94. Vol. 1 Ed. Z. Stewart. Oxford: The Clarendon Press, 1972).

Conversion: The Old and the New in Religion from Alexander the Great to Augustine of Hippo. Oxford: The Clarendon Press, 1933.

'Gnosticism' *HTR* 57 (1964) 225–79 (= *Essays on Religion and the Ancient World*, pp.940–59. Vol. 2. Ed. Z. Stewart. Oxford: The Clarendon Press, 1972).

Norden, E. *Die antike Kunstprosa vom VI. Jahrhundert v. Chr. bis in die Zeit der Renaissance*. Stuttgart: B. G. Teubner, 1915. 3rd ed. Repr. 1958.

'Jahve und Moses in hellenistischer Theologie'. In *Festgabe von Fachgenossen und Freunden A. von Harnack*, pp. 292–301. Tübingen: J. C. B. Mohr, 1921.

O'Brien, P. T. *Colossians, Philemon*. Word Biblical Commentary 44. Waco, Texas: Word Books, Publisher, 1982.

Ohlemutz, E. *Die Kulte und Heiligtümer der Götter in Pergamon*. Darmstadt: Wissenschaftliche Buchgesellschaft, 1968.

Olley, J. W. *'Righteousness' in the Septuagint of Isaiah*. Missoula, Mont.: Scholars Press, 1979.

Oostendorp, D. W. *Another Jesus: A Gospel of Jewish-Christian Superiority in II Corinthians*. Kampen: J. H. Kok, 1967.

Orr, W. F. and Walther, J. A. *1 Corinthians*. The Anchor Bible 32. New York: Doubleday & Co., 1976.

Painter, J. 'Paul and the Πνευματικοί at Corinth'. In *Paul and Paulinism: Essays in honour of C. K. Barrett*, pp. 237–50. Eds. M. D. Hooker and S. G. Wilson. London: S.P.C.K., 1982.

Payne, H. G. G. 'Archaeology in Greece, 1932–1933' *JHS* 53 (1933) 266–99. *Perachora: The Sanctuaries of Hera Akraia and Limenia*. Vol. 1. Oxford: The Clarendon Press, 1940.

Pearson, B. A. 'Hellenistic–Jewish Wisdom Speculation and Paul'. In *Aspects of Wisdom in Judaism and Early Christianity*, pp. 43–66. Ed. R. L. Wilken. Notre Dame: University of Notre Dame Press, 1975.

Pépin, J. 'Le "challenge" Moïse-Homère aux premiers siècles chrétiens' *RevScRel* 29 (1955) 105–22.

Peters, F. E. *The Harvest of Hellenism: A History of the Near East from Alexander the Great to the Triumph of Christianity*. New York: Simon and Schuster, 1970.

Peterson, E. '1 Kor 1, 18f. und die Thematik des jüdischen Busstages' *Bib* 32 (1951) 97–103.

Pfitzner, V. C. *Paul and the Agon Motif*. Leiden: E. J. Brill, 1967.

Pherigo, L. P. 'Paul and the Corinthian Church' *JBL* 68 (1949) 341–50.

Philadelpheus, A. 'Un hermès d'Hérode Atticus' *BCH* 44 (1920) 170–80.

Picard, C. *Ephèse et Claros*. Paris: E. de Boccard, 1922.

Powell, B. 'Greek Inscriptions from Corinth' *AJA* Ser. 2, 7 (1903) 26–71.

Pratscher, W. 'Der Verzicht des Paulus auf finanziellen Unterhalt durch seine Gemeinden. Ein Aspekt seiner Missionsweise' *NTS* 25 (1979) 284–98.

Preisendanz, K. 'Laminetta Magica Siciliana' *Acme* 1 (1948) 73–85.

Prinsloo, W. S. 'Isaiah 14:12–15–Humiliation, Hubris, Humiliation' *ZAW* 93 (1981) 432–38.

Proudfoot, C. M. 'Imitation or Realistic Participation? A Study of Paul's Concept of "Suffering with Christ"' *Int* 17 (1963) 140–60.

Provence, T. '"Who is Sufficient for These Things?" An exegesis of 2 Corinthians ii 15–iii 18' *NT* 24 (1982) 54–81.

Prümm, K. 'Gal und 2 Kor–Ein lehrgehaltlicher Vergleich' *Bib* 31 (1950) 27–72.

'Röm 1–11 und 2 Kor 3' *Bib* 31 (1950) 164–203.

Qwarnström, R. 'Paulinsk skriftanvändning – ett par observationer' *SEÅ* 22–23 (1957–58) 148–53.

Räisänen, H. *Paul and the Law*. Wissenschaftliche Untersuchungen zum Neuen Testament 29. Tübingen: J. C. B. Mohr (Paul Siebeck), 1983.

Ramsay, W. M. 'Unedited Inscriptions in Asia Minor' *BCH* 7 (1883) 297–327.

'Sepulchral Customs in Ancient Phrygia' *JHS* 5 (1884) 241–62.

'Artemis–Leto and Apollo–Lairbenos' *JHS* 10 (1889) 216–30.

The Church in the Roman Empire before A. D. 170. London: Hodder and Stoughton, 1903.

Rawson, B. 'Family Life among the Lower Classes at Rome in the First Two Centuries of the Empire' *CP* 61 (1966) 71–83.

Reekman, T. 'Juvenal's Views on Social Change' *AS* 2 (1971) 117–61.

Rehrl, S. *Das Problem der Demut in der profan-griechischen Literatur im Vergleich zu Septuaginta und Neuem Testament*. Münster: Aschendorff, 1961.

Reinach, A. 'Notes et Communications' *RE* 1 (1913) 227–49.

Reinach, T. 'Inscriptions d' Aphrodisias' *REG* 19 (1906) 79–150, 205–98.

Reinhold, M. 'Usurpation of Status and Status Symbols in the Roman Empire' *Historia* 20 (1971) 275–302.

Reisel, M. 'The Relation between the Creative Function of the verbs br'-ysr-'sh in Isaiah 43-7 and 45:7'. In *Verkenningen in een Stroomgebied*, pp. 65–79. Ed. M. Boertien. Amsterdam: Huisdrukkerij Universiteit, 1974.

Reitzenstein, R. *Poimandres*. Leipzig: B. G. Teubner, 1904.

Die hellenistischen Mysterienreligionen nach ihren Grundgedanken und Wirkungen. 2nd ed. Leipzig and Berlin: B.G. Teubner, 1920.

Richard, E. 'Polemics, Old Testament, and Theology: A Study of II Cor., III, 1 – IV, 6' *RB* 88 (1981) 340–67.

Rissi, M. *Studien zum zweiten Korintherbrief. Der alte Bund-Der Prediger-Der Tod*. Abhandlungen zur Theologie des Alten und Neuen Testaments 56. Zurich: Zwingli Verlag, 1969.

Robert, L. 'Hellenica' *Rev Phil* 13 (1939) 97–217.

'Inscription Agonistique de Smyrne' *Hell* 7 (1949) 105.

'Le grand nom de Dieu' *Hell* 10 (1955) 86–89.

'Le titre de "nourricier du peuple"' *Hell* 11–12 (1960) 569–76.

Robertis, F. M. de. *Lavoro e lavoratori nel mondo romano.* Bari: Adriatica Editrice, 1963.

Robertson, A. R. and Plummer, A. *A Critical and Exegetical Commentary on the First Epistle of St Paul to the Corinthians.* 2nd ed. ICC. Edinburgh: T. & T. Clark, 1911.

Robertson, A. T. *A Grammar of the Greek New Testament in the Light of Historical Research.* New York: Hodder & Stoughton, 1914.

Robinson, H. S. *The Urban Development of Ancient Corinth.* Athens: ASCSA, 1965.

Robinson, J. A. T. *Redating the New Testament.* London: S.C.M. Press Ltd., 1976.

Roebuck, C. *Corinth: The Asklepieion and Lerna.* vol. 14. Princeton, N.J.: ASCSA, 1951.

Rood, L. A. 'Le Christ Comme. ΔΥΝΑΜΙΣ ΘΕΟΥ' In *Littérature et Théologie Pauliniennes,* pp. 93–107. Louvain: Desclée De Brouwer, 1960.

Ross, J. M. '"Not Above What is Written": A Note on 1 Cor. 4:6' *ExpT* 82 (1971) 215–17.

Rostovtzeff, M. *The Social and Economic History of the Hellenistic World.* 3 vols. Oxford: The Clarendon Press, 1941.

The Social and Economic History of the Roman Empire. 2nd ed. 2 vols. Oxford: The Clarendon Press, 1957.

Rowland, C. *The Open Heaven: A Study of Apocalyptic in Judaism and Early Christianity.* London: S.P.C.K., 1982.

Ruppert, L. *Jesus als der leidende Gerechte? Der Weg Jesu im Lichte eines alt– und zwischentestamentlichen Motivs.* Stuttgarter Bibelstudien 59. Stuttgart: Verlag Katholisches Bibelwerk, 1972.

Saake, H. 'Paulus als Ekstatiker. Pneumatologische Beobachtungen zu 2 Kor. 12:1–10' *NT* 15 (1973) 153–60.

Salguerro, J. 'El Dualismo Qumranico y San Pablo'. In *Studiorum Paulinorum Congressus Internationalis Catholicus 1961,* pp. 549–62. Vol. 2. Analecta Biblica 17–18. Rome: E. Pontificio Instituto Biblico, 1963.

Sanders, E. P. *Paul and Palestinian Judaism: A Comparison of Patterns of Religion.* Philadelphia: Fortress Press, 1977.

Paul, the Law, and the Jewish People. Philadelphia: Fortress Press, 1983.

Sanders, J. A. *Torah and Canon.* Philadelphia: Fortress Press, 1972.

Sass, G. 'Zur Bedeutung von δοῦλος bei Paulus' *ZNW* 40 (1941) 24–32.

Schlier, H. *Die Zeit der Kirche. Exegetische Aufsätze und Vorträge.* Freiburg: Verlag Herder, 1956.

Schmithals, W. *Die Gnosis in Korinth. Eine Untersuchung zu den Korintherbriefen.* Göttingen: Vandenhoeck & Ruprecht, 1965.

Schneider, C. *Kulturgeschichte des Hellenismus.* 2 vols. München: Verlag-C. H. Beck, 1967.

Schneider, K. 'Isthmia' *PW* 9 (1916) 2248–55.

Schniewind, J. 'Die Leugner der Auferstehung in Korinth'. In *Nachgelassene Reden und Aufsätze,* pp. 110–39. Ed. K. Kähler. Berlin: Alfred Töpelmann, 1952.

Schoeps, H. J. *Paul: The Theology of the Apostle in the Light of Jewish Religious History.* London: Lutterworth Press, 1961.

Schottroff, L. *Der Glaubende und die feindliche Welt. Beobachtungen zum gnostischen Dualismus und seiner Bedeutung für Paulus und das Johannesevangelium.* Wissenschaftliche Monographien zum Alten und Neuen Testament 37. Neukirchen–Vluyn: Neukirchener Verlag, 1970.

Schrage, W. 'Leid, Kreuz und Eschaton: Die Peristasenkataloge als Merkmale paulinischer theologia crucis und Eschatologie' *EvT* 34 (1974) 141–75.

Schreiner, J. 'Jeremia 9, 22. 23 als Hintergrund des paulinischen "Sich-Rühmens"'. In *Neues Testament und Kirche*, pp. 530–42. Ed. J. Gnilka. Freiburg: Herder, 1974.

Schulz, S. 'Die Decke des Moses. Untersuchungen zu einer vorpaulinischen berlieferung in 2 Kor 3:7–18' *ZNW* 49 (1958) 1–30.

Schütz, J. H. *Paul and the Anatomy of Apostolic Authority.* Society for New Testament Studies Monograph Series 26. Cambridge, Eng.: Cambridge University Press, 1975.

Schwantes, H. *Schöpfung der Endzeit. Ein Beitrag zum Verständnis der Auferweckung bei Paulus.* Stuttgart: Calwer Verlag, 1962.

Scranton, R. L. *Corinth: Architecture.* Vol. 1, pt. 2, Cambridge, Mass.: ASCSA, 1941.

Corinth: Monuments in the Lower Agora and North of the Archaic Temple, Vol. 1, pt. 3. Princeton, N.J.: ASCSA, 1951.

Shaw, J. W. and Ibrahim, L. *Kenchreai: Eastern Port of Corinth.* Vol. 1. Leiden: E. J. Brill, 1978.

Scroggs, R. *The Last Adam: A Study in Pauline Anthropology.* Oxford: Basil Blackwell, 1962.

'Paul: ΣΟΦΟΣ and ΠΝΕΥΜΑΤΙΚΟΣ' *NTS* 14 (1967) 33–55.

'The Sociological Interpretation of the New Testament: The Present State of Research' *NTS* 26 (1979) 164–79.

Seeligmann, I. L. *The Septuagint Version of Isaiah.* Leiden: E. J. Brill, 1948.

Sellin, G. 'Das "Geheimnis" der Weisheit und das Rätsel der "Christuspartei" (zu 1 Kor 1–4)' *ZNW* 73 (1982) 69–96.

Sevenster, J. N. *Paul and Seneca.* Supplements Novum Testamentum 4. Leiden: E. J. Brill, 1961.

Shaw, G. *The Cost of Authority: Manipulation and Freedom in the New Testament.* Philadelphia: Fortress Press, 1983.

Shear, T. L. 'Excavations in the Theatre District of Corinth in 1926' *AJA* 30 (1926) 444–63.

Siber, P. *Mit Christus leben. Eine Studie zur paulinischen Auferstehungshoffnung.* Abhandlungen zur Theologie des Alten und Neuen Testamentes 61. Zurich: Theologischer Verlag, 1971.

Simon, M. 'Early Christianity and Pagan Thought: Confluences and Conflicts' *RS* 9 (1973) 385–99.

Smith, D. E. 'The Egyptian Cults at Corinth' *HTR* 70 (1977) 201–31.

Smith, J. Z. 'The Social Description of Early Christianity' *RSR* 1 (1975) 19–24.

'Too Much Kingdom, Too Little Community' *JRS* 13 (1978) 123–30.

Smith, M. 'Prolegomena to a Discussion of Aretalogies, Divine Men, The Gospels and Jesus' *JBL* 90 (1971) 174–99.

Smith, R. W. *The Art of Rhetoric in Alexandria: Its Theory and Practice in the Roman World*. The Hague: Martinus Nijhoff, 1974.

Snell, B. *Die Ausdrücke für den Begriff des Wissens in der vorplatonischen Philosophie*. Berlin: Weidmannsche Buchhandlung, 1924.

Solin, H. *Beiträge zur Kenntnis der griechischen Personennamen in Rom*. Helsinki: Societas Scientiarum Fennica, 1971.

Spencer, A. B. 'The Wise Fool (and the Foolish Wise): A Study of Irony in Paul' *NT* 23 (1981) 340–60.

Spicq, C. 'L'image sportive de II Cor 4:7–9' *ETL* 13 (1937) 202–29.

'Ἐπιποθεῖν, Désirer ou Chérir?' *RB* 64 (1957) 184–95.

Dieu et l'homme selon le nouveau testament. Lectio Divina 29. Paris: Les Éditions du Cerf, 1961.

Stachowiak, L. R. 'Die Antithese "Licht–Finsternis". Ein Thema der paulinischen Paränese' *TQ* 143 (1963) 385–421.

Staehelin, F. *Die Schweiz in römischer Zeit*. Basle: Benno Schwarbe and Co., 1948.

Stählin, G. 'ἐγκοπή, ἐγκόπτω' *TWNT* 3 (1938) 855–57.

Stambaugh, J. E. 'The Functions of Roman Temples' *ANRW* 16/2 (1978) 554–608.

'Social Relations in the City of the Early Principate: State of Research'. In *Seminar Papers: Society of Biblical Literature*, pp. 75–99. Ed. P. J. Achtemeier. Chico, Calif.: Scholars Press, 1980.

Stanley, D. M. *Christ's Resurrection in Pauline Soteriology*. Analecta Biblica 13. Romae: E. Pontificio Instituto Biblico, 1961.

'Paul's Interest in the Early Chapters of Genesis'. In *Studiorum Paulinorum Congressus Internationalis Catholicus 1961*, pp. 241–52. Vol. 1. Analecta Biblica 17–18. Romae: E. Pontificio Instituto Biblico, 1963.

Stephenson, A. M. G. 'Partition Theories on II Corinthians'. In *Studia Evangelica, II/1: The New Testament Scriptures*, pp. 639–46. Ed. F. L. Cross. Texte und Untersuchungen 87. Berlin: Akademie-Verlag, 1964.

Stillwell, R. *Corinth: The Theatre*. Vol. 2. Princeton, N.J.: ASCSA, 1952.

Stockhausen, C. K. *Moses' Veil and the Glory of the New Covenant*. Analecta Biblica 116. Romae: E. Pontificio Instituto Biblico, 1989.

Stowers, S. K. 'Social Status, Public Speaking and Private Teaching: The Circumstances of Paul's Preaching Activity' *NT* 26 (1984) 59–82.

Strack, H. L. and Billerbeck, P. *Kommentar zum Neuen Testament aus Talmud und Midrash*. 4 vols. Munich: C. H. Beck'sche Verlagsbuchhandlung, 1922–56.

Stuhlmacher, P. '"Das Ende des Gesetzes"' *ZTK* 67 (1970) 14–39.

Tannehill, R. C. *Dying and Rising with Christ: A Study in Pauline Theology*. Beiheft zur Zeitschrift für die neutestamentliche Wissenschaft und die Kunde der älteren Kirche 32. Berlin: Alfred Töpelmann, 1967.

Tarn, W. W. and Griffith, G. T. *Hellenistic Civilisation*. 3rd ed. London: Edward Arnold and Co., 1952.

Taylor, L. R. 'Freedmen and Freeborn in the Epitaphs of Imperial Rome' *AJP* 82 (1961) 113–32.

and West, A. B. 'The Euryclids in Latin Inscriptions from Corinth' *AJP* 30 (1926) 389–400.

Thackeray, H. St. J. 'The Song of Hannah and Other Lessons and Psalms for the Jewish New Year's Day' *JTS* 16 (1915) 177–204.

The Septuagint and Jewish Worship: A Study in Origins. London: Humphrey Milford, 1921.

Theissen, G. 'Soziale Schichtung in der korinthischen Gemeinde: Ein Beitrag zur Soziologie des hellenistichen Urchristentums' *ZNW* 65 (1974) 232–72.

'Legitimation und Lebensunterhalt. Ein Beitrag zur Soziologie urchristlicher Missionare' *NTS* 21 (1975) 192–221.

Thiselton, A. C. 'Realized Eschatology at Corinth' *NTS* 24 (1978) 510–26.

Thompson, M. E. W. 'Isaiah's Ideal King' *JSOT* 24 (1982) 79–88.

Situation and Theology: Old Testament Interpretations of the Syro–Ephraimite War. Sheffield: The Almond Press, 1982.

Thrall, M. E. *Greek Particles in the New Testament: Linguistic and Exegetical Studies.* Leiden: E. J. Brill, 1962.

'The Pauline Use of ΣΥΝΕΙΔΗΣΙΣ' *NTS* 14 (1967) 118–25.

'The Origin of Pauline Christology'. In *Apostolic History and the Gospel: Biblical and Historical Essays presented to F. F. Bruce on his 60th Birthday*, pp. 304–16. Eds. W. W. Gasque and R. P. Martin. Exeter: The Paternoster Press, 1970.

'Christ Crucified or Second Adam?' In *Christ and the Spirit in the New Testament: Studies in Honour of C. F. D. Moule*, pp. 143–56. Eds. B. Lindars and S. S. Smalley. Cambridge. Eng.: Cambridge University Press, 1973.

'Super-Apostles, Servants of Christ, and Servants of Satan' *JSNT* 6 (1980) 42–57.

'A Second Thanksgiving Period in II Corinthians' *JSNT* 16 (1982) 101–24.

Tiede, D. L. *The Charismatic Figure as Miracle Worker.* S.B.L. Dissertation Series 1. Missoula, Montana: Scholars Press, 1972.

Tod, M. N. *Sidelights on Greek History: Three Lectures on the Light thrown by Greek Inscriptions on the Life and Thought of the Ancient World.* Oxford: Basil Blackwell, 1932.

Travis, S. H. 'Paul's Boasting in 2 Corinthians'. In *Studia Evangelica* pp. 527–32. Ed. E. A. Livingstone. Berlin: Akademie, 1973.

Tuckett, C. M. 'Deuteronomy 21,23 and Paul's Conversion' In *L'Apôtre Paul: Personnalité, Style et Conception du Ministère*, pp. 345–50. Ed. A. Vanhoye. Leuven: Leuven University Press, 1986.

Ulonska, H. 'Die Doxa des Moses. Zum Problem des AT in 2 Kor 3:1–16' *EvT* 26 (1966) 378–88.

Van Unnik, W. C. '"With Unveiled Face", An Exegesis of 2 Corinthians iii 12–18' *NT* 6 (1963) 153–69.

Vermes, G. *Jesus the Jew.* London: S.C.M. Press, 1973.

Vermeulen, A. J. *The Semantic Development of Gloria in Early–Christian Latin.* Nijmegen: Dekker and van de Begt N. V., 1956.

Vielhauer, P. *Geschichte der urchristlichen Literatur.* Berlin and New York: Walter de Gruyter, 1975.

Ward, R. B. 'The Opponents of Paul' *RestQ* 10 (1967) 185–95.

Warmington, B. H. *Nero, Reality and Legend.* London: Chatto and Windus, 1969.

Watson, F. '2 Cor. X–XIII and Paul's Painful Letter to the Corinthians' *JTS* 35 (1984) 324–46.
Weaver, P. R. C. *Familia Caesaris: A Social Study of the Emperor's Freedmen and Slaves.* Cambridge, Eng.: Cambridge University Press, 1972.
Wedderburn, A. J. M. 'Adam in Paul's Letter to the Romans'. In *Studia Biblica 1978 III. Papers on Paul and Other New Testament Authors*, pp. 413–30. Ed. E. A. Livingstone. Journal for the Study of the New Testament Supplement Series, 3. Sheffield: JSOT Press, 1980.
'The Problem of the Denial of the Resurrection in I Corinthians XV' *NT* 23 (1981) 229–41.
'Paul and the Hellenistic Mystery–Cults: On Posing the Right Questions'. In *La soteriologia dei culti orientali nell' Impero Romano*, pp. 817–33. Eds. U. Bianchi and M. J. Vermasseren. Leiden: E. J. Brill, 1982.
'Hellenistic Christian Traditions in Romans 6?' *NTS* 29 (1983) 337–55.
Weiss, J. *Earliest Christianity: A History of the Period A.D. 30–150.* 2 vols. New York: Harper & Brothers, Publishers, 1959.
Der erste Korintherbrief. Kritisch–exegetischer Kommentar. Göttingen: Vandenhoeck & Ruprecht, 1970.
Welter, G. *Troizen und Kalaureia.* Berlin: Gebr. Mann, 1941.
Wendland, P. *Die hellenistisch–römische Kultur in ihren Beziehungen zu Judentum und Christentum.* Tübingen: J. C. B. Mohr (Paul Siebeck), 1912.
Wilckens, U. *Weisheit und Torheit. Eine exegetisch–religionsgeschichtliche Untersuchung zu 1 Kor. 1 und 2.* Tübingen: J. C. B. Mohr (Paul Siebeck), 1959.
'σοφία' *TWNT* 7 (1964) 497–529.
'Das Kreuz Christi als die Tiefe der Weisheit Gottes zu I. Kor 2, 1–16'. In *Paolo, A Una Chiesa Divisa (1 Co 1–4)*, pp. 43–81. Ed. L. De Lorenzi. Roma: Edizioni Abbazia di S. Paolo, 1980.
Wilcox, M. '"Upon the Tree"–Deut 21:22–23 in the New Testament' *JBL* 96 (1977) 85–99.
Will, E. *Korinthiaka: Recherches sur l'historie et la Civilisation de Corinthe.* Paris: E. de Boccard, 1955.
Williams, H. *Kenchreai: The Lamps.* Vol 5. Leiden: E. J. Brill, 1981.
Williamson, L. 'Led in Triumph. Paul's Use of *Thriambeuo*' *Int* 22 (1968) 317–32.
Willis, W. 'Corinthusne deletus est?' *BZ* 35 (1991) 233-241.
Wilson, J. H. 'The Corinthians Who Say There is No Resurrection of the Dead' *ZNW* 59 (1968) 90–107.
Wilson, R. McL. 'How Gnostic Were the Corinthians?' *NTS* 19 (1972) 65–74.
'Gnosis at Corinth'. In *Paul and Paulinism: Essays in Honour of C. K. Barrett*, pp. 102–14. Eds. M. D. Hooker and S. G. Wilson. London: S.P.C.K., 1982.
Windisch, H. *Paulus und Christus. Ein biblisch–religionsgeschichtlicher Vergleich.* Untersuchungen zum Neuen Testament 24. Leipzig: J. C. Hinrichs'sche Buchhandlung, 1934.
Winer, G. B. *A Treatise on the Grammar of New Testament Greek.* Tr. W. F. Moulton. Edinburgh: T. & T. Clark, 1882.

Wiseman, J. R. 'Ancient Corinth: The Gymnasium Area' *Arch* 22 (1969) 216–25.
'Excavations in Corinth, the Gymnasium Area, 1967–1968' *Hesp* 38 (1969) 64–106.
The Land of the Ancient Corinthians: Studies in Mediterranean Archaeology. Göteborg: Paul Åströms Förlag, 1978.
'Corinth and Rome I: 228 B.C.—A.D. 267' *ANRW* II, 7/1 (1979) 438–548.
Wissowa, G. *Religion und Kultus der Römer.* München: C. H. Beck'sche, 1912.
Wolff, C. *Der erste Brief des Paulus an die Korinther. Zweiter Teil.* Berlin: Evangelische Verlagsanstalt, 1982.
Woodhead, A. G. *The Study of Greek Inscriptions.* Cambridge, Eng.: Cambridge University Press, 1967.
Wright, K. S. 'A Tiberian Pottery Deposit from Corinth' *Hesp* 49 (1980) 135–77.
Wright, N. T. 'The Paul of History and the Apostle of Faith' *TB* 29 (1978) 61–88.
'The Messiah and the People of God'. D. Phil. dissertation, Oxford University, 1980.
'Adam in Pauline Christology' In *Society of Biblical Literature 1983 Seminar Papers*, pp. 359–89. Ed. K. H. Richards. Chico, Calif.: Scholars Press, 1983.
'ἁρπαγμός' and the Meaning of Philippians 2: 5–11' *JTS* 37 (1986) 321–52.
The Epistles of Paul to the Colossians and to Philemon: An Introduction and Commentary. Leicester: Inter-Varsity Press, 1986.
'Reflected Glory: 2 Corinthians 3:18' In *The Glory of Christ in the New Testament: Studies in Christology*, pp. 139–50. Eds. L. D. Hurst and N. T. Wright. Oxford: Clarendon Press, 1987.
Wuellner, W. H. 'The Sociological Implications of 1 Corinthians 1:26–28 Reconsidered'. In *Studia Evangelica VI*, pp. 666–72. Ed. E. A. Livingstone. Berlin: Akademie–Verlag, 1973.
Yadin, Y. 'Pesher Nahum (4Q pNahum) Reconsidered' *IEJ* 21 (1971) 1–12.
Young, F. and Ford, D. F. *Meaning and Truth in 2 Corinthians.* SPCK: London, 1987.
Zeilinger, F. *Der Erstgeborene der Schöpfung. Untersuchungen zur Formalstruktur und Theologie des Kolosserbriefes.* Vienna: Herder, 1974.
Zerwick, M. *Biblical Greek: Illustrated by Examples.* Adapted from the fourth edition by J. Smith. Rome: Scripta Pontificii Instituti Biblici, 1963.
Zmijewski, J. *Der Stil der paulinischen 'Narrenrede'. Analyse der Sprachgestaltung in 2 Kor 11,1–12,10 als Beitrag zur Methodik von Stiluntersuchungen neutestamentlicher Texte.* Bonner Biblische Beiträge 52. Cologne-Bonn: Peter Hanstein, 1978.
Zuntz, G. *The Text of the Epistles.* Oxford: The University Press, 1953.

INDEX OF PASSAGES CITED

Early Christian sources

INDEX OF MODERN AUTHORS

INDEX OF NAMES AND SUBJECTS

Dionysos, 33, 50
Discipline
Corinthian attitudes to it, 66–67
Paul's attitude to it, 67
Divine Man
in christology, 8–9, 155–56

Enyo, 50
Epictetus, 65, 170
Epigraphy, 15, 35
Erastus, 40
Etruscus, 39
Euelpistus, 51
Eurycles, 39, 40

Faustinus, 47
Favorinus, 41, 47
Fortunatus, 35
Freedmen
their traits, 37–40, 52, 78
their upward mobility, 37–40, 78
in Corinth, 20, 37, 52, 78

Gaius, 35
Galatians, 105
Games
at Isthmia, 44–45, 51
their glory, 45
Glory
of Adam, 148–50
of Christ, 128–29, 142, 160
of Israel, 123
of Moses, 105, 111, 129, 188
of Paul, 111–14, 127, 130, 143,
151–52, 161–63, 177, 182–85, 188,
190
of the cross, 143, 161–62
in LXX Isaiah, 112–14, 116, 118,
122–23, 126, 128–29, 188
the sheer brightness of, 112, 127, 129,
185, 188, 190
Gnosticism, 7–8, 75, 155, 165

Hadrian, 35
Handworker
despised vocation, 84
honoured vocation, 85
Hecate, 32
Helios, 26, 28, 29, 32, 50
Heracles, 32, 50
Hermes, 32, 50
Hicesius, 41
Hillel, 89
Horace, 36

Humility
of Christ, 152, 160, 189
of Israel, 120–22, 143
of Paul, 73, 93, 97, 142, 151–52, 156,
162, 167, 177, 186, 189
in relation to faith, 175, 177, 179–81,
185, 189
equated with 'weakness', 167–68,
186, 187, 189

Image
of God, 147–52
Isaac, 109
Isocrates, 71
Iuventianus, 50

Jacob, 109
Janneus, 132
Janus, 26
Jesus
the simple name 'Jesus', 172
the 'dying' of Jesus, 173
Jose, 168
Judgement, divine
its goal, 122, 126, 142, 151
its rationale, 120–22, 142
Julius Caesar, 35
Juvenal, 21, 26, 38

Kore, 26, 50
Kronos, 50

Laco, 39, 40, 42, 51
Law
its goal, 133
its inherent weakness, 130–39
its place in 2 Cor, 5, 10
Life, 175–78, 186, 189
Lucian, 22, 25, 44, 84, 86
Lucius, 35

Messiah, the Christ
afflictions of, 173–74
expectations of, 139–42, 143
Ministry, Christian
Paul's defence of, 6–7
the paradox of, 1, 162–63, 187–90
Mithras, 32
Moses, 8, 103–11, 132, 168
Mummius, 35

Nag Hammadi, 170
Nemesis, 26, 28, 50
Nero, 27, 36, 42, 48, 49, 50, 52
New age, 127, 139, 176, 186, 188–89